THE HISTORICAL METHOD
OF
FLAVIUS JOSEPHUS

ARBEITEN ZUR LITERATUR UND GESCHICHTE DES HELLENISTISCHEN JUDENTUMS

HERAUSGEGEBEN VON

K. H. RENGSTORF

IN VERBINDUNG MIT

G. DELLING, R. G. HAMERTON-KELLY, H. R. MOEHRING, B. NOACK,
H. M. ORLINSKY, H. RIESENFLED,
H. SCHRECKENBERG, M. STERN, A. WIKGREN, A. S. VAN DER WOUDE

XIX

PERE VILLALBA I VARNEDA

THE HISTORICAL METHOD
OF
FLAVIUS JOSEPHUS

LEIDEN
E. J. BRILL
1986

THE HISTORICAL METHOD
OF
FLAVIUS JOSEPHUS

BY

PERE VILLALBA I VARNEDA

LEIDEN
E. J. BRILL
1986

ISBN 90 04 07616 6

PRINTED IN THE NETHERLANDS BY E. J. BRILL

Iohannae,
uxori adamatae,
Georgio, Michaeli, Iohanni,
filiis dilectissimis.

CONTENTS

PRESENTACIÓ

El fenomen cultural és fruit de nombroses voluntats. En aquest sentit, l'anàlisi d'un aspecte del fenomen cultural esdevindrà molt complexa. Per tot això l'investigador s'haurà de plantejar, en primer lloc, el mètode que sigui més convenient per assolir els seus objectius.

Nosaltres hem intentat fer una anàlisi exhaustiva i profunda dels elements que vertebren l'obra de Flavi Josep. Com que l'objectiu que ens havíem proposat era l'estudi del mètode històric de Flavi Josep, hem hagut d'estudiar les estructures dels elements històrics i hem procurat de situar-los en una perspectiva historiogràfica, indicant, a vegades, l'ús que han tingut en els historiadors que l'havien precedit. Historicisme i estructuralisme formals, doncs, han estat per a nosaltres uns instruments vàlids per aconseguir el nostre objectiu: com escriu Flavi Josep la seva obra històrica.

La investigació que presentem sobre el mètode històric de Flavi Josep està ordenada en tres capítols. El primer capítol estudia el concepte de causa, tot preguntant-se si Flavi Josep fonamenta els fets històrics sobre les seves causes i si té una tipologia de causa històrica. Per tal d'esbrinar aquestes dues hipòtesis, he fet un estudi filològic dels mots indicadors de la idea de causa (αἰτία, ἀφορμή, πρόφασις, ἀρχή). A continuació, he intentat projectar el concepte de causa històrica flaviana sobre els plans humà (caiguda de Jerusalem, guerres del poble d'Israel i el subjecte històric) i el transcendent, summament ric aquest darrer en matisos (ἀλάστωρ, ἀλαστορία, ἀνάγκη, αὐτόματος, δαιμόνιον, δαιμόνιος, δαίμων, δεισιδαιμονία, fatum, τύχη, τὸ χρεών), i també m'estenc en l'estudi de la influència històrica dels fets de caràcter misteriós i en la intervenció directa de Déu en els esdeveniments humans.

Tot aquest primer estudi assenyala que Flavi Josep arriba a crear una història de caràcter intel.lectual, en la qual els hiatus històrics són emplenats amb raons lògiques i fonamentades. Hom hi observa també el dubte metodològic, propi d'un intel.lectual submergit en un procés de canvi profund de la societat en la qual viu.

El segon capítol presenta una anàlisi àmplia dels elements que integren els fets historiats. Aquesta anàlisi contempla el tractament dels personatges històrics, tot assenyalant el grau de coneixements psicològics per part de l'historiador. Els discursos, en sentit estricte i en sentit ampli, constitueixen un material força abundant i variat en l'obra flaviana, i en distingeixo tres grups ben clars: els d'estil directe, els d'estil indirecte i els tant al llarg de tota l'obra, i contribueixen poderosament a fer una història encarnada en un temps i un espai reals. Les freqüents referències a les institucions religioses i polítiques, tant les jueves com les d'altres pobles, han estat tractades en un estudi propi. L'arqueologia, entesa des del nostre punt de vista, és un element molt valuós per al coneixement de poblacions i edificacions de Palestina que l'autor conegué personalment, i la inclusió de llur descripció indica que Flavi Josep persegueix, moltes vegades, un objectiu historiogràfic. Les guerres són tractades des del punt de vista de la seva estructura i de la seva riquesa d'elements. També he prestat atenció a l'estil historiogràfic, concretant-lo en aspectes purament estilístics i, també, en tècniques que afecten més aviat els recursos narratius (dínosis, ècfrasis, anticipació narrativa).

Aquest segon capítol és clos amb set punts que recullen l'aportació personal de Flavi Josep a la seva obra. Així, doncs, hem vist que l'historiador mostra un balanceig freqüent entre la paradoxa i la raó, amb unes conclusions de tipus ètico-filosòfiques davant de la gran lliçó que ofereix la història, amb uns judicis personals sobre els personatges històrics. Els proemis i els epílegs, els advertiments historiogràfics, els elements novel.lístics i dramàtics representen un domini notable de la tècnica historiogràfica.

El capítol tercer presenta una mena de síntesi. Flavi Josep escriu una història pragmàtica, en el sentit concret d'història formada sobretot per fets de valor polític. Un segon punt respon al πῶς καὶ πότε καὶ διὰ τί de Polibi, i en ell s'estudien els principals predicaments en la seva aplicació als fets històrics. L'obra de Flavi Josep està també marcada pel seu caràcter apodíctic, en el sentit que l'historiador sap usar tot un conjunt de proves, argumentacions, referències i testimonis per donar un suport vàlid a les seves afirmacions. En un apartat dedicat a l'ús de les fonts, oferim un estudi breu sobre la manera com Flavi Josep usa la font literària, fent una anàlisi molt detallada de l'ús que fa de la Bíblia a les *Antiquitates Judaicae*. Finalment, cal dir que descobrim en Flavi Josep una actitud d'investigador que busca materials nous per a la construcció de la seva obra i fa una crítica de les fonts de què disposa, però que no reïx del tot a evitar de no ser parcial en certes apreciacions.

Així, doncs, si hom es pregunta a quina visió del món cal inscriure l'obra de Flavi Josep, caldria respondre que, sens dubte, correspon a una visió que tingui en compte la transcendència del fet humà, comparable, amb notables reserves, a la visió religiosa dels escriptors greco-llatins. Per a Flavi Josep, és evident que Déu és el governant del poble d'Israel, però amb un govern sense esperança perdurable, ja que el mateix Déu l'abandonà i es passà a les files romanes, símbol d'un ordre nou al món. En aquests darrers aspectes es diferencia notablement de la visió donada per

d'estil mesclat. També els elements cronològics i geogràfics són una cons-
Agustí d'Hipona, per al qual la història camina en una determinada
direcció, lineal i no cíclica, amb graus de progrés cada vegada més
elevats, basada en una doctrina plena d'esperança.

Aquest llibre és una revisió de la meva tesi doctoral presentada a la
Facultat de Filologia de la Universitat de Barcelona, l'any 1981, en el
Departament de Filologia Grega de la qual vaig poder trobar les fonts
bibliogràfiques i els mitjans financers per a dur-la a terme. Al Cap del
Departament i Director de l'Institut d'Estudis Hel.lènics, el Dr. Josep
Alsina i Clota, dec la meva iniciació en l'estudi de l'obra de Flavi Josep, i
li agraeixo les orientacions que, des de l'any 1972, m'ha estat fent.
També agraeixo els consells i suggeriments del Dr. Eduard Ripoll i
Perelló, Director del Museu Arqueològic Nacional, a Madrid, el qual ha
seguit molt atentament les vicissituds d'aquesta tesi doctoral. Així com
també al P. Alexandre Olivar, monjo de Montserrat, peritíssim conei-
xedor dels Sants Pares de l'Església, expresso el meu agraïment per
haver-me acompanyat moralment i científica al llarg de la meva investigació.
He d'agrair també aquí al Dr. Karl Heinrich Rengstorf la seva oferta
de publicació a ALGHJ que tan magistralment dirigeix, així com també
els seus consells, els quals he acceptat amb molta satisfacció, la revisió del
text i la correcció tan acurada de les proves d'impremta.
Finalment, vull expressar el meu agraïment més sincer a la ''Fundació
Enciclopèdia Catalana'', la qual ha comprès, des del començament,
l'abast d'aquesta investigació i, compromesa irreversiblement amb el
món de l'alta investigació a Catalunya, ha donat tot el suport econòmic a
aquesta publicació, tot revelant, així, la seva vocació de promotora cap a
l'exterior de les recerques científiques realitzades pels estudiosos
catalans. A ''Fundació Enciclopèdia Catalana'', doncs, gràcies!
Vaig redactar la meva investigació en llengua catalana, la llengua del
meu país, però ha estat necessari, per a la seva divulgació, publicar-la en
una llengua universal, la qual cosa m'omple de satisfacció. Vaig en-
comanar la traducció del català a l'anglès al Sr. John Matthews, pro-
fessor del Departament d'Anglès de la Universitat Autònoma de
Barcelona, el qual, tot i no haver nascut a Catalunya, ha sabut inter-
pretar perfectament la forma i el fons de les meves expressions més
genuïnes. Gràcies, a ell.

He procurat simplificar diversos aspectes que, a la meva tesi,
aparegueren tractats d'una manera més extensa, i he fet ressaltar, més
aviat, els punts principals, així com he substituït, excepte al capítol I, una

gran part de textos grecs per una traducció meva, inspirada, a vegades, en la versió de l'obra de Flavi Josep a la The Loeb Classical Library. No vull deixar de dir tampoc que el meu patró de treball ha estat l'obra de P. Pédech, *La méthode historique de Polybe*, així com també la *A complete Concordance to Flavius Josephus* ha estat un instrument usat per mi contínuament.

Per acabar, voldria només indicar que aquesta tesi doctoral representa l'inici, humil, de les investigacions sobre Flavi Josep al nostre país, la llengua del qual fou la primera que el publicà a l'àrea de les literatures romàniques.

Barcelona / Montserrat, Pasqua, 1982

Pere Villalba i Varneda

PREFACE

Culture is the fruit of a great many wills. Therefore any analysis of a given aspect of culture is bound to be a complex affair. As a result the investigator has to raise the issue, first and foremost, of the method which is best suited to his achieving his aims.

I have attempted to carry out a profound and exhaustive analysis of the elements which form the mainstay of the work of Flavius Josephus. Since the task I had set myself was a study of the historical method of Flavius Josephus, it has been necessary for me to look into the structures of historical elements, and I have tried to place them in an historiographic perspective by indicating, from time to time, the use made of them by historians who had preceded him. Therefore formal historicism and structuralism have served me as valid instruments in the pursuit of my aim: how Flavius Josephus writes his historical work.

This investigation into the historical method of Flavius Josephus is divided into three chapters. The first chapter is a study of the concept of cause, and the question is raised of how Flavius Josephus bases historical events on their causes and whether he has a typology of historical cause. So as to scrutinize these two hypotheses, I have made a philological study of the words which are indicative of cause (αἰτία, ἀφορμή, πρόφασις, ἀρχή). I have then attempted to project the concept of historical cause in Flavius Josephus onto two planes: the human plane (fall of Jerusalem, wars of the people of Israel and the historical subject), and the synonym-rich transcendent plane (ἀλάστωρ, ἀλαστορία, ἀνάγκη, αὐτόματος, δαιμόνιον, δαιμόνιος, δαίμων, δεισιδαιμονία, fatum, τύχη, τὸ χρεών). I also deal with the historical influence of events of a mysterious character and with the direct intervention of God in human affairs.

This introductory study shows that Flavius Josephus manages to create a history which is intellectual in character, and in which any historical hiatus is filled in with logical and well-founded reasons. Methodological doubt can also be observed here, as may be expected of an intellectual immersed in the profound change which the society he lives in is undergoing.

The second chapter presents a thorough analysis of the elements which make up events recorded as history. This analysis goes into the treatment given to historical personalities, and reveals the degree of psychological insight of the historian. The speeches, understood in the strict sense and the wide sense of the word alike, constitute extremely varied and abundant material in the work of Flavius Josephus, and can be divided into three distinct groups: those in direct speech, those in reported speech, and those which are a mixture of both. The chronological and geographical elements too are a constant throughout the work, and make a powerful contribution to the writing of a history which is firmly ensconced in real space and real time. The frequent references to religious and political institutions, those of the Jews as well as of other peoples, have been dealt with in their own study. Archaeology, understood from a modern-day point of view, is an extremely valuable element in providing information on the various conglomerations and buildings in Palestine of which Flavius Josephus had personal knowledge, and the inclusions of descriptions of them is indicative of the fact that Flavius Josephus is in pursuit of an historiographic objective. Wars are dealt with from the point of view of their structure and their wealth of elements. I have also given my attention to historiographic style, more specifically to aspects of a purely stylistic nature as well as to techniques which affect more the narrative recourses (dinosis, ecphrasis, narrative anticipation).

This second chapter is brought to a close with seven points which gather together the personal contributions of Flavius Josephus to his work Thus it has been seen that the historian offers a frequent to-ing and fro-ing between paradox and reason, and comes to certain conclusions which are ethical and philosophical in their nature when faced with the great lesson offered by history, together with personal judgement on historical personalities. Proems and epilogues, historiographic forewords, dramatic and novelistic elements all represent a remarkable command of historiographic techniques.

The third chapter presents a sort of summary. Flavius Josephus writes pragmatic history, in the specific sense that it is history formed above all by events of political value. A second point answers the πῶς καὶ πότε καὶ διὰ τί of Polybius, and in it are studied the main predicaments to its application to historical events. The work of Flavius Josephus is also noteworthy for its apodictic character, insofar as the historian is well-versed in the use of a whole series of evidence, arguments, references and testimonies so as to lend firm support to his statements. In a section devoted to the use of sources, I shall offer a brief study on the manner in which Flavius Josephus uses literary sources by means of a very detailed analysis of his use of the Bible in the *Antiquitates Judaicae*. Finally it should be said that in Flavius Josephus I find an investigative attitude which searches out new material for the making of his work, and is critical as regards the sources available to him, but an investigator who does not quite manage to avoid partiality in certain appraisals.

Thus, to the question of which world picture the work of Flavius Josephus belongs, the answer is bound to be that picture which takes into account the transcendence of human events, and which is comparable, with strong reservations, to the religious picture of the Greek and Latin writers. To Flavius Josephus' mind, it is obvious that God is the ruler of the people of Israel, but his reign is without hope of lastingness, since God himself abandons them and goes over to the Roman ranks, the symbol of a new world order. As regards these latter points there is a notable difference with that picture given by Augustine of Hippo, for whom history follows a definite direction, which is linear and not cyclical, in ever higher degrees of progress and based on a doctrine full of hope.

This book is a revision of my doctoral dissertation which was read at the Faculty of Arts of the University of Barcelona in 1981, in the Department of Greek Philology where I was able to find the bibliographic sources and financial means to carry it through. To the Head of Department and Director of the Institute of Hellenic Studies, Dr. Josep Alsina i Clota, I owe my initiation into the study of the work of Flavius Josephus, and I am grateful to him too for the corrections, criticism and guidance which he has given me since 1972. I am also grateful for advice, references and suggestions from Dr. Eduard Ripoll i Perelló, Director of the National Museum of Archaeology, at Madrid, who has closely followed the ups and downs of this doctoral dissertation. Also to Father Alexandre Olivar, a monk of Montserrat, with his unfathomable knowledge of the Holy Fathers of the Church, I express my gratitude for accompanying me on many of the scientific vicissitudes which my task has brought with it.

I also express my gratitude here to Dr. Karl Heinrich Rengstorf for his offer to publish with ALGHJ, which he so masterfully directs, as well as for his advice (which I have accepted with the greatest pleasure), his revision of the text and painstaking correction of the galley proofs.

Finally, I am bound to express my most sincere gratitude to the "Fundació Enciclopèdia Catalana". This foundation has, from the outset, realised the range of this investigation and, due to its firm commitment to the world of research in Catalonia, has given its full support to the publication of this volume. It has thus once again reaffirmed its vocation as the driving force behind Catalan scholars and their scientific research with a view to diffusion abroad. To the "Fundació Enciclopèdia Catalana", then, my thanks!

My investigation had originally been written in Catalan, the language of my country, but it has proved necessary to publish it in a universal language so that it should reach a wider audience, an event which has filled me with satisfaction. I entrusted the translation from Catalan into English to Mr. John Matthews, member of the English Department at the Universitat Autònoma de Barcelona, who, in spite of not being Catalan-born, has nevertheless interpreted perfectly the form and the substance of my truest feelings. To him, my thanks!

I have endeavoured to simplify divers aspects which were dealt with at greater length in my dissertation, and have brought out the principal points. Likewise I have replaced, except in chapter I, a great many Greek texts with a translation of my own which takes its inspiration at times from the version of the work of Flavius Josephus in The Loeb Classical Library. Neither do I want to omit the mention of my working guide, written by P. Pédech, *La méthode historique de Polybe*, Paris, 1964, nor of my constant companion and vademecum, the *A Complete Concordance to Flavius Josephus*.

By way of conclusion, I should simply like to point out that this doctoral dissertation presents the humble beginnings of research into Flavius Josephus in this country, whose language was the first to publish him in the sphere of the Romance literatures.

Barcelona / Montserrat, Easter, 1982

Pere Villalba i Varneda

STATUS QUAESTIONIS

As early as the second century the importance of the works of Flavius Josephus began to make itself felt. The Latin writers, starting with Tacitus, echo Flavius Josephus in their writings, and it is they who show that a recently-published oeuvre had not gone unnoticed. The writings of Flavius Josephus appear time and again by means of quotes, extracts, mentions and sketches up to the fifteenth century[1].

The period I have just mentioned synchronises with the interest in the work of Flavius Josephus which is shown by the numerous translations. The first Latin translation is that of Hegesipus (year 370), of the *Bellum Judaicum* only, in a free rather than literal rendering. In the fifth century there appeared Latin translations of the works of Flavius Josephus excepting the *Vita*: the Latin of the *Bellum Judaicum* translation was good, something which cannot be said for the other two works. Between the fourth and fifth centuries appears book VI of the *Bellum Judaicum* as the fifth Book of the Maccabees, amongst the books of the Syriac *Vulgate* bible.

The Hebrew translation of Josippon (tenth century) is not of outstanding interest for textual criticism, and the same can be said of the Slavic edition of the twelfth and thirteenth centuries.

Finally, the sixteenth-century vulgar Greek translation of the *Antiquitates Judaicae* and the *Bellum Judaicum* by Manuel Chartophylax should be mentioned[2].

As for the manuscripts of the works of Flavius Josephus, there exists the already-mentioned study by Schreckenberg. I should add that the incunabulas begin with Latin translations and with translations into the vernacular languages, from the Latin versions above all[3]. Thus the Latin *editio princeps* of the historical work of Flavius Josephus dates from the year 1470.

---

[1] H. Schreckenberg, *Die Flavius-Josephus-Tradition in Antike und Mittelalter*, Leiden, 1972, 68-171; G. Bardi, "Le souvenir de Josèphe chez les Pères", *RHE* 43 (1948), 179-191; P. R. Coleman-Norton, "St. Chrysostom's Use of Josephus", *CPh* 26 (1931), 85-89.

[2] H. Schreckenberg, *op.cit.*, 64.

[3] H. Schreckenberg, *Bibliographie zu Flavius Josephus*, Leiden, 1968, and *Bibliographie zu Flavius Josephus*, Supplementband mit Gesamtregister, Leiden, 1979. According to this author, the *Historia dos Judeos* was the initial edition in a vulgar language, in this case into "Limusinisch (Katalanisch)", in the year 1482, edited in Barcelona by Nicholas Spindeler.

It is from 1511 onwards that the first studies on the difficulties and interest provided by the work of Flavius Josephus begin to appear[4]. There begins a series of a vast number of articles all sharing the same subject, the *Testimonium Flavianum*[5], up to the present day.

The sixteenth century therefore is rich in translations, and it sees the first tentative beginnings of investigation publications in which religious themes, military harangues and ancient institutions were analysed. The Greek *editio princeps*, published in Basle in 1544 by Arnoldus Peraxylus Arlenius, should also be mentioned.

Editions continue to be published throughout the seventeenth century, but there is a remarkable increase in investigation studies, which deal with the historical aspects, insisting on the *Testimonium Flavianum*, sketch the historical person of Herod, and study various archaeological aspects.

There is an extraordinary increase in the number of investigation studies in the eighteenth and nineteenth centuries. In addition to enlarging on the subjects already dealt with in the previous century, the *Testimonium Flavianum* again comes under scrutiny, and theories alternate in favour of or against its authenticity. Editions are enlarged with extensive commentaries, and there is an increase in source-studies and textual criticism[6]. The historical authority of Flavius Josephus is questioned, and his chronological system and biblical canon are analysed[7]. Edersheim's article analyses Flavius Josephus' interpretation of the Holy Scriptures, under the headings of errors, alterations, additions, rationalism, apology, omissions and legends[8]. All these aspects are also dealt with in the present dissertation.

The first half of the twentieth century is characterized by a great proliferation of monographic studies, which delve into the most specific and

---

[4] For this analysis, I will borrow the ideas from Schreckenberg's works, cited in the previous note.

[5] Pallavicini, *Is liver continet: De Flenda cruce Baptistae ... Quaedam ex Josepho de Jesu Christo*, Wien, 1511.

[6] J. A. Ernesti, *Observationes philologico-criticae in Aristophanis Nubes et Flavii Josephi Antiquitates Judaicae*, Leipzig, 1795, 59; Holwerda, "Observationes criticae in Flavii Josephi Ant. Jud. librum XVIII", *Mnemosyne* 2 (1853), 111-141; S. A. Naber, "Observationes criticae in Flavium Josephum", *Mnemosyne* 13 (1885), 263-284, 353-399; F. Schemann, *Die Quellen des Flavius Josephus in der jüdischen Archäologie, Buch XVIII-XX = Polemos II, cap. VII-XIV, 3*, Hagen, 1887; C. Raab, *De Flavii Josephi elocutione quaestiones criticae et observationes grammaticae*, (Diss.), Erlangen, 1890; H. Paur, *Observationes et adnotationes ad Flavii Josephi elocutionem*, Nürnberg, 1892; G. Schmidt, *De Flavii Josephi elocutione observationes criticae*. Pars prior (Diss. Göttingen), Leipzig, 1893; completed in *JCPh*, Suppl. 19 (1894).

[7] M. Duschak, "Flavius Josephus. Seine Zeit und seine Bedeutung als Historiograph", *IMGIJ* 1 (1865), 53-59, 119-126, 300-306; B. Niese, "Zur Chronologie des Josephus", *Hermes* 28 (1893), 194-229.

[8] A. Edersheim, *s.u.* "Josephus", in *A Dictionary of Christian Biography*, III, ed. W. Smith and H. Wace, London, 1882, 441-460.

minutest detail of the contents of the work of Flavius Josephus. Even so, there is no study which offers an exhaustive treatment of his historiographic method.

Thackeray raises again the issue of the treatment of biblical sources in the works of Flavius Josephus, more specifically as regards the historian's additions, his omissions on account of clearly apologetic reasons, and explanations tinged with express rationalism[9].

Brüne researches into those points which constitute the real historiographic structure of the works of Flavius Josephus, such as, for instance, archaeology, rationalism, Jewish law, cults, divination and prophecy, rhetoric and τύχη, to name but a few. I should like to point out that these aspects also come under consideration in the present investigation[10].

Stein's article too deals with points of methodology, specifically in the sphere of the *ars narrandi*[11].

This brief bibliographical overview shows that there is in existence no piece of investigation which covers quite the same ground which I have set myself in this dissertation. I draw attention again to the fact that those general works—few and far between as it is—which deal with the works of Flavius Josephus do touch on some historiographic aspects which I have gone into more exhaustively, and never do they do so with sufficient breadth or in sufficient depth, nor do these historiographic aspects constitute their principal objective.

I should still like to put on record a mention of those studies which deserve special attention, for reasons of scientific honesty.

In 1947, P. Collomp published an article[12] in which he presents a brief review of the classical historiographic concept, a summary of the criticism of the works of Flavius Josephus, and states that the aim of Flavius Josephus, in his paraphrase, is simply to transmit what the Holy Scriptures say, without adding anything or taking anything away[13]. So Flavius Josephus would be numbered amongst the *narratores rerum*, *non exornatores*,

---

[9] H. St. J. Thackeray, *s.u.* "Josephus", in *A Dictionary of the Bible*, Extra Volume, ed. J. Hastings, Edinburgh, 1904, 461-473. — *Josephus, the Man and the Historian*, New York, 1929.

[10] B. Brüne, *Flavius Josephus und seine Schriften in ihrem Verhältnis zum Judentume, zur griechisch-römischen Welt und zum Christentume mit griechischer Wortkonkordanz zum Neuen Testamente und I. Clemensbriefe nebst Sach- und Namen-Verzeichnis*. Appendix: *Josephus der Geschichtsschreiber*, Gütersloh, 1913. Cf. also B. Niese, "Bemerkungen über die Urkunden bei Josephus Archaeol. B. XIII. XIV. XVI", *Hermes* 11 (1876), 466-488.

[11] E. Stein, "De Flavii Josephi arte narrandi", *Eos* 33 (1930-1931), 641-650.

[12] P. Collomp, "La place de Josèphe dans la technique de l'historiographie hellénistique" (Publ. de la Fac. des Lettres de l'Université de Strasbourg, 106), *Mélanges 1945, III. Études historiques*, Paris (1947), 81-92.

[13] A, I, 17.

and would condemn rhetorical history[14], and represents himself as being cast in the same mould as Polybius[15]. Collomp goes on to the analysis of one or two other historiographic aspects, but accords his study no other intent than that of indicating the need for a proper investigation, yet to be carried out.

Stern's[16] short article on the historic method of Flavius Josephus is limited to noting the main historiographic ideas in his work.

In 1971, at California State College, a dissertation was read whose title led me to believe that I was working on a subject which had already come under investigation[17]. But once in possession of the dissertation, I was able to see that the author had not intended to carry out a full-length investigation, nor had he reached a detailed analysis, and that, in short, the contents did not do justice to the ambitious title.

Cohen[18] has published recently a very critical work, in which different points referring to the historical method of Flavius Josephus are treated.

Problems and relations between *Vita* and *Bellum Judaicum*, questions on sources which Flavius Josephus uses and everything referring to his activity in Galilee and to the work produced in Rome are analysed in detail. But, here, we are only interested in saying that Cohen has been useful to us in some points, for instance, in the rhetorical character of Flavian work, in the thematic and not chronological order of some passages, in the dramatic effects, in the treatment of characters, and so on.

Ladouceur[19] analyses the vocabulary in the first part, with a criticism on different studies, but all this does not touch our investigation. The second chapter studies the problem of the "assistants", according to Thackeray's theory. Ladouceur denies the influence of Sophocles and Thucydides in books XV-XIX of the *Antiquitates Judaicae*. The third chapter investigates the sources of the *Bellum Judaicum*. For that, he mentions the different *commentarii* from which the historical narration is organized: the *commentarii* of Cicero (*Brutus*, 262) and Aulus Hirtius (*Bell. Gall.*, 8 *praef.*), the *commentarii* of Caesar, Tiberius, Vespasian and Titus. Ladoucer, however, concludes that by these indications on the *commentarii* it is not possible to infer their exact nature.

---

[14] A, I, 2; Ap, I, 24.

[15] XII, 25a, 3; XXXVI, 1.

[16] M. Stern, "Flavius Josephus' Method of Writing History" (in Hebrew), *IHS* (1962-1963), 22-28.

[17] S. G. Leuty, *An inquiry into the historical Methods and contributions of Flavius Josephus* (Thesis Calif. State Coll. at Fullerton), 1971 (Microfilm).

[18] Shave F. B. Cohen, *Josephus in Galilee and Rome. His vita and development as a historian*, Leiden, 1979.

[19] D. J. Ladouceur, *Studies in the Language and Historiography of Flavius Josephus* (Diss. Providence, 1977), Ann Arbor, Mich., 1979.

Ladouceur studies too the falsification of the sources and the access to official documents. The first one was possible and real; the second aspect was controlled, and the official documents were very restricted. For this reason, it is difficult to believe the use of official ὑπομνήματα by Flavius Josephus, when he quotes them, especially in *Contra Apionem*.

Nevertheless, Ladouceur's work has objectives other than we have had in our research.

For all these reasons, and above all because to my knowledge there is no investigation which takes in all of the historiographical problems of Flavius Josephus, providing an exhaustive analysis of his strategy as historian, I have felt it opportune to undertake this lengthy task in order to provide scientific service to many scholars of this universal Jewish writer.

ABBREVIATIONS

a) *Biblical*

Apoc.	Apocalypsis
Bar.	Baruch
Chron.	Libri Chronicorum
Dan.	Daniel
Deut.	Deuteronomium
Eccli.	Ecclesiasticus
Esdr.	Esdrae
Ex.	Exodus
Gen.	Genesis
Jos.	Josue
Jud.	Judices
Luc.	Lucas
LXX	Septuaginta
Mach.	Libri Machabaeorum
Marc.	Marcus
Matth.	Matthaeus
Num.	Numeri
Reg.	Libri Regum
Sam.	Samuelis

b) *Classical*

Anth. Pal.	Anthologia Palatina
Arstt.	Aristoteles
Aug.	Augustinus Hipponensis
Cato	M. Porcius Cato
Cic.	M. Tullius Cicero
Dem.	Demosthenes
Dio Cass.	Dio Cassius
Diod.	Diodorus
Dion. Hal.	Dionysius Halicarnasseus
Eus.	Eusebius Caesariensis
Harpocr.	Harpocration
Hecat.	Hecataeus
Hrdt.	Herodotus
Isocr.	Isocrates
Lucian.	Lucianus
Philo	Philo Alexandrinus
Phot.	Photius
Plat.	Plato
Plin.	Plinius
Pol.	Polybius
Quint.	Quintilianus
Sen.	L. Annaeus Seneca
S. Emp.	Sextus Empiricus
Strb.	Strabo
Suet.	Suetonius
Tac.	Tacitus
Thuc.	Thucydides

c) *Flavius Josephus*

A	Antiquitates Judaicae
B	Bellum Judaicum
Ap	Contra Apionem
Vit	Vita

d) *Periodicals*

AJPh	American Journal of Philology (Baltimore)
Ant	Die Antike (Berlin)
CM	Clio Medica. Acta Academiae internationalis historiae medicinae (Amsterdam)
CPh	Classical Philology (Chicago)
CQ	Classical Quarterly (Oxford)
Eos	Eos. Commentarii Societatis Philologae Polonorum (Vratislaviae — Varsaviae — Cracoviae)
Eranos	Eranos. Acta Philologica Suecana (Uppsala)
Hermes	Hermes. Zeitschrift für Klassische Philologie (Wiesbaden)
Historia	Historia. Revue d'histoire ancienne (Wiesbaden)
HThR	Harvard Theological Review (Cambridge, Mass.)
HZ	Historische Zeitschrift (München)
IHS	Israel History Society (Jerusalem)
IMGIJ	Illustrierte Monatshefte für die gesammten Interessen des Judenthums (Wien)
JCPh	Jahrbücher für classische Philologie (Leipzig)
JQR	The Jewish Quarterly Review (Philadelphia)
Klio	Klio. Beiträge zur alten Geschichte (Berlin)
MGWJ	Monatsschrift für Geschichte und Wissenschaft des Judent(h)ums (Breslau, Dresden, Krotoschin, Frankfurt, Berlin)
Mnemosyne	Mnemosyne. Bibliotheca Classica Batava (Leiden)
NJ	Neue Jahrbücher für das klassische Altertum, Geschichte und deutsche Literatur (Leipzig)
NT	Novum Testamentum. An international Quarterly for New Testament and related Studies (Leiden)
RBi	Revue Biblique (Paris)
REAug	Revue des Études Augustiniennes (Paris)
RHE	Revue d'Histoire Ecclésiastique (Louvain)
RhM	Rheinisches Museum (Frankfurt)
RPh	Revue de Philologie (Paris)
RSA	Rivista storica dell'Antichità (Bologna)
SCO	Studi Classici e Orientali (Pisa)
StudCPh	Studies in Classical Philology
TAPhA	Transactions and Proceedings of the American Philological Association (New York)
Theokratia	Theokratia (Leiden)
VChr	Vigiliae Christianae. A Review of early Christian Life and Language (Amsterdam)
WS	Wiener Studien. Zeitschrift für klassische Philologie und Patristik (Wien)
ZNTW	Zeitschrift für die Neutestamentliche Wissenschaft und die Kunde der älteren Kirche (Berlin)
ZRGG	Zeitschrift für Religions- und Geistesgeschichte (Köln)

e) *Collections*

AGJU	Arbeiten zur Geschichte des antiken Judentums und des Ur-christentums, Institutum Judaicum, Tübingen (Leiden)
AGSU	Arbeiten zur Geschichte des Spätjudentums und Urchristen-tums, Institutum Judaicum, Tübingen (Leiden)
ALGHJ	Arbeiten zur Literatur und Geschichte des hellenistischen Judentums (Leiden)
BzFchrTh	Beiträge zur Förderung christlicher Theologie (Gütersloh)

f) *Varia*

ed.	edidit, ediderunt, edition
FGH	*Die Fragmente der Griechischen Historiker* (F. Jacoby)
FHG	*Fragmenta historicorum graecorum* (C. Müller)
GGM	*Geographi graeci minores* (C. Müller)
op. cit.	*opere citato*
RE	*Paulys Realencyclopädie...*
s.u.	*sub uoce*
s.uu.	*sub uocibus*

CHAPTER ONE

THE THEORY OF HISTORICAL CAUSE

The chronological situation itself of Flavius Josephus makes him heir to an historical method which is already well-established and well-proved with regard to the subject of historiographical aetiology. Thus, one understands that Flavius Josephus goes to great lengths to show his knowledge of these points with a liberal use of formulae and appropriate words.

The great importance of this subject makes it necessary to begin a series of sections which, having a common denominator, will bring together those particular nuances of the concept of cause in Flavius Josephus.

First of all there will be a description of the concept within the personal philosophical system of Flavius Josephus. Later on, this concept will be dealt with on two planes: the human and the transcendent.

But before embarking on this, a study should be made of the concept of cause in historians previous to Flavius Josephus. Nevertheless, these *Precedents* do not form the main body of this dissertation, but merely serve to bring the subject into perspective. The same ideas may be said for the following *Precedents*. The contents of these *Precedents* have been taken from works and studies mentioned in their respective notes.

Precedents

According to some commentators, the oeuvre of Herodotus is eminently narrative, but this does not provide the key to the whole of his method. An effort on the part of the historian can also be seen there so as to avoid an ingenuous compilation of data and a searching out of those which contribute to a clarification of the precedents of each event together with the consequences, as well as demonstrating the interrelation of historical elements, thus providing evidence of the aetiological chain: affective elements and personal characteristics, such as ambition, vengeance, love, madness and so on, and a supernatural cause or the intervention of the gods[1]. In fact, and in short, his oeuvre turns out to be a grandiose

---

[1] Hrdt. I, 1-5; II, 161; III, 1, 36, 134-5, 139, 150; IV, 1, 180; V, 35, 37, 49, 81, 97, 102, 106, 124, 135, 145; VI, 1-3, 13, 32, 49, 86, 94, 137; VII, 1, 5-18, 150, 230. Cf. H. R. Immerwahr, "Historical causation in Herodotus", *TAPhA* 87 (1956), 244-247: αἰτίη implies personal responsibility, and πρόφασις the immediate cause. I have taken the principal ideas of these *Precedents* from P. Pédech, *La méthode historique de Polybe*, Paris, 1964, 54-98. Cf. too F. Hellmann, "Geschichte und Schicksal bei Herodot", in *Herodot. Eine Auswahl aus der neueren Forschung*, München (1965), 40-56.

drama, in which it is shown that ὕβρις is the principal cause of the downfall of the Persian empire.

Thucydides leaves us in no doubt as to his historiographic concept, by establishing a hierarchy of causes, going from those which are eternal and immutable to those which are physically provable, which, for Greek historiography, meant two basic aetiological notions: the profound cause and the immediate cause[2].

The other basic tenet of his concept is the confidence he had in being able to see into things beyond a simple autopsy, believing that the reason of the historian manages to create stable causes, since the deep underlying reasons of historical plurality can be described and summarised. Thucydides pays no more heed to the question and openly professes an uncompromising relativism, aware that all events, passing through the mental and psychological sieve of the historian, are an eternal ὡς ἐμοὶ δοκεῖ being accentuated and biased to varying degrees.

But his theory is also limited by the lack of a formulation concerning the aetiological character of the *entourage* which inevitable surrounds all historical events. He points out only those criteria which he has followed in the composing of the speeches, and how he has searched for clarity and has tried to avoid imagination. He also points out that historical truth is difficult to find, and that by avoiding the introduction of accomodating myths, an everlasting work may be achieved[3].

In the oeuvre of Xenophon, historiographic science loses vitality, in the sense that the author presents a narrative history, which is lacking in a hierarchy of causes. In his history, the concept of cause suffers something of a setback, even though he was a good disciple of Socrates. As a consequence, the historical personalities take on aetiological importance, and thus historiography makes gains in the field of individual psychology.

This latter aspect also prospered with Ephorus, Anaximenes and Theopompus, so that for them the will of a single man was the causative determinant of many events. Theopompus achieved the creation of a history based on temperamental personalities, going into the minutest of details as the conditioners of events in which human passions took no small part.

Plato upholds the Thucydidean idea, and understands history as having explicit knowledge of τὰς αἰτίας ἑκάστου, διὰ τί γίγνεται ἕκαστον καὶ διὰ τί ἀπόλλυται καὶ διὰ τί ἔστι[4].

---

[2] I, 23, 5-6; III, 13. Cf. P. Huart, *Le vocabulaire de l'analyse psychologique dans l'oeuvre de Thucydide*, Paris, 1868, 113 and 259.

[3] On the historical method of Thucydides, cf. J. de Romilly, *Thucydide et l'impérialisme athénien*, Paris, 1947.

[4] *Phaedon*, 96a.

Aristotle and his school exercised a profound influence, not only on the empirical sciences, but also on the sciences of the mind, politics and history, even on the impenetrable character of causes in the Stoic school[5]. Their definitions are significant enough: "to know is to know the causes"[6], "the essential of all knowledge is the examination of the reason why"[7]. They expound the theory of the four causes: the material, the formal, the efficient and the final causes[8]. These causes, translated into historical events were the equivalent of: means by which all events come to pass, manner of happening of primary or profound causes and human action.

In the political analysis of 158 constitutions and in his *Politica*, Aristotle applies his aetiological theory, providing Greek historiography with a new dimension: the idea of historical evolution. Any cause, however small, and even if it directed towards its own decline, brings about effects which, in their turn, bring about others afresh, thus forging the chain of drama of humanity[9].

The Stoic school, in addition to their concern with the establishing of a hierarchy of causes, contributed the concept of concomitant cause. Besides the supreme cause, they allowed a plurality of secondary causes, which could manifest themselves either as preceding conditions or as determinant causes or as concomitant causes[10]. This school exercized great influence on Polybius, who was a vehement postulator of their specification of historical causes[11].

The Hellenistic historians enriched the concept of cause rather than stating it with any greater accuracy. The loss of their works leaves a lot of points to be clarified. Even so, what remains of them still offers a certain possibility for the comprehension of their historiographic concept in its aetiological aspects.

Thus, the individual is all-important, and events are converted into the acts of important men. History is then dramatised. Aetiology is directed

---

[5] Strb. II, 38.

[6] Arstt., *An. post.* I, 2, 71c, 2.

[7] *Ibid.* I, 14, 79a, 23; II, 11, 94a, 20; *Phys.* I, 1, 184a, 12; *Met.* A, 2, 982a, 3; B, 2, 996b, 13; Γ, 2, 1003b, 16; 3, 1005b, 5; E, 1, 1025b, 1.

[8] Arstt., *Met.* Δ, 2, 1013a, 24; *Phys.* I, 3, 194.

[9] Cf. K. von Fritz, *Aristotle's contribution to the practice and theory of historiography*, Berkeley, 1958, 121 ff. The author also considers in this book the influence of the *Ethicae* on psychology studies. Indubitably there existed no real biographical genre before Aristotle. The *Agesilaus* of Xenophon is rather a eulogy to the virtues of man with anecdotes as illustrations. Historiography therefore appropriated Aristotelian psychological doctrine.

[10] Cf. M. Pohlenz, *Die Stoa*, II, Göttingen, 1955, 60-61.

[11] P. Pédech, *op. cit.*, 69; Pol. III, 6, 6; 31, 11-13; 32, 6-7; V, 21, 6; VI, 2, 3; VIII, 2, 3; XI, 19a; XXXIX, 8, 7. In the same sense: Cic., *De or.* II, 15, 63; Quint. IV, 2, 2; Diod., *Bibl.* XXX, 15.

towards an examination of responsibilities and an analysis of the motives. The importance of psychology therefore grows, with a basis in moral categories.

There also appear on the historiographic stage "supporting" personalities, together with the influence on matters of State of female personalities. It would seem that the New Comedy, by bringing women and confidents onto the stage, influenced historians to concede a certain role to these supporting actors.

Consideration is also due to the influence of political and military institutions themselves. The study of the institutions of various States, begun by Aristotle, discovered the field of customs and laws. Men do not last, but institutions survive them. In this manner history takes an interest in the besieging of cities, strategic arts, tactics of war and so on.

The beginnings of geographical studies too create the awareness of the influence of the environment on historical action, both on society and on customs and the future of the state[12].

Finally, such wide-ranging and diverse contacts proper to the expansion of the Hellenic world brought about the need to project events on the notions of fortune and chance (τύχη). Thus, sovereigns possess their own τύχη, as do cities and states.

In conclusion, as soon as an historical narrative is founded on causes and on all that might have had an influence on what it describes, then it differs substantially from the manner of annalmaking—ἐφημερίδες—and commentaries—ὑπομνήματα—, to become real history[13]. History therefore becomes intelligible insofar as it discovers the relationships between the different stages of human evolution, and thus the small instants which compose it remain united and not forgotten or unified within generalised concepts. It is true enough that history presents hiatuses in its development, but it is the mission of the historian to search out possible nexus therein[14].

Those histories which therefore omit the study of causes are not scientific. Even though Cicero made no distinction between the notions of annals and history[15], because the disposition of historical material is almost always presented according to the succession of years, he nevertheless marked the limits for the writers of each genre, by calling the former simply *narrators*, and the latter *composers of events*[16].

---

[12] Antecedents of this theory, in the Hippocratic treatise περὶ ἀέρων, ὑδάτων, τόπων.

[13] Cf. G. I. Vossius, *Ars Historica*, Lugduni Batavorum, 1623.

[14] H. I. Marrou, *El conocimiento histórico* (orig. title: *De la connaissance historique*), Barcelona, 1968, 131-135.

[15] *Ad fam.* V, 12.

[16] *De or.* II, 12, 51.

A. The concept of historical cause in Flavius Josephus

Historical explanation by means of causes is the all-important prime requisite for a historical text to be presented with guarantees of faithfulness to historical truth.

I therefore propose to analyse the two aspects announced at the beginning of this chapter. In the first section I shall classify the formulae and those words of a specifically aetiological content which allow for the establishing of a theoretical framework for the concept of historical cause in Flavius Josephus. In the second part I shall go on to the analysis of the aetiological concept itself and use specific expositions, both those in which the historical elements develop within the limits of the human plane and those where there is the intervention of elements which belong to a transcendent plane, elements which are justificatory of human activity. This latter aspect will then take me on to the study of the various denominations by which the intervention of a non-human force in human affairs is designated.

As regards the first objective, I should point out that, throughout the work of Flavius Josephus as a whole there appear numerous formulae, above all those of a prepositional structure, which announce or remind us of the statement of a fact: something happened "for the following causes"; that came to pass "for the causes already mentioned".

Therefore the relationship between these formulae, having considered their stylistic and historiographical function, is the following:

a. Introductory formulae:
- ἐξ αἰτίας τοιᾶσδε (B, I, 398),
- ἀπὸ τοιαύτης αἰτίας (B, VII, 219),
- διὰ τοιαύτην αἰτίαν (B, VII, 422; A, V, 338; A, X, 17; A, XV, 343; A, XVII, 148; A, XVIII, 91, 109, 343; A, XX, 17, 118; Vit, 31, 46, 125),
- ἐκ τοιαύτης αἰτίας (A, I, 53, 139; A, IV, 151; A, V, 135; A, X, 106),
- κατὰ τοιαύτην αἰτίαν (A, II, 1; A, XVIII, 39),
- ὑπὸ τοιαύτης αἰτίας (A, II, 8),
- αἰτίαν ἔλαβε τοιαύτην (A, IV, 101),
- ἐξ αἰτίας τοιαύτης (A, V, 175; A, VII, 162; A, X, 18, 212; A, XII, 11, 42, 187; A, XIV, 268; A, XV, 252; A, XVI, 271; Vit, 272),
- τοιαύτης ἀφορμῆς ἐγγενομένης (A, XV, 22),
- ἀφ' οἵας αἰτίας (A, XV, 372),
- ἐξ αἰτίας (A, XVI, 229),
- παρὰ τοιαύτην αἰτίαν (A, XVI, 300),

- κατὰ τοιαύτας αἰτίας (A, XVII, 299),
- αἰτίαν τοιαύτην (A, XVIII, 152),
- ἐκ τοιᾶσδε αἰτίας (A, XVIII, 340),
- ἐξ ἄλλης αἰτίας (A, XVIII, 347),
- δι' αἰτίαν, ἣν ἀφηγήσομαι (A, XVIII, 373),
- τοιαύτης ἐμπεσούσης αἰτίας (A, XX, 141),
- διὰ τὴν λεχθησομένην αἰτίαν (Vit, 13),
- προσγενομένης καὶ ἑτέρας τινὸς τοιαύτης αἰτίας (Vit, 24),
- τοιαύτης αἰτίας γενομένης (Vit, 179),
- τοιαύτης αἰτίας ὑποπεσούσης (Vit, 381).

b. Concluding and referential formulae:

- παρὰ τὴν αἰτίαν ταύτην (B, II, 532),
- διὰ δὲ τὰς αὐτὰς αἰτίας (B, IV, 498; Ap, II, 269),
- διὰ τοιούτους μὲν φόβους (B, VII, 303),
- ἀπὸ τοιαύτης αἰτίας (A, I, 59),
- τούτων δὴ τῶν προειρημένων αἰτιῶν (A, I, 4),
- διὰ ταύτην ... τὴν αἰτίαν (A, I, 180; A, II, 308; A, III, 265, 279, 313; A, IV, 106; A, VII, 285; A, IX, 74; A, XI, 300; A, XIV, 371; A, XVIII, 295; Ap, II, 21).
- διὰ τὴν αἰτίαν ταύτην (A, IV, 5),
- ὑπὸ δὲ ταύτης ... τῆς αἰτίας (A, IV, 156),
- ἐπί τοιαύτη ... αἰτίᾳ (A, V, 113; A, XIV, 173),
- ἐκ τῆς αἰτίας ταύτης (A, V, 197),
- κατὰ ταύτην τὴν αἰτίαν (A, VI, 61),
- διὰ τὴν προειρημένην αἰτίαν (A, VIII, 11; A, XIV, 32),
- κατὰ τὴν αὐτὴν αἰτίαν (A, IX, 25),
- διὰ τὴν αὐτὴν αἰτίαν (A, X, 194; Ap, II, 269),
- ἀπὸ τῆς αὐτῆς αἰτίας (A, XI, 55),
- ὑπὸ τοιούτων αἰτιῶν (A, XII, 88),
- ταῖς ὁμοίαις αἰτίαις (A, XII, 260),
- ὑπὸ ... λεγομένην αἰτίαν (A, XII, 359),
- ὑπὸ ταύτης ... τῆς αἰτίας (A, XIII, 235),
- τὴν αὐτὴν αἰτίαν (A, XV, 142),
- τὴν τοιαύτην αἰτίαν (A, XVI, 395),
- διὰ τοιαύτης αἰτίας (A, XX, 163),
- τὰς ὑπ' ἐμοῦ νῦν εἰρημένας ... αἰτίας (Ap, I, 69),
- διὰ τὴν λεχθησομένην αἰτίαν (Vit, 13).

The formulae διὰ ταῦτα and the adverbs διό and διόπερ should also be mentioned here, since their use is so frequent[17].

---

[17] Cf. K. H. Rengstorf, *A Complete Concordance to Flavius Josephus*, I-IV, Leiden, 1973-1983, *s.uu.* This work will be, henceforth, quoted only by the word *Concordance*.

The second point to come under study refers to those words which have a specifically aetiological content. Thanks to these words and, above all, the reiterated use of them in the Hellenistic historians, the aetiological concept in the work of Flavius Josephus can be deduced.

Αἰτία[18]. This word offers significant variants. In its active value it means "accusation, offence, claim", in the passive, "guilt, wrong, responsibility and, logically, cause"[19]. The adjective αἴτιος has the passive value, "guilty". The neuter αἴτιον leaves less doubt than αἰτία for the meaning of "cause"[20].

In the work of Flavius Josephus αἰτία has three sections. The first section has the meaning of "cause, reason, occasion and motive"[21]. A second section refers to the "responsibility and guiltiness"[22]. The third section embraces the values of "accusation and charge"[23]. The adjective αἴτιος means "causant, responsible and guilty"; ὁ αἴτιος means "instigator, perpetrator, sole responsible"; τὸ αἴτιον, "cause" and "reason"[24].

The fundamental concept, therefore, which is expressed by all these forms is that of the prime and profound cause, the justificatory reason for the entire sequence of causes which may accompany it and of the diversity of outcomes which may result.

Insisting on this point, there are further examples which may be mentioned. In αἰτία is to be found the prime reason for events. It is the principal cause within an aetiological hierarchy. It represents the foundation on which all other causes are founded, causes which are considered to be secondary, casual and concomitant. Thus Flavius Josephus tries to achieve those aims which are proper to an historian, and which consist of finding the closest possible relationships between facts which apparently are far removed from one another or which seem to bear no links. Therefore, we find ourselves in the presence of an intellectual history, in which previous intellectual elaborations are the causants of events and also rule over them. Therefore, it is not a question, in the work of Flavius

---

[18] Cf. *Concordance*, *s.u.*

[19] Cf. L. Pearson, "Prophasis and Aitia", *TAPhA* 83 (1952), 205-223.

[20] Cf. Gordon M. Kirkwood, "Thucydides' words for Cause", *AJPh* 73 (1952), 205-223.

[21] B, I, 83, 226, 503, 509, 578, 594, 611; B, II, 73, 296, 335, 353, 389, 455, 532, 629; B, III, 91, 170; B, IV, 244, 498, 519; B, V, 32, 482; B, VI, 251; B, VII, 299, 360; Vit, 51, 198, 390; Ap, I, 5, 19, 24, 69, 213, 224, 254, 298; Ap, II, 20-21.

[22] B, I, 502; II, 558.

[23] B, I, 539, 618; B, II, 28, 77, 92, 404, 418; B, IV, 255, 338, 364, 391; B, VII, 33, 60, 62, 207, 228, 299, 360, 445, 450; Vit, 13, 25, 56, 150; Ap, II, 150.

[24] Cf. *Concordance*, *s.uu.* and the verb αἰτιάομαι.

Josephus, of historical materialism in which phenomena of the economic type are those which determine events, but rather it is a question of mental elaborations which highlight the divers ranges of material and abstract causes which lie behind historical events[25].

'Αφορμή. The concept which this word expresses indicates the exterior occasion whence various reactions arise. Beneath the shades of meaning "pretext, chance, reason, cause, starting point, opportunity and possibility"[26], "living conditions, economic and diplomatic means and circumstances"[27], it establishes a nexus of aetiological continuity between the αἰτία and the ἀρχή of the action[28].

Thus, for example, the arrival[29] of the procurator Sabinus and the military occupation of the city of Jerusalem bring about circumstances which are appropriate for an urban war, for the burning of the portals of the temple and the stealing of the sacred treasure. At the same time these events constituted a weighty reason for delaying no longer the onset of the definitive war.

When mentioning Moses[30], Flavius Josephus presents him as having a two-fold mission, that is, with a two-fold reason (= cause) for his greatness: to humiliate the Egyptians and to raise up the Jews. He finds the moment, the occasion, the ἀφορμή for it: a spectacular victory over the Ethiopians marks a great step along the road to the liberation of the Hebrew people from the power of the Egyptians. Another occasion leading to his greatness[31] is found by Moses when he intervenes in the defence of some young men. This defence leads him towards a *"greater destiny"* (πρὸς τὸ κρεῖττον ἀφορμὴν): to find himself before God on Mount Sinai, the starting point for the greatness of Israel.

Elsewhere[32], it can be seen that the unbelieving of king Achab when confronted with divine revelation through the prophet Michaias was the ἀφορμή which destiny used (τὸ χρεών, 409) to bring about his death.

---

[25] Cf. B, VII, 77-79.

[26] B, I, 30, 447, 470, 502, 517, 612; B, II, 41, 324; B, VII, 441; A, II, 238, 257; A, III, 42, 214, 259; A, VI, 197; A, VII, 209; A, VIII, 369, 409; A, X, 251, 256; A, XIII, 185, 267, 305, 411; A, XIV, 159, 170; A, XV, 221, 238, 257, 308, 353; A, XVI, 71, 83, 134, 155, 200; A, XVIII, 333, 338, 375; A, XIX, 308-309; A, XX, 82; Vit, 375; Ap, I, 68. It is convenient to establish relations between the meanings of this word with those of πρό-φασις.

[27] B, I, 198, 523, 528; B, II, 371; B, V, 368, 397; A, I, 89; A, III, 6, 11, 23, 26; A, V, 57; A, XII, 184, 224; A, XIII, 427, 429; A, XIV, 51; A, XVIII, 149.

[28] Within these same aspects, it is necessary to include the meanings of the word καιρός, especially in B, VII, 78, 79; A, XIII, 267. Cf. *Concordance, s.u.*

[29] B, II, 41-54.

[30] A, II, 238-253.

[31] A, II, 257-263.

[32] A, VIII, 401-420.

The exceptional personality of Herod is well-known[33]. Now, from among the abundant evidence of his courage, he already had a unique *occasion*, at the age of fifteen, to demonstrate it by overwhelming bandits marauding along the frontier of Syria. What is more, this success won him great renown in the eyes of Sextus Caesar, the Roman governor of Syria.

On another occasion, Herod, who had already for a long time been going through a stormy relationship with Mariamme, finally comes to the end of his tether and condemns her to death[34]. In this case, the occasion brings about the end of a long uneasy wait, so as to initiate the fulfilment of what has been accumulating all along the days. For this accumulation Flavius Josephus uses a compound verb, both very descriptive and very little used: τὸ προοιχονομούμενον (No. 221).

The word ἀφορμή is also used in one place only with the value of cause, including that of profound cause[35]. For Josephus, the main cause (πλείων ἀφορμή) of Mariamme's misfortune was the set of circumstances on which she gave excessive rein to her tongue in the presence of Herod.

Πρόφασις. It is extremely difficult to be precise as to the semantic values of this word, since its field of action develops above all in the world of subjectivism. Considering the values found in the work of Flavius Josephus, πρόφασις means "reason placed before", "pretext" or "excuse", legitimate and real, simulated and apparent, and, finally, "occasion"[36]. It therefore seems to a certain extent the most distant cause from αἰτία, since, while the former indicates a profound and definitive reason, the latter expresses a justification or explanation which has varying force according to the intentions of the writer[37], in such a way that the truthfulness of a narrative could become subject to one of the many variants which exist between the two extremes of truth and untruth[38].

In fact, the πρόφασις embraces the idea of αἰτία, forming as it were a kind of secondary cause which could bring about the beginnings, the ἀρχή, of new situations[39].

---

[33] A, XIV, 158-160.

[34] A, XV, 218-231.

[35] A, XV, 238.

[36] Cf. *Concordance, s.u.* πρόφασις.

[37] Aristotle expressed the variety and the mutability of the excuse: προφάσεως δεῖται μόνον ἡ πονηρία (*Rhet.* 1, 1373a).

[38] ἀληθής, φευδής, Thuc. I, 23, 6; VI, 6, 1; Dem. XVIII, 226. καλή, φαύλη, Dem. XXI, 98; *Prooem.* XXXII, 2. διχαία, ἄδιχος, Dem. XI, 1; XVIII, 284; XX, 97; XXI, 98; XLIV, 39. εὔλογος, Thuc. III, 82, 4; VI, 79, 2. ἐπιειχής, Thuc. III, 9, 2. ἀχριβής, Thuc. IV, 47, 2. εὐπρεπής, Thuc. VI, 8, 4. ἄτοπος, Dem. XLVIII, 36.

[39] For the relations between πρόφασις and αἰτία, cf. K. Weidauer, *Thukydides und die hippokratischen Schriften*, Heidelberg, 1954, 8.

Its character therefore may be two-fold, the subjective character primarily, and then the objective character. The subjective character refers to the arguments which historical actors advance as justifications of their acts or events. The objective character is a result of the opinion which is given by the historian when confronted with historical material. Polybius makes wide use of the objective πρόφασις, impelled by his own interpretation of the facts and his constant passing judgement on the causes[40].

In the medical texts, the concept of profound cause is applied to αἰτία, whereas that of occasional, immediate and external cause is applied to πρόφασις[41]. Flavius Josephus, when commenting on the exterminating plague which ravages the people of Israel as punishment for an error committed by king David, adds to the biblical text that the plague, though no more than one, annihilated the Israelites through *real and apparent causes*[42].

In the work of Josephus, the subjective πρόφασις at times presents two sides. On the one hand, it symbolises what a given person wants to make understood to public opinion, or else the interpretation given to it by his enemies; on the other hand, it is the historian who judges that the truth is quite different (B, I, 229, 254, 276; A, IV, 167; A, X, 252; A, XIV, 151; A, XV, 365; A, XVI, 89; A, XX, 37).

The solely subjective pretext appears in certain attitudes of a war-like character (B, I, 115, 292, 299; B, II, 348, 412; A, IV, 177, 394; B, VII, 239, 368; A, VIII, 369; A, XIII, 427; A, XVI, 59; A, XIX, 311; A, XX, 162), and therefore serves to pass judgement on hostilities themselves or to justify them.

In its objective character, the word πρόφασις represents censure or simply a reasoning on the part of the historian as regards the acts of personalities (B, II, 285; B, IV, 146; B, VII, 256, 258; A, VII, 285; A, XIV, 372, 397; Ap, II, 276) or concerning delicate situations (B, IV, 363; A, XIV, 408).

Elsewhere the word πρόφασις is also used in expressions which apparently want to propose a reason, but which, in fact, achieve no more than to conceal the real cause of the situation: τῇ τοῦ θεοῦ προφάσει[43], προφάσει τιμῆς[44], προφάσει κυνηγησίων[45], ἐν προφάσει φιλίας[46]. In this sense

---

[40] P. Pédech, *op. cit.*, 88.
[41] Cf. περὶ ἀρχαίης ἰητρικῆς, Littré I, 616, 624-626; περὶ ἱερῆς νόσου, Littré VI, 366; ἐπιδεμίαι III, Littré III, 38-40, 70 and 74.
[42] A, VII, 324: αἰτίαις καὶ προφάσεσιν.
[43] A, IV, 22; cf. A, IV, 15.
[44] A, XV, 185.
[45] A, XV, 244; cf. also B, V, 424.
[46] Vit, 79; cf. also A, VII, 118.

there is a close approximation to Thucydides, for whom the separation of appearance and reality was a constant preoccupation.

The distinction made between πρόφασις and ἀφορμή is suggestive. The proximity of both words highlights their individual shades of meaning. In the words of king Achab to his people concerning problems occasioned by the demands of the king of Syria on their property it is affirmed that the Syrian king πρόφασιν βουλόμενος πολέμου λαβεῖν, εἰδὼς ὅτι τῶν μὲν ἐμαυτοῦ δι' ὑμᾶς οὐκ ἂν φεισαίμην, ἀφορμὴν δ' ἐκ τοῦ περὶ τῶν ὑμετέρων ἀηδοῦς πραγματευόμενος εἰς τὸ πολεμεῖν· ποιήσω γε μὴν τὰ ὑμῖν δοκοῦντα[47]. The πρόφασις conceals therefore what the king of Syria really wants, i.e. to wage war, and the moment previous to the outbreak of hostilities comes when the decision is made to attack the property of the citizens so as to exasperate them against him. This is in fact the ἀφορμή, and the king is thus justified[48], since the citizens, when confronted with the damage done to their property, will easily take to arms.

In another scene "the king of the Parthians, on finding no occasion (ἀφορμή) for a just excuse (πρόφασις), claimed those honours his father had accorded and declared war on him if he obeyed not"[49]. Thus, from the occasion, brought about by the natural rhythm of events or brought about expressly by reason of his absence, there arises the pretext as an immediate cause of events.

When comparing these two themes, there is still a slight distinction to be made, a distinction which, even though it may be rather frail, can sometimes help to delimit the differing degrees of causality when it comes to judging events. It seems therefore that the πρόφασις is rather a causal elaboration of the spirit, whereas the ἀφορμή always has a more tangible reality which is very localised within the aetiological scale. Doubtless, the ἀφορμή will very often take the place of πρόφασις, whereas elsewhere it will be difficult to make any distinction between them.

'Αρχή. This word indicates the beginning of an event. It includes the meanings of *occasion*, *non-profound cause*, the determining *motive* of the origin of either hostilities or human events. It is the circumstance in which an event begins plastically. It presupposes a set of reasons; it means the end of a more or less lengthy wait, and at the same a starting point or the bursting out into the exterior of a long accumulation of causes.

In the work of Flavius Josephus, to be more definite, the word varies between the meanings of *occasion*, *reason*, *cause*, *motivation*, *origin* and *basis*.

---

[47] A, VIII, 369.
[48] Similarly, A, XIX, 309.
[49] A, XX, 82.

Apart from these general ideas, the word ἀρχή has, in the work of Flavius Josephus, certain shades of meaning which should be considered separately[50]. It appears as a concomitant cause (B, I, 99, 171; B, III, 440; B, VI, 9); with the value of occasion for the taking place of an event (B, II, 284; B, VI, 73) or its motivation (B, II, 333; B, III, 72; Ap, I, 294); as a starting point (B, VI, 251; B, VII, 157); as the basis of a concept (Ap, II, 168) and as the prime cause, applied particularly to the Jewish concept of God "the beginning, middle and end of all"[51].

B. The aetiological question on the human plane

The aetiological theory which I have been expounding up to now is to be found in greatest detail in the descriptions of war which constitute the richest historiographical corpus in this sense. Wars sometimes begin in a surprising manner, and this very fact demands of the historian a labour of investigation so as to extract a detailed listing of the antecedents, of the motives and of the consequences. His examination will doubtless try to justify the reasons propounded by the belligerents.

1. *The fall of Jerusalem*

The first episode to come under study will therefore be the one concerning the fall of Jerusalem to the force of arms. Its very importance gives it pride of place.

The fall of Jerusalem into the hands of the Romans, on the 26th September of the year 70 A.D., takes up seven books, in other words a complete work of Flavius Josephus, the first of the four. I shall examine the causes for this fall, causes which are successively mentioned by the historian, and I shall base myself on the *Bellum Judaicum* mainly, making no more than the occasional reference to parallels in the *Antiquitates Judaicae* and the *Vita*.

Two circumstances which favour war: the worsening internal situation of the Roman Empire and the impetuous optimism of the Jewish revolutionary party, which took advantage of the general upheaval for insurrection (B, I, 4-5). These two motives constituted numerous occasions (ἀφορμαί) which led to the ἀρχή of definitive hostilities. It is therefore a question of concomitant and accumulative causes, and not of a prime cause. A date which can be taken as a starting point is the death of Nero, in June in the year 68. But in fact it can be seen that throughout the

---

[50] Cf. *Concordance, s.u.*
[51] Ap, II, 190: ἀρχὴ καὶ μέσα καὶ τέλος οὗτος τῶν πάντων. In similar senses, cf. A, I, 7 and Thuc. II, 1.

Bellum Judaicum there appear aetiological data concerning the war which have been noted intentionally by the author since he believes there to be a thread of continuity, however far-removed in time they may be. Therefore it is also necessary for them to be noted here and for an appraisal of their value to be made.

Here then are the most salient historical events, with strict respect for the narrative order of Flavius Josephus:

1. The first exchanges: alliances. The first occasion on which the Romans take a hand in the affairs of the Jews terminates in an alliance (162?B.C.), at the instigation of Judas Maccabaeus, an alliance whereby protection was required of the Romans so as to resist Antiochus Epiphanes (B, I, 38)[52]. The Jewish people derived very little benefit from the alliance. Jonathan renewed the treaty (144-143 B.C.) with the Romans (A. XIII, 163). Simon made another alliance (139 B.C.) with the Romans[53], and the high priest Hyrcanus renewed (132 B.C.) the treaty of friendship with Rome (A, XIII, 259-265).

2. In the year 65 B.C. the Romans again take a hand, in the person of the general Scaurus, because of the question of dissention between the brothers Aristobulus II and Hyrcanus II in a struggle for power. Scaurus received a substantial sum of money from the hands of Aristobulus, and Hyrcanus was forced to withdraw. But Hyrcanus and Antipater, a friend of his, had placed their hopes on the opposing side, i.e. on Pompey, who later captured Jerusalem (63 B.C.) and reduced Judaea, where he established the system of governors, the first of whom was Scaurus (B, I, 127-158). Thereafter there was a succession of Roman governors.

3. The second governor was Gabinius (57-55 B.C.), who, after various battles with pro-Aristobulus factions, reinstated Hyrcanus in Jerusalem, which henceforth was governed by an aristocracy (B, I, 169-170). Afterwards there followed a whole series of military interventions on the part of the Romans: against the renewed attempts of Aristobulus to win power, and against his son, Alexander.

4. The next governor of Syria, Crassus (54-53 B.C.), takes the treasure from the temple in Jerusalem to be used in his campaign against the Parthians. Cassius, his successor (53-51 B.C.), has to put down the pro-Aristobulus Jews and pacts peace with his son Alexander[54].

5. On Pompey's death, Antipater turns in favour of Caesar (B, I, 187), who names him procurator of the whole of Judaea (B, I, 199). In the meanwhile, Hyrcanus continued in his post as high priest. Antipater took consciousness of the power he wielded and, finding Hyrcanus unfit to be king,

---

[52] Anachronism: according to 1*Mach*. VIII, the treaty was made at the time of Demetrius (162-150 B.C.), a fact which seems to have been included in A, XII, 415. Cf. P. Viereck, *Sermo graecus quo senatus populusque Romanus magistratusque populi Romani usque ad Tiberii Caesaris aetatem in scriptis publicis usi sunt examinatur*, Göttingen, 1888.

[53] A, XIII, 227. The details of the treaty are to be found in 1*Mach*. XV, 16-24.

[54] For Crassus: B, I, 179-180; A, XIV, 104-119; Ap, II, 82. For Cassius: B, I, 218-242; A, XIV, 271.

entrusted the governing of Jerusalem to his son Phasael, and that of Galilee to Herod (B, I, 203).

6. After the death of Caesar (44 B.C.), the affairs of Judaea and the powers of its governors became increasingly dependent on the worsening situation in the Roman Empire. High tributes had to be paid (B, I, 219). Herod is named procurator of the whole of Syria. War between Caesar and Marcus Antonius. Malichus, then, conceives a revolt against Roman domination (B, I, 232), and stirs up internal unrest. Another Jew, Helix, instigates an uprising against Phasael (B, I, 236). Before Marcus Antonius, Jewish personages accuse Phasael and Herod of having usurped power from Hyrcanus (B, I, 242-244). Marcus Antonius names the two brothers tetrarchs of Judaea and condemns fifteen of the accusers to death. And Flavius Josephus adds: "Thus there came about, in Jerusalem, a greater confusion"[55]. Disagreement with the authority of the two brothers became increasingly pronounced. Antigonus, the son of Aristobulus II, is once again proposed as candidate to the throne by a large group of Jews (B, I, 248-252), a proposal which brings about the deaths of many citizens. A whole series of battles, with the participation of the Parthians, place Antigonus on the throne of Jerusalem. Afterwards, Phasael is assassinated (B, I, 271-272). Herod flees to Rome to plead for help. Marcus Antonius shows before the Senate the high regard in which he holds Herod and remarks on the anti-Roman attitude help by Antigonus. Finally Herod is unanimously proclaimed king of the Jews (B, I, 285): This happened toward the end of the year 40 B.C.

7. The reign of Herod represents a constant struggle to maintain himself in power. He could always depend on the help of the Romans, and in turn offered them his services in difficult cases, thus leaving Judaea marked by a continuous trail of bloodletting. A friend of Marcus Antonius, he also became an ally of Augustus Octavius Caesar, after the battle of Actium (31 B.C.), from whom he was confirmed in his sovereignty (B, I, 392). Dissentions within his own family put the finishing touches to a long reign filled with upheavals.

8. In the year 4 B.C. young Jews tried to throw down the golden eagle placed in the temple by Herod himself, possibly with the intention of making manifest the presence of Rome during his reign (B, I, 648-655). The young Jews were executed.

9. Archelaus, Herod's successor, also went to Rome to ask for the confirmation of his kingship (B, II, 2-3). During his absence from Jerusalem, Sabinus, the procurator of Syria, takes over the government of Jerusalem. Antipas also presents his candidature to kingship and in Rome his friends, although they prefer autonomy under Roman administration for Judaea, give him aid (B, II, 20-22). In the defence of Archelaus for his claims of rights to the throne, Caesar is recognised as the arbitrator of kingship (B,II, 34-36).

10. In the meantime the Jews are living through a situation of rebellion (B, II, 39-79 = A, XVII, 250-298) brought about by the sacking of the temple by the Roman procurator of Syria, Sabinus. At the same time, two usurpers of the throne, Simon of Peraea and Athrongaeus, strew the length

---

[55] B, I, 245.

and breadth of Judaea with corpses and guerrilla fighting (B, II, 57-65). Varus appears with his forces and imposes order (B, II, 72-79).

11. Archelaus, in Rome, sees opposition with the arrival of a Jewish embassy which asks from Caesar the administrative autonomy of their country (B, II, 80-95). Hence the result is that Caesar divides Judaea between an ethnarch, Archelaus himself, and two tetrarchies, Philip and Antipas.

12. There was no lack of revolutionaries against the power of Rome. During the time of the Roman procurator Coponius (6-9 A.D.), one Judas, a σοφιστής, announced the revolt against the power of Rome, since only God could be their Lord (B, II, 117-118). He, together with Saddok, was the downfall of the Jewish cause (A, XVIII, 10).

13. The Roman procurator in Judaea (26-36 A.D.), sent by the emperor Tiberius, sowed even greater discord amongst the Jews and turned them against Rome by introducing the standards of the Caesar into the city of Jerusalem and by laying hands on the sacred treasure (B, II, 169-177).

14. Under the procurator Cumanus (48-52 A.D.), there were new uprisings of the Jews, more particularly because of religious matters and unjustified deaths (B, II, 223-244).

15. With the arrival of the reign of Nero (54 A.D.), Flavius Josephus himself declares that he will deal only with Jewish affairs (B, II, 250-251). In the first place, thieves, *Sicarii* and false prophets created great unease amongst the whole of the Jewish people. In the second place, the rapid succession of procurators (Festus, 60-62 A.D.; Albinus, 62-64 A.D.; Florus, 64-66 A.D.) created no few problems. Florus especially carried his criminal acts to the extreme (B, II, 277-279). It was he who goaded the Jews into taking up arms (A, XX, 252-257), by his abusive government, his intentional religious insolence. And the flame of war spread from one Jewish city to another. The most virulent events took place in Jerusalem: a house-to-house massacre, on the orders of Florus, and the collision of the Jews with two Roman cohorts. In the meantime, the Jewish people were preparing their leaders for an uprising against Rome. On the other hand the priesthood played the role which was theirs to play: to calm down the populace so as to avoid a greater disaster. The role of Agrippa is also very clear from his long speech to the people[56]: you are on the verge of war with Rome, though it is clear that the honourable members of the community are striving to conserve the peace (B, II, 345); some for their lack of experience of the horror of war, others because of their hopes for independence; yet others because of their desire to amass riches; greater countries and greater states have submitted to the power of Rome; you can expect help from no one, only from God, but even his providence is on the side of the Romans (B, II, 390); maintain the peace in your cities, pay the tributes and restore the city. Thus the nobility, the patricians and the synagogue preferred the protectionism of Rome.

16. But the speech did not bear the expected fruit. The Jews who had instigated the hostilities attacked the fastness of Masada. The sacrifices in the temple in favour of the Roman people ceased forthwith. Flavius Josephus points out that it was this final event which precipitated the outbreak of hostilities (B, II, 409: τοῦτο δ' ἦν τοῦ πρὸς Ῥωμαίους πολέμου καταβολή).

---

[56] It is studied in the Chapter II, A, 2a (pp. 92-95).

17. Following on from this there is a whole series of consequences. The most salient of them was a civil war between the pro-Romans and the rebels, in the city of Jerusalem (B, II, 417-456): the deaths of the principal leaders and the destruction of the Roman garrison when betrayed by the Jewish rebels. Flavius Josephus assures us that in this last event the Jews saw the "irremediable cause of the war"[57]. At the same time there is increasing retaliation against Jews everywhere, even as far afield as Syria and Alexandria (B, II, 457-512), together with Jewish counteroffensives.

18. The situation reaches its most critical point with the attack of Cestius on the temple of Jerusalem (B, II, 527-555). The battle was manifestly between Romans and Jews. But unfortunately God would not allow that day to be the final one of the war. The retreat of the Roman army from the field of battle, an inexplicable retreat, raised the spirits of the rebels, described by Flavius Josephus as λῃσταί (B, II, 541), *bandits*, spirits which rose even higher with victory over the Romans (Vit, 24). The situation is communicated to Nero by Cestius, in such a way as to throw the responsibility for the war on to the shoulders of Florus.

19. From number 559 to number 646 in the book of *Bellum Judaicum*, Flavius Josephus describes the differences of opinion and the attitude of the Jewish leaders, together with a civil war which was brought on by them. During a moment of respite, the Jews of Jerusalem "devoted themselves to all manner of preparations against the Romans"[58]. The winter of 66-67 A.D. was drawing on.

20. Nero decides to put an end to the Jewish rebellion and to assert his power over the surrounding countries. The person chosen to execute this is called Vespasian, whose military exploits against the Jews were a never-ending series of successes. Galilee was harshly attacked and finally dominated by Vespasian (B, III, 115 - IV, 120). Then, the state of rebellion became centred on the capital, Jerusalem, where three Jewish factions disputed control over the city. Of these factions it was the Zealots who, by their attacks on the populace, brought about the beginning of the downfall of the city (B, IV, 3). To this must be added the acts headed by John of Gischala (B, IV, 9 ff.).

21. As for the Jewish side, the rivalries between those in favour of war and those who wanted peace did not stop (B, IV, 131 ff.). To this was added the notorious activity of the extremist group of Zealots, who brought about the insurrection of the populace of Jerusalem. The Zealots were guilty of a veritable urban war, by creating a situation of chaos such as had never been seen before (B, IV, 196 ff.). John of Gischala was the ruin (παραίτιος) of the two groups of antagonists (B, IV, 208 ff.) and the prime mover of the situation by advising the Zealots to ask for help from the Idumaeans[59]. These were the criminals of the high priest Ananus, the guiding light of the salvation of the Jews, and whose death meant the beginning of the end of the city (B, IV, 318).

22. The Roman reaction was very soon in coming, and the plight of the Jewish people was interpreted as a divine sign (ἕρμαιον πρόνοιαν θεοῦ) to ad-

---

[57] B, II, 455.

[58] B, II, 647.

[59] For the Jewish parties, cf. H. Drexler, "Untersuchungen zu Josephus und zur Geschichte des jüdischen Aufstandes 66-70", *Klio* 19 (1925), 277.

vance on Jerusalem (B, IV, 366 ff.). Flavius Josephus makes use of the moment to show that the Romans were not the ones who started the war, and also to praise the wisdom of Vespasian who had counselled a wait. Jews deserted in ever-increasing numbers to the Roman camp. Finally Flavius Josephus interprets the disastrous conduct of the Zealots as the fulfilling of a prophecy concerning the destruction of the sanctuary (B, IV, 385 ff.).

23. John of Gischala takes control of the situation (B, IV, 389). On the other hand, the *Sicarii* overrun Masada and cause havoc the length and breadth of Judaea, which constitutes for Flavius Josephus a fourth point with grave consequences (B, IV, 398).

24. Vespasian reacts and marches on Jerusalem (B, IV, 410 ff.). Meanwhile, he is informed of the uprising in Gaul (B, IV, 440). It is the winter of the year 67-68. In June in the year 68 Nero dies.

25. Another war breaks out in Jerusalem between Simon, the ally of the *Sicarii* of Masada, and the Zealots, who destroy Idumaea (B, IV, 503 ff.). Jerusalem finds itself at the mercy of the two antagonistic forces.

26. Galba and Otho die in Italy (January-April in the year 69). Vitellius is proclaimed emperor. Vespasian and his army are loath to accept the government of Vitellius. The army forces Vespasian to accept their proclamation of him as emperor (B, IV, 603). The change-over of power, in the midst of grave difficulties, does not fully come about until the month of December in the year 69.

27. Another faction was brought about in the midst of the party of Zealots by Eleazar, and sows confusion throughout the city (B, V, 5 ff.). The resulting civil war, fought between the three factions, that of Eleazar, that of John and that of Simon, carried the city to hunger and disaster (B, V, 19 ff.).

28. Titus advances towards Jerusalem with four legions (B, V, 39) and lays siege to the city.

29. In the meantime, the three Jewish forces become allied and present a common front to the Roman army (B, V, 71 ff.).

30. The previous situation, in spite of the common front presented to the Romans, is characterised by its internal fighting. Flavius Josephus proposes this struggle as the principal cause of the Roman intervention and destruction of the city (B, V, 257). He even goes so far as to justify the Romans for their just action. (B, V, 19).

31. From number 258 to number 347 there is a whole set of war activities, by which the Romans take the first and second walls. The internal situation was such that the destruction of the city is already a foregone conclusion, and reality bears this out (τὸ χρεών, B, V, 355).

32. Before the last great scaling operation by the Romans, Titus orders Flavius Josephus to convince his fellow-citizens to lay down their arms. It is a long speech, which is practically a carbon copy of Agrippa's speech at the beginnings of the hostilities (B, II, 345-401), insisting on their surrender to the stronger power (B, V, 362-419, pp. 95-97).

This analysis can be reduced to the following basic points: Αἰτίαι. It seems that there is a fundamental cause (αἰτία) underlying the whole process, which could be defined as a rejection on the part of the Jews of everything which was Roman. It is possible that the first alliance of concord brought about by the Maccabees may have become a situation of force and of domination accompanied by contempt for Jewish nationalistic positions on the part of the Romans[60]. Indeed, what was at the beginning no more than temporary aid ended up by becoming a debt, interference and a suppression of liberties. All this can be deduced, in spite of the few notes which Flavius Josephus leaves us, due to his wellmeaning effort to leave the Roman intervention in a good light. Neither should we forget, as a basic thesis of Flavius Josephus himself, that opinion according to which it was God himself who had vowed the downfall of Jerusalem (B, V, 19, 559; B, VI, 371, 411), and that it was this same God who for a long time (πάλαι) had destined it to the flames (B, VI, 250), and that there also existed a premonition of its undoing, which the Jews had not managed to understand with sufficient justice (B, VI, 310-315).

᾽Αφορμή, ἀρχή and πρόφασις: The other causes are accumulative and concomitant, and gradually reduce the gap towards the outbreak of hostilities, and at the same time are a justification of them. The ἀφορμή could be placed in the mandate of the procurator Florus, the person evidently responsible for the beginnings of hostilities[61], and the ἀρχή of the downfall of the city is centred on the acts of the Zealots and on the death of the high priest Ananus at the hands of the Idumaeans. The πρόφασις may be plural. Thus, the suppression of the sacrifices in favour of the Roman people (B, II, 409), the death of the Roman guard (id. 455), the Jewish victory over Cestius (id. 540), the internal civil war and the dissentions amongst the Jews, the involvement of the Sicarii in Masada and throughout Judaea (B, IV, 398) seem to intend a justification of the conduct of the Romans and, in short, a declaration of the need for the end of Jerusalem. As regards the over-long duration of the war, Flavius Josephus points out that it might have finished without creating such ruin if Cestius had continued with his offensive. But, convinced by his commanders who had been bribed by Florus with that aim in mind, he abstained from attacking and so from finishing things. That short-lived episode had great repercussions on the lengthening of the war[62]. All in all, Flavius Josephus, in his lengthy speech before the walls of Jerusalem, tries to minimise the reasons for which the Jews wish to wage war against the Romans: "for insignificant motives ... to wage war"[63].

---

[60] Cf. the Roman decrees cited in A, XIV, 185-267.

[61] Cf. Tac., Hist. V, 10. For causes in general, cf. M. Braun, "The prophet who became a historian", The Listener 56 (1956), 53-57. For the struggles of the parties against the Jerusalem hierarchy, cf. B. Brüne, Josephus der Geschichtsschreiber des heiligen Krieges und seine Vaterstadt Jerusalem, Wiesbaden, 1912, 51-57.

[62] B, II, 532.

[63] B, II, 353.

But this must be seen in the context of an exhortatory speech, written after events themselves had taken place, written with the full benefit of hindsight, knowing the consequences of the war, and composed from the high standing enjoyed by a Jew favoured by Rome.

2. *The wars of the people of Israel*

I shall now go on to an analysis of the interpretation which Flavius Josephus makes of the war footing which is kept up by the people of Israel during their pilgrimage to the Promised Land. I shall make especial mention of those causes which Flavius Josephus adds to the biblical text.

There are a great many battles which the people of Israel fought against those peoples they came up against in their journey towards the Promised Land. They are therefore wars waged due to the necessity of advancing along their road, inspired by an uncompromising nationalism, wars usually started by the opposing nations, who block their path. The causes of these wars are not looked at in detail either by Flavius Josephus or the biblical text, possibly because there was a supreme objective overriding everything: the divine commandment to reach the land of Canaan by whichever means were deemed necessary. These battles therefore are due to the leadership of the supreme leader of the people, who is no other than God himself, who, at the propitious moment, makes his voice heard. It is also clear that Flavius Josephus finds this divine aetiology in the Scriptures, but that neither denies him credit nor detracts from his worth. Flavius Josephus is writing for an audience which is ignorant of the customs of the people of Israel and does not hesitate to accept even wars as emanating from divine will. Neither does he deny them the rationalist character which he shows at other times. It must have been very difficult for him to give an explanation for wars using other, more materialistic bases. There is a general rule according to which the Hebrews are bound to suffer defeat if they turn their backs on God in their acts. If they are faithful to Him, victory is assured and complete. These victories therefore represent situations of difficulty which are overcome due to the privileged position of the people of Israel. Defeat, I repeat, means a rejection of divine guidance.

I shall list here only the most significant exploits of war:

A, III, 39-58 (Moses places the army in the hands of God: victory); A, IV, 1-8 (action contrary to divine will: defeat); A, IV, 85-99 (God is favourable: two victories); A, IV, 100-164 (God provident: victory); A, V, 1-34 (victory); A, V, 35-48 (defeat-victory); A, V, 49-61 (victory); A, V, 62-67 (victory); A, VI, 19-28 (victory due to divine will); A, VI, 271-274 (victory); A, VIII, 274-285 (defeat); A, VIII, 379-388 (victory);

A, IX, 7-15 (victory); A, IX, 29-43 (victory); A, X, 40-41 (defeat-victory).

On the other hand, there exist a great number of battles which could be dealt with conjunctly, since in them there appears a common denominator as the supreme cause, on which the other causes are based, causes which for the most part accompany it.

This group of battles can be located in the time when the people of Israel had already gained the land which was due to them by inheritance. To the semitic mind in general, and more particularly it can be seen in the Islamic world, the fact of finding oneself in the midst of material well-being, of settling in comfortable and rich cities, of abandoning the wealth of the nomadic life, are causes of the deterioration of the real spirit of the man of the desert, and constitute the quintessence of the semitic soul. This spirit is insistently recalled in the Holy Scriptures, and Flavius Josephus admits it as such. The Jew therefore who leads an easy life forgets his God, and this forgetfulness is the αἰτία of a series of battles which I shall now go on to look at.

When the people of Israel had overcome the Canaanites and the out-skirts of Jerusalem, they lay down their arms and set to working the land[64]. Their wealth increased, and they forgot the laws of God. Lust and corruption took possession of them and they led a life of debauchery which ended in a civil war. This war was brought about by the lustful treatment received by the wife of a Levite, of the tribe of Ephraim, in the city of Gaba, of the tribe of Benjamin, and which led to the death of the woman. The Levite and his wife, who had been passing through that city, had lodged at the house of a stranger, an occasion which Flavius Josephus uses to bring together the greatest number of causes which justify the hospitality accepted: διὰ συγγένειαν καὶ διὰ τὸ τὴν αὐτὴν φυλὴν νέμειν καὶ διὰ τὴν συντυχίαν[65].

The war begins, and the Israelites are twice vanquished by the tribe of Benjamin, in spite of their numerical superiority. Then the Israelites have recourse to the aid of God and are victorious[66].

Later, the Israelites once more stray from their constitution and forget their God, and are thus subjected to the yoke of the Assyrians with tributes included[67]. Later, delivered by Keniaz, they lived honourably for forty years under his leadership. On his death the Israelites ceased honouring God, and fell under the power of the Moabites[68].

---

[64] A, V, 132-174.
[65] A, V, 142.
[66] A, V, 159.
[67] A, V, 179-184.
[68] A, V, 185-197.

The Hebrews did not learn from the divine teachings as made manifest in those calamities which resulted from their acts of impiety, and once more failed to honour God and began to disobey his laws[69]. This time they fell under the sway of the Canaanites. Flavius Josephus reiterates that the principal motive for their misfortune is the contempt they show for God's laws[70]. In this case, at the end of twenty years, the people of Israel are delivered from the hands of their enemies, since God yet again promises them their salvation[71], since during the battle God sends a tempest against the Canaanites and renders their hands useless because of the cold[72]. Yet once more the Hebrews stray towards disorder, insulting God and showing contempt for His laws[73]. They fell this time into the hands of the Ammanites and the Philistines. But Israel came to its senses in the face of its calamities, and God provided them with a deliverer.

After the death of king Solomon, his son Roboamus sits on the throne, but ten tribes of the people of Israel prefer Jeroboam, and so they proclaim him king. The insistence with which Flavius Josephus alludes to the failure of Roboamus is obvious, and three times he indicates that this came to pass thus since it was κατὰ τὴν τοῦ θεοῦ βούλησιν[74]. Flavius Josephus makes no reference to the prolonging of the war exploits between these two kings, who protagonize in a political schism in Israel, and is unaware of the contribution of the LXX, according to which "there was ceaseless warfare between Roboamus and Jeroboam"[75].

To quote the biblical text, king Roboamus behaved in a manner which was contrary to divine will, and, for that motive, the king of Egypt invaded the kingdom of Roboamus, including Jerusalem. On this matter therefore, Flavius Josephus follows the text of the Chronicles (2 *Chron.* XII, 1 ff.), but insisting on the fact that it is God who thus punishes the conduct of Roboamus[76]. However, Flavius Josephus makes some remarks designed to justify the acts of Roboamus—remarks which are completely abiblical—before beginning the narration of the war of the king of Egypt. These remarks deserve to be considered at length.

"The vastness of the affairs of a kingdom and the betterment of those same affairs"[77] are the αἴτιον of the misfortunes and the transgressions of

---

[69] A, V, 198-209.
[70] A, V, 200.
[71] A, V, 201.
[72] A, V, 205.
[73] A, V, 255-266. In the same sense, cf. A, V, 338-340 and 352-360.
[74] A, VIII, 218. Similar ideas in A, VIII, 216 and 217.
[75] 3*Reg.* XIV, 30.
[76] A, VIII, 246-265.
[77] A, VIII, 251: αἴτιον... πολλάκις γίνεται κακῶν καὶ παρανομίας ... τὸ τῶν πραγμάτων μέγεθος καὶ ἡ πρὸς τὸ βέλτιον αὐτῶν τροπή.

the law on the part of men. That refers only to significant and important men. Consequently there is generated a chain of ills and illegal acts on the part of the great mass of the populace, since it is not capable of maintaining an upright moral conduct when it sees that the king himself leads a life of debauchery. He affirms that the morality of the subjects becomes corrupt through the corruption of their legislators[78], and that correct conduct on the part of the people could represent an act of censure against the governor.

God, as Flavius Josephus remarks, takes his revenge on king Roboamus by sending him the king of Egypt, Isokos. The Israelites plead to heaven, but God has abandoned them just as they had abandoned him[79]. They insist in their supplications, God forgives them, but of necessity has to hand over the city of Jerusalem to Isokos.

The conduct of king Jeroboam is also based on his moral and religious behaviour, in a struggle to make his own will prevail, in spite of divine warning. The entire exposition is sprinkled with references to the observance of divine law, without which there is no salvation[80].

Finally, the war which Jeroboam wages against the king of Judah, Abias, ends with the victory of the latter, in spite of his also leading a disorderly life. But the Bible adds (1Reg. XV, 4) something which is not mentioned by Flavius Josephus, that God, out of consideration for king David, gave protection to the descendants of his family tree. Flavius Josephus insists a great deal on the fact that this victory was conceded by God[81].

In the work of Flavius Josephus, the fact of the godless behaviour of the kings of Israel being the source of numerous misfortunes for the people as a whole is continuously reiterated. It is true that the causes already appear in the Bible, but it is also true that Flavius Josephus in many cases extends the aetiological references[82].

As regards the transportation of the ten tribes of Israel to Persia and to the cities of Media[83], Flavius Josephus notes the religious causes which brought about this event. He makes a distinction between the most recent causes and the initial cause. The most recent and concomitant causes were the violation of the laws and the contempt shown to the prophets (id., 281), the behaviour of various kings and of the people. On the other hand the beginning of the misfortunes of the Israelites is centred on their

---

[78] A, VIII, 252.
[79] A, VIII, 255-259.
[80] A, VIII, 265 ff.
[81] A, VIII, 282-285.
[82] A, IX, 159-160, 166-176, 186-204, 243-257, 258 ff.; A, X, 36-46.
[83] A, IX, 278 ff. According to the Bible (2Reg. 17, 23), "Assyria".

rebellion against Roboamus, by preferring his servant Jeroboam as king, a sinner and an enemy of the Divinity (*id.*, 282).

This entire succession of wars and difficult situations, created essentially because of questions related to the religious world of the Jews, lead us to the conclusion that Flavius Josephus was extremely sensitive to detecting and testifying to one of the most fundamental causes in the history of the people of Israel, and, in a certain sense, one of the most fundamental causes in universal history, something which had already been noticed first of all by the Hellenistic and, later, the Christian historians: the intervention of the transcendent plane on the acts of man, of peoples, and of political events. This aspect will be dealt with later on at greater length.

I shall now make a brief analysis of some other battles, making a special mention of the aetiological contributions of Flavius Josephus.

King Saul defeats Naas, king of the Ammanites, with the aid of the God of Israel[84]. The causes of the war are explained with a whole wealth of detail by Flavius Josephus[85], who here enlarges on the text of the Scriptures. The expression ἔνθεος γενόμενος[86] does not come from the Scriptures either. This inspiration enables Saul to pledge his aid to the inhabitants of Jabis, who are terrified by the threats of Naas.

In the battle of Saul and the Philistines, Flavius Josephus uses the same elements which he reads in the Bible, but with a different aetiological slant. Both the Bible and Josephus say that the Philistines encamped at Machma, since the Hebrews had destroyed a fortress of theirs which was near Gebala[87]. This event constitutes the excuse proper (πρόφασις) for the begining (ἀρχή) of hostilities, but there was no doubt an underlying and profound cause. Then Flavius Josephus adds other causes which, in the Bible, appear as a simple enumeration of the privations to which the Jews had been subjected by the Philistines[88]: here we are dealing with the real cause which pushes the Jews to rebellion. Flavius Josephus introduces this series of events as causes with the conjunction γάρ and leads us to believe that the Jews overran the stronghold of the Philistines as an act of rebellion against the state of prostration to which they were subjected[89]. One may observe that the intention of Flavius Josephus to search out the aetiological processes is both persistent and thorough.

---

[84] A, VI, 82.
[85] A, VI, 68-71.
[86] A, VI, 76.
[87] 1*Sam.* XIII, 3.
[88] 1*Sam.* XIII, 19-22.
[89] A, VI, 95 ff.

Antiochus Epiphanes marches on Egypt for two reasons which I have not read in the Scriptures: "Since he had been overwhelmed by a desire to possess it and because of the contempt which he felt towards the sons of Ptolemy, still weak and unfit to rule over so great a state"[90]. I have no knowledge of the source which Flavius Josephus used for A, XIII, 135 ff., but the fact is that the historian gives the causes for the revolt of the people of Antioch against king Demetrius II. He writes: "The people of Antioch, who hated Demetrius because of the ill-treatment which they had suffered at his hands, and were hostile to him on account of his father Demetrius, who had wronged them greatly, hoped to have an occasion to fall on him"[91]. That occasion was the arrival in Antioch of Jewish troops sent by Jonathan as a replacement for Demetrius' own troops. The biblical parallel does not give the reasons for the uprising, only the occasion (1Mach. XI, 42 ff.).

The generals of Demetrius want to regroup after the defeat inflicted on them by Jonathan, and manage to get together a larger army than the previous one[92]. The biblical text makes no mention of the cause which puts them on the path to war.

At times wars are brought about by subjective causants, affecting rather the feelings of people. In the case of Antiochus, it is ὑπὸ πλεονεξίας καὶ φαυλότητος[93] that he begins the attack on Simon, or because of the resentment he feels on account of the defeats he has suffered at the hands of Simon[94] who invades Judaea.

So as to avoid unnecessary repetition on this subject, I shall simply note here other situations of war, which contain the defining traits of the technique of Flavius Josephus: B, I, 216-224 = A, XIV, 268-270; A, XV, 108-160, 349-353; A, XVI, 271-285; A, XVII, 149-163; A, XVIII, 109-125, 257-308, 310-379.

3. The historical subject as cause

In this section, I shall study historical cause as embodied in human action and human enterprise. Man, in his role as the forger of situations, as the coordinator of differing tensions, may set himself up as the centre, the nucleus and the cause of political, social and economic, cultural and sentimental events. According to whether the historian uses this aetiological resource to a greater or lesser degree, the history produced will have varying degrees of dynamism and psychological insight.

---

[90] A, XII, 242 = 1Mach. I, 16-20.
[91] A, XIII, 135.
[92] A, XIII, 174.
[93] A, XIII, 225.
[94] A, XIII, 236.

Now, historical events are brought about by man in his twofold role: as an individual and as a productive cause of human community.

Were we to take a purely historicist stand, then it would be necessary also to delimit the quality of human acts, so that they could be classified within the historiographic category. When an historiographic agent is the perpetrator of an act which has an influence on the historical future, and, given the case, it is, when all is said and done, the reason for a chain of events, then we find ourselves face to face with an act which is worthy of being recorded in history, in such a way as to differentiate it from all those other acts which do not go beyond the boundary of the personal world of the individual, and which therefore do not intervene in History and cannot be recorded as such.

It is nevertheless true that everything is history; any detail which were to contain existential elements is worthy of forming part of the corpus of historiography[95], and the attitude of the ancient historian when confronted with historical facts was not so much a selection of facts which were explicable by means of their causes as a vital experience which provided the opening to every anecdote, so that in any historian one finds any number of simple pieces of news, which can be considered useful or useless, but which have been recorded by the historian without any further intentions than the fact of recording them. Therefore it must not be forgotten that these unimportant pieces of news make up the historiographic corpus and contribute to maintaining the balance of the narrative.

Since the historicist attitude sets itself a subjective history which is the fruit of the intellectual efforts of the historian, it suffices to relegate this personal attitude to the simple fact of the free choice of subject on the part of the historian and not to project it on to the facts which are narrated.

In this sense, then, in the work of Flavius Josephus, as we have seen, there is an abundance of acts of an historiographic character, both individual and collective, which can be classified within the historicist school. Thus to avoid unnecessary repetition we must choose those personages whose acts will no doubt be worthy of becoming history in the mind of the ancient historians. However, the multitude of minor events contained in the work of Flavius Josephus must not be forgotten.

This manner of centring attention in the historical narrative on persons and communities has gone through a lengthy period of development.

---

[95] Cf. P. Veyne, *Comment on écrit l'histoire*, Paris, 1971, 43-44 (with a very extensive bibliography on this subject); E. Ripoll Perelló, *Sobre els orígens i significat de l'art paleolític*, Barcelona, 1981, 17-18 (the author applies the question to the simple vestiges and to Paleolithic art).

This development, beginning from initial inaccuracies, eventually gives rise to a manifest historiographical technique.

Thus it can be seen that the unitarian and universal concept of the historical subject, man and peoples, produce a national and a universal history respectively. For Polybius, for example, the historical subject is the Roman people, which becomes a suprapersonal historical subject, transcending the limits of action of the individual. In that, therefore, there has been an evolution.

While for Thucydides man is the receiver of the forces of power, for later historians the individual grows in importance with all the wealth of his psychology. In this sence, the portraits of Pericles, Nicias and Alcibiades[96] stand out because of their desire to dominate, while lacking greatly in psychological traits. In this first part of classical historiography, we can see that it is the communities—the Athenians, the Lacedaemonians, the Syracusans and so on—which speak and act as if they were individuals. After Thucydides, thanks to the psychological analysis of philosophical thought, the knowledge of the internal aspects of man is gone into much greater profundity, there is exploration into the distinction between sensations and thought, and the conclusion reached is that the interior life of man influences the conditions of life in a country[97].

As is to be expected, when human thought has overcome certain stages, the use to which men put that progress is never presented with a clear-cut distinction of fields, but rather with a mixture of the same. Thus, Hellenistic historiography offers a mixture: it is possible to combine both the acts of outstanding personalities with the great acts of communities. The preeminance of one or the other will depend above all on psychological knowledge and on the idea of historical universality which the writer possesses.

On general lines, Flavius Josephus presents a mixture of the two techniques: he is able to create personages who are responsible for and the perpetrators of historical good and evil; on the other hand he presents communities, organisms and peoples who show a totally personalising role. But let us go on to a more detailed analysis.

An example which is to hand and which perhaps synthesises this manner of writing of Flavius Josephus appears in his proem to the *Bellum Judaicum*[98]. Here can be seen the alternating use he makes of the concepts

---

[96] Thuc. II, 65, 5-13; VI, 15; VII, 8.

[97] On the contributions of the philosophers in this field, cf. P. Pédech, *op. cit.*, 204-206. On the antithetic typology of characters in Tacitus, cf. J. Lucas, *Les obsessions de Tacite*, Leiden, 1974.

[98] Cf. its study in Chapter II, C, 4a (pp. 208-210).

of the individual and the community as historical factors. As regards the Roman world, he mentions the Romans, the Roman Empire, the Roman army, and centres events around the persons of Titus, Sossius, Quintilius Varus, Cestius; as for the Jewish camp, he speaks of the Jewish people, of the Jewish revolutionary party, of Jewish fellow citizens from beyond the Euphrates, of Herod, of the Jewish tyrants and the gangs of bandits; a third group is formed by the mention made of the troubles in the countries of the east, of the Gauls, Celts, Parthians, Babylonians, the tribes of Arabia, of the Euphrates, of Adiabene, the Greeks, of the Assyrian and Median Empires, of Antioch Epiphanes and the Hasmonaeans.

It cannot be asserted that there is a preponderance of one tendency over the other, it is wiser to offer an opinion that—and I repeat—together with the acts of the outstanding personalities also move the great acts of the communities. I propose to analyse these aspects now in greater detail.

Still dealing specifically with the *Bellum Judaicum* and looking closely at the statistics, it can be seen that the historiographical construction which Flavius Josephus creates rests on the personalities. In this sense, the same expressions are centred on actor-personalities, individuals and communities, around whom revolves the whole of history. Examples abound[99]. Here I shall comment on the most significant ones.

The figure of king Herod, the subject of so much study elsewhere from a different perspective, cannot be ignored. In short, Flavius Josephus paints a whole series of scenes in which Herod appears as the central figure on whom all action hinges: "Herod lays waste the enemy territory and overruns five towns, puts two thousand inhabitants to the sword and razes their houses to the ground..."[100]. With reference to the passages devoted to the description of the building carried out by Herod[101], one may appreciate that it is the king who is the maker of history, on whom Flavius Josephus confers insistent personalism: he it is who restored (No. 401), raised up (No. 401), enlarged (No. 401), built (No. 403), erected (No. 403), remade (No. 408), and embellished (No. 408).

The historian himself makes his own person the object of special treatment[102]. Thus it is Flavius Josephus who organises resistance in Galilee against the Romans: he chose and appointed seventy people as

---

[99] B, I, 35, 39, 63, 127, 155, 195-200, 242-247, 634-646; B, II, 553; B, III, 229-234; B, IV, 37-38, 56, 112-120, 592-604; B, V, 88-89, 460-465; B, VI, 417-419; B, VII, 26-36, 190-215, 220-243.

[100] B, I, 334.

[101] B, I, 401-430.

[102] B, II, 569-583.

magistrates for the whole of Galilee, and seven for each city (Nos. 569-571); fortified the most important cities (Nos. 572-576), remodelled the army with a discipline based on the Roman model (Nos. 577-578), trained it (Nos. 579-583), organized the infantry, the cavalry and the mercenaries, and formed a guards corps consisting of six hundred hand-picked men (No. 583).

All this activity, however, was guided by a previous mental activity and a thorough comprehension of the problems and the remedies necessary. The historian does not let this go by without a mention: he intended (ἐφρόντισεν, No. 569) to attract the affection of the inhabitants of Galilee, fully aware (εἰδώς, No. 569) that this was the most important thing; he fully realised that the leaders of the people would be reconciled to him (συνιδών, No. 570) were he to give orders through them to the populace; he discovered (γινώσκων, No. 573) that Galilee was the prime objective of the Romans, and consequently fortified the cities; he understood (συνιδών, No. 577) that the Romans owed their successes to their discipline and their military training, and so organised his own army on the basis of discipline and drilling.

As can be seen, Flavius Josephus undertakes mental activity before making resolutions. Likewise, to judge from the indications which abound in his writings, one may come to the conclusion that his is a history which belongs to the intellectual type of history, in the sense that he bases many events on the reasoning of historical subjects previous to any action.

On the other hand, the personal enemy of Flavius Josephus, John of Gischala, is shown as having an important role as a prime mover of historical events. Although Flavius Josephus treats his rival in a very biased manner, he does present him as the leader of an ever-increasing multitude (No. 587), with capacity of thought (φροντὶς δ' ἦν αὐτῷ, No. 588) for choosing his followers, with whom he pillaged the length and breadth of Galilee. He persuaded Flavius Josephus to rebuild the walls of his city, but did so only for personal gain. He obtained authorisation to import oil, and amassed an enormous fortune which he used against Flavius Josephus. He assumed (ὑπολαβών, No. 593) that he would eventually govern Galilee, and increased his attacks in Galilee with his *Sicarii* so as to lay an ambush for Flavius Josephus. Finally he spread a rumour according to which Flavius Josephus was intending to hand over the country to the Romans (Nos. 593-594).

Whole groups are also treated as historical actors in the sense that they too make speeches[103]. Flavius Josephus has the crowds make their own

---

[103] Cf. Chapter II, A, 2a and c.

decisions and have a powerful influence on historical action and at the same time they are the agents of events which are worthy of being recorded in history. Crowds also have feelings and can embark on a tragic course of action[104]. Thus mention is made of combatants, peoples, soldiers, sentinels, the inhabitants of towns, assassins, factions and so on, who are the agents of war exploits, attract to themselves the attention of other forces, cause disasters and end up either victorious or annihilated.

In book IV of the *Bellum Judaicum*[105], an extensive narrative provides a magnificent sample of what is under study. Flavius Josephus manages to combine both the individual acts and the acts of whole communities. The individual personality who most predominates in this fragment is that of John of Gischala who, by means of his harangues, excites the passions of the people to war against the Romans[106] and spreads confusion amongst the citizens. The community who has the most influential effect on historical action is that of the Zealots[107] who assume control of Jerusalem, arrest and put to death the eminent citizens, and appoint high priests of their own choice[108]. It is they who are the cause of an uprising of the people led by Ananus who makes a long and magnificent speech during a general assembly[109] with the aim of inciting the people to attack the Zealots[110]. As a consequence there is warring in the city[111]. Once more John of Gischala makes an appearance on the scene, betrays Ananus before the Zealots[112] as an ambassador, and encourages them to ask for outside help[113]. His advice brings about the arrival of the Idumaeans[114]. Jesus, the most important priest after Ananus, makes a speech[115] to them from the city walls[116], and is answered by Simon, the head of the Idumaeans[117]. Finally the Zealots manage to open the city gates to the Idumaeans[118]. The two factions, now united, bring about a general massacre, and Ananus and Jesus[119] are numbered among the dead; then

---

[104] B, IV, 26-29, 62-69, 85-96, 400-439; B, V, 71-84; B, VII, 244-251, 410-419, 437-453.
[105] Nos. 135-365.
[106] B, IV, 126-128.
[107] B, IV, 135-137.
[108] B, IV, 138-150.
[109] It is studied in Chapter II, A, 2a (pp. 100-101).
[110] B, IV, 151-192.
[111] B, IV, 193-207.
[112] B, IV, 208-215.
[113] B, IV, 216-223.
[114] B, IV, 224-235.
[115] It is studied in Chapter II, A, 2a (p. 101).
[116] B, IV, 236-269.
[117] B, IV, 270-282.
[118] B, IV, 283-304.
[119] B, IV, 305-325.

it is the turn of the nobility to be tortured and put to death[120]. The Idumaeans leave, and this action is the cause of renewed atrocities and fresh victims[121].

This internal situation in Jerusalem puts Vespasian on the road to Jerusalem, by the express will of his generals[122]. The three calamities which are the causants of the situation in Jerusalem are the war, the tyranny of John and the factions. Added to these there is now another calamity: the occupation of Masada by the *Sicarii*[123].

The whole of this chaotic situation starts up the vast Roman operation which will end with no less than the total destruction of Jerusalem itself.

Reflecting on this analysis, especial mention should be made of the rhetorical character of the moderate class on the one hand, and the violence and tensions brought about by the entire opposition. This incompatibility was the immediate cause of destruction at the hands of the Romans.

Another personality emerges in the *Bellum Judaicum* as the creator of new situations of violence which help only to hurry the already existing situation of chaos towards its inevitable outcome. Simon, expelled by Ananus, joins the *Sicarii* in Masada[124]. He will create new motives for a Roman intervention:
  - he gets together an army to attack towns (Nos. 509-513),
  - and the Zealots at Jerusalem (Nos. 514-515),
  - he invades Idumaea (Nos. 515-528),
  - he takes Hebron (Nos. 529-533),
  - he lays waste Idumaea (Nos. 534-357), and
  - he rescues his wife from the hands of the Zealots (Nos. 538-544);
  - Simon takes Jerusalem (Nos. 556-584).

In book VII of the *Bellum Judaicum*[125], Flavius Josephus recapitulates concerning all those who are guilty of creating such a situation. He speaks of emulation in evil, of the oppression of power over the masses and of the desires of these masses to destroy that power. He mentions the *Sicarii*, he speaks again of John of Gischala, who is less moderate than the former, of Simon, the perpetrator of a variety of crimes, of the Idumaeans and of the Zealots. The text constitutes a digression which

---

[120] B, IV, 326-344.
[121] B, IV, 345-365.
[122] B, IV, 366-388.
[123] B, IV, 389-409.
[124] B, IV, 503-544, 556-584; B, V, 110.
[125] B, VII, 259-274.

aims at completing the general situation on the occasion of the beginning
of the narration of the destruction of Masada.

In the story of Abraham, the inhabitants of Sodom are dealt with *en
bloc*. Flavius Josephus, reducing the biblical text to its bare bones, makes
them the receivers of divine wrath. According to Flavius Josephus, but
not the Bible, the Sodomites, "proud of their number and of the
magnitude of their wealth, were insolent towards men and impious
towards God, in such wise that they no longer remembered the benefits
received from Him, they hated strangers and avoided all contact with
others"[126]. Here it can be seen how the abstract concepts constitute the
αἴτιον of the consequent events: ὑπερφρονοῦντες ... ἦσαν ὑβρισταὶ καὶ ...
ἀσεβεῖς, ὡς μηκέτι μεμνῆσθαι τῶν ... ὠφελειῶν, εἶναί τε μισόξενοι.

Flavius Josephus makes a long presentation of the person of Moses (A,
II, 201 ff.), surrounding the preparation for his birth with a great wealth
of details which he takes from the rabbinical tradition[127]. The biblical text
is much more austere. All this process makes us infer that there is an intention of Flavius Josephus to hint to the readers that we are dealing with
an important personage.

In the—abiblical[128]—story of the war between the Ethiopians and the
Egyptians, it can be seen that the perpetrators of the acts are two communities, in other words the two enemy peoples. In the face of the
hostilities, the Pharaoh charges Moses with the solution to the conflict.
Moses acts after previous reasonings: he wants to advance to meet the
enemy (φθάσας, A, II, 244), and attacks by the path which is least expected, given the situation of the enemy army, an attack which brings
him victory. By his stratagem, Moses creates a situation of surprise attack on the Ethiopians (οὐδὲ προμαθοῦσι, A, II, 48), and promotes the in-
exhaustible energy of the Egyptian army (πονεῖν οὐκ ἔκαμνεν, A, II, 248).

Further on, Flavius conceives the Egyptians as a community with the
same faculties which are possessed by the individual: "They *hated* him for
this and *intended* to carry out their decisions against him (Moses) with the
greatest pleasure, *suspecting* that for his success he would bring about a

---

[126] A, I, 194.

[127] From the *Mechilta* commentary, according to Thackeray in his edition of Flavius
Josephus in The Loeb Classical Library, vol. IV, 257, note a. On the other hand, there is
no enlargement in the Palestinian Targum: A. Díez Macho, *Neophyti 1, Targum
palestinense, ms. de la Biblioteca Vaticana*, vol. 1, Génesis, C.S.I.C., Madrid-Barcelona,
1968.

[128] Based on the biblical allusion (*Num.* XII, 1) of the *Cushita woman* whom Moses was
due to marry.

revolution in Egypt, and *instructing* the king on his death''[129]. The community ''Egyptians'' is the causant, the αἴτιος, which forces the king's hand. Here too special mention should be made of the abstract concepts as the αἴτιον which trigger off events. Thus, there are the words φθόνος, μῖσος, δέος and ταπείνωσις. As regards the attitude of the king, we should keep in mind that he too rules by mental processes which are previous to action: ''He (the king) also, for his part, was intending to do so''[130].

Moses is motivated by acts which he judges unjust (A, II, 260). The route which led the Israelites to Palestine was chosen, in spite of the hardship involved in following it, by Moses and not by God (as the biblical text has it) in the opinion of Flavius Josephus (A, II, 322-323). The route was chosen so as to avoid any encounter with the Egyptians were they to follow their trail, or with the hostile Palestinians.

The figure of Joshua is also filled out in comparison with the biblical text. Joshua is portrayed as a far-sighted man with regards to the future fate of his people, when the Jordan has been crossed and Jericho gained. After sending out scouts to Jericho— in this he concords with the biblical text—Flavius Josephus explains the mission: ''So as to have knowledge of their strength and their intentions, and he reviewed his army to cross the Jordan at a suitable moment''[131]. Neither is it God—according to Flavius Josephus—who orders the priests to stop half-way across the Jordan until the whole people has passed over, but the idea comes from Joshua, who even establishes a crossing order among the different classes of the people of Israel (A, V, 17). The logical fact of the Israelites setting up camp (*Jos.* IV, 19) near Jericho is interpreted by Flavius Josephus as an explicit order from Joshua to lay siege to the city[132].

The style of the historian is another reflection of the personalist character imparted to his work. When Joshua attacks, it is he who puts to death—''having caused great carnage there...''[133]—, it is he who goes out to meet the enemy (*ibid.* 65), it is he who goes off in pursuit, who destroys the entire enemy army, butchers the horses and burns the chariots, and leaves a trail of destruction wherever he has passed by (*ibid.* 66-67).

Within this same historical episode, Flavius Josephus coincides with the same literary style as the Bible, when he has a whole crowd speak out in its own defence, as the subject therefore of its own claims (*Jos.* XXII,

---

[129] A, II, 254.
[130] A, II, 255.
[131] A, V, 2.
[132] A, V, 22: πολιορκεῖν αὐτοὺς ᾽Ιησοῦς ἔγνω.
[133] A, V, 62.

21 ff. = A, V, 111 ff.). We can see that Flavius Josephus, in the first thirteen books of the *Antiquitates Judaicae*, personalises the individuals and communities in the same way as the Bible does. But although he paraphrases the biblical text, he adds to it on many occasions.

King Solomon appears at the centre of the whole time lapse which the description of his reign takes up, so that the history of the people of Israel has as its epicentre the figure of its king. So it is that the history of the reign of Solomon became the very history of the people of Israel. In view of the magnitude of the story, I shall limit analysis to the two main aspects of the reign of Solomon: the building of the temple of Jerusalem and Solomon's military exploits and successes.

The temple which king David was not able to erect was built by his son Solomon. By comparing the text of the LXX with that of Flavius Josephus, two conclusions may be drawn: that the inspiration and artificer of the construction of the temple is none other than Solomon himself, and that the manner of describing the conduct of the king coincides even in the use of entire quotes. There is no doubt that the historiographical styles of both the Bible and of Flavius Josephus reveal, in the case of the history of king Solomon, a similarity of concept as regards historical narration. I shall here make a comparative study of the texts, and more specifically those texts which are demonstrative of the preeminent role of the king and of the stylistic similarity of the sources:

a. Comparative texts:

- 1*Reg.* VI, 2: ὁ οἶκος ὃν ᾠκοδόμησεν ὁ βασιλεύς,
- 1*Reg.* VI, 3 i 9: ᾠκοδόμησε τὸν οἶκον,
- *Ibid.* 10: ᾠκοδόμησεν[134] τοὺς ἐνδέσμους,
- A, VIII, 61: τῆς δ'οἰκοδομίας τοῦ ναοῦ Σολομὼν ἤρξατο,
- *Ibid.* 62: τὸν ναὸν ᾠκοδόμησε Σολομών.

b. Texts without biblical parallels:

- A. VIII, 63: βάλλεται μὲν οὖν τῷ ναῷ θεμελίους ὁ βασιλεύς,
- *Ibid.* 64: ἀνήγαγε δ' αὐτὸν ἄχρι τῆς ὀροφῆς ἐκ λευκοῦ λίθου πεποιημένον,
- *Ibid.* 65: περιῳκοδόμησε δὲ τὸν ναὸν ... τὰς εἰσόδους αὐτοῖς δι' ἀλλήλων κατεσκεύασεν,
- *Ibid.* 68: τὴν δὲ ὑπὸ τὰς δοκοὺς στέγην τῆς αὐτῆς ὕλης ἐβάλετο.

---

[134] The same verb is used many times throughout Chapter VI.

c. Comparative texts:

- 1*Reg.* VI, 9: καὶ ἐκοιλοστάθμησε τὸν οἶκον κέδροις,
- 1*Reg.* VI, 15: ᾠκοδόμησε τοὺς τοίχους ... διὰ ξύλων κεδρίνων,
- 1*Reg.* VI, 18: κέδρῳ περιεσκέπασε τὸν οἶκον ... πάντα κέδρινα,
- A, VIII, 68: τοὺς δὲ τοίχους κεδρίναις διαλαβὼν σανίσι χρυσὸν αὐταῖς ἐνετόρευσεν,
- A, VIII, 70: διέλαβε δὲ τὸν ναὸν καὶ ἔνδοθεν καὶ ἔξωθεν ξύλοις κεδρίνοις,

- 1*Reg.* VI, 8: καὶ ἑλικτὴ ἀνάβασις εἰς τὸ μέσον,
- A, VIII, 70: ἐφιλοτέχνησε δὲ ὁ βασιλεὺς ἄνοδον εἰς τὸν ὑπερῷον οἶκον,

- 1*Reg.* VI, 32: δύο θύρας ... καὶ περιέσχεν χρυσίῳ,
- A, VIII, 71: διελὼν δὲ τὸν ναὸν εἰς δύο ... τὸν δὲ τεσσαράκοντα πηχῶν ἅγιον ναὸν ἀπέδειξεν. ἐκτεμὼν δὲ τὸν μέσον τοῖχον θύρας ἐπέστησε,

- 1*Reg.* VI, 36: ᾠκοδόμησε τὸ καταπέτασμα τῆς αὐλῆς,
- 2*Chron.* III, 14: καὶ ἐποίησε τὸ κατεπέτασμα ὑακίνθου καὶ πορφύρας καὶ κοκκίνου,
- A, VIII, 72: κατεπέτασε δὲ ταύτας ὕφεσιν εὐανθεστάτοις ἐξ ὑακίνθου καὶ πορφύρας καὶ κόκκου,

- 1*Reg.* VI, 23: καὶ ἐποίησεν ἐν τῷ δαβὶρ δύο χερουβίμ,
- 1*Reg.* VI, 28: καὶ περιέσχε τὰ χερουβὶμ χρυσίῳ,
- A, VIII, 72: ἀνέθηκε δ᾽ εἰς τὸ ἄδυτον ... δύο χερουβεῖς ὁλοχρύσους,

- 1*Reg.* VI 27: καὶ διεπέτασε τὰς πτέρυγας αὐτῶν,
- A, VIII, 73: ἀπ᾽ ἀλλήλων αὐτὰς (= πτέρυγας) ἀνέστησεν,

- 1*Reg.* VI, 30: καὶ τὸ ἔδαφος τοῦ οἴκου περιέσχε χρυσίῳ,
- A, VIII, 74: κατέστρωσε δὲ καὶ τοῦ ναοῦ τὸ ἔδαφος ἐλάσμασι χρυσοῦ,

- 1*Reg.* VI, 35: περιεχόμενα χρυσίῳ καταγομένῳ ἐπὶ τὴν ἐκτύπωσιν,
- A, VIII, 75: οὐδὲν εἴασε τοῦ ναοῦ μέρος ... ὃ μὴ χρυσὸς ἦν,

- 1*Reg.* VI, 31: καὶ τῷ θυρώματι τοῦ δαβὶρ ἐποίησε θύρας ξύλων ... καὶ περιέσχεν χρυσίῳ,
- A, VIII, 74: ἐπέθηκε δὲ καὶ τῷ πυλῶνι τοῦ ναοῦ θύρας ... καὶ ταύτας κατεκόλλησε χρυσῷ,

- 1*Reg.* VII, 48: καὶ τὴν τράπεζαν, ἐφ᾽ ἧς οἱ ἄρτοι ..., χρυσῆν,
- 2*Chron.* IV, 8: καὶ ἐποίησε τραπέζας δέκα,
- A, VIII, 89: τραπεζῶν τε πλῆθος ἀνέθηκεν ὁ βασιλεύς, καὶ μίαν μὲν μεγάλην χρυσέαν, ἐφ᾽ ἧς ἐτίθεσαν τοὺς ἄρτους τοῦ θεοῦ,

- 1*Reg.* VII, 49: καὶ τὰς λυχνίας πέντε ἐξ ἀριστερῶν καὶ πέντε ἐκ δεξιῶν,
- 2*Chron.* IV, 7: ἐποίησε τὰς λυχνίας τὰς χρυσᾶς δέκα ... πέντε ἐξ δεξιῶν καὶ πέντε ἐξ ἀριστερῶν,
- A, VIII, 90: καὶ λυχνίας δὲ μυρίας ἐποίησε.

d. Texts without biblical parallels:

- A, VIII, 75: κατεπέτασε δὲ καὶ ταύτας τὰς θύρας ὁμοίως ταῖς ἐνδοτέρω καταπετάσμασιν,
- A, VIII, 91: οἰνοχόας δ' ὁ βασιλεὺς μυριάδας ὀκτὼ κατεσκεύασε,
- A, VIII, 94: καὶ σαλπίγγων ... μυριάδας εἴκοσι ... κατεσκεύασε,
- A, VIII, 95: περιέβαλε δὲ τοῦ ναοῦ κύκλῳ γείσιον,
- A, VIII, 96: ἱερὸν ᾠκοδόμησεν ... στοὰς ἐγείρας μεγάλας,
- A, VIII, 98: περιλαμβάνει δ' αὐτὸ καὶ στοαῖς διπλαῖς.

e. Texts with biblical parallels:

- 1Reg. VII, 50: καὶ τὰς θύρας ... τοῦ ναοῦ χρυσᾶς,
- A, VIII, 98: τὰς δὲ θύρας ... ἐπέστησεν ἐξ ἀργύρου,

- 1Reg. VI, 37-38: ἐν τῷ ἔτει τῷ τετάρτῳ ἐθεμελίωσεν τὸν οἶκον κυρίου ἐν μηνὶ Ζιοῦ καὶ τῷ δευτέρῳ μηνί. Ἐν ἑνδεκάτῳ ἐνιαυτῷ, ἐν μηνὶ βαάλ, οὗτος ὁ μὴν ὁ ὄγδοος, συνετελέσθη ὁ οἶκος,
- A, VIII, 99: τὰ μὲν οὖν ἔργα ταῦτα ... Σολομὼν ὁ βασιλεὺς ἐν ἔτεσιν ἑπτὰ[135] συντελέσας.

These texts, both those which coincide and those which do not, show that the author quite naturally accepts the manner of narrating the Bible, without doing stylistic violence to it. Confirmation of this can be seen in the fragments (1Reg. IX, 15; 2Chron. VIII, 1 = A, VIII, 150-154) which refer to the works of fortification and reconstruction undertaken by king Solomon, to his military successes (1Reg. IX, 20; 2Chron. VIII, 7 = A, VIII, 160-162), to the building of his fleet (1Reg. IX, 26; 2Chron. VIII, 17 = A, VIII, 163-164) and to roads (A, VIII, 187), and to the construction of chariots (1Reg. X, 26; 2Chron. IX, 25 = A, VIII, 188-189).

Finally Flavius Josephus, but not the Bible, follows a line of reasoning concerning the tragic end of the wise king, which is indicative of an attempt to create a justificatory substratum for the historical facts: "nonetheless, though he was the king of greatest renown and most loved by God, and surpassed in intelligence and riches all those who before him had ruled over the Hebrews, he did not remain thus till the end of his days, but he became negligent in the keeping of paternal customs..."[136]. Thus through the straying of his religious behaviour and as man of God, Solomon brought down great calamities on to the last days of his life (A, VIII, 203 ff.).

---

[135] The number seven is borrowed from the Hebrew text, since it is not mentioned in the LXX.

[136] A, VIII, 190.

Beginning with number 304 of book XI of the *Antiquitates Judaicae*, the biblical paraphrasing of Flavius Josephus all but comes to an end. The sources used from this point onwards are various and not so splendid as the strictly biblical sources. This can be seen in the literary treatment which Flavius Josephus gives to Alexander the Great.

It is doubtless true that the unremitting pressure of the Macedonian king is what brings about the reaction of the Persian king Darius, pressure which even makes him set about organising a great army capable of halting the conquests of the Macedonians (A, XI, 313). The whole of Asia was convinced that Darius would conquer Alexander, Flavius Josephus remarks laconically. The outcome, however, was quite another at the city of Issus in the year 333 B.C. Alexander's personality is highlighted by Flavius Josephus: Δαμασκὸν αἱρεῖ καὶ Σιδῶνος κρατήσας ἐπολιόρκει Τύρον[137], and further on, λαμβάνει τὴν Τύρον ... ἐπὶ τὴν τῶν Γαζαίων πόλιν ἦλθε καὶ τήν τε Γάζαν καὶ τὸν ἐν αὐτῇ φρούραρχον ... ἐπολιόρκει[138].

At the beginning of book XII of the *Antiquitates Judaicae* there is a laconic statement that Alexander destroyed the Persian Empire. And thus the story of Alexander is brought to a close. Previously, however, in book XI, the arrival of Alexander in Jerusalem is given great importance. In this story, one can appreciate the outstanding role of the Macedonian king and how all the action revolves around him. Alexander's acts, according to the interest of Flavius Josephus, are worthy of being recorded in history. In the first place, Flavius underlines the fact that it was Alexander who on bended knee was the first to salute the high priest of Jerusalem[139]. Just then, he puts some words into his mouth in direct speech which reveal themselves to be rather excessive if we bear in mind that what the king actually says is somewhat far-fetched. Having arrived at the temple, Alexander "offers a sacrifice to God ... and did honours in a worthy manner"[140]. He was considered to be the one who would destroy the Persian Empire as shown in the Book of Daniel[141], and finally, whatever the Jews wanted, "he gave to them"[142] and "promised to do as they asked"[143].

Another source, a very rich one from the historical point of view, was found by Flavius Josephus in the Books of the Maccabees. For the Jewish

---

[137] A, XI, 317.
[138] A, XI, 320.
[139] A, XI, 331.
[140] A, XI, 336.
[141] A, XI, 337.
[142] A, XI, 338.
[143] A, XI, 338.

historian, the Books of the Maccabees represent a period of strong nationalistic feeling, during which the people of Israel struggle to conserve
their independence in the face of other nations. It is therefore a situation
which resembles that of the uprising against the Romans in the times of
Flavius Josephus himself.

Although Flavius Josephus follows the biblical text very closely, one
can see his personalising tendency in all that refers to the actors of
history. I shall limit my comments to the person of Judas Maccabaeus.

Once in power, Judas sets himself up immediately as the head of
organised resistance among the Jews against foreign domination. Before
anything else, he sweeps the country clean of enemies and traitors[144].
Then come his victories in war: πολλοὺς μὲν αὐτῶν ἀπέκτεινεν... πλείους δὲ
τραυματίας ἐποίησε καὶ πολλὴν λείαν ἐκ τοῦ στρατοπέδου λαβὼν τῶν πολεμίων
ἀνεχώρησεν[145]. In the battle against the commander Seron, it is Judas who
takes the initiative: he comes out to meet him, and tries to attack before
the enemy does, even though he has to rally his soldiers who are
disheartened at the sight of such a numerous enemy army: συμβαλὼν
τρέπει τοὺς Σύρους... ἐπιδιώκων... κτείνει τῶν πολεμίων ὡσεὶ ὀκτακοσίους[146].

The great military rise of Judas places the Seleucian king Antiochus
Epiphanes on his guard against a possible attack on a large scale. Judas,
after convincing his own men using concepts of liberty and eternal glory,
which can only with difficulty be deduced from the biblical text, "left
alight many fires in his camp and marched for the whole of the night
against the enemy who was at Emmaus"[147]. The fires do not appear in
the biblical version, and it could be interpreted as a trick, attributed to
Judas by Flavius Josephus, to take the enemy by surprise. The enemy,
who had also tried to launch a surprise attack, is disorientated, and
"Judas shows himself before the enemy at Emmaus..., orders the
trumpet-players to sound their instruments. Having flung himself on the
enemy straightway, and having shaken their resolve and perturbed them,
slew many of those who would resist"[148]. An attempt to attack on the part
of the enemy is a failure, and Judas breaks off to take booty[149]. A final
enemy attempt ends with victory for Judas.

Throughout this text (A, XII, 287-315), one may appreciate that the
descriptions of war are not over-long, and that attention in the telling is
centred on the person of Judas. And on him alone, since whenever men-

---

[144] A, XII, 286.
[145] A, XII, 287.
[146] A, XII, 290 and 292.
[147] A, XII, 306.
[148] A, XII, 307.
[149] A, XII, 312.

tion is made of his soldiers, they are portrayed as unhappy beings, seeing that their lack of courage makes Judas rally them to him, he being the sole possessor of the reason (αἴτιον) by which the war progresses, and at other times it is the enterprise of Judas (ἀρχηγός) that makes events turn one way or another.

In addition to vanquishing these particular enemies, Judas also has to fight against communities: "the surrounding nations"[150], "the Idumaeans"[151], "the Baanites"[152], "the Ammanites"[153], "the city of Jazora"[154] and "the city of the Emphraeans"[155].

The exploits of Judas will still extend to two great actions: his victory over the garrison which was stationed on the acropolis of Jerusalem, and his final battle with the Syrian king Demetrius.

Judas begins the siege of the acropolis, "having prepared siege engines and having thrown up embankments"[156]. The besieged manage to alert king Antiochus Eupator. When Judas finds out about the arrival of the royal army, "he raised the siege of the acropolis, marched out to meet the king and set up camp..."[157]. In the face of an attack from the magnificent army of the king, "all 'according to the *Books of the Maccabees*[158]' felt consternation on hearing the shouts of the multitude", but Flavius Josephus mentions no more than the fact that "Judas did not tremble at the sight, rather, receiving the onslaught of the enemy with courage... slew some six hundred of them"[159]. Nevertheless, taking into consideration the superiority of the enemy, retreats to Jerusalem and prepares for a siege[160].

The involvement of king Demetrius in the affairs of Judaea also revolves around the attitude of Judas when confronted with the corruption in his country. Thus, the high priest Alcimus, a supporter of Syrian power, appeals to Demetrius for his aid against Judas[161]. In the face of the unjust deaths of pious Jews at the hands of Alcimus, Judas "slew those who were on the side of the former"[162]. Shortly afterwards,

---

[150] A, XII, 327.
[151] A, XII, 328.
[152] *Ibid.*: τοὺς υἱοὺς τοῦ Βαάνου.
[153] A, XII, 329: ἐπὶ τοὺς ᾿Αμμανίτας ἐξώρμησε.
[154] *Ibid.*: τὴν ᾿Ιαζωρῶν ἐξαιρεῖ πόλιν.
[155] A, XII, 347.
[156] A, XII, 363: κατασκευάσας οὖν μηχανήματα καὶ χώματα ἐγείρας. The book of the Maccabees does not explicitly say that these deeds were carried out by Judas (1*Mach.* VI, 20).
[157] A, XII, 369.
[158] 1*Mach.* VI, 41.
[159] A, XII, 372.
[160] A, XII, 375.
[161] A, XII, 389 ff.
[162] A, XII, 400.

Nicanor, Demetrius' general, attempts to seize Judas by a trick. Judas defeats him for the moment[163]. Finally Judas completely destroys Nicanor.

Judas brought to fruition an important political plan, by foreseeing the pressing need for an alliance with Rome. This represents an act which was carried out with intelligent foresight, since Rome was gradually asserting herself as mistress of the world[164].

The final act of Judas was that of his own courageous death. Abandoned by some of his soldiers, he joins battle and dies, vanquished by the superiority of the enemy[165].

Finally mention should be made of a short text which I believe is very demonstrative of the intentionality of Flavius Josephus in wishing to give historiographic relevance to certain historical figures.

Part of the Jewish army, under the command of Joseph and Azarias, joins battle with the enemy, in defiance of the orders of Judas not to attack without him, and is defeated[166]. So far Flavius Josephus coincides with the biblical text. But then he adds his own comments: "since, besides his other qualities, he (Judas) could also be admired for having foreseen the disaster which would overtake the men of Joseph and Azarias if they were to take no heed of his instructions"[167]. In other words, none of his collaborators could act on his own initiative, no-one could seek glory for himself[168]: no-one but Judas could go out to an encounter with the enemy, since he was "of the family of those men to whose hands the salvation of Israel had been entrusted"[169].

C. The aetiological question on the transcendent plane

During the Hellenistic epoch there was a manifold increase, due to the influence of oriental religions, in the superstitions and beliefs whereby spiritual beings and powerful forces took a hand in human activities. The most widespread fear was motivated by the belief that there existed forces which were antagonistic to man, who thus was forced to great efforts so as to prevent their intervening in his works.

---

[163] A, XII, 405 ff.

[164] A, XII, 414.

[165] A, XII, 420-434.

[166] A, XII, 352.

[167] *Ibid.*: πρὸς γὰρ τοῖς ἄλλοις αὐτοῦ στρατηγήμασιν καὶ τὸ κατὰ τοὺς περὶ τὸν Ἰώσηπον καὶ τὸν Ἀζαρίαν πταῖσμα θαυμάσειεν ἄν τις, ὃ συνῆκεν, εἰ παρακινήσουσί τι τῶν ἐπεσταλμένων αὐτοῖς, ἐσόμενον.

[168] *1 Mach.* V, 57 = A, XII, 350.

[169] *1 Mach.* V, 62: ἐκ τοῦ σπέρματος τῶν ἀνδρῶν ἐκείνων οἷς ἐδόθη σωτηρία Ἰσραὴλ διὰ χειρὸς αὐτῶν.

The process which therefore had begun with the imperialistic expansion of Alexander the Great had already reached its religious heights in the time of Flavius Josephus. In this sense then, the historian is sensitive to that religious revolution, and the analysis of these aspects in his work highlights the need to embody human events in broad religious concepts. To this must be added the effort of Flavius Josephus aimed at safeguarding his own religious concept of the world by expressing himself in Hellenistic terminology[170].

1. Diversity of the transcendent concept in Flavius Josephus

'Αλάστωρ/ἀλαστορία[171]. Among those forces superior to man, there was that which embodied the idea of vengeance, and was personified in the figure of the demon of vengeance, who was charged with the mission of carrying out the revenge which might arise from some wrongdoing. Such was the extent of the panic which this higher spirit spread in popular belief, that man was even vulnerable after death. This idea is enshrined in the sentence of Antipater, when he confesses to his surreptitious attempt to poison his father Herod: "lest I should take the demon of vengeance off with me even to Hades"[172].

At the beginning of book XVII of the *Antiquitates Judaicae*, the historian, when referring to the intrigues of Antipater himself against his brothers, says that Antipater "involved his father in the greatest of iniquities and exposed him to divine vengeance"[173].

'Ανάγκη[174]. Among the manifold forces which have transcendency and which impinge on human will, forcing man to behave in a certain manner, Flavius Josephus counts *necessity*. Not simply the necessity for material and temporary things, even though the former may be originated by the latter at times, but rather transcendent necessity, a necessity which surpasses man's capacity to resist, which can only with difficulty be made concrete as to its beginning and end, irresistibly oppressive, which to a certain extent comes very close to the concept expressed in the word "fate".

---

[170] W. Nestle, *Griechische Religiosität von Alexander dem Großen bis Proklos*, Berlin, 1934; Th. A. Brady, "The reception of the Egyptian cults by the Greeks (330-30 b. Ch.)", *The University of Missouri studies* 10 (1935); Th. von Scheffer, *Hellenismus, Mysterien und Orakel*, Stuttgart, 1940.

[171] Cf. *Concordance, s.uu.*

[172] B, I, 596: ἵνα μὴ καὶ καθ' ᾅδου φέροιμι τὸν ἀλάστορα.

[173] A, XVII, 1: ἀσεβείᾳ τε τῇ ὑστάτῃ καὶ ἀλαστορίᾳ τῇ ἐπ' αὐτοῖς τὸν πατέρα περιβεβληκότι.

[174] Cf. *Concordance, s.u.* On questions of free will, chance and necessity, cf. A. Meyer, *El historiador y la historia antigua*, Buenos Aires, 1965, 3-53; G. Stählin, "Das Schicksal im Neuen Testament und bei Josephus", *Festschrift O. Michel* (1974), 319-343.

This kind of necessity makes man follow a certain path of action at a given moment and brings about a change in the natural path undertaken up to any given moment.

This transcendent necessity therefore springs up on earth and arises from circumstances of the moment[175]. In this sense, when the leaders of the Jewish rebellion decide to abandon the towers, the historian points out that "their courage was not in proportion to the demands made on them by that occasion"[176], thus indicating that in the word ἀνάγκη he encodes a force which is imposed on them, makes them inoperative, and therefore incapable of acting to bring about their salvation.

In a positive sense, necessity sharpens even the dullest wit and spurs it to action, "since there is nothing in war which excites the urge for warfare more than necessity"[177].

Continuing with the oppressive aspect of necessity, he brings the meaning more into focus by writing that "Josephus, in that critical situation, took necessity for a counsellor, a counsellor extraordinary for making decisions when desperation urges"[178]. Within this aspect of desperation, necessity can channel the feelings of a mother to committing the most terrible acts of cruelty, such as killing her own child and eating it[179], as well as driving people to do things which even beasts would not do[180].

Necessity can also be personified in the sense that it can influence human will in the same manner as a warning given by a real person: "others harvested it (the wheat) according to the dictates of necessity and fear"[181]. And again "necessity will quickly reconcile them"[182].

These aspects are more definite when the historian uses the word ἀνάγκη in conjunction with verbs which are proper to the activity of man: "shame led some of them; others were led by necessity"[183]. And again "necessity spurred them on to fight"[184].

---

[175] B, I, 3, 220; B, II, 199; B, III, 186; B, IV, 207, 320; B, V, 339, 449, 497, 548, 568, 571; B, VI, 78, 230, 319, 433; B, VII, 61, 195, 212; A, II, 114; A, III, 1, 22; A, V, 145; A, VI, 334; A, XI, 47; A, XIII, 382; A, XIV, 44; A, XV, 151, 227; A, XVI, 2, 232, 253, 290, 324; A, XVII, 77, 105; A, XVIII, 148, 186; A, XIX, 35, 209; A, XX, 53; Vit, 74, 161. 171, 291; Ap, II, 143.

[176] B, VI, 402: χρησάμενοι δὲ ταῖς τόλμαις ἀγενεστέραις τῆς ἀνάγκης. Similarly A, III, 5.

[177] B, III, 149: οὐδὲν γὰρ ἀνάγκης ἐν πολέμῳ μαχιμώτερον.

[178] B, III, 271: ὁ δὲ Ἰώσηπος ἐν ταῖς ἀμηχανίαις σύμβουλον λαβὼν τὴν ἀνάγκην, ἡ δ' ἐστὶν δεινὴ πρὸς ἐπίνοιαν, ὅταν αὐτὴν ἀπόγνωσις ἐρεθίζῃ. Similarly in B, III, 496; B, IV, 434; B, V, 548; B, VI, 78, 197, 230, 397, 433; B, VII, 195, 330.

[179] B, VI, 204-205: σύμβουλον λαβοῦσα (= the mother) τὴν ὀργὴν μετὰ τῆς ἀνάγκης. Similarly in B, VII, 392-393; A, IX, 43 (bis).

[180] B, V, 571; B, VI, 197.

[181] B, V, 427: οἱ δ' ἔπεσσον ὡς ἥ τε ἀνάγκη καὶ τὸ δέος παρήνει. Similarly in B, VI, 397: διέφυγον γὰρ ὅπη τινὶ συνεβούλευεν ἡ ἀνάγκη.

[182] B, III, 496: οὓς ἀνάγκη διαλλάξει ταχέως.

[183] B, VI, 160.

[184] B, IV, 434.

Fear, however, can be more persuasive than necessity itself: "the tyrants (leaders) were invaded by a fear far greater than necessity"[185]. It is also the case that both may be the determining factors without one prevailing over the other[186].

Necessity can also arise as an elaboration of the mind of the person, as a response to the multiple options and ambitions to which the person is subject: "for those who had achieved the highest honours in an unworthy manner were in the necessity (felt obliged) of obeying those who had conceded them"[187]. When wishing to justify the attitude of The Jews in the war against the Romans, Flavius Josephus shows necessity to be the determining factor in their decision: "The Jews did not decide on the war against the Romans, but rather it was necessity that made them do so"[188].

Necessity also gives rise to an acute feeling of pessimism, especially when necessity becomes inevitability, as is the case with death. In this aspect, the concept of the adjective ἀναγκαία applied to τελευτή approximates fully to the concept of fate which is expressed in the word χρεών: "If inevitable death is honed for men, and the sword is a servant which takes us hence much more quickly than any disease, how cannot it be an ignoble act not to give to pressing necessities what we surrender to destiny?"[189]

In another passage we also find the idea of death together with the concept of necessity: "We must die by the decision of God or through necessity"[190]. Finally, necessity can also be sent by God[191].

In the face of the violence which necessity sometimes implies, it is understood that necessity also exonerates the cruelty of certain acts: "Indeed, it would have been less cruel if done through necessity"[192].

With an ascetic sense, Flavius Josephus does not forget to point out that there comes a time in life when the will of man cannot be bent, however much necessity presses, since the strength of the spirit surpasses

---

[185] B, VI, 394.

[186] A, IX, 201; A, XX, 42.

[187] B. IV, 149: τοῖς γὰρ παρ' ἀξίαν ἐπιτυχοῦσι τῆς ἀνωτάτω τιμῆς ὑπακούειν ἦν ἀνάγκη τοῖς παρασχοῦσι. Similarly B, IV, 207; B, VI, 120; B, VII, 212; Vit, 161, 291.

[188] Vit, 27.

[189] B, VI, 49: εἰ δὲ κέκλωσται μὲν ἀνθρώποις ἀναγκαία τελευτή, κουφότερον δ' εἰς αὐτὴν νόσου πάσης σίδηρος ὑπηρέτης, πῶς οὐκ ἀγεννὲς μὴ διδόναι ταῖς χρείαις ὃ τῷ χρεὼν ἀποδώσομεν; Similarly in B, VII, 362, 380, 382; A, VII, 322; Vit, 153.

[190] B, VII, 358.

[191] B, VII, 387.

[192] B, V, 436: καὶ γὰρ ἧττον ἂν ὠμὸν ἦν τὸ μετ' ἀνάγκης. Also in B, VI, 120: "since the Romans would never venture, except under the direct necessity, to set fire to the holy places" (οὐ γὰρ ἂν τολμῆσαι Ῥωμαίους μὴ μετὰ μεγίστης ἀνάγκης καταφλέξαι τὰ ἅγια). Similarly in A, V, 169; A, VI, 219.

the weakness of the flesh[193]. This notwithstanding, the will can also give way before certain demands made by necessity[194].

Norms and conventions may constitute a necessity to take a certain line of action. Thus, Laban is forced to surrender first his daughter Leah to Jacob, going back on his promise to give him Rachel, according to the custom of marrying off daughters in order of age. Confronted with the protests of Jacob, Laban asks his forgiveness, but he alleges, according to the historian, that he had acted in this manner by force of necessity: "He begged his pardon however, since he had acted thus because of necessity"[195].

The suffering of humanity seems to respond less to certain events which may occur than to realities which of necessity succeed each other. Thus Flavius Josephus justifies the existence of laws, which are designed to provide man with the means by which he may overcome his problems[196].

Necessity reaches its climax when it must be understood as an irresistible destiny. The divergence of lessons in the manuscripts is symptomatic. Some of them qualify the word ἀνάγκη with the participle πεπρωμένη (P¹LV, SP²). There is no doubt that here necessity brought about by destiny must be understood; in other words, and in short, destiny itself: "reasoning that that by which they (the presents promised) had been given was something of his (king Balthasar's) own and of destiny"[197].

Human acts, when guided by all-powerful chance, "are previously dedicated by it to the inevitable necessity of coming to pass"[198]. Here may be observed a grading of powers, so that it seems that the necessity of having things happen is planned, and consequently activated by force of chance, which predetermines their happening without their being able to escape it.

Αὐτόματος. This word has two significant meanings: that which comes about by itself, and that which, bearing this point in mind, must come about without any kind of outside influence. In this latter sense, reference is to "chance", i.e., that which happens without logical prediction, but which impinges directly on the acts of men[199].

---

[193] B, VII, 418-419. Similarly in A, III, 223; A, XII, 280-281.
[194] A, VI, 41, 103; A, X, 178.
[195] A, I, 302.
[196] A, IV, 293.
[197] A, X, 246: τὸ μὲν ἐφ᾽ οἷς δοθήσονται λογιζόμενος ἴδιον αὐτοῦ καὶ τῆς ἀνάγκης [πεπρωμένης P¹LV: πεπρωμένης ἀνάγκης SP²]. With the meaning of dire fate, cf. Vit, 153.
[198] A, XVI, 397.
[199] Cf. Concordance, s.u.

There is a text in which the αὐτόματος is placed on the same operative level as divine will, indicating thus accidents which were to come about. Thus, after the crossing of the Red Sea by the Israelites, Flavius Josephus comments on the fact that Alexander the Great also had similar fortune: his soldiers managed to cross over the sea, even though they had to get themselves wet "up to their navels"[200], "by the will of God or by chance"[201]. This expression makes one think of an alternative to the divine will which facilitates the way and the fact that the soldiers crossed the sea because it had to be thus, "since they were to destroy the Persian Empire through divine will"[202]. It seems, therefore, that the existence is also possible of a superior force which makes it easier for the Greeks to overcome their difficulties so as to accomplish their objective: the destruction of Persia.

On the other hand, elsewhere, he annihilates the αὐτόματος in the face of divine providence, leaving it firmly established that "all is guided by Your (God's) divine providence and that nothing happens fortuitously (αὐτομάτως) but according to Your will which guides it towards its outcome"[203].

Within the idea of spontaneity and fortuity may be concealed the workings of God. In this sense, that which simply comes to pass before the eyes of men is charged with latent significance. In the story of the destruction of Jericho by Joshua, the walls crashed down, and God handed the city over to the Israelites, "the walls collapsing spontaneously, without any effort on their part"[204].

The world moves automatically, and is not guided by an immortal being, according to the beliefs of the Egyptians. Here we are dealing with the inexorable laws which make the cosmos move in an unchangeable direction: "The Egyptians say that the universe moves automatically, free from any control of a guide and with no help from another"[205].

In his defence of the people of Israel in the face of the accusations of Apion, Flavius Josephus tries to refute the calumny according to which the Israelites had invented Saturday as a day of rest because they were prey to tumours in the groin: that is simply not possible—writes Flavius Josephus—in people who traverse an entire desert and fight against their enemies, since it is nature itself which does not suffer it in people who have to walk day after day, "nor is it possible that this should come

---

[200] Strab. XIV, 666.
[201] A, II, 347: εἴτε κατὰ βούλησιν θεοῦ εἴτε κατὰ ταὐτόματον.
[202] A, II, 348.
[203] A, IV, 47.
[204] A, V, 24.
[205] A, X, 278.

to pass by chance, for it were the most absurd thing"[206]. In this case rationalism is stronger than casualness, and the happenings of life are subject to the imperatives of nature and logic.

Δαιμόνιον, δαιμόνιος and δαίμων. The semantic basis of these three words is formed by the following: "deity, destiny, evil spirit, demon, celestial, miraculous, supernatural, spectre and fate"[207]. One can therefore see the intervention of the beyond with differing shades of meaning. In this study, however, I shall analyse only those circumstances which are brought about by the direct involvement of this power.

From Flavius Josephus himself we may take the definition which is common to all these words, when he writes: "Since these called demons, that is, those spirits of evil men which enter into the living and slay them if they find no help..."[208]. In principle therefore, and in a general sense, one is dealing with malignant spirits which:
– interfere in the will of men[209] and
– cause them problems and upset their lives[210].

There is, however, the positive aspect of these supernatural forces, which show themselves to be on the side of men by helping them to succeed in their undertakings and intentions. In this case, the idea of δαίμων is intimately linked to that of God or his providence over men. Naturally, when one says that the δαίμων is positive, one means that it helps people in a favourable fashion, in certain specific circumstances, and from the point of view of the historian or of the multiple actors who take part in the historical event, and, something which must not be forgotten, from the point of view of the historian himself or of the historical actors themselves, since, in the eyes of the people in the opposite camp, it may even take on a complete reversal of meaning, that is, harmful intervention[211].

These spirits, in spite of their strong influence on all human affairs, can be cast out and dominated by some men, and using methods which are not exactly reasonable. Thus, the root of a plant may have sufficient force to expel these spirits[212] from within a person. King David too[213]

---

[206] Ap, II, 24.

[207] Cf. Concordance, s.uu.

[208] B, VII, 185.

[209] B, I, 613; B, IV, 501; B, VII, 82.

[210] B, I, 370, 376, 556, 599, 607, 628; A, VI, 166, 168, 211, 214; A, XIII, 314, 315, 415; A, XIV, 291; A, XVI, 76; Vit, 402.

[211] B, II, 457; B, III, 341, 485; B, IV, 217, 622; B, V, 502; B, VI, 59, 252, 296; B, VII, 318; A, XIII, 314; A, XVI, 210. Cf. Concordance, s.uu. κακοδαιμονέω, κακοδαίμων.

[212] B, VII, 185.

[213] A, VI, 166-169, taken from the Bible (1Sam. XVI, 14 ff.), and A, VI, 214 (= 1Sam. XIX, 9).

and his son Solomon had received from God the power to cast out these supernatural spirits or demons[214].

Δεισιδαιμονία. Religious fear and superstitious motives may sometimes direct the will of a person towards the most heinous acts. However, the range of meaning of this compound word should be stressed: fear of divinity, unbending religious persuasion, religious scruple and superstition[215]. Understood thus, one sees that the person in the clutches of this fear cannot be master or mistress of his or her acts, and consequently the will is not subject to the guidance of reasoning or logic. At the same time there is a feeling of justification in the sense that the responsibility for the consequences of his or her acts is placed on that superior force which has forced the action.

In this sense, the queen Alexandra allows the most eminent citizens to be condemned to death[216]. On the other hand, this religious zeal may lead to the sacrifice of one's own life[217] and may pool the efforts of a group who have the same aim in common[218].

Even the Jewish people owe their submission to the power of Rome to their own religious superstition, according to which they were not permitted to take up arms[219], in accordance with the testimony of the historian Agatharchides of Cnidos.

Fatum. The idea of fate is already to be found in Homeric poetry. It was a basic concept of Greek theology. Everything was subject to fate. All men had a part of the universal fate assigned to them, including the gods, which was inevitably to come to pass. It therefore, at times, went far beyond the bounds of human reasoning.

In Flavius Josephus, this concept appears expressed in various words: εἱμαρμένη, εἱμάρθαι, εἱμαρμένος; πεπρωμένη; ἄτροπον[220]. The meanings for the first idea are the following: εἱμαρμένη: "destiny, fate (divine), providence"; εἱμάρθαι: "to be decreed by fate"; εἱμαρμένος: "predestined, decreed by fate". To the word πεπρωμένη corresponds the simple meaning of "fate" or "marked by fate". The ἄτροπον means "unbending fate"[221].

---

[214] A, VIII, 45-48, without biblical parallel (LXX, 1*Reg.* IV, 28 ff.).

[215] Cf. *Concordance*, *s.u.*

[216] B, I, 113.

[217] B, II, 174.

[218] B, II, 230.

[219] A, XII, 5-6. Similarly in A, XIV, 228, 232, 234, 237 and 240; Ap, I, 208.

[220] Cf. *Concordance*, *s.uu.* For πεπρωμένη, cf. A, X, 76; A, XIX, 347; Ap, I, 247, 266. The word μοῖρα too has a value of "divine destiny" in A, I, 333.

[221] Appears on a single occasion (A, IV, 114) and only then if we accept the reading proposed by Thackeray.

On making an exposition of the religious tendencies among the people of Israel in the times of Flavius Josephus, an occasion arises for discussing the idea of fate. According to the sect of the Pharisees, εἱμαρμένη appears in cooperation with divine involvement in human affairs, and they believe that righteousness is mostly dependent on men (B, II, 162-163), and not all acts are executed under its influence (A, XIII, 172). On the other hand, the Essenes declared that fate is absolute master of all and that nothing ever comes to pass without his decree (*ibid.*); later on however, Flavius Josephus says that they place everything in the hands of God (A, XVIII, 18). The Sadducees separate fate from the influence which it might exercise over man, and believe in the free will of man, so that not even God himself can have any influence over human will; responsibility for one's acts therefore is with man (B, II, 164-165; A, XIII, 173).

This notwithstanding, in a passage which is difficult to translate, Flavius Josephus delimits more sharply the limits of this concept, and says that the Pharisees "though maintaining that all things are brought about by fate, do not deprive human will of striving to carry them out, since it was God's pleasure that there should be a fusion and that the will of man with his virtue and vice should be admitted to the council-chamber of fate"[222]. Here Flavius Josephus sidesteps the problem of the free will of man, without denying fate, by expressing his belief in man's capacity of choosing between good and evil. These latter points also appear in Talmudic and Biblical literature[223].

In B, II, 162-166, there is the statement that the sect of the Pharisees attribute all "to fate and to God, and righteousness or no, in the majority of cases, rests with men, and fate also takes a hand in each act"[224]. Here we find three elements: fate, which intervenes in acts, God, and the free will of man. Next there is the statement that the Sadducees do not admit fate, and believe in the free will of man, and affirm that God can cause them no harm.

---

[222] A, XVIII, 13: πράσσεσθαί τε εἱμαρμένη τὰ πάντα ἀξιοῦντες οὐδὲ τοῦ ἀνθρωπείου τὸ βουλόμενον τῆς ἐπ' αὐτοῖς ὁρμῆς ἀφαιροῦνται δοκῆσαν τῷ θεῷ κρᾶσιν γενέσθαι καὶ τῷ ἐκείνης βουλευτηρίῳ καὶ τῶν ἀνθρώπων τὸ ἐθελῆσαν προσχωρεῖν μετ' ἀρετῆς ἢ κακίας. My translation has taken into account that of Feldman and that of Thackeray, in *HThR* 25 (1932), 93 (transcribed by L. H. Feldman in his edition of The Loeb Classical Library). For intervention of human will and fate Flavius Josephus says the same thing as in A, XIII, 172.

[223] Cited by L. H. Feldman in the note to A, XVIII, 13 of his edition: *Abot* III, 19; *Berachot* 33b; *Niddah* 16b; *Eccli.* XV, 11-17. For all the aspects related to *fatum*, cf. G. F. Moore, "Fate and Free Will in the Jewish Philosophies according to Josephus", *HThR* 22 (1929), 371; L. Waechter, "Die unterschiedliche Haltung der Pharisäer, Sadduzäer und Essener zur Heimarmene nach dem Bericht des Josephus", *ZRGG* 21 (1969), 97-114.

[224] εἱμαρμένη τε καὶ θεῷ προσάπτουσι πάντα καὶ τὸ μὲν πράττειν τὰ δίκαια καὶ μὴ κατὰ τὸ πλεῖστον ἐπὶ τοῖς ἀνθρώποις κεῖσθαι, βοηθεῖν δὲ εἰς ἕκαστον καὶ τὴν εἱμαρμένην.

In A, XIII, 171-173, he repeats the same ideas concerning the sects of
the Pharisees and the Sadducees, but extends the explanation by expounding the concept which the Essenes have of fate: "The sect of the
Essenes declares that fate is master of all, and that nothing comes to pass
without his decree"[225].

The conclusions which can be drawn from these texts dealing with
historical events lead us to think of the belief in a cosmic force, named
God, the guiding force of human destiny, which, with its providence, fate
(= εἱμαρμένη), though respecting the alternative of human will, directs
man's acts. According to Moore, this determinism of the Jews was only
theological and not philosophical, and the term εἱμαρμένη is an equivalent
which is adapted to the non-Jewish mind of what the Jews understood by
divine providence[226].

Scattered throughout the work of Flavius Josephus, we find the following details and applications of fate. It can hold sway over the life of men
(B, IV, 297; A, XIX, 347), over an entire nation (B, VI, 428) or over the
end of a city (B, IV, 257). To it are subject all human plans and aspirations since "no mortal can avoid it"[227]. It can also predestinate the place
where a death is to occur (B, I, 79). It is possible to make destiny become
reality before its allotted time (B, I, 662). Logically, fate is qualified as
unjust by Herod (B, I, 628).

When dealing with the death of Mattathias, Flavius Josephus places in
the mouth of the dying man the words which refer to inevitable fate instead of the simple expression of death, as is the case in the Scripture: "I,
my sons, am about to follow the fated path"[228].

When satirizing the mythological concepts of the Greeks, Flavius
Josephus remarks that even the gods are subject to fate (Ap, II, 245).

One cannot allow as strictly exact the opinions of some authors who excuse Flavius Josephus by saying that he used the word εἱμαρμένη instead
of divine πρόνοια as a concession to his readers who had not been brought
up in the religion of the Jews[229].

In this sense I believe that the ideas of fate and of God, which appear in
conjunction in the text B, II, 162 are complementary, fate being placed in
a lower level. The two ideas are presented as if it were a question of two
independent entities, and Flavius Josephus emphasises only that fate
which cooperates in all human activity (No. 163). Neither in A, XIII,

---

[225] A, XIII, 172.
[226] G. F. Moore, *op. cit.*, 379.
[227] B, VI, 84.
[228] A, XII, 279.
[229] H. St. J. Thackeray, in a note to B, II, 163 in his edition, and R. Marcus, also in a
note to A, XIII, 172 in his edition, both in The Loeb Classical Library.

172 is fate divine providence, because Flavius Josephus makes sure of attributing it with involvement limited to certain acts.

There is still a complex text which, though juggling with three transcendent concepts, nevertheless marks off very sharply the field of the transcendent concept which now concerns us. It goes thus: "Fortune (τύχη) smiling on him everywhere, as was his desire, and the political situation for the most part being to his advantage, the idea immediately came to Vespasian that without divine providence (δαιμονίου προνοίας) he would not have achieved the Empire, and that a just fate (δικαία τις εἱμαρμένη) had placed the sovereignty of the world in his hands"[230].

I find, in the first place, that the attribution of *divine providence* when applied to a Roman personality to be outside the bounds of historical reality. It is difficult to admit such great theological foresightedness with regards to a personality who has been formed in a polytheistic world. Here I interpret this expression as one of the historian's, and no more.

This notwithstanding, the text is presented to us with these three concepts, and it must be interpreted thus. Therefore, I should like to point out that I see there a grading of the transcendent context in so far as it has an influence over the activity of Vespasian. On the one hand Vespasian's own good fortune is constituted by an accumulation of events which bring about the aggrandizement of the emperor; but on the other hand there is the recognition of a superior force, thanks to which the magnificent situation of the present has been possible. In the third place, the writer believes that all had come to pass in this way because it was decided by fate. In other words, although the aggrandizement of Vespasian had to come about because of the inexorable force of fate (εἱμαρμένη), divine providence was vigilant so that those steps should come about which would lead to a felicitous outcome, since Vespasian was of necessity a man of fortune, protected by *good* fortune.

Referring to the destruction of the temple of Jerusalem, Flavius Josephus is very clear with regard to the fatalistic character of this event. He says: "God, from ancient times, had vowed (κατεψήφιστο) the burning of the temple, and now, with the passage of time, the appointed day had arrived: the tenth day of the month of Lous, the same day in which it was burned for the first time by the king of Babylon"[231]. Once more, two hierarchized ideas are related. It is God who by his vow[232] takes it on himself to see to the destruction of the temple by fire. On the other hand,

---

[230] B, IV, 622.
[231] B, VI, 250.
[232] God gives, sometimes, His vow: B, VI, 250; B, VII, 359; A, XVII, 43.

there is a force which has appointed a specific day, which happens to coincide with the day of the first destruction, and brooks no delay.

In a later text, Flavius Josephus observes, with no doubt, the inevitability of fate: "A person who profoundly laments a work, the most worthy of admiration of all those which we have seen and heard mention made of, because of its grandeur and also for the richness of every detail and for the glory of its holy places, might be able to accept fate as the greatest consolation, since it is not avoidable either by living beings or by works of art and places"[233]. He brings his idea to an end by referring once more to the exactitude of the day appointed by fate, and makes use of a great wealth of chronological information.

Flavius Josephus tries to obtain some spiritual benefit from a paradoxical line of thought. He believes quite simply that, if all things and all men are subject to fate, then it must follow that there is no thing and no man who will escape it, and therefore, the misfortune of all could bring with it veritable consolation for the disconsolate.

The family of king Herod also had its fate, and to it all members of the family were subject. Flavius Josephus wonders on whom the responsibility for the domestic tragedy should fall, whether on the sons of Herod, or on the king himself, or whether "on fortune, which has a greater power than all cautious reflexion, and by this too we are convinced that human acts are previously dedicated by it to the inevitable necessity of coming to pass, and which is named fate, since no thing happens which is not through it"[234].

Here a definition of fate is to be found. It is, therefore, that superhuman force which, having arisen from fortune (τύχη) which accompanies each person and having arrived to the dire necessity (ἀνάγκη) of influencing men, has events come about in an inevitably predetermined way (εἱμαρμένη). It can be quite clearly seen here that Flavius Josephus does not use the idea of fate in the stead of that of divine providence to thus adapt himself better to the religious training of his future Roman and Greek readers, but rather that he reaffirms his belief in those forces which can influence the acts of men[235].

---

[233] B, VI, 267.

[234] A, XVI, 397: ἢ καὶ τὴν τύχην παντὸς εὐγνώμονος λογισμοῦ μείζω τὴν δύναμιν ἐσχηκυῖαν, ὅθεν καὶ πειθόμεθα τὰς ἀνθρωπίνας πράξεις ὑπ' ἐκείνης προκαθωσιῶσθαι τῇ τοῦ γενέσθαι πάντως ἀνάγκῃ, καὶ καλοῦμεν αὐτὴν εἱμαρμένην, ὡς οὐδενὸς ὄντος ὃ μὴ δι' αὐτὴν γίνεται.

[235] There are doubts on the part of critics as to whether this text may be integrally attributed to Flavius Josephus. Cf. G. C. Richards and R. J. H. Shutt, "Critical Notes on Josephus' Antiquities", CQ 31 (1937), 170-177. Thackeray considers it an addition to the second edition of the work and that it is possibly not of the hand of the author (Josephus, the Man..., 67). For Seneca, fatum was that "ex quo suspensa sunt omnia, causa causarum" (Nat. Quaest. II, 45). Cf. Cic., De fato 18, 41; Diu. I, 55; Aug., Ciu. Dei V, 1-8.

Τύχη. The τύχη or *Fortuna*, apart from its personification as a divinity, is a kind "of capricious and mobile influence" which may present itself in the lives of men as the bearer of misfortunes (δυστυχία, ἀτυχία) or successes (εὐτυχία), without being ruled by a logical or moral law[236].

This general definition of τύχη may serve as an introduction to the search for its limits in the thought of Flavius Josephus. One can see there an inevitable and unthinkable dominion over human acts. The outlook may therefore show itself to be very pessimistic. This latter aspect also appears in the thought of Demetrius of Phalerum: "To the destructive and capricious power as defined by Demetrius of Phalerum, he (Polybius) opposes a constructive and almost reasonable finality which chooses the means and combines the effects so as to achieve a specific goal, such as the supremacy of Rome"[237]. For Polybius then, τύχη may have its beneficial side[238].

One must, as in all philological analysis such as this, search to see whether the writer himself, at some stage throughout his work, throws some light on the concept which he encapsulates in any given word. In the present case, I believe that Flavius Josephus manages to give an explanation of his concept of τύχη at the stage where he goes into a digression, thus interrupting the historical thread, so as to meditate concerning the domestic tragedy of king Herod (A, XVI, 395 ff.). Three possibilities present themselves to the historian of the ill-fated life of the king: either to throw the blame on his sons, on Herod himself, because of his burning desire to govern, or on τύχη[239].

In this text, emphasis is laid on the fact that what τύχη lays in store for human acts comes about inevitably, so that that which was simply thought to be the changing fortune of a person becomes his inevitable fate, and which is present in all events. Thus fate exercises irremediable influence over the acts of man, and therefore over his will, which brings into question the free will of man, and to what extent he is responsible for his merits and shortcomings, and therefore for the consequences of his acts.

Flavius Josephus himself strives to come up with some kind of answer (A, XVI, 398), since, at bottom, he experiences a critical situation within himself, who is used to monotheistic and providentialist religious con-

---

[236] M. M. Ch. Daremberg et Edm. Saglio, *Dictionnaire des Antiquités Grecques et Romaines*, Paris, 1896, *s.u.* "Fortuna". Cf. A, Nordh, "Virtus and Fortuna in Florus", *Eranos* 50 (1952), 111-128; V. Alba, *La concepción historiográfica de Lucio Anneo Floro*, Madrid, 1953, 46-49. For the word τύχη, cf. *Concordance*, *s.u.*

[237] P. Pédech, *op. cit.*, 341.

[238] I, 4, 4.

[239] A, XVI, 397.

cepts. I do not think that Flavius Josephus extricates himself in a very graceful manner by wishing to give an idea of transcendence which is adapted to the minds of his Hellenistic readers. The marriage is not possible. Deep down, I should like to suppose that the contradiction is simply *in terminis*, and that he remains faithful to Jewish religious ideas. Flavius Josephus in this aspect is a clear example of the intellectual who is deeply affected by the religious and social crises of his times.

Going back to the various aspects offered by the term τύχη, one may observe that it acts in a favourable (εὐτυχία) or unfavourable way (ἀτυχία, δυστύχημα, δυστυχία)[240] towards men and it may also operate by means of those acts which are proper to a human being, without taking into account the social standing of the person on whom it falls.

Taking up once again the life of king Herod, which for Flavius Josephus represents one of the most brilliant moments in the history of the Jewish people, we can see that it is marked by a series of specific oc-curences, part of which comes from his good τύχη. But this εὐτυχία is also curbed by evil forces—κακοδαιμονεῖν—, caused by the τύχη, by vengeance or envy of his prosperity[241]. Here Flavius Josephus or his literary assistants echo the classical concept according to which the gods —in this case the τύχη—meted out punishment, through the intervention of the νέμεσις, to any mortal who had aspired to things beyond human possibilities, or else simply through envy of his well-being. In this sense therefore, the etymological identity between the word νέμεσις and the verb applied by Flavius Josephus to the τύχη, ἐνεμέσησεν, is suggestive: ''Fortune, however, was envious of his evident prosperity, thus bringing down vexations on his household, and there began his misfortune because of the woman he passionately desired''[242].

A case which is parallel to the previous one is the sin of ὕβρις represented in the conduct of the emperor Gaius, who aspired to being considered a god[243] and ordered images of himself to be placed in the temple of Jerusalem. The untrammelled behaviour of Gaius has given rise to an abundant literature[244]. Here we shall see how Flavius Josephus echoes it.

---

[240] Cf. *Concordance*, *s.uu.*

[241] Τύχη may feel the effects of jealousy (B, I, 431; B, VI, 63).

[242] B, I, 431.

[243] B, II, 184; A, XVIII, 256.

[244] Suet., *Calig.* 32; Philo, *Leg. ad Gaium* 31; Dio Cass. LIX, 29, 1; Tac., *Ann.* XI, 3, and Sen., *De const. Sap.* 18, 1, cited by J. P. V. D. Balsdon, *The emperor Gaius (Caligula)*, Oxford Univ. Pr., 1964 (1rst. ed. 1934), 212.

Flavius Josephus is very explicit: "The emperor Gaius insulted fortune to the point where...[245]. He also showed himself to be extremely insolent towards the Jews and subjects of the Empire[246].

In the *Bellum Judaicum*, Flavius Josephus is very sparing in his consideration concerning the fortune of Gaius[247], but gives himself a much freer rein in the *Antiquitates Judaicae*[248], giving over some paragraphs to transcendent reflection.

Flavius Josephus introduces the affair of the placing of the images by order of Gaius in the temple of Jerusalem, together with the sentencing to death of recalcitrants and other abominable orders with a sentence which is full of mystery: "The orders did not go unnoticed by God"[249]. He then brings the narration to a close with the bare mention of the murder of Gaius. It seems, therefore, that the historian believes that the behaviour of Gaius was kept track of at all moments by divine power. He is even more explicit in the *Antiquitates Judaicae*, where he says twice that God did not forget the good works of Petronius in favour of the Jews[250], adding that the fact that Petronius was saved from the execution of the death sentence, given by Gaius for not having carried out his orders concerning the matter of the images, came about in an unexpected way.

In A, XIX, 15-16, Flavius Josephus gives four reasons why he will write a complete narrative of the death of Gaius: because it meant a freeing of the whole world; because history offers proof of divine power; because the miserable are comforted and these who believe that good fortune is everlasting should know that, without virtue, it too is mortal.

Immediately there spring up three conspiracies against Gaius[251]. There are three points on which the historian dwells. The first text is corrupt, but the idea of divine intervention is clear: "but if no sign as if issuing from the gods were to give him the power of death..."[252]. Here we interpret that, until the divinity should express its disapproval of the death of Gaius, then the conspirator Chaerea continued with his plan until he

---

[245] B, II, 184: Γάιος δὲ Καῖσαρ ἐπὶ τοσοῦτον ἐξύβρισεν εἰς τὴν τύχην. This expression is always used in the case of the personality acting in an inconsiderate manner against fortune (B, II, 250; B, V, 120), against God (B, II, 230; B, V, 394; A, I, 100; A, VIII, 245, 265, 299; A, IX, 196; A, X, 39), the laws (A, IV, 13; A, VI, 35, 92; A, IX, 168) and people and peoples (B, I, 196, 438; B, VI, 122; A, I, 188; A, IV, 13, 189, 260); the same verb again is used in the negative when the personality does not go beyond the bounds of his attributes (B, I, 140, 206; A, 273; A, XIV, 161).

[246] A, XIX, 1.
[247] B, II, 184-204.
[248] A, XVIII, 224-309; A, XIX, 1-161.
[249] B, II, 186.
[250] A, XVIII, 306 and 309.
[251] A, XIX, 17-23.
[252] A, XIX, 72.

saw it through. But the role of Fortune has still to be added to this, which delayed the day of the consummation of the plot[253]. The third aspect is that represented by the interpretation which is given to the fact of a senator's soiling his clothes with the blood which spurted from the sacrifice made in honour of Augustus, at the beginning of the games: it was a question then of an omen concerning the death of Gaius[254].

It is difficult to determine to what extent divine power is the hidden actor behind these events, and to what extent the τύχη. It would seem that Flavius Josephus leaves rather the fulfilling of events in the hands of τύχη, which then leads the life of the emperor, punctually, against the plans of the conspirators, until the final reckoning.

A vision which is really all Flavius Josephus' own is projected onto the τύχη of the Romans, possibly as a result of the influence of Jewish apocalyptic literature.

In the Jewish eschatological view, empires came to form part of divine determinations. So, while ancient prophetism had to contemporize with circumstantial disasters, at the time, the great powers of the world, according to the Jewish mind, served to justify a series of divine plans on the future of humanity. In this way, so as to harmonize the historical difficulties, rising empires played a role in divine plans. Therefore a type of determinism appeared in the Jewish apocalyptic outlook[255].

Let us analyse the quotes following the order of edition of the works. Flavius Josephus is very clear on the idea that τύχη corresponds, at the present moment, to the Roman people, in the same way as it previously corresponded to Alexander the Great (B, II, 360) and to other peoples. In the speech, therefore, which Agrippa gives to the Jews so that they should lay down their arms against the Romans, it is left quite clear that the powerful peoples of yesteryear are now subjects of Rome, and that the terrible Macedonians "bend before those towards whom τύχη has turned"[256].

Later on, Flavius Josephus, moved by the clearsightedness which he has of the situation of disaster, will counsel his companions to surrender to the Romans, will state that the fortune of the Romans is absolute, and not simply partial: "All fortune has passed over to the Roman side"[257].

---

[253] A, XIX, 77.

[254] A, XIX, 87 and 123.

[255] R. H. Charles, *Eschatology*, New York, 1963 (2nd. ed.), 205. In this same sense, cf. D. S. Russell, *The Method and Message of Jewish Apocalyptic*, London, 1964, 230.

[256] B, II, 360: πρὸς οὓς μεταβέβηκεν ἡ τύχη προσκυνοῦσιν. The Gauls too have submitted to the Romans "because of the power of Rome and her fortune, which gave them more victories than their arms" (B, II, 373).

[257] B, III, 354.

This sentence is significative. It is the whole fortune of the world that has gone over to the Roman Empire. I believe that Flavius Josephus centred the whole force of his expression in the word πᾶσα. But the fellow-citizens of Flavius Josephus do not share his own pragmatic outlook, and they place their patriotic ideal before the reality which is being imposed on them: "If the τύχη of the Romans has brought about in you the forgetting of yourself, then it behoves us to have providence of the glory of our homeland"[258].

And it is not only political power which has passed into the hands of the Romans, but also material power (B, V, 366). This idea of a τύχη on the material plane is completed by the idea of a God who hangs over Italy: "Since τύχη has gone over to them (the Romans), from all corners, and God, who concedes in turn power everywhere, is now over Italy"[259]. These words are harsh, if we keep in mind that they were spoken by Flavius, already a prisoner of the Romans, before his fellow-citizens who were still prepared to resist behind the walls of Jerusalem. I believe that these words, whether spoken *in situ* or written later, are highly charged with the justification of the realist or betrayalist stance of Flavius Josephus, according to the point of view from which his acts are judged. In short, they mean that he too has gone over to the Romans, without being a deserter, since, if the powerful τύχη and the omnipotent God are on the side of the Romans, then he and the Jews must act likewise. And he speaks to them thus: "Fools forgetful of your real allies, you struggle against the Romans with weapons and with your hands? What other enemies have you vanquished thus? When has God the creator not been the avenger of the Jews when they have suffered injustice?"[260] Later on, and in the same speech, Flavius Josephus says the most senseless thing that a Jew could ever utter, and which, in my opinion, must have caused substantial impact on the listeners behind the walls, if we keep in mind the number of deserters to the Roman camp, even though the impact was not total: "I believe that God has fled the holy places (the *sancta sanctorum* of the temple of Jerusalem) and that He now resides amongst those against whom you fight"[261].

In the use which he makes of various historiographic aspects, Flavius Josephus shows that he is familiar with Polybius' history-writing[262]. In the case of τύχη, Flavius Josephus agrees with Polybius as regards his

---

258 B, III, 359.
259 B, V, 367.
260 B, V, 376-377.
261 B, V, 412.
262 P. Collomp, *op. cit.*, *passim*.

teleological conception, but differs from him with regard to changing τύχη. For Polybius the μεταβαίνειν of τύχη does not exist. The duration of τύχη as regards the Roman people has a more profound significance for Polybius than for Flavius Josephus[263].

On a different level, more profound, there can be seen throughout this analysis a gradation of the influencing power over historical events. God is seen here as the maximum superiority and influence, and τύχη is placed alongside the idea of God, without their being mutually exclusive, and τύχη represents no more than a part of God. God allows the Jewish people to be annihilated on earth; hence the fact of τύχη floating over the Romans[264]. All in all, the power of the Romans has been the result of their valour (B, III, 71), of their keen foresight (id. 98-100) and of their perfect discipline (id. 105-106), rather than as the consequence of chance (id. 71 and 100), and the Romans place more trust in their own foresight than in fortune (id. 106). It is obvious that this last idea reveals a strong streak of rationalism and that the intellectual attitude of Flavius Josephus tends to a pragmatic and realistic stance, in the face of a whole world of mysticism which cannot be evaluated.

As a postscript to what I have been dealing with here, it should be said that Flavius Josephus places τύχη alongside the idea of God, and that this does not mean that God replaces the idea of τύχη, but rather that this idea is a part of God[265]. Therefore, as is supposed by Lindner, τύχη is a synonym of the idea expressed by εἱμαρμένη, by πρόνοια, and by κηδεμὼν θεός (B, III, 387-391)[266].

In these commentated texts, the repeated use of certain words is significant. This indicates that the fact of Roman supremacy was an obsession with Flavius Josephus, that it was something which was irrevocable and which spread to the four corners of the world, and that the rebellious attitude of the Jews was indefensible, and, above all, that the fact that the Romans were the masters of the world was part and parcel of divine plans. In this latter sense, the use of the verb ἐμπεριάγοντα is very significant. It is a polysemic verb. It indicates two types of movement, the one static (ἐν) and the other dynamic (περί), in a circular sense, and finally the verb ἄγω, with a dynamic value. Movement and change therefore prevail over a static situation, and if there were a desire to point out through the structure of the word itself that the permanence of power

---

[263] H. Lindner, *Die Geschichtsauffassung des Flavius Josephus im Bellum Judaicum*, Leiden, 1972, 47-48. Polybius qualifies τύχη as πανοῦργος which Flavius Josephus also echoes: πανουργήσασαν τὴν τύχην (B, IV, 591).

[264] H. Lindner, *op. cit.*, 45.

[265] *Ibid.*, 45.

[266] *Ibid.*, 88.

is shortlived, almost reduced to a point (ἐν), whereas change, by means of a circular movement spiralling (περί) through the various empires which have existed, is everlasting, and in it is to be found the very essence of power. It is, lastly, a very impressionistic verb, since one can imagine a god circling the earth and looking for a place where he may place temporal power[267]. Here, then, we are dealing with a cyclical concept of power (B, V, 367).

The idea of the totality (τύχη πᾶσα, B, III, 354) of the fortune of the Romans is completed by physical totality (πάντοθεν, B, V, 367), and the fortune which had been the lot of scattered empires has now come to rest *in toto* on Rome.

The force of the verbs (μεταβέβηκεν, B, II, 360; μετέβη, B, III, 354; μεταβῆναι, B, V, 367) should also be observed. They are used to indicate the change of fortune of a people and its passing to another. It is indisputable, therefore, that the peoples have had and have their τύχη, but that this is changeable, and swings from one kind to another (μεταβολή, B, II, 360). Individuals are also subject to the misfortune of changing τύχη; thus, for example, fortune passes from Antonius to Octavius (μεταβαινούσης τῆς τύχης, A, XV, 191; B, I, 390), and Flavius Josephus himself is the object of a change towards good fortune (μεταβολή, B, III, 395).

There are doubtless a great many examples of the involvement in events of τύχη, considered as a superior power which is imposed, as an independent being, and as a divinity. Flavius Josephus has it intervening in the lives of specific persons and of large groups, leading them along a specific path.

In the personal case of Flavius Josephus, τύχη will decide on the order in which he and his companions are to die (B, III, 389), to the point where, when there are only two left, he himself and another, he asks himself whether it has been because of the intervention of τύχη or because of divine providence (B, III, 391). Here we are dealing with a forced doubt, which makes us suspicious of the feelings expressed in it, since the conviction of Flavius Josephus is not at all clear. Were the sentence to be attributed to one of his literary assistants, the problem in question would be sufficiently clarified. If this is not the case, we should be forced to consider that Flavius Josephus was no more than a beggar of circumstances, a refined product of the philosophy of *carpe diem*. On the other hand, his reflexion, once having fallen into the hands of the Romans, concerning the power of τύχη (B, III, 396) leads one to think of Josephus' adherence

---

[267] Philo had expressed the same idea: χορεύει δὲ ἐν κύκλῳ λόγος ὁ θεῖος ὃν οἱ πολλοὶ τῶν ἀνθρώπων ὀνομάζουσι τύχην (*Quod deus sit immutabilis*, XXXVI, 176).

to that transcendent reality which, in this final instance, freed him from death.

Τύχη is in a constant state of flux with regard to the destiny of men (B, IV, 40, 622; B, VI, 66; A, XVII, 122; A, XVIII, 239), collaborates even with perverse people (B, IV, 238), its intervention is not understood by humans (B, IV, 243), it forestalls human decisions (B, IV, 591) or delays them (A, XIX, 77), it may betray human hopes (B, III, 100; B, VI, 173; A, XI, 56) and effects changes in the personalities of people (A, XV, 17). Man places his trust in it (A, XV, 165, 246). Τύχη may be favourable (A, XVII, 191; A, XVIII, 54; A, XIX, 233)[268] or unfavourable (A, XVI, 188, 300)[269], and may be the object of oath (A, XVI, 344). On a personal level, men have their τύχη, which may be beneficial (B, I, 68, 430, 622, 665; B, II, 207; B, IV, 365, 438; B, V, 46, 78, 88, 465; B, VI, 57, 66, 280; A, II, 39; A, XIV, 9; A, XVI, 7, 344; A, XVIII, 46, 254; A, XIX, 193, 214, 293; A, XX, 70; Vit, 419), unfavourable (B, I, 390, 606; B, III, 202, 438; B, IV, 626; B, V, 474; B, VII, 231; A, IV, 266; A, XIV, 97, 140, 354, 451; A, XVII, 13, 94, 109, 148, 192; A, XVIII, 178, 200, 209; A, XIX, 29, 177, 294, 318; A, XX, 60; Vit, 180; Ap, II, 227) and changeable (B, I, 353; B, IV, 607; A, I, 8, 13; A, XIV, 381, 481; A, XV, 179, 191, 374; A, XVIII, 142, 197, 267; A, XIX, 317; A, XX, 57, 61; Vit, 417), but it never remains either beneficial or unfavourable for long (B, I, 374). Titus is especially singled out for favourable τύχη (B, V, 88; B, VI, 57, 413).

Finally, the second aspect of the interventions of τύχη is that it holds in its hands the fate of whole peoples and nations, with the two-fold character of good and ill fortune: B, I, 28, 45; B, II, 213, 360, 373, 387; B, III, 9, 24; B, IV, 179; B, V, 120, 121, 122, 367, 486, 548; B, VI, 14, 44, 352, 399, 400, 413; B, VII, 7, 115, 203; A, I, 6; A, XI, 343; Vit, 142; Ap, II, 130, 228.

The prepositional expressions also play the part of the unexpected and add a kind of fortuity to scenes: κατὰ τύχας (A, XVII, 24), κατὰ τύχην (B, I, 341; B, II, 494; B, III, 327) and ἀπὸ τύχης (B, IV, 155)[270].

Τὸ χρεών. The conclusion which the historian writes to the life of king Achab is suggestive on account of the presence of another term, τὸ χρεών. Two prophecies hang over the king of Israel, that of Elijah and that of

---

[268] Cf. in the *Concordance* the following words: εὐτυχία, εὐτυχέω, εὐτύχημα, εὐτυχής.

[269] Cf. in the *Concordance* the following words: δυστυχής, δυστυχέω, δυστυχία, δυστύχημα, ἀτύχημα, ἀτυχία.

[270] Cf. F. Rösiger, *Die Bedeutung der Tyche bei den späteren griechischen Historikern, besonders bei Demetrios von Phaleron*, Konstanz, 1880.

Michaias[271], which predict his end. This ending does not appear in the parallel position in the Holy Scriptures[272]; it is, therefore, a short *excursus*, of Flavius Josephus' own doing. Previously, however, to the prophecy of Michaias, Achab had consulted with his own prophets, who had predicted the victory of the king over the Syrian king Adados. This prophecy coincided exactly with the king's wishes, and war is undertaken, and the king inevitably dies on the first day of the hostilities.

At this point in the story of king Achab, the historian brings the narrative to a close with a reminder of the precise fulfilment of the prophecies, and adds that man must recognise the greatness of God and do Him honour, and that he must not prefer the words of those who flatter him to the truth, but rather realise that a prophecy gives him previous knowledge of what will happen to him, that path which God offers to him so that he should know what he must avoid[273]. And he adds: "It behoves us to reflect on the force of *that which must come to pass* (τὸ χρεών), since it is impossible to escape from it even with fore-knowledge of it, for it insinuates itself by adulating human spirits with good hopes, by means of which it leads them where it will"[274].

The atmosphere of this text points towards fatalism[275], an idea which supposes the possession of the faculty of thought itself (διάνοια), which τὸ χρεών deceives: "It is seen, therefore, that Achab too was deceived in his mind by this power, so that he believed not in those who prophesied his downfall..."[276].

All this suggests two ideas: that it is a question of the predestination of man, and that Flavius Josephus tinges with a Hellenistic outlook the concept of divine providence as a concession to the understanding of non-Jewish readers, so that there is a resulting mixture, according to which human future is not simply protected by God, but is inevitably directed.

Whenever the τὸ χρεών appears it reaffirms its character of *that which is bound to come to pass*, as the expression of a cosmic necessity, without the fulfillment of which there would come about an imbalance in the future of human history. Death, for example, is something which is inevitable, forms part of destiny, and which, for the historian, may be brought forward through some lofty ideal: to obtain a military victory. Flavius Josephus places these words in the mouth of Titus: "How can it not be

---

[271] A, VIII, 360-362, 404-410.
[272] 1*Reg.* XXI, 17-XXII, 40; 2*Chron.* XVIII, 14.
[273] A, VIII, 418.
[274] A, VIII, 419.
[275] The inevitability of τὸ χρεών on the part of the man, even having fore-knowledge, is very clear in the historian: B, VI, 314.
[276] A, VIII, 420.

an ignoble act not to give to pressing necessities that which we shall surrender to fate?''[277] I notice here, in the use of the words χρεία and χρεών, a similarity of root, something which brings into close relationship the irreversibility of circumstances—which are inevitable—and of fate.

The linking of the idea of death to that of τὸ χρεών will appear again and again[278].

This mortal fate often omits to take into account the moral quality of the person who is to suffer it, for there is no distinction made between people, and thus ''τὸ χρεών brought about the destruction of the innocent as well as the guilty, and the city together with sedition (i.e. citizens together with rebels)''[279].

Finally, the active character of τὸ χρεών should be pointed out, as well as the personalizing treatment accorded it by the historian, though dealing with an abstract concept. I refer to the verbs which accompany it, verbs which are more in line with human conduct: ἐπεγέλα (B, I, 233)[280], ἐφθάχει (B, I, 275), ἐκράτει (B, V, 355), πεπήροντο (B, V, 572), ἐφθάσθη (A, VIII, 307), ἐνίκα, ἐποίει (A, VIII, 409), εὗρε (A, VIII, 412), κολακεῦον, κρατήσει, περιάγει, ἀπατηθείς (A, VIII, 419-420).

2. Events mysterious in nature

Flavius Josephus does not leave to one side the possibilities offered by certain episodes which are a mixture of unusual events and those of a certain transcendence.

The presence of an enigmatic animal shrouds the narrative in a prophetic atmosphere, as well as serving as an aetiological explanation for certain events (A, XVIII, 195; A, XIX, 346).

The mystery created by the dreams dreamed by certain personalities is also mentioned by Flavius Josephus. This working method is fully parallel to the same literary genre in the Old Testament. For Flavius Josephus, dreams too have a prophetic nature (B, II, 112-113 and 116; B, III, 351; Vit, 208 ff.).

Certain acts which are carried out without forethought are also signs which are pregnant with transcendence. When the Pharaoh had seen the infant Moses, he placed his crown on his head, but the infant threw it down (A, II, 234 ff.). This event is considered as an omen of ill-fortune (οἰωνόν). And it is interpreted thus by the priest who is in attendance.

---

[277] B, VI, 49.
[278] B, I, 233, 275; B, V, 514, 572; A, VII, 383; A, VIII, 307, 409, 412.
[279] B, V, 355.
[280] The same verb applied to God: ὁ δὲ θεὸς κατεγέλα (A, XI, 247).

This incident may respond to an intellectual elaboration of the historian so as to create the mystery, since this anecdote is not to be found in the Scriptures (*Exod.*, II, 10).

When dealing now with contemporary events, Flavius Josephus sees here too omens of ill-fortune (A, XIX, 87: οἰωνόν) and of good fortune (B, I, 45).

Going even further, Flavius Josephus wraps the end of the temple of Jerusalem up in extraordinary phenomena[281], which he describes as "divine warnings". He notes the exact day, month and hour of the events[282], and the names of those people who have a hand in it[283].

He also expounds two prophetic oracles, which he interprets in the light of harsh reality, since other Jews had made light of them[284], and which have brought about the downfall of the city through their folly. If it is called for, he adjusts the interpretation of the omens to their historical necessity, thus echoing other sources, Latin ones[285] in the case of wanting to see in Vespasian the master of the world, as had been predicted by the Jewish oracle, in spite of its "ambiguity" (ἀμφίβολος).

The oracular interpretation too of the death of Eleazar is an interpretation of Flavius, so that the events came to mean for Judas a warning of the importance of the undertaking[286].

The world beyond is also quoted by Flavius Josephus, but as the underworld, according to the classical concept contained in the term ᾅδης. In a certain sense, and in view of the quotes, rather few and far between, the next world may exercise great influence on human activity[287].

By way of concluding this collection of unusual events, Flavius Josephus assures that in them will be found a sign of divine preoccupation for men, since God shows his people the path to salvation by any means which may be necessary, and that ill-fortune is no more than the product of human folly[288]. A wise manner of justifying his Hellenized faith, or a conciliatory attitude which takes into account the diverse religious training of his readers, or an addition of his literary assistants.

Flavius Josephus mentions further elements which he interprets as omens of that which may come to pass. Thus, he says that the Roman

---

[281] B, VI, 288-315.
[282] B, VI, 290, 296, 299, 300.
[283] B, VI, 300, 305.
[284] B, VI, 310-315.
[285] Tac., *Hist.* V, 13; Suet., *Vesp.* 4. For the relations between Flavius Josephus and Tacitus, cf. E. Norden, "Josephus und Tacitus über Jesus Christus und eine messianische Prophetie", *NJ* 16 (1913), 637-666, and P. Corssen, "Die Zeugnisse des Tacitus und Pseudo-Josephus über Christus", *ZNTW* 15 (1914), 114-140.
[286] B, I, 45.
[287] B, I, 596; B, II, 156, 165; B, III, 375; A, VI, 332.
[288] B, VI, 310.

soldiers see, in the symbol of the eagle of their legions, an omen of future victory (B, III, 123).

Ill-treatment of a body was an object of condemnation, but the Jews, impelled by the fury of their desperate situation, pass over the pestilent mounds of the bodies of their dead fellow citizens, in a vain attempt to defend themselves. They do so, says Flavius Josephus, "without pity and without a thought for the dreadful omen which their trampling underfoot of the dead meant for them"[289].

While the temple of Jerusalem was burning down, there occurred some prodigies which, according to Flavius Josephus (though he must have collected them from oral sources) are to be believed, if we accept his final words as being written in all sincerity. After describing new prodigies which surrounded the fall of the temple[290], he says that the Jews interpreted them in a very superficial and disdainful manner "until such time as they (the prodigies) refuted their wickedness by bringing about the ruin of their homeland and their own destruction"[291].

Finally, Flavius Josephus also entrusts himself to the imperatives of chance, and so lots are drawn amongst the various personalities for posts of responsibility in his army[292].

3. *Biblical God and historical event*

The idea of God in Flavius Josephus covers broad theological horizons, as is to be expected in a Jew and priest of the ancient people of Israel. God is therefore the creator, king and lord, father, God of Israel, the only true God, God the spirit, God the judge, the kind God, the angry God[293]. All these concepts are doubtless borrowed from the Holy Scriptures[294].

However, my aim in this section cannot contemplate the theological concept of the God of Flavius Josephus, but rather a God in the role of historical actor, who becomes mixed in with human acts, and to whom may be attributed specific implications in the affairs and the interests of men. It is therefore necessary to study Him as the efficient cause, as the instigator of human acts and as the force responsible for numerous moments in human development.

---

[289] B, VI, 3.

[290] B, VI, 288-314.

[291] B, VI, 315.

[292] B, I, 258.

[293] For all these aspects, cf. M. Duschak, *Mor Deror. Josephus Flavius und die Tradition*, Wien, 1864, 33; A. Schlatter, *Wie sprach Josephus von Gott?*, Gütersloh, 1910, and *Die Theologie des Judentums nach dem Bericht des Josefus*, Gütersloh, 1932; J. B. Fischer, "The term δεσπότης in Josephus", *JQR* 49 (1958-1959), 132-138.

[294] Cf. *Concordance*, s.u. θεός, and derived words.

I should also like to draw attention to the restricted use which I have made of literary sources. No reference has been made to the first eleven books of the *Antiquitates Judaicae* since Flavius Josephus follows closely the same theological ideas which are in the biblical books he paraphrases.

It seems to me that the most succinct method, given the wealth of quotes offered by the *Concordance* under the word θεός, may be a simple interpretation of divine intervention, by making a kind of list of the different moments and the various acts which bear clear witness to His intervention.

Therefore, the historical God from the viewpoint of Flavius Josephus can be attributed with the following interventions:

He is a God who
– has in His hands the multiple circumstances of wars (B, I, 215 (if this lesson is allowed), 373; B, II, 539, 582; B, III, 28, 144, 293, 484, 494; B, IV, 26, 104, 370; B, V, 60, 386, 404; B, VI, 98, 100, 371, 401; B, VII, 387),
– concedes power to men and allies Himself to them (B, I, 390; B, II, 140, 214, 390; B, III, 6, 404; B, V, 2, 39, 367-368, 412, 459; B, VI, 110, 411; B, VII, 319, 325; A, XII, 25, 316; A, XIII, 80, 163, 299; A, XV, 138, 374),
– is attentive to human decisions and collaborates in them (B, I, 457, 465, 558, 584, 595, 639; B, II, 186, 401; B, III, 341, 387, 391; B, IV, 219, 288, 362, 366, 573; B, V, 278; B, VI, 38-39, 310; A, XIII, 300; A, XV, 4, 376, 383, 387; A, XVI, 318; A, XVII, 158, 330, 354; A, XVIII, 245, 284, 288, 306; A, XIX, 314; A, XX, 18, 84-85; Ap, II, 160),
– punishes men (B, I, 378, 593, 631; B, III, 371, 375; B, IV, 323, 573; B, V, 39, 343, 392, 396, 398, 559; B, VI, 40, 108, 250, 285, 433; B, VII, 32-34, 271, 331, 333, 359, 453; A, XII, 111, 413; A, XIV, 25; A, XV, 243, 299; A, XVI, 43, 60, 64; A, XVII, 60, 168, 170; A, XVIII, 116, 119, 255, 260; A, XIX, 294; A, XX, 72, 81, 166),
– is needed by men (B, V, 400, 519; A, XII, 112-113, 285, 300, 314; A, XIII, 13; A, XVII, 195; Vit, 15; Ap, II, 165),
– is the best of leaders (B, III, 373),
– shows His will to men by means of dreams (B, III, 351; A, XIII, 322),
– sends rain (A, XIV, 22, 391; A, XVIII, 285-286),
– sends snow (A, XIV, 414),
– brings peace (A, XIV, 312) and
– protects His own from evil (B, V, 383; A, XIV, 455, 462, 470; A, XV, 146; A, XX, 48, 88-91; Vit, 83, 301, 425).

CHAPTER TWO

ARS NARRANDI

Precedents

Hellenistic historians take great care when it comes to choosing historical subjects and the literary form to be followed. Thus they reason on the qualities which the historical subject should contain so that it make its contribution to mankind's store of knowledge. They dictate norms and profess tendencies with regards to the material form of their histories, so that their works should also be products with literary value.

They thus consider that the subject must be chosen with wisdom, so that it be beautiful, pleasing, grandiose and useful, and has to be carried out with the greatest of vigour[1]. It may not be a simple subject, μονοειδής, but a fairly complex one, πολύμορφος, so that the reader is not wearied[2]. The historian must investigate the causes of events and must exercise great prudence in his use of sources[3].

Again, there are historians who, when giving their methodological guide-lines, censure those others who have made the wrong choice, and have dealt with mediocre and nugatory subjects[4].

Insisting on the limitations of the subject of an historical work, Dionysius criticises the working method of Thucydides in the sense that he has not taken care to note the beginning and the end of his history, the very least that can be demanded, since it may be seen that they are observable even in nature itself[5]. More specifically, the general subject of the work must be well-defined, and all the other monographic subjects must fit well within the framework of the main argument.

Polybius is very explicit on these points, and of the writer asks that, before he settle down to write, he should conceive the whole of the argument from beginning to end, in such a way that a singleness of spirit per-

---

[1] Dion. Hal., *Arch.* I, 1, 2; 2, 1; *Ad Pomp.* 3, 2; 4, 1; 8, 10. Diod., *Bibl.* I, 3; Pol. I, 2, 1; 4, 4; III, 4, 13; V, 31, 6; VIII, 4, 3 and 7; IX, 21, 14.

[2] Dion. Hal., *Arch.* I, 8, 3; *Ad Pomp.* 3, 3-4; 6, 3; 11-12; *De Thuc.* 5; 331, 20; Diod., *Bibl.* XX, 2, 1.

[3] Dion. Hal., *Arch.* I, 1, 4-5; 6, 1; 7, 3; VII, 71, 1; *De Thuc.* 6, 332, 21. Diod., *Bibl.* I, 4, 1; 39, 8; 69, 7; III, 11, 1; 38, 1.

[4] Dion. Hal., *Arch.* I, 1, 3; V, 75, 1; *Ad Pomp.* 3, 4; *De Thuc.* 5, 331, 22; Pol. VII, 7, 6; XXIX, 12, 1. We borrow the ideas from P. Scheller, *De hellenistica Historiae conscribendae arte*, Leipzig, 1911.

[5] *De Thuc.* 10; 11; 341, 5. He praises Xenophon for his observance of these norms (*Ad Pomp.* 4, 2).

vades the whole of the work[6]. That the beginning and end of the historical work are well-marked is of the greatest importance, so that a unified, ἕν, and complete, αὐτοτελές, product should be the end-result[7].

On the other hand, Aristotle rejects the unity of an historical work when it includes many and varied narratives[8]. But nevertheless there is no clear rejection on his part of the possibility of constructing a rich and varied work.

Polybius, in contrast, is in favour of this unity, in spite of the fact that subjects which differ in content and time are dealt with in the same work. This sense of unity seems to have been the obligatory precept of the art of ancient history[9].

Dionysius compares history to a body, which may be considered in two ways: as a unit with various parts (as in the case in history with Thucydides) or as various parts which form a symphonic ἓν σῶμα (in history, Herodotus). He later on compares history to a *living body*[10].

But this metaphorical unity will be born only from a strict ordering and laying out of historical events. With a view to this, the speeches must be reduced and placed in the most convenient and opportune places; events referring to cities and to kings must be perfectly developed from beginning to end; digressions must not be over-long[11], and are to be included only when useful[12].

When observing the magnitude of his work, Polybius confesses to having had πρόνοιαν καὶ τοῦ χειρισμοῦ καὶ τῆς οἰκονομίας, so as to σαφὲς τὸ σύνταγμα γίνηται τῆς πραγματείας (V, 31, 7; X, 23, 1). When accused by other historians of having dealt with too many events in a single work (XXXIX, 1), he defends himself by saying that the variety in his work is not incompatible with the exigencies of order and continuity and that the readers easily relate what goes together (XXXIX, 2, 1; 2, 3-6). For reasons of clarity, he brings together everything relating to a given subject in a single narrative moment[13], or else anticipates the end at the

---

[6] III, 1, 4-5; V, 32.

[7] I, 5, 3; 12, 6 ff. These aspects concord with what Aristotle says concerning epic poetry: δεῖ τοὺς μύθους ... συνιστάναι δραματικοὺς καὶ περὶ μίαν πρᾶξιν ὅλην καὶ τελείαν, ἔχουσαν ἀρχὴν καὶ μέσα καὶ τέλος, ἵν' ὥσπερ ζῷον ἓν ὅλον ποιῇ τὴν οἰκείαν ἡδονήν (*Poet.* 23, 1459a 1).

[8] *Poet.* 23, 1459a 21.

[9] I, 3, 4.

[10] *Ad Pomp.* 3, 14; XX, 1, 5.

[11] Dion. Hal., *Ad Pomp.* 3, 13 ff; *De Thuc.* 9. Diod., *Bibl.* XX, 1, 12, 2; XVI, 1, 1-2; II, 31, 10. Diodorus praises Ephorus for his narration of events (V, 1, 4). Dionysius follows the same line (*Ad Pomp.* 3, 13) as does Appian (*Praef.* 12-13).

[12] Dion. Hal., *Ad Pomp.* 6, 11; *Arch.* VII, 70, 1.

[13] XIV, 12; XXXII, 25, 7.

beginning[14], or groups together things of a similar kind[15], and devotes the whole of book XXXIV to geography[16]. By observing this discipline, related material is not cut up (XXXII, 25, 3-4).

So much for the general principles which must govern good historical narrative. The next point deals with a look at the most important elements which form part of the historical narrative.

One of the essential virtues so as to be able to form a ἕν σῶμα is symmetry, i.e. things and events should be dealt with and described to an extent in keeping with the moment, with their importance, and also bearing in mind the harmony of the whole of the remaining historical corpus. Speeches, therefore, will be composed only of important affairs[17]; things which are equal in importance must be dealt with in a similar manner[18]. In the same way, the books and inner divisions of the work must be balanced in their length and in their treatment. In short, the art of historiography demands balance and ponderation, τὸ μέτριον[19].

By this yardstick, Thucydides is severely criticised for leaving a narrative unfinished to go on to another, thereby confusing the reader[20]. Digressions should be both moderate and justified[21].

Diodorus postulates symmetry very often, both that referring to the equal length of books[22], and that of the subjects and particular aspects within them[23].

Polybius takes the same line[24]. For reasons of symmetry too, he prohibits epilogues for those personalities who are undeserving of them[25].

Lucian recommends a correlation between the proem and the rest of the work with regard to thematic quality, and also requests reasonable proportions in the narratives in keeping with the importance of the matter dealt with[26].

In view of the fact that, in classical historians, the importance of the personalities practically monopolises historical action, it follows that historiographical ideas should refer to significant acts of those per-

---

[14] XV, 24a; cf. 25, 19; XXVIII, 16, 10 ff.

[15] XII, 11, 6; III, 57, 4; II, 16, 14.

[16] Both Ephorus (E. Schwartz, *RE*, *s.u.* "Ephoros") and Theopompus had already done so.

[17] Dion. Hal., *De Thuc.* 18; 353, 4; for the word συμμετρία cf. X, 4; 362, 11.

[18] *Ibid.*, 15; 17; 350, 4-8.

[19] *Ibid.*, 16; 344, 4; 349, 13 ff.; 19.

[20] Dion. Hal., *De Thuc.*, ἀτελῆ, ἡμιτελῆ, 337, 3; 6; 337, 17; 9; 336, 23 ff.

[21] *Ad Pomp.* 6, 11; *Arch.* VII, 70, 1.

[22] I, 8, 10; 9, 4; 41, 10.

[23] IV, 5, 4; 68, 6; VI, 1, 3.

[24] XXIX, 12, 6. In the same line, XIV, 1a, 5; XXIX, 12, 4.

[25] VII, 7; XV, 34, 3; 35, 1 and 7.

[26] *De hist. conscr.* 23; 27-28.

sonalities and should guide and exercise control over the inclusion of these actions in the historical narrative. Restraint should therefore be the guiding hand behind the entire narrative style. The precepts of symmetry must be observed in the case of praise[27], and the writer must never stray from the imperative of art[28] or strict truthfulness[29] whether his attitude is neutral[30] or whether he expresses an opinion[31].

Diodorus and Polybius demand of the writer the virtue of being able to choose the right moment for either praise or censure[32]. In contrast, Lucian proposes that praise and blame should be restricted both in length and frequency, and should always be faithful to the truth. The historian should always avoid making his history an encomiastic and panegyrical work[33].

Here too a discussion of the use and place of the speeches and descriptions within the narrative continuity would fit in well, but both points will be sufficiently dealt with[34].

The art of narrative has as its mission the presentation of events, personalities and institutions in an intelligible and reasoned manner. Even so, this may lead the historian into such exaggerated flights of emotion that the integrity of historical truth is affected. So it is therefore worthwhile to study the varying opinions on the subject. The problem comes down to two basic questions: what are the bounds which the πάθος of the writer has to respect, and, again, can the historian use his history to arouse feelings of sympathy in his readers?

There are many answers, some differing only slightly from others, and some even being in complete contrast to each other.

Dionysius is of the opinion that the historian should take advantage of important moments to rouse the feelings of his readers, and criticises Thucydides and Herodotus for their lack of πάθος[35].

Polybius is in favour of separating the tragic aspect from the historical aspect proper[36], and alludes to the errors committed against truth if narrative drama is allowed to get the upper hand. He calls to mind writers who used epilogues and descriptions in their works with this very aim.

---

[27] Dion. Hal., De Thuc. 18; 353, 4.
[28] Dion. Hal., Ad Pomp. 5, 6.
[29] Pol. I, 14, 5; XVI, 28, 5; VIII, 10, 7; 12, 2; 13, 1 ff.
[30] Pol. VIII, 13, 2.
[31] Pol. II, 61, 6.
[32] Diod., Bibl. XI, 46, 1; XV, 1, 1 and 88; Pol. VII, 7; XV, 34, 3; 35, 1 and 7; XVIII, 41, 1; XXIX, 21, 8.
[33] De hist. conscr. 59; 7 and 14.
[34] Cf. Chap. II, A, 2 and B.
[35] De Thuc. 15; 347, 15; 23; 360, 23. Plutarch, in contrast, is of the opinion that Thucydides wished to arouse emotions (De gloria Athen. 3).
[36] II, 56, 7, 8 and 10; III, 47, 6; VII, 7, 1 ff.; X, 27, 8; XV, 34; XVI, 18, 2.

Again Dionysius, concerned for what he names μιμεῖσθαι τὴν ἀλήθειαν[37], says that readers demand to know the places, the causes, and leaders *inter alia* which have intervened in the events narrated[38], together with the resulting consequences[39]. In short, here we are dealing with the difficult art of explanation and the historiographic predicaments.

By way of conclusion. I should like to draw attention to the idea of Polybius who, for all his rationalism and thirst for truth, eventually admits that it is impossible to exclude absolutely all shades of πάθος, συμπάθεια or ἔκπληξις within human drama. What he does want to make quite clear is that the *rousing of feelings* should be relegated to the writers of tragedy, and that the historian should set his sights on creating a work which will have everlasting usefulness, not simply provide passing delectation[40].

On the question of the style and the form of historical narrative[41], we may recall that for Polybius[42], the historian must take great literary care so that historical narrating enlightens and does not confuse.

Thus historical diction must be καθαρός, σαφής and σύντομος, and must have τὸ κοινὸν καὶ σύνηθες τῆς διαλέκτου with a certain literary embellishment[43]. These qualities which are postulated for history come from the stylistic and literary theories of Isocrates and Theophrastus.

Bearing these concepts in mind, a sort of style proper to history is the result, τὸ λεγόμενον ἰδίως πλάσμα ἱστορικόν[44], a style which Herodotus did not possess, which Xenophon[45] endeavoured to achieve and which Thucydides, according to his detractors, never achieved, his style being described as ἀσαφής and considered as being particularly complex, πεπληγμένη λέξις. This special πλάσμα ἱστορικόν is in complete contrast to the rhetorical atmosphere of the forum and court cases[46], and has more in common with the fluid, unconstrained, moderate Isocratean period[47].

---

[37] *De Thuc.* 45; 402, 3.
[38] Proem to the book XI. Cf. Pol. III, 32, 6.
[39] *Arch.* V, 56, 1. Cf. too Demetrius, *De eloc.* 217.
[40] II, 56, 10. In Chap. II, B, 2 and C, 1, it has been seen that the θαύματα and παράδοξα may have their place in history, if they contribute to the clarification of events narrated.
[41] The part named τὸ λεκτικὸν μέρος by Dionysius (cf. Chap. III, *Precedents*).
[42] XVI, 17, 9 ff.
[43] Dion. Hal., *De Thuc.* 51; 411, 7.
[44] Dion. Hal., *Ad Pomp.* 4, 3.
[45] Dion. Hal., *De Imit.* III, 2; 208, 9.
[46] Dion. Hal., *De Demosth.* 24; 182, 15 and 18; 166, 10 ff.
[47] Cicero is extensive on this point and regarding the last mentioned: *Brut.* 83, 286; *Orat.* II, 37; 20, 66; 61, 207; *De Orat.* II, 15, 64; *De op. gen. or.* 5, 15. Cf. Quint. IX, 4, 18; X, 1, 31; XI, 4, 129; Plin., *Ep.* V, 8, 9. Strabo made a distinction between ἱστορικὴ φράσις and δικανικὴ φράσις (I, 18c).

The historical source of this distinction seems to spring from the stylistic triptych propounded by Demetrius[48] of ἱστορική, διαλογική, ῥητορική, placing the historical period as a middle term between the other two.

Cicero is a rich source for questions relating to the epideictic aspect of historical style[49]. The principal information concerning this matter is dealt with in Chapter II, A, 2.

A. HISTORIOGRAPHIC ELEMENTS

1. *Historical personalities*

In this section I shall make a study of the manner in which Flavius Josephus treats historical personalities as regards their personal and psychological aspects. We have already seen[50] how Flavius Josephus organises his historiographical system around people, and how his history is highly personalist. Now is the time to go on to a study of the individual as such, observing the qualities both of an external and intrinsic nature in which the historian envelops them, so that the reader is able to conjure up a plastic image of these history-makers.

I shall proceed by first of all giving a general analysis of the question, and then I shall deal more specifically with some important personalities. In addition, I shall offer the most relevant psychological vocabulary.

In the first place, the statistics confirm that Flavius Josephus always provides his personalities with an introduction, in which the physical and moral qualities, as well as the defects, are described. Let us take several examples.

Alexander Jannaeus ascends to the throne "because of age and because of his apparent moderation of character"[51]. His life, full of war exploits[52], is brought to a close by the historian with a short reminder of his illness, his death and the years of his reign.

The next person in line of succession is his wife, Alexandra, who had won the affection of the people, and Flavius Josephus says of her: "This lady takes power firmly into her hands thanks to her reputation for piety"[53]. Alexandra exercised strict observance of national traditions.

---

[48] *De eloc.* 19 ff.
[49] *Orat.* 62, 209.
[50] Chap. I, B, 3. Cf. D. Daube, *Typologie im Werk des Flavius Josephus* (Bayerische Akad. d. Wissenschaften. Philos.-hist. Kl., 6), München, 1977.
[51] B, I, 85.
[52] B, I, 86-106.
[53] B, I, 108.

Her sons on the other hand are described in less exalted terms: Hyrcanus is said to be lethargic, and Aristobulus a hothead[54]. Hyrcanus is
even described as being inferior to his brother "in capacity and in intelligence"[55].

Herod's introduction is very simple: "He is energetic by nature"[56] at
the age of fifteen, and "a young man of noble spirit"[57].

The general qualities and the introduction of social groups also take
place in the work of Flavius Josephus. Thus, when mentioning a pact
with the Parthians, he says of them: "The barbarians are by nature per-
fidious"[58].

Of Simon he says: "One of the royal slaves, made proud by the beauty
and stature of his body..."[59]. Later on he complements his psychological
portrait: he was less shrewd than John of Gischala, but was his superior
as regards physical strength and daring[60], a thing which led him into frequent brushes with authority. He aspired to despotic power and great
ambitions. Of a shepherd pretender to the throne he says: "Physical
strength and a soul which was contemptuous of death procured him
hope, and he had, besides, four brothers resembling himself"[61].

Of a second Simon, his physical qualities and his daring are emphasised[62].

With regard to the introduction of John of Gischala, Flavius Josephus
goes into much greater detail. With his introductory words, he practically
maps out his entire life. He writes: "There appeared an instigator, a man
of Gischala, son of Levi, named John, the most malicious and deceitful of
all those who distinguished themselves in these misdeeds. Poor at the
outset, his poverty was for a long time the impediment to his wrong-
doing; ever ready to lie, skillful in obtaining credibility for his lies, he
considered lying a virtue and used it against even his best friends; a
simulator of humanity and the most sanguinary in the hope of gain; ever
cherishing great ambitions, he fed his hopes on wrongdoings most vile.
He was therefore a lone brigand, he later too found company for his daring; at the outset it was not great, but was fuelled by success. He took
care not to choose simply anyone who was easily enlisted, but rather
picked those who excelled in the constitution of their bodies, in firmness

---

[54] B, I, 109.
[55] B, I, 120.
[56] B, I, 204.
[57] A, XIV, 159.
[58] B, I, 255. Too B, II, 482; A, XIV, 160, 165, 302, 324, 327, 348.
[59] B, II, 57.
[60] B, IV, 503-508.
[61] B. II, 60.
[62] B, II, 469.

of spirit, and in experience of warfare''[63]. Some points of this description bring to mind the description made of Catiline by Sallust[64]. It should also be supposed that Flavius Josephus is not impartial in the moral and personal appraisal of his greatest enemy. There is, no doubt, some degree of exaggeration.

Flavius Josephus will not leave this personality aside for any length of time, and, in book IV of the *Bellum Judaicum*, insists on other aspects, some of which are reiterative, which gradually make up the figure of John of Gischala. Thus, John is mentioned as being garrulous (γόης, No. 85) and shrewd (ποικιλώτατος, No. 85), ready to expect great things (πρό-χειρος, No. 85) and skillful at carrying them out; everyone knew that he wanted war for his own aggrandizement. Later on he insists on his character as a trickster (δολιώτατος, No. 208), on his desire of despotic domination (ἔρωτα τυραννίδος, Nos. 208 and 389), and on his ability to pretend (Nos. 209-210) and to win people over to him by means of deceit and rhetoric (No. 391).

I shall, by means of a note, bring together a good many quotes where Flavius Josephus gives only a very bare introduction to his personalities[65]. I shall then focus my comments on the better-known actors.

A whole people may also be the holder of virtues and of intelligence, especially in moments of difficulty[66]. Thus, the inhabitants of Sepphoris were the only people to maintain an attitude of welcome with the arrival of the Romans. In this sense, Flavius says that the inhabitants of Sepphoris showed peaceful feelings (εἰρηνικὰ φρονοῦντες, No. 30). He also attributes intellectual activity to the whole group when he says that they are not lacking in foresight (οὐκ ἀπρονόηται, No. 31) as regards their salvation, and neither as regards the strength of the Romans, and consequently they accept a Roman garrison.

In the *Antiquitates Judaicae* too, there appear a great number of introductions of personalities, together with a great wealth of psychological vocabulary. I shall therefore offer a statistical collection firstly, and then secondly a detailed study of two personalities: Abraham and Herod. Reference should also be made to chapter I.B.3., where an analysis will be found of many elements which complement the study I shall make in this present section.

The *Antiquitates Judaicae* contain a eulogy in honour of Epaphroditus, the patron of Flavius Josephus, in which he is introduced as a scholar,

---

[63] B, II, 585-588.
[64] *De Cat. coni.* 5.
[65] B, III, 4; B, IV, 140, 151, 155, 335, 358; B, V, 11, 12, 312, 317, 474, 527, 532, 534; B, VI, 54-55, 81, 161, 169, 186-189.
[66] B, III, 30-33.

with an especial interest in history. Even though he is not a historical actor as such, I have thought it convenient to make mention of him so as to
demonstrate once more the almost natural tendency of Flavius Josephus
to introduce personalities by two or three of their most important
characteristics.

Here too I shall offer a list of those quotes which belong to the type of
the typical and brief introductions, so as to comment on only the richer
ones[67].

The person of Cain is introduced by his aspects of wrongdoings, which
do not appear in the paraphrased biblical writings[68]. They are, therefore,
an elaboration on the source and indicate an entire mapping out of the
future life of Cain. Thus Cain grew in evil, gave himself up to all kinds of
pleasures, insulted his companions, practised robbery and violence, and
incited others to follow in his ways. He did away with the simplicity of the
others with the invention of weights and measurements, he was the first
to mark out fields, and raised a city.

It should be noted that, under the pen of Flavius Josephus, Cain turns
out to be a highly active and enterprising historical personality who was
in the vanguard of the men of his time. What is more, it is also worth
noting that those aspects which in principle are positive are considered as
downright damaging for a simple human life.

As has been already been pointed out, none of these qualities has been
mentioned by the corresponding biblical text[69]. This is an indicative example of the characteristic traits of the historiographical biography in
Flavius Josephus.

The person of Joseph, son of Jacob, is extensively embellished by his
moral and physical virtues[70]. As this personality will be dealt with under
the heading of his novelistic aspects[71], let a simple mention suffice here.

The person of Moses, extensively studied in this investigation[72], is introduced with those qualities as are befitting to the greatest leader which
the people of Israel will know[73]. He begins by explaining the etymology of
the name Moses, and then goes straight on to comment on the excellen-
cies of the new-born child: ''... all agree that, according to the prediction of God, Moses is the noblest of the Hebrews by the grandeur of his
intellect and by his disdain of fatigue.... His capacity for comprehension

---

[67] A, I, 68. 238, 259; A, II, 7, 9-10; A, IV, 14, 98, 152-153; A, V, 182, 188, 230, 257,
276, 339; A, XIII, 320-321.
[68] A, I, 60-62.
[69] Gen. IV. 16.
[70] A, II, 9-200.
[71] Cf. Chap. II, C, 6 (pp. 221-225).
[72] Cf. Chap. I, B, 3 (pp. 31-32) and II, C, 6 (pp. 225-227).
[73] A, II, 228-331.

was not in accord with his age, but was much greater than the measure of his years, and he showed the mature excellency of it in games, and his acts of yesteryear announced the greater works he would undertake when he reached manhood. At the age of three years, God granted him an admirable stature for his age, and no-one was so indifferent to his beauty that he was not amazed, when seeing Moses, at his handsomeness, and it happened that many who met with him upon their way turned, attracted by the look of the boy, to leave their serious affairs and to enjoy his contemplation: verily the infant grace which enshrouded him was very great and pure, and captivated all those that saw him''[74].

A magnificent introduction, a presage of the greatness of a far-from-ordinary personality! In it stand out the intellectual and physical qualities, together with his precocity as regards the understanding of things, and his behaviour as a child, something which was an announcement of his greater acts to come. A large part of this introduction is devoted to singing the physical praises of Moses. It really is a very novelistic and exaggerated finish. As is the case in many other excellent aspects of his life, these ideas elaborated by Flavius Josephus do not come from the biblical text[75].

Joshua too, the successor to Moses, is adorned with good qualities: a man of great courage, capable of enduring hardship, endowed with intelligence and eloquence, pious towards God and admired by the Hebrews[76] qualities all befitting the second leader of Israel.

The remaining books which paraphrase the Holy Scripture offer personalities around whom the historical event is woven. The treatment given to the personalities carries on in the same vein as those already studied above. However, something still remains to be said of the personalities in the books whose source is not biblical, but another. Let us see.

The personality of Hyrcanus is amply detailed[77]. His life abounds in war exploits. In him three great privileges are combined: being a ruler, being a high priest, and having the gift of prophecy. With a man of his ilk, what is there that is not possible to achieve?

His son Aristobulus is also introduced as having a very marked character. This can be gathered from the expressions used by the historian: "He conferred many benefits in his country, he waged war

---

[74] A, II, 229-231.
[75] *Ex.* II, 10. With regard to the moment of his death, cf. Chap. II, C, 3. Cf. E. Meyer, *op. cit.*, 273-285.
[76] A, III, 49.
[77] A, XIII, 230-300.

on..., he annexed a goodly tract of land..., he expelled the inhabitants..."[78].

I should also like to mention the fact that the historian brings to a close the lives of these personalities with some words of praise. This aspect, however, comes in later for its own study[79]. Here I simply want to point out that, at the end of the life of the personality, Flavius Josephus makes a summary of his human, intellectual and moral qualities, so that the life, as it were, comes full circle[80].

In this very general introduction, I have marked out an area for study. Now I shall embark on a detailed study of the treatment which Flavius Josephus gives to those personalities of great importance in his work. One of those personalities, Abraham, comes from biblical paraphrase; the other, Herod, comes from more recent sources.

Abraham

The biography of Abraham in the work of Flavius Josephus contains those same elements which are offered by the paraphrased biblical text. Leaving to one side the reasons why Flavius Josephus should have changed the biblical order with regard to some points, the subject of the present chapter impells us to investigate into those specific aspects of the historiographic treatment which Flavius Josephus gives to the personalities, the actors of history. There are therefore two points to come under study:

– whether or not the Abraham of Flavius Josephus and the Abraham of the Bible are presented as exactly the same,

– whether there exists any psychological deepening of the personality on the part of the historian.

The first point will comprise an analysis of those descriptions where the biblical source and Flavius Josephus either differ or complement one another. With regard to this, I shall analyse only points A, I, 154-157, 166-168 and 256.

At the beginning of the biography of Abraham[81], the text of Flavius Josephus is parallel to the biblical text as regards the genealogical tree of Abraham. Then, however, Flavius Josephus makes an unusual abridgement of the description of the divine call of Abraham, by which he is to take himself to the land of Canaan[82], and, on the other hand, lengthens

---

[78] A, XIII, 318.
[79] Cf. Chap. II, C, 3.
[80] B, I, 68-69, 226, 665; B, II, 476; A, I, 256; A, II, 198; A, V, 118; A, XIII, 299, 300, 318, 430; A, XIV, 283.
[81] A, I, 154-157.
[82] A, I, 154 = LXX, *Gen.* XII, 1-9.

the introduction of the personality as a man[83], an introduction which is not offered by the text of the LXX nor by the Hebrew text. Let us see.

According to Flavius Josephus, Abraham, at the age of seventy five, "left for Canaan by order of God, settled there and left it to his descendents" (No. 154). These brief words intend to sum up the nine verses of Genesis, where the writer specifies the call of Abraham by God (verse 1), the promise to make him father of a great people and the promise of his attendance (verses 2-3), details the appurtenances and goods which the patriarch takes with him (verses 4-5) and the place where he first settles, Shechem (verse 6). The phrase used by Flavius Josephus "left it (the land) to his descendants" is a summing up of the great divine promise itself "to your descendants I shall give this land" (verse 7), which is the ultimate reason for the constitution of the people of Israel as a people and as a nation in a land of their own. Flavius Josephus lessons the importance of this. Why? Political and circumstantial reasons which can hardly have been in his favour must have surrounded the life of Flavius Josephus at the time of writing these lines. Or perhaps due to his rationalism? For the moment, the investigator can reach no conclusion. The truth is that Flavius Josephus silences the choice of the Jewish people as a people of God, and takes away all the transcendent character from the fact of Abraham's change of abode together with his family.

Verses 8 and 9 of the Bible should be understood within the concept of the life of the epoch. Here we are dealing with the continuous wandering of a nomad family. Abraham's life should be placed within the framework of the migratory movements of a desert people. Who is to say whether the departure of Abraham coincides with a customary migration which is simply used by the biblical writer to show his readers, also of a similar mentality to desert people, the divine vocation of the patriarch? If this were the case, we should once again have a pedagogical system embodied to a great degree in the methodology of a routine event.

Flavius, however, has to create an entire system to justify the journey of Abraham. Even though in paragraph 157 he has said Abraham occupied Canaan "according to the will and with the help of God", immediately before he has said that "for that (i.e. because of his unorthodox reasonings concerning the world and God), the Chaldaeans and the remainder of the Mesopotamians rose up against him, and, preferring to emigrate according to the will and with the help of God, he took possession of the land of Canaan, and, once established there, set up an altar and made a sacrifice in honour of God".

---

[83] A, I, 151-153, without parallel in the LXX.

Let us then analyse the motives which brought about the emigration of Abraham, according to Flavius Josephus, and which are totally absent from the biblical text.

In the first place, three words provide the introduction of Abraham: δεινὸς (ὢν συνιέναι τε περὶ πάντων) καὶ πιθανὸς (τοῖς ἀκροωμένοις) (περί τε ὧν εἰκάσειεν) οὐ διαμαρτάνων[84]. Each one of these words will be completed in greater detail in paragraphs 155 and 156.

Thus, to δεινὸς ὢν συνιέναι corresponds the reasoning which follows: ''For that, having begun to have higher thoughts than the others concerning virtue, he also proposed to himself to reform and change the idea which all had currently of God''[85]. Therefore, the first quality is of an intellectual order. Abraham was for Flavius Josephus a thinker, an intelligent person, who would devote himself to the blessed idleness of thinking: in conclusion, one of the forerunners of philosophy. In this respect, the Greek philosophers also concerned themselves with virtue, and would make it the subject of their deepest reasonings.

To πιθανὸς τοῖς ἀκροωμένοις correspond the following ideas: ''He was the first, therefore, to dare to present God as the creator of the universe, as unique, and that any other, if he contributes in happiness, does so by command of Him and not through his own power''[86]. With these words a dialectic Abraham can be glimpsed, whose tongue is ever ready to give reasons to prove that God is the creator, unique and providentialist. Here, therefore, we can see the rhetorical dimension of the patriarch. For the mind of the Classical and Hellenistic age, the ideal of a citizen was the orator, who brought together in himself the subtleties of the philosopher, the arguments of the legislator and the strength of the leader. Therefore Abraham makes political use of a religious subject, and is forced to emigrate. Without doubt, the new religious values should undo the mental processes and the religious and social structures of the society which surrounded him.

Finally ''he was not wrong in his conjecturing''[87]. Here Flavius Josephus projects the scientific dimension of Abraham. We are dealing with an Abraham who is an investigator into nature, since he says: ''he made these conjectures by the changes of the earth and the sea, by the changes of the sun and the moon, and all that happened in the heavens''[88]. To the extent of deducing regular physical laws and a

---

[84] A, I, 154.
[85] A, I, 155. Cf. L. H. Feldman, ''Abraham the Greek Philosopher in Josephus'', *TAPhA* 99 (1968), 143-156.
[86] A, I, 155.
[87] A, I, 154.
[88] A, I, 156.

guiding being behind them: "For these beings, had they power, might have the providence of their own good order[89]; however, since they are lacking in it, it is clear that that in which they collaborate for our greater good is not by virtue of their own faculty, but rather they provide the service by virtue of the strength of the one who commands it, to whom alone it is just to render honour and gratitude" (A, I, 156).

This whole line of argument is missing in the biblical text. Whether Flavius Josephus borrows it from another source[90], or whether it is his own contribution, Abraham appears in the *Antiquitates Judaicae* as a very rounded personality, very self-assured, and is prepared so as to be a good leader. The Abraham of the Bible, on the other hand, is an envoy of God, an idealist, who all of a sudden hears the voice of God—*in medias res*— and willingly accepts his commands.

Not content with that, Flavius Josephus brings to bear the testimony of three literary sources: Berosus, Hecataeus and Nicolas of Damascus. If all that he has said is not sufficient proof of the existence of Abraham, there is a need for documentary evidence to substantiate it. It is, therefore, a history which is based on an apodictic method[91].

When Abraham arrives in Egypt, he has occasion to show the full extent of his capabilities. It is a text of Flavius Josephus' own doing[92], and not one single detail of a similar style is to be found in the biblical text. Therefore an investigation must be made into the historiographical reasons which might move the historian to make an enlargement of this kind, with contents of this kind, of the biblical text.

When confronted with the diversity of customs and practices existing amongst the Egyptians—the cause of enmity among them— "Abraham takes them up with each of them in turn and, belittling the reasonings which they made on their particular points of view, showed that they were empty and contained not a grain of truth"[93]. The Abraham who acts here is an orator who undoes puzzles and censures the conduct of others, so as to have his own reasonings outshine the reasonings of others. The verb ἀπέφαινε should be noticed again; it is the same one which is used in paragraph 155, ἀποφήνασθαι, the repeated use of which indicates an insistence on the characteristic traits of the personality.

These two aspects of the character of Abraham, that of thinker and that of orator, once more come together in his scientific capacity, as can be gathered in the following lines: "Admired, then, by them in their con-

---

[89] That is to say, "regularity".
[90] Possible influences of Philon of Alexandria, *De migrat. Abrah.*
[91] A, I, 158-160.
[92] A, I, 166-168.
[93] A, I, 166.

versations as the most intelligent man, and as a man with the capacity
not only of reflexion, but also of persuasion concerning that which he
proposes to teach, he graced them with arithmetic and he bestowed on
them his knowledge of astronomy''[94].

The points which are dealt with in this text are already reiterative in
Flavius Josephus, which provides the person of Abraham with a special
importance, above all in his human dimension, and he is without any
doubt set up as the undisputed protagonist of his own history. On the
other hand, in the biblical text there is insistence above all on the
religious dimension of the acts of the patriarch.

Another fragment which is Flavius Josephus' own insists on the rational and religious aspects of Abraham. The Holy Scripture makes the
attitude of Abraham crystal clear when faced with the sacrifice of his son
Isaac: it is an attitude which is based, without reasonings, on faith. The
version given by Flavius Josephus of this event is also based on faith, but
it is a faith which is full of humanity, rooted in human weakness, in the
reasonableness of the most illogical thing a god could order, the death of
the son whom, in his very presence, he promised and conceded. Thus,
when the altar is prepared to receive the sacrifice, Abraham lays his son
on it and takes hold of the knife to sacrifice him, according to the biblical
story. Now, immediately previous to this, Flavius Josephus composes an
entire speech, in direct speech, which is briefly answered by Isaac, in indirect speech[95].

Three ideas make up the backbone of Abraham's words:

1. Isaac has been a greatly desired son, to the point of being a token of
the vocation of Abraham as father of a people (No. 228);

2. God now claims the son in sacrifice, in return for the benefits which
He has conceded to him (Nos. 229-230); and

3. Isaac is not to die in the manner normal for a human being, so
Abraham hopes that by dying thus, Isaac should be his protector and
help him in his old age, things for which he had waited for him for so
long.

The first point mentioned develops in the following way: ''Son, with
thousands of prayers did I ask of God thy birth; when thou camest into
this life, no effort did I spare in thy upbringing, nor did I believe there to
be anything which hast made me more joyous than to see thee become a
man and to leave thee, on my death, heir to my dominion''[96]. Without

---

[94] A, I, 167.
[95] A, I, 228-231 and 232.
[96] A, I, 228.

any doubt, these words are a natural and necessary complaint, when a man, bowed down with years, see that all his plans for succession are undone. For the mind of a patriarch, a son is the carrier on of a work begun and a help in old age. It is a way of transmitting culture, tradition, and not simply material goods which have been mounting up through the years of life. In a nomadic society, a son means the survival of one's own culture and of one's own social structure.

The second point is that of the thesis: "But since I became thy father by divine will and anew I am to let thee go according to His wont, undergo nobly the sacrifice, for it is to God to whom I cede thee, He who deems it suitable to receive now this obeisance, in return for having been for me a propitious helper and an ally. Since thy birth..., depart now this life not in a common manner, but rather sent by thine own father to God, the Father of all, by means of the rite of sacrifice"[97]. Even though this text is not in the Holy Scriptures, all in all it condenses the profound religious feeling which is to be found in the person of the biblical Abraham. In short, these lines present Abraham the theologian, since the concepts which are handled constitute the quintessence of the religious mind: a divine will which intervenes in favourable and unfavourable affairs, and a god who is inevitable, in other words, who is found at the beginning and end of any act which man might undertake.

The third point: "Since, according to what I think, He believes thee to merit leaving this life, not through illness, nor through war, nor through any other disaster which is wont to fall on men, but rather through prayers and a sacrifice, may He receive thy soul and may He keep it close to Himself; thou shalt be for me as a protector and a helper in my old age, and for that above all did I set about thy upbringing, since thou hast given me God in thy stead"[98]. On this point, the theological line which was set out in his previous words is followed. Here, however, there comes about a change: God, in exchange for Isaac. Without doubt, this exchange says a great deal in favour of an Abraham with a great religious sense.

The life of Abraham is brought to a close with praise, a summing up of his life: "Abraham died a short while after, a man eminent in all virtue and deservedly honoured by God for his zeal shown towards Him"[99].

In short, I believe that the figure of Abraham in the time of Flavius Josephus was, in all justice, ennobled and aggrandised. The human traits

---

[97] A, I, 229-230.
[98] A, I, 230-231.
[99] A, I, 256.

are notably emphasised, something which is not the case in the biblical text, without losing the spiritual density of his mind, perhaps with more theology than the biblical Abraham who accepts unquestioningly. To be more specific, there is a predominance of theology over faith, as we can see from the commentary on the last fragment but one.

As I have already pointed out at the beginning of this commentary on the story of Abraham, a study should also be made of the degree of psychological knowledge which may be attributed to Flavius Josephus. The method I shall be following is the philological one, so that the analysis of the quality of the lexis used by Flavius Josephus to describe the spiritual and emotional life of the personality and the mental activities which preceded his acts is, as it were, the key piece in this investigation.

With regard to this, there are, in the biography of Abraham, some phrases of a highly stereotyped character which should be reviewed:

1. Abraham μετοικεῖν δοκιμάσας ... τὴν Χαναναίαν ἔσχε γῆν (A, I, 157);

2. Ἄβραμος ... πυθόμενος μεταίρειν πρὸς αὐτοὺς ἦν πρόθυμος ... ἢ ... ἄμεινον φρονῶν (A, I, 161);

3. Abraham φοβούμενος ... τέχνην ἐπενόησε τοιαύτην (A, I, 162);

4. Abraham συμβαλὼν ... καὶ διαπτύων ... ἀπέφαινε ... (A, I, 166);

5. Abraham θαυμασθεὶς ... ὡς συνετώτατος καὶ δεινὸς ἀνὴρ (A, I, 167);

6. Abraham βοηθεῖν αὐτοῖς δοκιμάσας οὐκ ἀνέμεινεν, ἀλλ' ἐπειχθεὶς καὶ ... ἐπιπεσὼν ... καὶ φθάσας ... ἀπέκτεινε (A, I, 177);

7. Ἄβραμος δὲ διώκων εἵπετο ... ἐπιδείξας ὅτι τὸ νικᾶν οὐκ ἐν τῷ πλήθει καὶ τῇ πολυχειρίᾳ κεῖσθαι συμβέβηκεν, ἀλλὰ προθυμία ... καὶ τὸ γενναῖον κρατεῖ ... (A, I, 178).

8. Abraham νομίσας ... ἠσπάσατό τε καὶ ... παρεκάλει (A, I, 196);

9. Ἄβραμος δὲ ἐπὶ μηδενὶ κρίνων παρακούειν τοῦ θεοῦ δίκαιον ἅπαντα δ' ὑπουργεῖν ... ἐπικρυψάμενος ... ἀλλὰ μηδὲ ... δηλώσας ... λαβὼν ... καὶ ... ἐπισάξας ... ἀπῄει πρὸς τὸ ὄρος (A, I, 225);

10. ... γυναῖκα γνοὺς ἀγαγέσθαι ... Ἄβραμος ... πέμπει (A, I, 242).

In these ten examples, it can be seen that the act which Abraham undertakes is generally presided over by mental activity, which rules the action which takes place straightway (Nos. 1, 2, 3, 6, 8, 9 and 10). This mental activity may be motivated by fear (No. 3), by a social act (No. 4) and by an external opinion expressed by others (No. 5) or by himself (No. 7).

It cannot be concluded that Flavius Josephus has been successful in the introduction of his personality, from a psychological point of view. What must be concluded however is that Abraham becomes a rational man, before the people who surround him, far above the biblical Abraham.

Herod

In view of the information gathered, one may see that the figure of king Herod is treated as no other is, above all if we take in account space devoted to him. Indeed, in the *Bellum Judaicum* the history of Herod takes up almost three-quarters of the first book (Nos. 203-673), and in the *Antiquitates Judaicae*, it fills four books (XIV, 158-XVII, 199), apart from other references scattered throughout other books. Without any doubt, easy access to the work of Nicolas of Damascus favoured this lengthy treatment, which has no parallel either in the most important biblical personalities, nor actors contemporary with Flavius Josephus. This reminds us, when confronted with the structuring of the two works, that Flavius Josephus does not bear in mind the norm of symmetry in historiographic composition, which was so much postulated by the Hellenistic historians[100].

It is also true that according to whether the extension is greater or smaller, the treatment given to the personality is different. In the *Bellum Judaicum*, the life of Herod is presented under specific headings, such as his public life, his building, and his family tragedy. In the *Antiquitates Judaicae* however, a rather more chronological order is maintained.

If one takes into account the arrangements of the dramatic family conflicts, the language and the presentation of Herod as a victim of destiny, Thackeray concludes that the narrative of the *Bellum Judaicum* is indebted more to the source of Nicolas[101]. There is an attitude more in keeping with the historical image of king Herod. One should also keep in mind the information according to which Nicolas of Damascus was the author of tragedies and comedies[102], which are lost to us, and which would mean that there is a dramatic influence in the manner of presenting the life of the king.

In the *Antiquitates Judaicae* on the other hand, the treatment, which is much more extensive, shows some discrepancies as regards the above, and there appears an anti-Herod feeling, which probably comes from other sources, such as the case of the "commentaries" (ὑπομνήματα) of king Herod[103].

The biographies, therefore, of the Idumaean King are not uniform in the work of Flavius Josephus. Herod, bedecked with praises, due in part to the work of Nicolas of Damascus, is also presented with acts of cruelty towards his subjects, enemies or relatives, a thing which the historian

---

[100] Cf. Chap. II, *Precedents*.
[101] H. St. J. Thackeray, *op. cit.*, *Josephus, the Man...*, 65.
[102] *Suidae Lexicon*, *s.u.* "Νικόλαος".
[103] A, XV, 174.

could not pass over in silence. The literature of the New Testament echoes this cruelty[104].

Character. The first introduction of Herod in the *Bellum Judaicum* includes all of his later characterological development: ''Being energetic as he was by nature, he quickly found material for his spirit''[105].

The words φύσις and φρόνημα comprise the irrational and rational aspects of human psychology. On the other hand, δραστήριος[106] implies activity in its widest sense: to do, to keep oneself in constant activity, and to finish what has been begun.

The word φρόνημα comprises the faculty of thinking and feeling, sometimes in moderation, and sometimes with pride and immoderacy. It may be the bearer of noble thoughts and feelings, or else may approach ὕβρις, μεγαλαυχία and ὄγκος. With these meanings, the following sentence is revealing: ''His spirit soared to the heights and his great magnanimity tended toward piety''[107]. The acts of Herod were always accompanied by lofty spirits and great magnanimity.

Φρόνημα makes Herod show his generosity to other cities outside his realm[108], makes him the object of the attention of the emperor Octavian, attracted by his generous spirit[109], makes him give an instance of his liberality[110] with regard to Ionia and of his munificence in the founding of cities[111], as well as showing great affection for his friend Agrippa[112], his father[113], and his children[114]. The word φρόνημα has a meaning similar to the word ὄγκος: ''He presents himself to him without a diadem ..., but with the pride of a king''[115].

Herod, guided by his great φρόνημα, was the perpetrator of many other acts and attitudes. Let the short references made here suffice.

The other great quality of the king is expressed in the word δραστήριος. If this is allowed thus, then a whole series of acts by Herod could be understood. He would therefore have to be a farsighted man, and would have to be, especially in his thoughts, one step ahead of the enemy, given

---

[104] *Matth.* II, 3-17.

[105] B, I, 204.

[106] His enterprising character (B, I, 283: τὸ Ἡρώδου δραστήριον) is contrasted with his incapability of doing nothing, when it says ''he did not remain motionless'' (B, I, 303: οὐχ ἠρέμει).

[107] B, I, 400.

[108] B, I, 422.

[109] B, I, 397.

[110] B, I, 425.

[111] B, I, 403.

[112] B, I, 416.

[113] B, I, 417.

[114] B, I, 466.

[115] B, I, 387.

that an uncontrolled act of the mind could lead to disaster. With regard to this should be included the departure of Herod for the encounter with king Hyrcanus in the company of a large army, "in such wise as not to make it seem that he was going to depose Hyrcanus with a substantial force nor that he should fall without protection to the price of envy"[116]. This savoir-faire with foresight dictated by φρόνημα manages to give an eminently practical man (δραστήριος) insight into the right method or way at the right moment. Doubtless suspicion and caution are mixed up here, qualities which, properly administered (a rather difficult task for a human being, as can be seen in the case of Herod), can lead to a very accurate foretelling of immediate events.

All this, however, is theorising, and the reality of the matter is that we find a king Herod who is immersed in a world of suspicion and unease: "He suspecting the barbarians from the very beginning..."[117]; or else, and in a much clearer manner, one may appreciate the complexity and richness of his character when Flavius Josephus writes: "For Herod had him, who was the father-in-law of Alexander, under suspicion. He took not his sons to trial very prudently, for he knew that, no sooner had they appeared, they would be an object of compassion"[118].

The other facet which comes from his φρόνημα is to be seen in the change of action and of plan when the reasons and advice of others are logical and timely. This correction of action no doubt enhances the sovereign. With regard to this, one may observe a repetition of πείθεται τούτοις, being convinced that Herod, although he changes his plan by accepting the advice of another, always obtained some benefit during the preparation of that plan. Thus, he refrains from attacking Hyrcanus on the advice of his father and his brother, but he is convinced that he has satisfied his future expectations with the display of his forces before the nation[119].

Herod also gives examples of his feelings when, in different situations, he is presented without the roughness which characterizes the warrior, resembling, in a certain way, the heroes of the epic poems. Just as he is capable of killing in order to avenge himself, so too he can be sensitive in the face of misfortunes. With regard to this, his conduct on the occasion of the campaign against brigands hiding out in caves is very significant[120]. While his soldiers are in the process of killing all those they find, Herod decides to spare some of them, but they prefer death to cap-

---

[116] B, I, 210.
[117] B, I, 261.
[118] B, I, 538.
[119] B, I, 214. Other cites: B, I, 267, 487, 538, 655.
[120] B, I, 309 ff.

tivity. It is at this time when he sees a father who is killing his sons one by
one, so that they shall not fall into the hands of Herod. Before this
gruesome and awful spectacle, Flavius Josephus says that Herod "was
afflicted by that misery, and raised his right hand up to the old man im-
ploring him that he spare his sons"[121].

On receiving the news of the death of his brother, "Herod, making a
short lament for this misfortune, and adjourning the ceremony of mourning, set off against the enemy"[122]. In this fragment, one can see how
Herod combined his feelings with his action, with rather greater
predominance on the part of his reasoning.

In his old age and illness, Herod understands the mistakes of his life.
The death he has inflicted on his sister has left him profoundly afflicted[123].

At the sight of the orphans which his criminal act has left in the family,
Herod weeps disconsolately[124]. And, at the end of the speech, in which he
has publicly arranged the marriages of the orphans, the historian once
again makes manifest the feelings of Herod: "Having said this, he wept
and joined the hands of the children; then, lovingly embracing them one
after the other, he dismissed the assembly"[125].

When faced with the final illness of his brother, Herod, who shortly
before had sent him into exile, goes to visit him in a display of humanity,
"for he went to him and cared for him with great affection"[126].

All these examples are sufficient to characterise a Herod who is capable
of showing deep feelings, in spite of having behaved cruelly throughout
his life.

The range of the activities of king Herod is enormous, and, as a consequence, the historian has to present Herod the builder, magnanimous
and magnificent. In times of peace and prosperity, Herod raises
numerous buildings in Judaea and abroad. As I have already mentioned,
Flavius Josephus brings together his activity as an architect and town
planner in one narrative unit (B, I, 401-430)[127].

Thus, Herod rebuilt Samaria, and set up a city which he names
Sebaste in honour of Octavian (B, I, 403; A, XV, 292 ff., 296-298),
rebuilds Caesarea (B, I, 408 ff.; A, XVII, 87), finances the reconstruction of the temple of Pythian Apollo in Rhodes (B, I, 424; A, XVI, 147)

---

[121] B, I, 312.
[122] B, I, 328.
[123] B, I, 644.
[124] B, I, 556.
[125] B, I, 559.
[126] B, I, 580.
[127] Cf. H. Drüner, *Untersuchungen über Josephus*, Marburg, 1896, 57.

and the holding of the Olympic Games (B, I, 427 ff.; A, XVI, 149). In Palestine, he builds fortresses and military colonies (B, I, 265, 419 ff.; A, XIV, 360; XV, 323-325; XVI, 13), doubles the area of the temple of Jerusalem, adds new buildings to it, and embellishes it with unequalled magnificence (B, I, 401-402; A, XV, 380 ff.).

Family life. Τύχη (B, I, 431), envious of Herod, visited great family tribulations on him. There is a whole mentality which surrounds the biography of king Herod, especially that which is in the *Bellum Judaicum*, according to which his life was directed and ruled by a "malignant spirit"[128], which he himself expressly admits.

Keeping this precedent in mind, it may be seen that Herod appears as a man who is passionately jealous of his wife Mariamme, a passion which slowly burned away inside him until it makes him decree the death of his own wife[129]. Herod never ever recovers from this misfortune and from his amorous passion[130].

Parallel to this terrible background situation should be placed the number of executions of relatives and other persons which Flavius Josephus cannot pass over in silence, deaths due to suspicions[131], to other diverse reasons[132]; neither can he omit the mention of tortures[133] and punishments which he inflicted throughout his life[134].

Since it is not my intention in this investigation to go into an exhaustive study of the life of king Herod, a subject which has already been dealt with by other writers, but rather to select those details which are useful as regards his psychological characterisation and an important historical actor, my conclusion as regards the point just dealt with is that Herod acted basically as a violent man, and it is obvious that violence is one trait which characterises his person δραστήριος, and that this king is not always guided by his φρόνημα in his acts. Given this panorama, and from an impartial historiographic viewpoint, one is bound to attribute the cause to a transcendent force.

Going deeper into this latter aspect, it is evident that Herod believed himself to be under the influence of the transcendent world, and Flavius Josephus emphasises this fact with terms which are proper to his religious spirit, composed of a mixture of biblical, Jewish, and Hellenistic elements. It is a matter, therefore, of a religious syncretism which is

---

[128] B, I, 556: σκυθρωπὸς ... δαίμων.
[129] B, I, 443.
[130] B, I, 444.
[131] B, I, 433, 443 (Joseph), 543, 550-551, 664.
[132] B, I, 357, 437.
[133] B, I, 527, 584, 586, 598, 655.
[134] B, I, 535, 578, 600, 640.

proper to the Hellenistic intellectual. With regard to this, the following terms are made use of: θεός[135], χρεών[136], δαιμόνιος[137], τύχη[138] and δαίμων[139].

For Herod, God is a god who intervenes in political affairs, by surrendering empires[140], by blessing willing marriages[141], preventing misfortunes[142], and is the object of sacrifices[143], and gratitude in the same way as Caesar himself[144], and therefore restores and extends the temple of Jerusalem[145].

For Flavius Josephus, destiny—χρεών—is both beneficial[146] and harmful[147] to the king, who has been the target of heavenly warnings—δαιμόνιος—which have worked in his favour[148] or against him[149], so that they even dishearten his army[150], even though a Jew can conquer by his courage alone[151]. Meanwhile, fortune, whether good—δεξιὰ τύχη—or ill —δυστυχεῖν—does not last for ever[152], and either takes revenge on account of his successes[153] or blesses him[154].

The character of king Herod either gives way, reacts or becomes exasperated under the influence of the outside world. Let us see.

He knows when to give way in the face of the evidence of reality (B, I, 214-215), but reacts with war and bloodshed to smallscale attacks (B, I, 252). Confidence in future victory spurs him into action (B, I, 339). He is capable of becoming utterly exasperated (B, I, 443-444, 473, 526, 534-535, 564, 571, 654; A, XV, 213), or knows how to control his own reactions until he becomes fatherly (B, I, 480-481, 504, 508), he is afraid of a possible coup d'état (B, I, 492-497), is not immune to flattery (B, I, 565).

---

[135] Cf. Concordance, s.u.
[136] B, I, 233, 275. Cf. Chap. I, note 278.
[137] B, I, 331, 370, 373, 376.
[138] B, I, 374, 390, 430, 431, 665.
[139] B, I, 556, 628.
[140] B, I, 390: καὶ θεὸς ὁ σοὶ τὸ κρατεῖν χαριζόμενος.
[141] B, I, 558.
[142] B, I, 593.
[143] B, I, 380.
[144] B, I, 457.
[145] B, I, 401.
[146] B, I, 233-235.
[147] B, I, 275: τὸ χρεὼν ... τὴν αὐτοῦ σπουδὴν ἐφθάκει.
[148] B, I, 331.
[149] B, I, 370.
[150] B, I, 373.
[151] B, I, 376.
[152] B, I, 374, 390, 430.
[153] B, I, 431.
[154] B, I, 665: κατὰ μὲν τὰ ἄλλα πάντα τύχη δεξιᾷ ... ἐν δὲ τοῖς κατ᾽ οἶκον ἀτυχέστατος.

Popular opinion did not respond to the efforts of the king to win it over to him. In spite of the rebuilding of the temple of Jerusalem, of the reduction of taxes (A, XV, 365) and of the good economic situation all over the country, the impression that one gets, not taking into account that information which has a slightly favourable tendency, is that Herod was a harsh and cruel ruler, who decreed numerous executions of his political enemies (A, XVII, 305 ff., 366), and deprived the people of the right of assembly by spying on their every move and thought.

His persecution mania led him to commit all manner of aberrations. He had his beloved wife, Mariamme, put to death, as well as his mother and Hyrcanus, and his three sons. It is no surprise therefore that other crimes, real or imagined, have been imputed to him, the most famous of which appears in the literature of the New Testament.

The extraordinary aspects of the life of king Herod appear extensively amplified, after the custom of the historians of the epoch of adorning historical personalities with acts which went beyond the bounds of human possibilities. Herod therefore is informed through dreams—ὄνειροι σαφεῖς[155]—, has miraculous escapes from danger[156], from his enemies[157], and even from earthly disasters[158].

Mention should also be made of the figure of the king as a great soldier who wins victory after victory. Even though these victories are accompanied by a great deal of bloodshed, the figure of Herod is not presented as being sanguinary; far from it, he takes on particular importance because of his desire for justice rather than for vengeance, and at the same time his fame grows the world over[159]. Military defeats are simply noted[160] or attributed to others[161].

Herod gives five important speeches: to encourage his troops[162], to win the friendship of Octavius[163], to declare his sons as his heirs before the people of Jerusalem[164], to show his compassion for those he has orphaned[165] and to accuse Antipater[166].

---

[155] B, I, 328.
[156] B, I, 331.
[157] B, I, 340-341.
[158] B, I, 370.
[159] B, I, 204-205, 238-240, 252-253, 265, 292-294, 301-311, 315-316, 321-322, 329-330, 336-339, 342-353, 366-385.
[160] B, I, 251-252, 332, 339, 366-368, 370.
[161] B, I, 367-368, 430.
[162] B, I, 373-379, studied in Chap. II, A, 2a-b (pp. 102-103 and 107-108).
[163] B, I, 388-390.
[164] B, I, 457-465.
[165] B, I, 556-558, studied in Chap. II, A, 2a (p. 104).
[166] B, I, 622-628.

In the face of all this information given in the *Bellum Judaicum*, some conclusion must be drawn. In the first place it is obvious that the figure of king Herod, while alive, occupies the centre of attention of all the history. Around him revolves a multi-coloured present. It is a highly personalised history, where the figure of Herod is indispensible for the history to advance, to progress.

From the point of view of maintaining interest, Flavius Josephus is capable to keeping up a narrative intensity which is striking for the reader and, at times, reaches climaxes of emotion and terror. The entire text on the life of king Herod becomes drama, and ends only with his death. One fact should be insisted on however: it is that Flavius Josephus values above all else the psychological traits of his personality, and for that reason places especial emphasis on his changing states of mind. The treatment given therefore to the historical personalities in Flavius Josephus falls squarely within the literary requirements of classical biography and the sphere of psychological historiography[167].

With no claim to being exhaustive, I shall make here a list of the principal words which indicate intellectual activity and the moral and characterological behaviour of the historical personalities. To a certain extent, one could include the degree of psychological knowledge which Flavius Josephus possessed:

ἀκρασία, εἰλικρινέστατος, τολμηρός, πάθος, ὁρμή, ἐπιμανής, μακάριστος, ἀφόρητος, φρονῶν, ὠμότης, τόλμη, οἶκτος, φθόνος, ἐπίβουλος, βάσκανος, μετριότης, φιλανθρωπία, ζηλωτός, τρόπον τ.ἀνώμαλον, ὑποκριτής, κοπωθείς, νωθέστερος, θρασύτατος, μεγαλαυχία, θερμότης, δολιώτατος, ἐγκράτεια, δύναμις, δεινός, σωφροσύνη, φρόνημα, φονικώτατος, φιλοτιμία, διαμισούμενος, ἐπιθυμέω, διαβολή, δραστήριος, ἔνθους, μετάνοια, γενναῖος, γόης, ἄπραγμον, ἀνθυποκρίνω, ποικιλώτατος, μεγαλόψυχος, θυμός, πρόχειρος, ἐκκαίω, μισέω, παροξύνω, ὀργή, ἔρως, μισοπόνηρος, μετριότερος, ἄπιστος, φιλελεύθερος, πάθος, πανοῦργος, ἐγκράτεια, συμπαθής, φιλοφρόνησις, σύνεσις, συνετωτάτη, θυμός, ὑποψία, φλεγμονή, ὕδρας κεφαλαί, ἦθος, ἐπιθυμία, φιλεῖν, ἐμμανής, λύπη, νήφοντες, δαιμονάω, διάθεσις, θερμότερος, φιλοστόργος, ὑπόνοια, συνοράω, συμφιλοκαλέω, ὑποψία, θρασύτερος, ζηλοτυπία, ἄφρων, κακοήθης, ἀπραγμοσύνη, καθαρώτατος[168].

---

[167] Cf. A. v. Mess, "Die Anfänge der Biographie und der psychologischen Geschichtsschreibung in der griechischen Literatur", *RhM* 70 (1915), 337-367; A. Posner, "Römische Persönlichkeiten in Josephus' bellum", *MGWJ* 80 (1936), 246-261. On the treatment of Vespasian and Titus, cf. W. Weber, *Josephus und Vespasian. Untersuchungen zu dem jüdischen Krieg des Flavius Josephus*, Stuttgart, 1921.

[168] Cf. *Concordance*, *s.uu.*

2. *The speeches*

In the face of more than one thousand quotes where Flavius Josephus transcribes the thoughts of another, necessity calls for philological statistics which might group together those fragments which have something in common and a certain quality. We cannot, therefore, speak of generalisations, but we must rather follow an objective method, based on the number of speeches and direct quotes.

In a classification which gives attention above all to style, the statistics offer one hundred and seventy-three speeches written in direct speech, six hundred and ninety in indirect speech, together with one hundred and eighty-eight which are mixed. As to the contents, I shall analyse those speeches which pursue an objective, those which are simply expository and inflated, I shall analyse the manner of using the speeches and words from the Bible, I shall attempt to show the differences between the speeches in the *Bellum Judaicum* and those in the *Antiquitates Judaicae*, and I shall make reference to the manner of transferring textual quotes.

Precedents

The speeches which appear in the works of the Greek historians are not motivated solely by an epideictic influence, even though they are very often used with epideictic aims. The speeches come to constitute literary means by which the historian records a given situation or expresses the arguments of parts in disagreement. They may therefore have a political, ethical or dramatic slant, according to the kind of situation. In authors with epideictic leanings, epideictic speeches are often found.

Cicero saw the history of the Greeks as being the work of writers with great rhetorical power, and was convinced that history-writing demanded such power[169].

Speeches may be presented as being either direct or reported. Direct speech seemed more contrived, hence its condemnation and the preference for indirect speech which allows for a picture more in keeping with the moment[170].

With the exception of Herodotus, all the historians fell under the influence of the rhetorical canons. Herodotus' speeches are natural and simple[171]. The speeches of those of Tegea and of Athens contain certain epideictic commonplaces which demonstrate a use which is already stereotyped.

---

[169] *De Orat.* II, 12, 57; *De leg.* I, 2, 5.
[170] Dion. Hal., *De Thuc.* XVI, 349, 9; *Arch.* VII, 66, 3.
[171] Even so, some rhetorical traits also show through in it: I, 32; III, 36, 80-82; V, 91; VII, 8.

There is a listing of epideictic commonplaces in IX, 27. Bischoff has pointed out the exhortative and panegyrical character of their speeches in which the conduct of their personalities is made to stand out[172].

The degree of rhetorical influence varies from historian to historian, and even within the work of a single historian[173].

Thucydides wrote his history before the time of the rhetorical school of Isocrates, but even so his work was influenced by those same stylistic trends which were later to flourish so much. His frequent speeches are a reproduction of what might possibly have been said or what is most in keeping with the situation or the character of the speaker[174]. They are a perfect model of rhetorical style, and their vividness creates a highly realistic atmosphere. For the most part they are not epideictic[175]. Nevertheless, this system entails the risk of the historian replacing the real reasons behind an event by those which he judges to be most suitable, thus falling into a subjective situation. It is for this reason that the speeches of Thucydides came in for criticism from Dionysius of Halicarnassus[176].

Xenophon usually used fairly un-epideictic speeches[177], and, in *Anabasis*, offers some formal ones; at times they are indeed commonplaces. They too were criticised by Dionysius[178], above all for the lack of suitability of the speech to the personalities.

So great was the following amongst the majority of 4th century historians of rhetorical theories that Polybius tried to separate history from rhetoric so as to reduce it to its own limits[179].

Theopompus and Ephorus, as the most outstanding disciples of Isocrates, were the ones who properly speaking introduced the stylistic ideas of their master into historiography[180].

---

[172] H. Bischoff, *Der Warner bei Herodot*, Marburg, 1932.

[173] C. Th. Ch. Burgess, "The Epideictic Element in History", *Stud. in Class. Philology* 3 (1902), 198.

[174] I, 22, 1-4.

[175] Except in a few cases: the funeral oration of Pericles, and in III, 53; IV, 95; VII, 82.

[176] *De Thuc.* 41; 395, 11; *Ad Pomp.* 3, 20.

[177] *Cyrop.* VI, 4, 12; *Hellen.* VI, 5, 38. Cf. E. M. Soulis, *Xenophon and Thucydides*, Athens, 1972, 129 (influences of speeches of Thucydides on those of Xenophon).

[178] *De Imit.* III, 2; 208, 10; VI, 3, 2; *Ad Pomp.* 5, 6.

[179] I, 1, 14, 35; II, 35, 56; III, 31, 57, 58; V, 75; X, 21; XII, 7, 12, 25.

[180] Cf. Müller, *FHG* 64 (Ephorus) and 279 (Theopompus); Dion. Hal., *De comp. Verb.* 23. For Ephorus, cf. Quintil. IX, 4, 87; Pol. V, 33; VI, 45; XII, 4a, 22, 23, 25, 27, 28; Cic., *De Orat.* 57, 191; *Brut.* 204; Strb. IX, 3, 11. For Theopompus, cf. Dion. Hal., *Ad Pomp.* VI; Quintil. X, 1, 74; Pol. VIII, 10-13; XII, 25, XVII, 12; Cic., *De Leg.* I, 1; *Brut.* 66; *De Orat.* II, 57. According to Croiset, Theopompus was the creator of a new manner of writing history (vol. IV, 653).

The speeches of the ancient historians may be broadly divided into two blocks: situational speeches and character speeches[181]. Callisthenes was the introducer of the character speeches whereby the historian has to tailor the speeches to the character of the personality and the surrounding circumstances[182]. This new exigency is no doubt born of the psychological theories of the peripatetics, at a time very close to the *Characters* of Theophrastus and in an era when man was caught up in his own individuality, as appearing in the works of the New Comedy.

Polybius is not in favour[183] of the repeated use of speeches, notwithstanding his recognition of them having their place at critical historical moments[184]. Pédech discovers great originality here: "L'originalité de Polybe est d'avoir dégagé le discours de la technique oratoire et de l'avoir rattaché d'une part à sa théorie étiologique, d'autre à sa conception psychologique de l'histoire..."[185]. But even though the use of speeches is allowed, it must be strictly controlled, by rules which are very different from rhetorical norms, and an attempt must be made to reproduce the exact words originally spoken[186].

The very few speeches of Diodorus are fully epideictic in tone (XIII, 20-27; 28-32; 52; XIV, 65-69). He uses antithesis, rhetorical questions, asyndeton, shows an intentionally moralising character, which is also present in other historians[187].

Dionysius of Halicarnassus is essentially an orator, and hence his history suffers as a consequence. His speeches are at times anachronic, lacking in harmony and proportion (XI, 7 ff.), extremely epideictic (VI, 72-80; VII, 40-46, 48-53; VIII, 29-35; IX, 36; XI, 7, 26) and full of antithesis, even though he is a stalwart defender of speeches which are adapted to the temperament and qualities of the speaker. At best, he makes a poor imitation of the speeches of Thucydides.

The long speeches of Dio Cassius are epideictic (XXXVI, 25, 26), antithetic, panegyrical (XXXVI, 27-29; XXXVIII, 20 ff.) and circumstantial (XXXVI, 31-37; XLI, 27 ff.; XXXVIII, 36 ff.; XLIV, 36-49; LVI, 35 ff.).

---

[181] P. Pédech, *op. cit.*, 255-256.

[182] *FGH* 124 F 44; cf. P. Scheller, *op. cit.*, 25. In the same line, Lucian, *De hist. conscr.* 58; cf. G. Avenarius, *Lukians Schrift zur Geschichtsschreibung*, Meisenheim-Glan, 1956, 149-157. On Duris, cf. *FGH* 76 F 1.

[183] III, 44, 63, 108, 111; XII, 25; XV, 11; XVIII, 11; XXXVI, 1.

[184] I, 27, 1; III, 108-111.

[185] P. Pédech, *op. cit.*, 29.

[186] XXXVI, 1, 2-7. Cf. P. Pédech, *op. cit.*, 257.

[187] Diod., *Bibl.* XIII, 20, 21; Dion. Hal., *Rom. Ant.* IV, 11; *Ad Pomp.* VI; Dio Cass. I, fragments 33, 40, sections 30-34; XXXVIII, 22; LII, 2 and 14.

It is from Theopompus onwards then that history appears adorned according to rhetorical canons so as to delight the mind of the reader[188]. In short, as regarded its rhetorical aspects, history fell under the great genre of rhetoric[189].

This trend persisted up to the era of Flavius Josephus, and is given expression in him thus: "History therefore, and the revelation of events which to most are unknown because of their antiquity, should have, for the readers, not only beauty of exposition, which springs from the choice of words and their harmony, but also all that adds beauty to them in the exposition, so that readers receive the information with a certain elegance and satisfaction"[190].

a) Direct speeches in the Bellum Judaicum

The longest and most elaborate speeches are to be found in the *Bellum Judaicum*[191], something which indicates a more painstaking undertaking and a greater degree of concern for the art of rhetoric. In the *Antiquitates Judaicae* the speeches are more lax, and at the same time are no more than a reproduction of the speeches already contained in the biblical texts which Flavius Josephus paraphrases, and which for the most part are in indirect speech[192].

The longest speeches are: the speech of Agrippa (B, II, 345-401), the speech of Flavius (B, V, 362-419), and the two-part speech of Eleazar (B, VII, 323-336, 341-388); a fair way behind, the speeches of Ananus and Jesus (B, IV, 163-192, 238-269), with the short speech of reply by Simon (271-283), the other speeches of Titus (B, VI, 328-350 and 34-53) and another speech by Flavius Josephus on suicide (B, II, 362-382). The remaining speeches in direct speech are very short (fewer than fifteen paragraphs, according to the edition of Niese).

The first three speeches, even though already studied[193], still deserve attention. The speech given by Agrippa II offers the following parts:

---

[188] E. Stein, *op. cit.*, 641.

[189] Cic., *Orat.* 11, 37; 20, 66.

[190] A, XIV, 2. Since this dissertation cannot touch on all of the many varieties of use and constructions of the speeches of all the historians, whether Greek and Latin, I shall give here the bibliography consulted: H. Tränkle, *Livius und Polybius*, Basel-Stuttgart, 1977, 120; R. Ullmann, *La technique des discours dans Sallust, Tite Live et Tacite*, Oslo, 1927; A. Lambert, *Die indirekte Rede als künstlerisches Stilmittel des Livius*, (Diss.), Zürich, 1946, and R. Syme, *Tacito*, vol. 1, Brescia, 1967, 153 and 422.

[191] E. Stein, *op. cit.*, 641. Cf. D. R. Runnalls, *Hebrew and Greek sources in the speeches of Josephus war* (Diss. Univ. of Toronto), 1971; B. Nadel, "Quid Flavius Josephus sermoni atque colori dicendi invectivarum Romanorum debuerit", *Eos* 56 (1966), 256-272.

[192] As to a general idea on the speeches in Flavius Josephus. cf. H. St. J. Thackeray, *op. cit.*, *Josephus, the Man...*, 41-45.

[193] H. Lindner, *op. cit.*, 21-42. These three long speeches of the *Bellum Judaicum* have no parallels in the *Antiquitates Judaicae*. Cf. too O. Bauernfeind and O. Michel, "Die

A. Agrippa tries to persuade the Jews into giving up the war against the Romans (B, II, 345-401);

B. Corpus of the speech (Nos. 348-399):

– the reasons the Jews have for waging war are by no means clear (Nos. 348-349);

– the pretexts (προφάσεις) of the Jews do not justify war: nor do their accusations against the procurators from Rome (Nos. 350-355), nor does their desire for independence (Nos. 356-357), seeing that many other greater states have submitted to Rome (Nos. 358-361);

– here he introduces the comparative method: he analyses the power of the Jews and the power of some fifteen nations who have bowed before Rome (Nos. 362-387);

– the Jews can expect no help from other Jews and, what is even more serious, neither is any help forthcoming from God, since He has placed himself on the side of Rome (Nos. 388-391); the religion of the Jews commands them to place their hopes in God, not in their weapons, since this latter choice would mean distancing God from them (Nos. 392-394): it would be madness (Nos. 395-396).

C. Conclusions (Nos. 397-401):

– the danger of the Jews is all over the world, since their defeat is assured (Nos. 397-399);

– the emotional finishing touches: have pity on your sons and daughters, your wives, your city and your temple (Nos. 400-401).

Having made this short outline, now is the time to inquire into the historiographic meaning of the speech. This speech is made at a time of suffering and of hatred towards the Roman procurator Florus on account of his abusive use of authority and the victims and destruction which he has caused in the city of Jerusalem. The priests exhort the Jews to submit to the power of Rome (No. 320). The Jewish magistrates, on the other hand, sent notification of the disastrous situation to Cestius, the Roman governor of Syria (No. 333). He then sends the tribune Neapolitanus to investigate into the truth of the matter and to search out those who are guilty (No. 335). But all too soon Neapolitanus returns to the side of Cestius, without having given any consolation to the Jews; quite the opposite, he insists on their fidelity to Rome and the keeping of the peace (No. 341).

However, the Jewish people pressure the king and the high priests for them to send an embassy to Nero, so as not to remain under suspicion of

---

beiden Eleazarreden in Jos. bell. 7, 323-336; 7, 341-388'', *ZNTW* 58 (1967), 267-272; E. Gabba, ''L'impero romano nel discorso di Agrippa II (Joseph., B, II, 345-401)'', *RSA* 6-7 (1976-1977), 189-194.

rebellion as well as to denounce the person who was really guilty (No. 342). Then Flavius Josephus makes concrete the attitude of Agrippa in the face of the people's proposal, a stance which I believe to be most indicative for understanding the intentionality of the speech which he will now embark on. Flavius Josephus writes: "It was odious for Agrippa to choose accusers for Florus, but on the other hand it did not seem advantageous to him either to disdain the wishes of the Jews when their spirits were inflamed for war"[194]. In this preparatory text, there are two words which are significant for the understanding of the spirit of the speech which follows straight on: ἐπίφθονον and λυσιτελές. The first indicates the real attitude of Agrippa: he had no desire to compromise himself with regard to the Romans since they represented the security of his power. In other words, Agrippa placed his own interests over the interests of the Jewish people. On the other hand, the second word reveals that Agrippa is aware of the reality of the situation, and even fears for his own safety were he not to heed the people's request. I believe that these two attitudes are clearly reflected in his speech, and thus we can understand, on the one hand, the expositive effort concerning the power of Rome over other more powerful nations and, on the other, the appeal to the feelings of the listeners in the conclusion. It is quite clear that Agrippa is on the side of the colonizers, and his attitude of not wishing to solve the problems is left without any doubt when he says to them that if they want to remove the accusation of rebellion which is hanging over them, then they must rebuild the gates and pay the taxes[195].

Bearing this in mind, then the speech is exhortative (συμβουλεύειν, No. 345), because many of the Jews are disorientated and have chosen wrongly in wanting to go to war (No. 346). Agrippa therefore considers himself to be the only one who can reconcile such widely differing options, and he states explicitly that he has brought them together to "state what I consider is of [greatest] advantage"[196]. The analysis he makes of the reasons the Jews have for waging war is that they are confused (Nos. 348-349), and so Agrippa at the very outset throws a wet blanket over the eager listeners.

The speech is therefore aimed at coaxing his audience away from what they are thinking, something which is completely opposed to the idea of the orator, and for this purpose he follows the method of trial speeches, presenting as evidence the fortune which has befallen many nations before the power of Rome, the lack of allies (Nos. 388-389), the desertion

---

[194] B, II, 343.
[195] B, II, 404.
[196] B, II, 346.

of their own God to the Roman camp (Nos. 391-394), and concludes with an attempt to appeal to the listeners' feelings, as members of a jury, so that they should pass a verdict in favour of continuing the peace; a peace, naturally, made to fit the interests of its counsel for the defence.

The speech of Flavius Josephus to his fellow-citizens[197] has, from a formal point of view, two parts; from the point of view of contents, it is very similar in idea content to the speech of Agrippa. Let us proceed by parts.

With regard to the form, the speech of Flavius Josephus opens with a long exposition in indirect speech (Nos. 362-374), which links up, after the beginning of paragraph 375, with a lengthy speech in direct speech (Nos. 376-419). This way of solving the problem of the transmission of words spoken in public presents a mixed composition, which, as we shall see later on, is the recourse which is most favoured by Flavius Josephus. The mixture, therefore, of part indirect speech and part direct speech, or the other way round, substantially abbreviates the historical scene, and provides the reader with a variety of exposition.

During the speech in indirect speech, Flavius Josephus does no more than expound the superiority of the Romans, their magnanimity if they surrender, and the disastrous state of the city and its citizens who are already starving to death: their end is clear. He insists on one point[198] which is already clear, and it is that God is over Italy at that moment, that fortune is in the hands of the Romans, and that one must give way in the face of the strongest and most trained in arms. The part of the speech in direct speech provides the historical proof, according to the spirit of which the Jews should no longer continue in their struggle. And he again repeats that God is on the side of those against whom they are waging war.

Two parts, therefore, which are perfectly clear: the first, in indirect speech, brings together advice; the second, in direct speech, presents the proof. Let us see[199].

A. Indirect speech. Advice to capitulate (Nos. 362-374):
– they must submit to the Romans (Nos. 363-366); God is over Italy (Nos. 367-369); the famine which is spreading throughout the city does not go unnoticed by the Romans (Nos. 370-371);
– the Romans will be sympathetic if the Jews surrender peaceably (Nos. 372-374).

---

[197] B, V, 362-419.
[198] B, V, 367.
[199] H. Lindner, *op. cit.*, 25-33.

B. Direct speech. Historical proof so that the Jews should capitulate (Nos. 376-414):

1. Evidence for: the struggle cannot be maintained if God is not in alliance (Nos. 376-378);

– Abraham overcame the vexing situation with the Pharaoh thanks to the help of God and without arms (Nos. 379-381);

– the Hebrews are spared by God from the plagues of Egypt (Nos. 382-383);

– the ark was retrieved from the Philistines with the help of God (Nos. 384-386);

– Sennacherib, the king of Assyria, was defeated by the angel of God (Nos. 387-388), and

– God brought the Jewish people out of exile in the time of Cyrus without the need for arms (Nos. 389-390).

2. Evidence against: when the Jewish people have not placed their hopes in God, they have been defeated (Nos. 391-400):

– by the Babylonians (Nos. 391-393),

– by Antiochus Epiphanes (No. 394),

– by Pompey (Nos. 395-397) and

– by Herod and Sossius (No. 398);

– arms have not been granted to the Jews (Nos. 399-400).

3. Their secret sins do not allow God to be their ally (Nos. 401-411).

4. God has abandoned the holy places and has passed over to the side of their enemies (Nos. 412-414).

C. Conclusion. The final appeal to salvation (Nos. 415-419):

– lay down your arms (Nos. 415-417),

– have pity on your families (No. 418),

– myself, in exchange for your salvation (No. 419).

By way of conclusion therefore, here too we are dealing with an exhortative speech, the aim of which is to persuade the Jews to give themselves into the hands of the Romans. However, the construction of the speech hinges on a theological aspect. Flavius has recourse to the transcendent plane so as to appeal to the spirit of his fellow-citizens, seeing that he is well acquainted with the Jewish mind. This speech is a summing up of the Jewish concept of traditional social life and the theocratic State. The remaining elements of the speech are a simple complement which answer the need of form rather than substance.

I believe that this speech participates in the two characteristics which are to be found in the historical speeches of the Greek writers. It is a speech with a very strong circumstantial character: it is made at the supreme moment of the destiny of Jerusalem, and as the last hope for the salvation of the Jewish people. On the other hand, it is also a speech which demonstrates close adaptation to the character of the person who makes it and is very much in harmony with the circumstances which surround it. We shall never know whether these were the very words spoken by Flavius Josephus, but the possibility must be considered as very real, since the historian and orator are here one and the same person.

With regard to this latter point, the speech of Flavius Josephus before the fallen walls of his beloved city may be, in certain sentences, a faithful reproduction of the words spoken at the real historical moment. It would therefore form part of the innovative doctrine of Polybius concerning historical speeches.

The third great speech is that of Eleazar[200], the leader of the Jewish *Sicarii* who occupied the fortress of Masada, in the year 73 A.D. The whole of Judaea was under Roman rule, except for the fortress of Masada, manned by those who did not recognise submission to Rome (B, VII, 252 ff.). The Roman governor, Flavius Silva, lay siege to the rock of Masada, impregnable by its very nature, with the most sophisticated devices (B, VII, 305 ff.).

The circumstances in which Eleazar speaks to his followers are extreme. Doubtless they are circumstances which do not offer even a single glimmer of hope of salvation. It is, therefore, a very different case from that of the fall of Jerusalem, where there were certain promises of salvation. Still to be added is the fact that Flavius Josephus sees here a decisive intervention of God in favour of the Romans (B, VII, 318-319). The only solution in the eyes of Eleazar is death, collective suicide, since the Romans, once victorious, will show no pity.

In principle therefore, this speech is the result of circumstances, and its aim is to persuade the listeners to give themselves over to death.

This speech too has two parts, both of which are given in direct speech, and are separated by the historian by a few short considerations of the effect of the first words of Eleazar on his listeners (B, VII, 337-340).

The contents of the speech are as follows:

A. Part one (Nos. 323-336):
– we can serve no other than God, and He has granted us the favour of dying freely (Nos. 323-326),
– the Jewish race has come to an end, and God has allowed this to be so (Nos. 327-332) and

---

[200] B. VII, 323-336, 341-388. Cf. H. Lindner, *op. cit.*, 33.

– we must die, therefore, with honour, and leave evidence for the Romans that we have preferred death to slavery (Nos. 333-336).

In view of the fact that his first words have not achieved the desired effect, Eleazar again insists with new elements of persuasion, this time on a metaphysical level "with words more brilliant concerning the immortality of the soul"[201] and concerning death as a freeing of the soul.

B) Part two (Nos. 341-388):

– censure for the subject of death and thesis based on tradition: "living is a misfortune for men, not death"[202]; what is more, there appear here ideas of Greek poetry and philosophy (Nos. 341-348);

– evidence: dreams and the example of the self-sacrifice of the Indians (Nos. 349-357).

C. God has sentenced us to destruction (Nos. 358-359).

D. The Romans cannot claim victory as theirs (No. 360).

E. Information which bears witness to the definitive end of the Jewish people (Nos. 361-367).

F. Conclusions:

– when hearing of the disastrous situation of the Jewish people the world over, who can bear to see the light of the sun? (Nos. 378-380),

– we were born to die (No. 381), and,

– before seeing our women outraged and our sons and daughters killed, we shall all die together (Nos. 382-388).

There is no doubt that this speech has the aim of making collective suicide acceptable. In order to persuade, it is necessary to bring forward convincing evidence, it is necessary to use words which are proper to all exhortation. This speech is, therefore, an exhortation, and Flavius Josephus himself recognises this fact in the words which make up its introduction (παρακέλευσις, No. 340) and those which constitute its conclusion (παρακαλεῖν, No. 389).

We can see here a great adaptation of the speech to the circumstances, though we do not have sufficient elements to be able to judge whether a speech of this calibre could come from the mouth of Eleazar, who, if Flavius Josephus is to be believed[203], was no more than the head of a gang of criminals. But it is certainly very well adapted to the needs of the moment.

---

[201] B, VII, 340.

[202] B, VII, 343. Cf. Euripides, *Fr.* 634, Dindorf, and W. Morel, "Eine Rede bei Josephus (Bell. Jud., VII, 341 sqq.)", *RhM* 75 (1926), 106-114.

[203] B, VII, 253-258.

A comparison therefore is called for of the three long speeches of the *Bellum Judaicum*, so as to draw attention rather to the historiographic recourses which are used there. In general, it can be said that the structure is very similar, and that all three speeches follow a standard model. The synopsis must therefore be made:

1. Introduction to the speech so as to check or channel the spirits of the listeners:

– the war must be renounced (Agrippa, Nos. 345-347),

– since God is now on the side of the Romans (Flavius Josephus, Nos. 362-369),

– and he has delivered us into their hands (Eleazar, Nos. 323-336).

2. Evidence in favour of desisting in their war footing:

– much more powerful states have submitted to Rome (Agrippa, Nos. 348-399),

– it is not by force of arms that the Jewish people have freed themselves from their enemies through their history (Flavius Josephus, Nos. 376-414),

– material needs and divine condemnation force us to suicide (Eleazar, Nos. 349-359).

3. Conclusions: arms must be laid down:

– out of pity for sons and daughters, and the temple (Agrippa, Nos. 400-401),

– out of pity for your families (Flavius Josephus, No. 418), and

– so as not to see violence done to our loved ones (Eleazar, Nos. 382-388).

I believe that these are the invariable elements which form the mainstay of the three speeches; the remainder is a complement. There is, however, an element on which Flavius Josephus touches time after time: without God, the Jews can do nothing (Agrippa, Nos. 388-391; Flavius Josephus, Nos. 367-369, 376-415; Eleazar, Nos. 327-332).

The other speech of Flavius Josephus[204] is the result of pressing needs: the followers of Flavius Josephus threaten to put him to death if he surrenders to the Romans without a fight[205]. Therefore the words of Flavius Josephus are a set of reasonings (φιλοσοφεῖν ἐπὶ τῆς ἀνάγκης, No. 361), with the aim of making them see that the suicide that they are looking for is unjustified, both if the situation is looked at from the point of view of immediate defeat, and if it is contemplated from the divine viewpoint. In his reasonings, Flavius Josephus literally falls into pantheism (No. 372),

---

[204] B, III, 362-382.
[205] B, III, 356-359.

and bases them on human laws which punish suicide in the case of the person who has brought about his own death (No. 378).

This short speech is given a framework of a few introductory words and a few concluding words. Flavius Josephus makes it seen that he is convinced that God has revealed to him the destiny of the Jews (Nos. 351-352), and that confers on him sufficient clearsightedness so as to surrender to the Romans, not as a traitor, but rather as a minister of God (No. 354). But his companions in misfortune are not of the same mind, and give him two alternatives: to commit suicide with them or to die a traitor (No. 360). Then follows the set of reasoning which I have already commented on. I should like to point out that this speech of Flavius Josephus is suspect with regard to the authenticity of his words and with regard to the reality of the event: it is difficult to believe that the companions of Flavius Josephus should put up with such a torrent of rhetoric on suicide at such a critical moment.

The speech ends too with words which Flavius Josephus uses to propose the drawing of lots to establish a roster for the acts of suicide. He draws the last place.

Another speech which sees the light during times of war and unrest is that which Flavius Josephus places in the mouth of Ananus, at a time of widespread indignation due to the occupation of the holy places by a sector of the Zealots. The people are called to a general assembly, anxious that an end should be put to the uncomfortable situation created by these uncontrollables.

There are a few brief clear points in the speech of Ananus:

A. Introduction:

– he would sooner die than see the sacrilegious situation brought about by the Zealots (B, IV, 163-165);

– his listeners are partly to blame, for not having shown their opposition in time (Nos. 166-172).

B. What is to be done?

– the Romans will give us no aid against the Zealots (Nos. 173-174);

– have we lost our desire for freedom? (Nos. 175-177);

– we must accept neither the domination of the Romans nor that of our internal enemies (Nos. 178-179).

C. Comparative method:

– the Romans have given signs of better conduct than the Zealots (Nos. 180-185).

D. Conclusions:

– the acts of the Zealots have shaken us (Nos. 186-188);

– we must therefore attack them (No. 189);

– God, whom they have offended, will punish them (Nos. 190-191);

– I offer you all the help I can give (No. 192).

The speech opens and closes with emotive words, and the words included in it are exactly adapted to the mind of an old man and priest, who feels, in his heart of hearts, the feelings of a father before that disorientated people. It is a pragmatic speech, natural to a man of experience, and is full of reasonings which provide the doctrinal basis and content of the decision which the listeners have already taken to resist the sacrilege of the Zealots. It is not, therefore, an epideictic speech, since circumstances are not favourable for such elaborate declamation, nor is it simply exhortative, since the listeners are already convinced of what must be done: all that is lacking is the first thrust, and thus the speech assumes all the prerogatives of an aetiological speech, in so far as it fully accomplishes the aim it pursues, i.e. to spur into action a whole community so as to achieve something of which they were already convinced.

The Zealots find the opportunity to have the Idumaeans come to their aid, and the latter show up before the gates of Jerusalem without delay. The Zealot emissaries had evaded the watchfulness of Ananus, but the arrival of the Idumaeans suddenly brought about the fidelity of the population to their principles in the face of a new problem, this time internal. On this occasion, Jesus, the oldest of the high priests, addressed a few words[206] to the Idumaeans in these terms:

A. Introduction. An attempt to separate the Idumaeans, so that they should not heed the appeal of the Zealots:

– I am greatly surprised that fortune (τύχη) should cooperate with undesirable men (the Zealots, Nos. 238-239);

– comparative method: you are not like them (Nos. 240-244).

B. Reasons for our presence:

– we are not traitors, we have not sold ourselves to Rome: that is a calumny (Nos. 244-257).

C. You have three alternatives:

– to defend the metropolis and join forces with us (Nos. 258-264);

– to take a neutral stance and act as arbitrators (Nos. 265-266);

– to take your leave without supporting either side (Nos. 267-268).

D. Conclusions:

– if you do not accept any of these three proposals, be not surprised that the gates remain shut (No. 269).

This speech is incomplete without the answer of the Idumaeans to the harsh words with which Jesus ends (No. 269). Simon replies at first in in-

---

[206] Direct speeches (B, IV, 240-269) are opened by a few words in reported speech (B, IV, 238-239). The use of mixed speeches is a constant tendency in the work of Flavius Josephus.

direct speech (No. 272-275) and later goes on in direct speech (Nos. 276-282):

A. A harsh reply to the high priests:

– you have imprisoned in the temple the champions of liberty (i.e. the Zealots, No. 272);

– you adorn yourselves to receive the Romans and you parley with the Idumaeans so that they lay down their arms (No. 273);

– you accuse the others of deaths, and you condemn the entire nation to dishonour (No. 274).

B. Why are we here?:

– to make you free men (Nos. 276-277);

– because you are tyrants and your acts belie your words (No. 278-279);

– because the Zealots have done no more than eliminate traitor members (No. 280), held by you to be distinguished people;

– to defend the house of God from outside invaders and inside traitors (No. 281).

This speech of Simon is therefore aetiologic: and the Idumaeans remain where they are.

On various occasions I have noted the aetiological function of the speeches. At this moment, and at the beginning of another speech which I propose to examine, Flavius Josephus himself is explicit on two points: "Titus, believing that the spirits of the soldiers can be excited greatly by expectations and by words, and that exhortations and promises, very often, achieve a forgetting of danger and, at times, contempt of death"[207]. Two points should be picked out from these words:

– speeches can be an ideal instrument to spur the spirit to action;

– he will make an exhortative speech.

There are no more noteworthy speeches in direct speech in the *Bellum Judaicum*. All in all, four of them must be studied, which, although they do not strictly speaking offer the wellmarked parts of the speech proper, are still words expressed in public and addressed to a public which has gathered to listen. In historical order they are the following: B, I, 373-379; B, I, 556-558; B, II, 605-607 and B, III, 472-484.

The first short speech, B, I, 373-379, though it rises to no great heights, nevertheless has an historical repercussion comparable to that of the great speeches. Flavius Josephus says: "Herod called them and tried

---

207 B, VII, 33. The speech comprises the numbers 34-53.

to encourage them to resist with these words''[208]. From the start then, it is an exhortative speech, a speech with the sole aim of preparing the spirits of the soldiers for resistance against the Arabs. The circumstances in which the speech was given are also extreme: the troops are demoralised and have lost heart, after an unexpected setback (No. 368), after a series of battles without reaching a conclusive outcome (Nos. 369-370), after an earthquake which, according to the news, destroyed the whole of Judaea, after the invasion of the Arabs and the slaughter which they caused among the Jewish people.

The scheme is very simple, but steeped in doctrine:

A. Introduction. It weakens the impact of present reality, and expounds metaphysical and objective reasonings so as to convince them:

– present misfortunes, and especially those brought about by earthly elements should not be allowed to dishearten us (No. 373);

– hopes which are based on the misfortunes of others, and not on one's own strength, are false hopes (No. 373).

B. Corpus of the speech:

– philosophic reasonings: chance is not everlasting; fear teaches us caution (No. 374);

– demagogy: your doubt and our disheartenment are for me a token of victory (No. 375);

– nationalistic pride: no disaster will ever undermine the courage of the Jews (No. 376);

– objective reasonings concerning the little importance which those misfortunes caused by earthly elements have (No. 377).

C. Conclusions:

– the enemy has sacrificed our ambassadors and has broken the treaties (No. 378);

– let us all go into battle so as to avenge our ambassadors (No. 379);

– courage! (No. 379).

Indeed, from the historiographical point of view, the speech had an aetiologic charge with overwhelming effects. Flavius Josephus says: ''With these words he instilled spirit into the army, and on seeing them so full of valour...''[209]. Later on, he recounts the destruction which Herod wreaked on the Arab army.

As can be seen from the scheme which I have given, Flavius Josephus loses no time either in the introduction or in the conclusion. All his efforts are directed towards the idea of convincing them to resist. And he succeeds.

---

[208] B, I, 372. Cf. the study of the parallel speech in the *Antiquitates Judaicae* (A, XV, 127-146), in this same section (pp. 107-108).

[209] B, I, 380.

The other speech is very short and is of a different character[210]. It is not a speech strictly speaking, in the style of the others. What I here call a speech is rather a noting down of some words which Herod must have spoken, and which proceed from a family scene which is authentic. They are words which are perfectly fitting to the personality and the moment. They could almost be taken as being literal.

The content is made up by an expression of the feelings of Herod, and by commitments as regards political marriages. It may well be that the act had no other objectives than political ones with regard to the succession to the throne. In fact, the act brought about a reaction of insecurity in Antipater, the heir to the throne of Herod (No. 559). The scheme of the words includes three points:

– feelings of compassion and pity towards the three fatherless children (No. 556);

– the arrangement of the marriages (No. 557);

– a plea to heaven for a blessing on the marriages (No. 558).

The third short speech is also formed by some very concise sentences, but with them Flavius Josephus pursues a much more explicit aim[211]. Flavius Josephus asks to be allowed to speak to make a confession of his behaviour with regard to some money so as to calm down over-excited spirits[212]. Flavius Josephus, therefore, makes a speech of justification and exhortation.

The scheme is as follows:

– explanations as to the purpose of the money collected (No. 605);

– the money which has been entrusted to me will be invested for your benefit (Nos. 606-607).

These words achieve two aims: the saving of the life of Flavius Josephus and satisfying the wishes of the people of Tarichaeae (No. 608).

Then (No. 609), Flavius Josephus briefly repeats the same ideas, but in indirect speech.

The fourth speech is given by Titus, before a huge demonstration of power on the part of the Jews. The Roman soldiers are divided between two alternatives: attack, without waiting for the reinforcements from Vespasian, and faintheartedness and discouragement at the sight of such a huge host of Jews[213]. The words of Titus achieve some degree of encouragement, and with regard to this it can be said that the speech is

---

[210] B, I, 556-558. Other speeches of Herodes: B, I, 388-390, 457-465, 622-628.

[211] B, II, 605-607.

[212] B, II, 604.

[213] B, III, 471.

highly exhortative and is the cause of an unexpected change of heart in the soldiers.

Its outline is the following:

A. Introduction. Two basic ideas[214]:

– remember who you are (Nos. 472-473);

– remember against whom you are fighting (Nos. 472-473).

B. Comparative method:

– the Jews are a starving rabble, we are an experienced army (Nos. 474-475);

– our military training and the equipment at our disposal multiply our strength (Nos. 476-477);

– it is not the number of soldiers that has won battles, but their efficiency (No. 478);

– the Jews have launched themselves into the fray through daring, fear and desperation; we, through courage, discipline and heroism (No. 479);

– your reason for fighting is greater than that of the Jews (No. 480).

C. Conclusions:

– our help is numerous (No. 481);

– we shall be victorious (No. 482);

– and I shall go at the head (No. 483);

– God is with me (No. 484).

The results are immediate. Flavius Josephus writes: "Titus having spoken thus, there invaded the men supernatural spirits..."[215].

This speech is a jewel among those exhortative speeches which use comparison as a technique of persuasion. It is doubtless a coercive method, but it ostensibly gives the listener freedom of choice as to which of the two proposals expounded is the better[216].

Still within the *Bellum Judaicum*, we can find quotes in direct speech that cannot really be classed as speeches. Thus, Flavius Josephus takes an interest in transcribing directly the sentence of a person who is on his death-bed, sentences and words of encouragement, interior prayers of one kind or another, words and sentences spoken by a whole group of people at the same time, interior expressions and laments in the face of a disastrous situation, exclamations and passwords[217].

---

[214] B, III, 472-484.

[215] B, III, 485.

[216] In a similar vein is to be found the speech made by Titus in the presence of Simon and John, once they have been taken prisoners: B, VI, 328-350.

[217] B, I, 76, 79, 272, 442, 500-501, 503, 522, 547, 584, 595-597, 618, 639, 660; B, II, 116, 201, 211, 472-473; B, III, 204, 354, 356-360, 388-389, 494-496; B, IV, 343, 626, 628; B, V, 19-20, 74, 272, 535-537; B, VI, 56-57, 124-128, 188, 205-207, 210-211, 300-301, 304, 308-309, 411; B, VII, 109.

b) *Direct speeches in the Antiquitates Judaicae*

In the *Antiquitates Judaicae*, and within direct speech, no more than nine speeches can be counted, some of which have been invented by the historian[218], and speeches which have been reworked using biblical speeches as a model[219]. But a distinction can still be made, when dealing with the invented speeches, between those which correspond to biblical narratives[220] and those which come from the post-biblical period. On general lines, it may be stated that Flavius Josephus usually enlarges on the texts of the biblical speeches.

The first non-biblical speech of a biblical narrative appears in the story of Joseph (A, II, 101-104). At the moment when Joseph wishes to test the feelings and intentions of his brothers, Rubel begins a speech which constitutes a summary of the words which, in the Bible, are spoken by the ten brothers[221], since they "found themselves in a state of perturbation and fear, believing that the greatest of dangers was hanging over them..."[222]. The words of Rubel touch on the three principal points of the whole story:
 – we are not spies and we have come solely out of necessity (No. 101);
 – we are sons of Jacob, who is alive (Nos. 102-103), and
 – we want grain too for our father and for our smaller brother Benjamin, who has stayed at home (No. 104).
It is thus that Joseph, concludes Flavius Josephus, comes into the knowledge that his father and smaller brother are still alive (No. 105).
Possibly the words which the biblical writer had the whole group speak simultaneously seemed very impersonal to Flavius Josephus, who then directed his reworking towards placing these same words, spoken by the group, in the mouth of one particular speaker.

One speech which has no parallel in the Holy Scriptures is placed in the mouth of Moses on the occasion of his presenting the Decalogue to the people of Israel[223]. Just then, the Israelites were in very low spirits, since there was no sign of Moses returning to the camp, after a blaze of glory, together with thunder and lightning, on Mount Sinai. The people of Israel imagined that Moses had died through the wrath of God and

---

[218] A, II, 101-104, 140-159; A, III, 84-88; A, XV, 127-146; A, XVI, 105-120; A, XIX, 167-184.
[219] A, II, 161-165; A, IV, 177-193; A, XII, 279-284.
[220] A, II, 101-104, 140-159.
[221] *Gen.* XLII, 8-17.
[222] A, II, 100.
[223] A, III, 84-88.

that the same fate was in store for them (No. 82). However, with the appearance of Moses, even the air became serene and pure (No. 84).

The historiographical value of this speech is simply occasional. Flavius Josephus wishes to make a dramatic introduction to the making public of the Ten Commandments, to which he does not give the solemn tone which they would seem to merit, and pays more attention to the reasons why the Decalogue should be accepted, rather than to the contents of the same. Here a desire can be seen to justify the laying down of the Ten Commandments, which present a summing up of the religious and moral life of the people of Israel.

In the first redaction of the Decalogue in *Exodus* (Chap. XX), there appears no similar introduction, even though it is the fruit of "priestly" recension. In the redaction of *Deuteronomy* (Chap. V), the author places a brief introduction at the head, but very distant, no doubt, from that of Flavius Josephus, and brings the proclamation of the Commandments to a close with a series of recommendations which exhort the acceptance, fulfillment and transmission of the same to their descendents. Perhaps Flavius Josephus, taking inspiration from the Deuteronomical redaction, composed his speech (A, III, 84-88).

The outline therefore of the speech of Moses is as follows:

– God has dictated some rules to me, whereby you may lead a happy life (No. 84);

– disdain not these Commandments, for they come from no human being but from God, who has worked marvels of salvation amongst His chosen people Israel (Nos. 85-87);

– conclusions: fulfill them, since they come from God, and are proof of the care which He takes of your race and of its perpetuity (No. 88).

Another speech outside the context of the Bible is made by Herod as the result of a situation of chaos. The words which Flavius Josephus uses are explicit[224]. After an earthquake which has created havoc in the country, has killed both human beings and livestock, and has encouraged the Arabs to invade a country in ruins, the Jews fall prey to acute disheartenment (ἀθύμως διακείμενοι, No. 125), and desperation (οὐ γὰρ ἦν οὔτε ἰσοτομίας ἐλπίς, No. 125). To this must be added the illegal act which the Arabs committed by killing the Jewish ambassadors sent to make peace treaties.

As a consequence, Herod's intention is to raise wilting spirits (ἀναλαμβάνειν αὐτῶν πεπτωκότα τὰ φρονήματα, No. 126) by first of all ad-

[224] A, XV, 127-146.

dressing words of encouragement (παραθαρρύνας, No. 126) to men in his confidence, and then an exhortation (παρεκάλει, No. 126) to the rest.

The parallel speech in the *Bellum Judaicum*[225] is of a very different structure, but the contents of both speeches agree with regard to the essential points: it is necessary to have hope of victory with the help of God, and the barbarity of the Arabs must be condemned. Here, then, is the outline:

A. Introduction:

– we have been hard pressed by great difficulties, and that has disheartened us (No. 127);

– the position could be improved by the right action (No. 128);

– firstly, I shall say to you that the war has been cause by the outrageous acts of our enemies (No. 129);

– secondly, we may have hope of victory (No. 129).

B. Corpus of the speech:

1. Part one:

– the Arabs are an ungrateful people, since they do not requite my aid, thanks to which caesar Antonius did not utterly destroy them (Nos. 130-133);

– the Arabs are people who do not respect their friends and do not honour treaties (Nos. 134-138).

2. Part two:

– our position is that of the conquerors (Nos. 138-140);

– the Arabs lay more store by our misfortunes than by their own capability (Nos. 141-143).

C. Conclusions[226]:

– we have not suffered the punishment of divine wrath, as some believe (No. 144);

– everything is happening according to divine will (No. 145), and

– having God as our eternal protector, we can attack such sacrilegious men (No. 146).

This speech, made in the midst of a bad situation and before embarking on a war, obtains results which could not be better: "The Jews became much more prepared in spirit to undertake the war"[227].

Another speech is made up of the words which Alexander addresses to his father Herod, in view of the accusations of which he, together with his

---

[225] B, I, 373-379.

[226] Through these conclusions, the speech takes on a more theological air than its counterpart in the *Bellum Judaicum*.

[227] A, XV, 147.

brothers, is the object[228]. According to Herod, his sons intended to kill him and take his throne from him (A, XVI, 92). The matter is taken to Rome by Herod himself, for Caesar to give a solution.

Outline of the speech[229]:

A. Introduction:

– tries to win his father's affection, by saying that Herod could have punished the person guilty, with no need to go and lay the problem before Caesar (Nos. 105-106);

– but he wants to clear up the misunderstandings and take away the suspicion of guilt (Nos. 107-108).

B. Corpus of the speech:

– the accusation of wanting to kill a father is logical, when sons are left without a mother (Nos. 109-111);

– all that refers to their intention of poisoning him is calumny (Nos. 112-113);

– kill our father to occupy the throne? We shall inherit the throne by natural right, and, if we were to occupy it by means of a crime, our lives would be fraught with misfortune (Nos. 114-117).

C. Conclusions:

– before Caesar, we ask you to remove any suspicions you have of us (Nos. 118-120).

The speech of Alexander achieves what it has set out to do. It is therefore a speech of defence, the consequences of which bring about a clarification of a confusing situation and the agreement of the two parts.

As regards its historiographic value, this speech can be placed among the situational speeches, offering an analysis of the situation and giving rise to solutions. The atmosphere which is created is entirely in harmony with the feelings of filial piety and fear of the speaker.

After the murder of the emperor Caligula (41 A.D.), there arises a grave situation as regards succession. It was the Praetorian guard who, with a view to their own interests, proclaimed Claudius, the uncle of Caligula, emperor. Claudius embodied two conditions: that of being a member of the imperial family, and of being a very learned man. It was believed that the continuity of the imperial dynasty was a guarantee for the maintaining of a vast empire. Thus the Praetorian guard put an end to the hesitation of the Senate between restoring the old régime or looking for some member of the Julia family for the principate, or else choose a head by voting[230].

---

[228] A, XVI, 105-120.

[229] Regarding its stylistic form, note the great number of rhetorical questions contained in this speech.

[230] A, XIX, 166-184.

In these circumstances, the consul Gnaeus Sentius Saturninus makes a speech before the Senate, in which he aims at persuading the senators with regard to the path which must be followed. It is exhortative in character (ποιεῖται παραίνεσιν, No. 166):

A. Introduction:
– after so long a time, we are finally enjoying freedom (Nos. 167-169);
– I ask that that freedom should last for ever (Nos. 170-171).

B. Corpus of the speech:
– an analysis of the dangers which a tyrannical régime brings with it (Nos. 172-177).

C. Conclusions:
– we have succumbed to peace and we have learned to live as prisoners of conquest (Nos. 178-181);
– we are grateful to Chaerea for ridding us of the tyrant (Nos. 182-184).

The words of the consul Saturninus fill the hearts of the listeners with satisfaction, and so Chaerea was given their vote of confidence and freedom to act as he saw fit.

In the *Antiquitates Judaicae* there still remains a considerable number of speeches, quotes, words and so on, which are either transcribed literally or in direct speech by Flavius Josephus. The quantity, however, is not significant in so far as defining Flavius Josephus as an historian who was a lover of rhetorical ornamentation. Rather, one may see in him a writer who keeps the use of speeches to a limited number of occasions. It should also be remembered that many of these literal quotes are proper to the biblical source which Flavius Josephus paraphrases.

Be that as it may, I think this is a suitable place to list the main quotes in direct speech: A, I, 34, 46-47, 57, 100-102, 228-231, 252-255, 271-273, 280-283, 288-290; II, 55-57, 67-69, 80-86, 106, 136, 172-175, 235, 270-271, 286, 309, 330-333, 335-337; III, 69-72, 84-88, 189-191, 300-302; IV, 18-19, 25-34, 40-50, 114-117, 119-123, 127-130, 134-138, 145-149, 261-262, 314, 315-319; V, 93-98, 123, 203, 297-298, 323; VI, 12, 20-21, 24, 54-57, 66, 81, 86-87, 88, 104, 110-111, 126-128, 160, 172-173, 184-185, 216, 251-253, 273, 284-291, 355; VII, 50-52, 291, 312, 371-374, 383-388; VIII, 107-108, 111-117, 171-173, 227-228, 232, 269-272, 276-281; IX, 26, 69, 145-146, 151-152, 153, 155, 169, 181, 189, 194-198, 206-207, 262; X, 33, 203-209, 243-244; XI, 230, 300-301; XII, 302-304; XIII, 197-200, 399, 403-404; XIV, 24, 165-167, 172-174; XV, 28, 382-387; XVI, 31-57, 209-212, 379-383; XVIII, 77, 213, 219-222, 229, 279-283, 292-297, 301-304, 320-322, 326; XIX, 78-83, 92, 217-219, 303-311, 323-325, 345; XX, 27, 56-59; we include here too Vit, 172, 141-142, 209, 221, 256-258, 259-261, 386-387.

Within, therefore, the *Antiquitates Judaicae*, the list of speeches and transcriptions of words in direct speech provides the following percentage: in direct speech, 20 per cent; in indirect speech, 50 per cent; mixed, i.e. speeches transcribed partly in direct and partly in indirect speech, 30 per cent.

c) *Indirect speeches in the Bellum Judaicum*

A very considerable number of speeches, words, quotes and summaries of speeches are used in indirect speech by Flavius Josephus in a very elegant way, something which provides agility in the narrative of the events as such and also great historical conciseness. Comment on them will not be based on the most significant parts of each speech, but rather on their repercussion on the historical moment; in other words, I shall try to evaluate their global historiographic value. Along general lines, I have chosen only those speeches which, because of their contents, affect historical action, and I have taken as samples of text a minimum of five paragraphs, from the edition of Niese.

The first quote comprises two short defence speeches before a tribunal which is presided over by Augustus. The subject revolves around the question of the succession to the throne of the sons of Herod[231].

Antipater, the most skilfull orator among the opponents[232] of Archelaus, bases his accusation on two points: a) Archelaus, though showing his doubts as to his right to the throne, in practice has behaved like a king; b) his mourning for the death of his father has been no more than hypocrisy, to which should be added his criminal conduct in the massacre he inflicted on the people who were present in the sanctuary. This second point is the one his father fears, and he does not name him as his successor until the day when he is no longer capable of recognising the name which he was writing in his will. And he concludes that, if value is to be given to the decision of an exhausted man like Herod, then Archelaus has lost his royalty through his outrages against it.

These are the most important points of the accusation of Antipater. And Flavius Josephus, to summarise the rest, says in a very laconic tone that "Antipater expounded many similar facts"[233] and brought forward testimony for them.

The refutation of this speech and the defence of Archelaus is placed in the hands of Nicolas, who simply says the opposite, point for point, of

---

[231] B, II, 26-36. See pages 114-115.
[232] B, II, 26.
[233] B, II, 33.

what he has just heard: the slaughter in the temple was brought about by the attitude of the masses against the reign and against Caesar; the will is valid, since in it Caesar provides the guarantee of the succession.

As can be seen, these two speeches—short in the literary form given by Flavius Josephus—contain no more than needs to be said. There is no ecphrasis, nor rhetorical questions, nor introductions nor conclusions. It is simply the skeleton of a speech which, in the hands of a rhetorical historian, would have turned out to be a highly noteworthy piece, given the especially delicate circumstances: the proving of rights to the throne before Augustus.

Another speech which is potentially very important was made by Titus before his army after the destruction of Jerusalem[234]. No doubt he transmits to his soldiers what a general usually transmits after a victory. Flavius Josephus, however, is sober in form and precise in ideas. This summary or précis he offers could have been raised to the category of an elaborate speech with a triumphalist bent. But none of this is made use of by Flavius Josephus. The entire speech is a listing of ideas, but within a rhetorical structure. Thus:

A. Introduction:
– Titus thanks the soldiers for their fidelity (No. 6) and
– praises their obedience and courage (Nos. 6-7).
B. Corpus of the speech:
– glorious has been the end to such a long war (No. 8),
– but what is even better is the fact that those they have chosen to be the governors and administrators of the Empire have been accepted with satisfaction by all (No. 9).
C. Conclusions:
– I hold you all in great esteem (No. 10);
– those who have excelled in their exploits will be correspondingly rewarded (No. 11);
– he will reward deeds and will not punish errors (No. 12).

This speech has great historiographic value, and seems to be entirely moved by a single idea, that given in B: now that you have put an end to the war in a victorious manner, stand by your Emperor, who is none other than Vespasian. In all its parts, therefore, a situational speech: because there has been a great victory, because there will be rewards, because there is a need too to support the head of the Empire. Therefore

---

[234] B, VII, 6-12. One finds stylistic traits of Thucydides here: No. 7, ἀλόγιστοι τόλμαι = Thuc. III, 82, 4, τόλμα ἀλόγιστος; No. 8, εἰς αὐτὸν καθίσταντο = Thuc. IV, 23, πόλεμον καθίσταντο.

one would be nearer the mark in seeing here an authentically political content than the words expected to commemorate a victory.

Within his tendency towards the speech which is reported indirectly, Flavius Josephus goes even further in strictly reducing the words which a given personality might have used, being reduced to the transcription solely of the ideas which might have been expressed[235].

Nor does he refrain from mentioning those good qualities which should adorn an orator, and thus says that "Alexander was aided by the strength of his words together with a clear conscience, for he was a very skilful orator"[236].

The ideas are the following: an exposition of the faults of Herod, the calumnies of which he has been object, the innocence of his brother Antipater and the ignominy to which they have been exposed. The conclusions take on a dramatic mien: if the accusations levelled against them are true, his father Herod can condemn them to death. At that moment the historian remarks that the hearers all broke into tears, and that even the Caesar was not unmoved.

This speech outline also comprises a final closure by the author with a noting of the consequences which follow it: Caesar reconciles Herod to his sons. So here we have an example of the care which Flavius Josephus takes to provide his narratives or episodes of the same with a neat finish, however insignificant they may be.

This technique of speech summarising, used a great many times throughout the work of Flavius Josephus[237], not only provides his oeuvre with a great sense of condensing, but also avoids the feeling of literary vacuum which may be produced by the repeated use of extensive speeches. This technique of summarising also avoids the loss of the narrative thread, since the end of the preceding narrative is not excessively far from the taking up of the thread in the following narrative.

d) Indirect speeches in the Antiquitates Judaicae

In the Antiquitates Judaicae as well as in the Vita and Contra Apionem, there appear no speeches in indirect speech which might have a definite structure and relevance. It has been possible to ascertain that Flavius Josephus limits the speeches to simple collection of the ideas which the

---

[235] B, I, 453-454; B, II, 216-223; B, V, 55-561; also a collected group (B, II, 411-418; B, IV, 122-125) of certain emissaries (A, XVII, 304-316).

[236] B, I, 453.

[237] B, I, 637-638; B, II, 2-4, 26-36, 84-92, 580-582; B, III, 194-200; B, IV, 93-102, 216-223.

personalities defend[238] in such a simple way that very often the speeches are reduced to a sort of concise dialogues of the kind ''he said to them... the others answered him...[239].

There is, nevertheless, the description of a speech and its reply, the parallel of which I have already analysed[240]. Flavius has at his disposal the written source of Nicolas of Damascus, who was one of Herod's most intimate collaborators and well acquainted with all the domestic problems. In the *Antiquitates Judaicae* the speech made by Antipater ''the most skilful orator''[241], is much longer, and in spite of revolving around the question of the legitimacy of the succession to the throne by Archelaus and his lack of religious feelings on the day of Herod's death, it is enriched with other accusatory information. The speech must have been extremely solemn and must have represented the most important appeal ever made against the successor to a king who was protected by the power of Rome. Indeed, Caesar gives no ready reply (A, XVII, 249).

Due to the importance which I find in this speech, a detailed analysis should be made of it, so as to evaluate the volume of offences and its historiographic relevance:

1. Archelaus has assumed royal power before Caesar has conferred it on him (No. 230);

2. Archelaus has been sanguinary in his dispersal of the multitude in the temple. His action cost hundreds of people their lives (Nos. 231-232);

3. Archelaus has made changes among the officers of the army (No. 232) and has behaved as if he had been appointed king by Caesar (No. 233);

4. he has released prisoners (No. 233);

5. Archelaus has been negligent at the funeral of his father (No. 234), which has provoked the multitude to rebellion (No. 235);

5. worst of all: Archelaus has come to Rome to obtain power which he already exercises in reality (No. 236);

7. insistence: the deaths in the temple and the impiety of Archelaus are the most damaging points of the accusation (No. 237);

8. Herod, in prevision of the sanguinary character of Archelaus, named Antipater as his successor, while he was yet in possession of his faculties (No. 238);

9. Archelaus has shown what kind of king he would be, on two counts: by having taken from Caesar the right to confer power and by not having hesitated in the slaughter in the temple (No. 239).

---

[238] A, XVII, 93-105.

[239] A, XII, 12-15, 110-115, 160-166, 188 ff.; A, XVI, 90-99.

[240] B, II, 26-36 commented in the beginning of this section (pp. 111-112).

[241] δεινότατος εἰπεῖν: this expression appears in two places (B, II, 26 and A, XVII, 230).

According to Flavius Josephus therefore, there are certain ideas which are repeated throughout the rhetorical turn of Antipater, which have been gathered under the numbers 1, 2, 5, 6, 7 and 9. It can certainly be seen here that Antipater is obsessed with an idea which he is not willing to accept under any circumstances: that Archelaus should have acted as if he were the master of power, acting on his own initiative, and heeding no man (Nos. 1, 3, 6, 9). This accusation can certainly be considered as the most suitable to an accusation made before the only person who may confer power. It should be recognised, therefore, that Flavius Josephus or Nicolas spun a speech which was greatly in keeping with the circumstances, or, if it is allowed as real, that they were very faithful to the historical reality.

Now comes the speech by Nicolas in defence of Archelaus. At the beginning of the speech, he refutes the slaughter in the temple, and affirms that Archelaus sent his forces so as to prevent any excesses by the multitude (Nos. 240-241). The speech ends with a defence of the appointment of Archelaus as successor, made when Herod was still of a sound mind (No. 244). On the other hand, the Caesar will not annul the decision of a man who is faithful to him and an ally (No. 246), nor will he condemn a man of royal rank who has left succession to his son, on the basis of mental disturbance (Nos. 246-247). Herod had sufficient sense to place everything under the judgement of the Caesar (No. 247).

Half-way through his speech, Nicolas links the accusations against Antipater and against the accusers (Nos. 242-243), and minimises the virulence of those other acts which have been presented as evil so as to harm Archelaus, the man who has done them nothing but good (No. 243).

Here Nicolas is more extensive than in the *Bellum Judaicum*[242] and it seems that his speech provides two accusatory phrases which Antipater passes over, without going into detail: "by his general conduct"[243] and "by many other acts"[244]. Nicolas extends his defence to all this, too.

e) *Mixed styles*

The investigator however is still left with a host of quotes which refer to the manner of transmitting of the thoughts of another, his words, his prayers and so on, which offer another very widespread resort in the work of Flavius Josephus. This particular system represents a mixture of the techniques already described; in other words, it represents a balance be-

---

[242] B, II, 34-36.
[243] A, XVII, 232: πάντων διάπραξιν.
[244] A, XVII, 233: πολλὰ τὰ μὲν γεγονότα.

tween indirect and direct speech. I should add, however, that this system comes to represent a characteristic touch of the historiographic style of Flavius Josephus. Let us see.

This historiographic style is channeled in two different ways: by means of speeches in mixed speech which are made by one orator or speaker, and by means of speeches made by different people, expressed in a mixture of the two styles. As a subsection to this latter way, should be added the dialogues which are reduced to a mixture of the two styles.

In this section then, in addition to the speeches proper, mention is also made of dialogues and prayers. The term "speech" must therefore be understood in its widest sense.

The first point deals with those speeches made by a single person and presented with the mixture of styles. Vespasian, before his troops who are disheartened on account of the disaster they have suffered at the hands of the Jews, is forced to address them with words of consolation[245]. He begins his peroration in indirect speech, making them reflect on the nature of the war and the changes in fortune, ideas all of which are very profound[246]. He then goes on to address them in direct speech, so as to encourage them[247]. The speech of the priest Jesus which is made from the walls and addressed to the Idumaeans who are trying to enter Jerusalem by invitation of the Zealots who are within[248] is made up of a first part in indirect speech[249] and by a long second part in direct speech[250]. One of the leaders of the Idumaeans, on hearing the words of the high priest, addresses his troops so as to give them heart[251]. His speech starts off in indirect speech[252] and goes on in direct speech[253].

The Roman general Petronius poses a religious problem for the Jews by sending them the order to erect statues in honour of the Caesar in each of their cities[254]. The Jews, together with wives and children, beg him to respect their laws. The scene follows this outline:

– indirect speech (supplication of the Jews, No. 192);
– the general replies in indirect speech (he threatens them, if the order is not complied with, Nos. 193-194);

---

[245] B, IV, 39-48.
[246] B, IV, 40-41: παλίμπους δ' ἡ τύχη παρίσταται.
[247] B, IV, 42-48.
[248] B, IV, 238-269.
[249] B, IV, 238-239.
[250] B, IV, 240-269.
[251] B, IV, 272-282: Simon, son of Caathas and the Idumaean chief.
[252] B, IV, 272-275.
[253] B, IV, 276-282.
[254] B, II, 192-198.

- the Jews insist on their point of view, in indirect speech (No. 195);
- Petronius insists, in direct speech (No. 195);
- the multitude of the Jews protests, in indirect speech (No. 196);
- Petronius, in direct speech: "Will you therefore wage war on the Caesar?"[255];
- the Jews promise him two sacrifices daily in honour of the Caesar and of the Roman people, in indirect speech (No. 197).

In this historical event one may observe that the speakers who begin each of the speeches end up in dialogue form.

Here I shall give a list of the main items which repeat this procedure: A, III, 99-101, 308-310, 311-314; A, IV, 15-19; A, V, 134-138, 235-239; A, VII, 289-292; A, IX, 250; A, X, 6-10; A, XI, 89-96; A, XIII, 43-45, 88-90; A, XX, 87-91.

The second section is very extensive, and, as I have already mentioned, included in it are all those possible ways of transmitting thought, words, dialogues and so on. I should like to insist on the matter of the mixture, since Flavius Josephus is just as likely to transmit words, a short speech, or a prayer in direct speech as in indirect speech. With regard to this, I give here the main items:

- speeches: B, III, 197-204, 399-408; B, IV, 366-376; B, VI, 95-110; A, VI, 40-44; A, XII, 176-179; A, XIII, 288-296, 399-404; A, XVI, 361-372; A, XVII, 48-51; A, XVIII, 334-337;
- sentences and prayers: B, I, 76; B, V, 463; B, VI, 300-309; B, VII, 109; A, I, 271-273; A, II, 136; A, V, 312; A, IX, 35; A, XI, 64; A, XIX, 159;
- speeches or words spoken by a whole group: B, II, 195-198; A, IX, 34-36, 250; A, XII, 424-425; A, XVIII, 263-268.

Finally mention should be made of the well-known personal stamp of Flavius Josephus, which is that the dialogues of the texts which he paraphrases from the Bible are reduced to a mixture of direct and indirect speech. The tendency in the biblical text is towards predominant direct speech; in Flavius Josephus, towards the mixture of both[256].

Taking the oeuvre of Flavius Josephus as a whole, the *Bellum Judaicum* stands out above the others on account of its rhetoric[257].

---

[255] B, II, 196.
[256] The most notable samples are the following: A, I, 294-296, 313-319; A, II, 60-90, 210-216, 267-271; A, V, 11-14, 243-250; A, VI, 145-155, 205-212, 255-261, 310-319, 327-336; A, VII, 150-153, 215-221, 250-257; A, VIII, 27-34, 81-84, 404-408; A, IX, 110-111; A, X, 34-38, 124-130, 203-210, 239-244; A, XI, 250-267, 230-233, 238-243.
[257] Cf. Shave F. B. Cohen, *op. cit.*, 90.

3. *Chronology*

The chronological form which an historian gives to his work may consist of a great wealth of items or a great lack of them. Flavius Josephus belongs to that group of historians who forget neither the hour, nor the day, nor the month, nor the year, nor the Olympiad, nor the reign, nor the consulship in terms of which events are measured in time or with which they have a simple temporal relationship. This then is what I hope to demonstrate.

First of all, a distinction should be made between what is understood by the chronological system which is used by an historian and the chronological resourses which form the backbone of the work and give a temporal dimension to events. The first does not fall strictly within the scope of this investigation, and to take it up would be to touch on a subject which has already been studied by others[258]; it alone could constitute the object of a doctoral thesis which might review and provide fresh data to be added to the studies already edited. This investigation will therefore analyse no more than the temporal recourses as historiographic elements, and not the chronological system of Flavius Josephus.

Bearing these premises in mind, one may observe that Flavius Josephus is very rich in typically chronological expressions. Among them there are formulae which are indicative [of the past] of an act which happened in the past, of the type κατὰ ⟨δὲ⟩ τοῦτον τὸν καιρόν[259], κατὰ δὲ τὰς αὐτὰς ἡμέρας[260] and similar ones[261]. Temporal indications which are approximative to an act are noted with expressions of the type περὶ δὲ τὸν αὐτὸν καιρόν[262], εἰς τὸν αὐτὸν χρόνον[263], ὑπὸ δὴ τοῦτον τὸν καιρόν[264], and ἐν τῷ χρόνῳ τούτῳ[265]. Simultaneity is expressed by ἐν δὲ τούτῳ[266], ἐν δὲ τῷ τότε[267], and κατ' αὐτό[268]. The duration of the historical act is indicated by

---

[258] Cf. H. Schreckenberg, *Bibliographie...*, *passim*.

[259] B, I, 218; B, II, 309; B, IV, 585; B, VI, 213, 271; A, VI, 325; A, VIII, 176, 363; A, IX, 7, 239; A, X, 15; A, XI, 304, 313; A, XII, 196, 265; A, XIII, 351, 395, 419; A, XVII, 89, 213, 224; A, XVIII, 63; A, XX, 17, 169, 179, 189, 211; Vit, 112, 271, 373, 390, 398.

[260] B, II, 485; B, VI, 169.

[261] B, II, 595; B, III, 336; B, VI, 387; A, I, 41, 171, 174; A, VIII, 26; A, IX, 88; A, XI, 347; A, XII, 223; A, XVI, 6; A, XIX, 278.

[262] B, VII, 216; A, XV, 300.

[263] A, VII, 100.

[264] A, I, 194; A, IX, 258; A, XI, 158; A, XII, 237, 354, 389; A, XIII, 18, 103, 180, 365; A, XIV, 268, 420.

[265] A, XIX, 360.

[266] B, I, 261, 309, 323; B, II, 55; 101, 178; B, III, 414; B, IV, 550, 633; B, V, 261, 460; B, VI, 149; A, XIII, 330; A. XIV, 86; A, XV, 121; A, XVII, 79, 269; A, XVIII, 109; A, XIX, 24.

[267] A, XV, 5.

[268] B, I, 195.

the formulae παρὰ δὲ τὸν χρόνον τοῦτον[269], τοῦτον δὲ ἅπαντα τὸν χρόνον[270]. The chronological following of one act in relation to another already realised is marked by a remarkable wealth of expressions: μετ' οὐ πολύ[271], οὐ πολὺ ὕστερον[272], χρόνοις δ' ὕστερον οὐ πολλοῖς[273], μετ' ὀλίγον δὲ χρόνον[274], and similar ones[275], and with verbal formulae, such as χρόνου δ' ὀλίγου διελθόντος[276]. Finally, there still remain diverse expressions with prepositions: οὐκ εἰς μακράν[277], ἐν δὲ τῷ μεταξύ[278], πρὸ δὲ τούτων[279], and adverbs[280].

Flavius Josephus pays attention to the beginning of spring (A, XII, 293: VIII, 381), to the constellations (A, XIII, 237), to an eclipse (A, XVII, 167), the only one, which serves to mark exactly the night when Matthias the high priest was removed from his post and when Matthias the revolutionary met his end, i.e., the 13th March, in the year 4 B.C.

The passing of days is marked[281], above all, in expressions such as τῇ ὑστεραίᾳ, τῇ ἐπιούσῃ and other similar ones[282], and indication is also given of whether the act happened in the morning, in the afternoon, in the evening, at night[283] or at dawn[284].

---

[269] B, I, 286.

[270] A, XIV, 390.

[271] B, I, 513; A, VIII, 225; A, IX, 102, 182; A, X, 96, 247; A, XII, 132; A, XIII, 367, 430; A, XIV, 34, 37, 53, 285, 447; XV, 289; A, XVIII, 31, 34, 49; A, XIX, 316; A, XX, 5, 74, 92, 141; Vit, 309, 326, 407, 419, 427.

[272] A, I, 237; A, VII, 298.

[273] A, VI, 170.

[274] A, VII, 383.

[275] B, II, 175; A, V, 35; A, VI, 310; A, VII, 294; A, VIII, 398; A, X, 68, 216; A, XI, 140, 207; A, XII, 154, 341; A, XIII, 422; A, XIV, 82, 123, 126, 324, 336; A, XV, 244; A, XIX, 272; A, XX, 43.

[276] A, VII, 96, 303; A, VIII, 328; A, IX, 27; A, X, 17; A, XII, 199; A, XIX, 300; similar: A, XVIII, 179.

[277] A, IX, 170; XX, 153.

[278] A, XIV, 434.

[279] Vit, 179.

[280] ποτε, B, I, 556; B, II, 179, 270; A, II, 2; A, XVIII, 81, 91; τότε, B, VII, 451; A, XIV, 140; A, XV, 27; A, XX, 118; ἔνθεν, B, I, 656; τηνικαῦτα, B, II, 206.

[281] B, IV, 547, 660-661; A, VI, 236.

[282] B, I, 342, 620; B, II, 172, 199, 289, 301, 315, 430, 441, 634; B, III, 145, 150, 155, 505; B, IV, 112, 646, 650; B, V, 291; B, VI, 236, 244, 363; A, I, 178; A, VI, 2, 209, 235, 374; A, VII, 18, 382; A, IX, 37; A, XI, 109, 110, 167, 289, 292; A, XII, 215; A, XIV, 73, 456; A, XVIII, 211, 234; Vit, 15, 293, 331, 384, 400.

[283] B, I, 139, 340; B, II, 5, 552; B, VI, 407; A, V, 60, 330; A, VI, 145, 306; A, VII, 195, 218; A, VIII, 382, 414, 416; A, IX, 12, 129; A, X, 137; A, XII, 307; A, XVIII, 336; A, XIX, 254; Vit, 91, 404. Cf. Concordance, s.uu. νύξ, ἑσπέρα, δείλη and their derived.

[284] B, I, 332; B, II, 598; B, III, 87, 253, 422; B, V, 51, 538; B, VI, 249; B, VII, 124, 402; A, VI, 40, 215; A, VIII, 414; A, IX, 54; A, XVIII, 211. Cf. Concordance, s.uu. ἔωθεν, ἑωθινός.

Duration is expressed from two viewpoints, i.e., fixing attention on the duration itself of the event[285], or else marking the term after which another action begins[286].

The system of marking the day, year, name of the month (according to the Jewish and Greek calenders), and the Olympiad, all together is frequent in the work of Flavius Josephus. In this way the historian pays tribute to his Jewish public and also to his Greek and Roman readers. An example: ''It came to pass that two years later, in the year 145, on the 25th day of the month which is called Chasleus amongst us, and Apellaeus amongst the Macedonians, in the 153rd Olympiad, the king came up to Jerusalem with a great army...''[287]. At times the chronological recourses are mixed, that is, Flavius Josephus makes a mixture of indications of time proper and references to periods presided by kings[288], consuls[289], priests[290], prophets[291], emperors[292], or the date of the exodus of the Israelites from Egypt[293].

Within this same chronological orientation which is under study, I believe that there is one point which, on account of its complexity and wealth of data, should have more detailed comment: ''In the month of Xanthicus, which is called Nisan amongst us and is the beginning of the year, on the fourteenth lunar day, when the sun is in Aries, for in this month we were released from slavery under the Egyptians, (our legislator...)''[294]. The elements are multiple: the names of the months (Greek Xanthicus, Hebrew Nisan); the beginning of the Jewish year, that is, in spring, according to the priestly tradition; the sun in Aries, which indicates the days half-way through March to half-way through April, the time when the Israelites came out of Egypt. The biblical verses

---

[285] B, I, 70, 343; B, II, 168, 180, 203, 204, 219, 248, 528; B, III, 157, 289, 444, 530; B, IV, 491, 652; B, V, 109; B, VI, 147, 269, 308, 378; A, II, 316; A, III, 11; A, V, 200; A, VI, 19, 378; A, VIII, 55, 287, 316; A, IX, 156, 204; A, X, 185; A, XIV, 270; A, XVIII, 224; A, XIX, 350.

[286] B, I, 248, 305, 399; B, II, 203, 645; B, III, 316, 317; B, V, 356; B, VI, 165, 392, 437; A, I, 177; A, V, 79; A, VII, 392, 394; A, VIII, 18; A, XIV, 330, 416; Vit, 13, 157.

[287] A, XII, 248. Parallel places: B, II, 315, 430, 555; B, III, 142, 282, 306, 315, 409, 542; B, IV, 63, 69, 83, 413, 449, 577; B, V, 302, 466, 567; B, VI, 22, 67, 94, 177, 220, 250, 290, 296, 374, 407, 435; B, VII, 401; A, I, 80; A, II, 311, 318; A, III, 248, A, IV, 78, 84, 327; A, VIII, 61, 146, 230; A, IX, 186; A, XI, 148, 151, 154, 286, 290, 291; A, XII, 264, 319, 321, 412; A, XIII, 236.

[288] A, XI, 106-107, 202; A, XIII, 236; Ap, II, 16.

[289] A, XIV, 4, 389, 487.

[290] A, XIV, 148.

[291] A, XI, 106-107.

[292] B, II, 284, 555; B, III, 339; Ap, I, 184.

[293] A, VIII, 61.

[294] A, III, 248.

which Flavius Josephus paraphrases (*Lev.* XXIII, 5 and *Deut.* XVI, 1) are not as explicit.

Finally, within my statistics there are a great many items in which one may see that Flavius Josephus uses other data of a mere historical type in relation to which he places the new event which he intends to narrate. This technique is a simplified version of the one which I have analysed in the previous point. The simple reference, therefore, to a ruler, a death, a battle, a project or undertaking, a Jewish religious institution, or a historical period (the Seleucids for instance) suffices to orientate the reader as regards the event which is to follow and to situate it within the chronological coordinates of the whole work[295].

4. *Geography*

The geography of the historical oeuvre of Flavius Josephus can be divided into two distinct parts. The first refers to the geographical realities which influence historical action. The second has the purpose of fitting historical events in a suitable setting, so that the event described appears embodied in an earthly reality. It is in this second sense that I shall analyse the data given in this section[296].

The data collected which refer to the use of geographical elements may be grouped under three headings. The first heading refers to simple geographical indications. The second heading groups together climatological data. The third heading brings together those longer descriptions which give details of the historical setting and give a special candour to the entire oeuvre.

There are, therefore, in the first place, geographical indications of the following type: "Afterwards, having passed through Pella and Scythopolis, he reached Corea, where begins the country of the Jews who go up into the interior"[297], or else: "in a village named Gema, situated on the great plain of Samaria..."[298], or again: "...Ascalon is an ancient city, five hundred and twenty stadia from Jerusalem..."[299], and again:

---

[295] B, I, 31, 70, 364, 370, 398, 401, 665; B, II, 219, 284, 457; B, III, 339, 532; B, V, 331; B, VI, 157, 269, 435; B, VII, 219, 436; A, I, 148, 171; A, II, 318; A, VII, 1, 68, 130; A, VIII, 254, 287, 312, 395; A, IX, 19, 173, 177, 184, 203, 205, 216, 260, 277, 278; A, X, 84, 87, 116, 135, 145, 195, 248; A, XI, 1, 6, 75, 79, 135, 168, 178, 325; A, XII, 246, 285, 320, 361; A, XIII, 35, 236, 304; A, XIV, 465; A, XV, 380; A, XVII, 191, 242; A, XVIII, 26, 106, 143, 238; A, XIX, 351; A, XX, 1, 34, 104, 106, 138, 145, 158, 257; Vit, 414; Ap, I, 105; Ap, II, 16.

[296] The historical use of geography as an element which may influence human action is too indicated in Chap. III, B.

[297] B, I, 134.

[298] B, II, 232. Similarly B, II, 511.

[299] B, II, 9-10.

"Vespasian, having gathered together his forces of Antioch, which is the metropolis of Syria, and because of its extension and affluence occupies third place, with no doubt, among all the cities under the sway of Rome..."[300], and also: "he ordered them to set up camp six stadia from Jerusalem, at the foot of the mount called of Olives, which lies opposite the city, towards the east, and is separated by a dividing deep torrent, called Kedron"[301].

In view of these examples, and in the face of others which provide the same tonic and variety[302], one may conclude that Flavius Josephus concieves his history as the receiver of all those geographical details which serve to situate the fact he is recording in space.

The simple listing of cities at a given moment is of less historiographic importance[303]. There is, however, a text which is fairly long and which I shall transcribe, since it may be very indicative of this manner of inserting a geographical detail within the historical event. The text says: "When Vespasian reached Alexandria..., though it is the greatest city after Rome, it is poorer in inhabitants... Vespasian lets his thoughts go to the troops he had in Judaea. All in all, he was preparing to embark for Rome, now that the winter had drawn to a close..., and he sent his son Titus with a picked force to take Jerusalem. He came first, by land, to *Nicopolis, twenty stadia distant from Alexandria*, and thence embarked his army on great ships and went *up the Nile to the nome of Mendes as far as the city of Thmuis*. There he disembarked, began to march and camped for the night by the side of *small Tanis*. The second stage was the city of *Heracleopolis*, and the third *Pelusium*... On the third day he crossed the estuary of the *river Pelusis*, and advancing another day across the desert, camped before the *temple of Casian Zeus*, and, on the following day, *at Ostracine*; this last stage was lacking in water, and the natives have water brought from outside. After he rested at *Rhinocorura* and thence advanced on to *Raphia*, the fourth stage, a city which is the very threshold of Syria; on the fifth stage, he set up camp at *Gaza*, after which he went on towards *Ascalon*, and thence, towards *Jamnea*, after to *Joppa*, and from Joppa he reached *Caesarea*, and decided to gather together in that very place the other forces"[304].

In this text, the following details can be appreciated: definite and numerous names of cities, explicit reference to the importance of the city

---

[300] B, III, 29. Similarly B, III, 34, 464; B, IV, 105.
[301] B, V, 70.
[302] B, VII, 39, 305; A, I, 170; A, II, 315; A, VI, 14, 135, 140; A, VIII, 348; A, IX, 7; A, X, 84; A, XI, 340; A, XIII, 338; Vit, 349.
[303] B, I, 156, 166; B, II, 458, 573; A, XIV, 18.
[304] B, IV, 656-663.

of Alexandria, indications of distances, mention of the end of the corresponding annual season, stages of the journey made by Titus from Alexandria to Joppa, with indications of the kind of journey (overland, across a river, through the desert) and of the limits of Syria. All of this gives the journey a fluidity which brings to mind the skill of the historian in making his own corpus for his narrative, in contrast to the various sources from which Flavius Josephus borrows.

The second section comprises the insertion of atmospherical accidents and of the climate type within the narrative. Thus, Flavius Josephus places his attention on dry climate (B, I, 298), or hot climate (B, III, 312-313, 413), on rains (B, I, 287), hail (A, II, 305), on tempests (B, I, 304, 330, 339, 343; B, III, 181-182; A, V, 205; A, XIV, 377, 461, 543), on earthquakes (B, I, 371; A, XV, 121) on winds (B, I, 413) and on pollution caused by putrefact bodies (B, III, 530). The historian makes his own all these elements which are circumstantial to historical events, and integrates them into a unity which is really dramatic. Here then, is one more attempt on the part of the historian to want to imitate nature, to want to confer cohesion on the parts.

A third section comprises the descriptions of places, cities and rivers at fair length. It is no longer simply a question of quoting the name of the city or of the place, but of enlarging on it with a brief description of its components. Thus "Joppa is not provided with a natural harbour, since it ends on a rocky coast, and all the rest is placed on a abrupt place, slightly converging at its farthest points on both sides; these are sheer scarps and jutting reefs towards the sea, where the still visible imprints of the chains of Andromeda bear witness to the ancientness of the legend. The boreal wind lashes the coast head on and dashes there the foam whipped up against the piled-up crags, and makes the port more dangerous than the desert. Against it the violent wind dashed those people of Joppa who were tossed hither and thither by it towards the dawn; "black from the north" is the name given to it by those who sail thereabouts"[305].

In this really dramatic description[306], there is a combination of methods. The description of the natural situation of Joppa is linked to a mythological reference, which gives a great deal of colouring to the whole narrative, and at the same time there is the adding of the winds and the dawn. These headings could almost be grouped with the long ecphrasis which I shall now go on to describe.

Mount Tabor is given a short, full description at a time of full war footing. The description, far from breaking the historiographic thread,

---

[305] B, III, 419-422.
[306] In the same vein, see also the fragment which continues this description.

opens a door onto the surroundings which is both pleasing and instructive for the reader. Flavius Josephus says: ''This (Mount Tabor) is in the middle, between the great plain and Scythopolis. Its height is of thirty stadia[307], hardly accessible by the northern slope, and the summit is a flat of twenty-six stadia[308], completely walled around''[309].

Description of rivers: ''And, finally, they arrived at Saba, the capital of Ethiopia... The place offers considerable difficulties for siege, since the Nile embraces it and encircles it, and other rivers, the Astapus and the Astaboras, make the crossing of the current for those who attempt it. The city, therefore, which is within rises like an island...''[310].

These details are repeated in numerous descriptions of this kind[311].

Finally, I have managed to collect four fairly extensive items which represent a veritable geographical ecphrasis within the historical narrative. All four belong to the *Bellum Judaicum*, and, in a certain sense, it may be said that this work has a greater wealth of descriptions, of cities as well as of geographical places, than I have found in the *Antiquitates Judaicae*. Thus, the Lake of Gennesar (B, III, 506-521), Gamala (B, IV, 2-10), the description of the surrounding countryside of Jericho (B, IV, 452-475) and the description of Egypt (B, IV, 607-615) cut the narrative thread, but do not distort either the preceding or following historical events, nor do they distract the reader; rather they constitute an extraordinary contribution to the historiographic picture[312].

5. *The Institutions*

In this section a study will be made of the contributions of an institutional nature which Flavius Josephus provides from time to time and in certain cases so as to make clearer or enrich the setting, or else to situate it within a real context. Thus, leaving to one side the first eleven books of the *Antiquitates Judaicae*, where Flavius Josephus is in debt to the biblical source which he paraphrases, I shall make an analysis of the principal moments when the historian quotes or analyses an institution.

In principle, ninety per cent of the institutions quoted by Flavius Josephus are of a religious nature. Thus the Jewish Passover is men-

---

[307] A mistake in numbers, it actually measures 1,312 feet from the base.

[308] In reality 3,000 feet for 1,300 feet.

[309] B, IV, 55.

[310] A, II, 249-250. As to the description of Sabbatical river, cf. B, VII, 96-99.

[311] B, I, 310, 406, 408-411, 657; B, II, 371; A, II, 18; A, III, 76; A, IV, 85; A, VI, 108; A, VIII, 186; A, XV, 96; A, XVII, 171; A, XVIII, 31, 36, 311; A, XX, 25.

[312] I also include those geographical elements in Flavius Josephus which are not to be found in the Bible: A, II, 18; A, III, 1 and 9 (enlargement); A, IV, 85 (enlargement); A, V, 205 (enlargement). The geographical ecphrases concerning Gennesaret, Jericho and Egypt are studied in Chap. II, B, 3, pp. 171-172.

tioned various times: on the occasion of the drawing up of a census in the times of Nero, under the direction of Cestius, the Roman governor of Syria[313], with the intention of checking the strength of the city; the feast of the Passover was an ideal time to carry it out. It is here that Flavius Josephus draws out his explanation: "During the Passover, sacrifices are made from the ninth hour up to the eleventh hour, in such a way that a fraternity of no fewer then ten people gather together around the sacrifice, for it is not suffered that one single person should make the sacrifice, but many gathered a score... For those who had leprosy or gonorrhoea, and women in menstruation, and those who had other impurities could not participate in this sacrifice, and a great multitude of them congregated without"[314].

This text is highly revealing as regards the historiographic use which Flavius Josephus makes of institutions. The motive of the census is a good occasion to explain each one of the details which made up the feast, and they provide a valuable contribution of institutional data.

The Feast of the Tabernacles is also mentioned, although Flavius Josephus does not offer such a detailed account as he gives for the Passover. For example, Alexander Jannaeus, king of Judaea, was pelted with lemons because the people held him in enmity, since "it is the custom amongst the Jews that each, for the feast of the Tabernacle, bear palm or lemon branches, as we have mentioned elsewhere"[315]. It is not true that he mentions lemons "elsewhere", but a different tree whose fruit is similar to the lemon[316].

As to the sabbatical year, he says: "Whilst the siege drew out for such a length of time, there arrived that year during which the Jews must remain inactive: every seven years they observe this, like the seventh day"[317].

As to resting on the sabbath there are two different formulations. He assures us that Mattathias ordered his supporters to fight even on the sabbath, since, if they observed the law, they would end up falling victims to the enemy, who would not rest on the sabbath. And Flavius Josephus adds: "With these words he did persuade them, and even to this very day endures the practice amongst us of fighting even on the sabbath, were it ever necessary"[318]. A few lines earlier, however, he explains that the

---

[313] B, VI, 422.

[314] B, VI, 423-427. In similar sense: A, XIV, 25; A, XVII, 214; A, XVIII, 29; A, XX, 106.

[315] A, XIII, 372. Other places: B, VI, 300; A, XV, 50.

[316] A, III, 245.

[317] A, XIII, 234. Similarly, A, XIV, 475.

[318] A, XII, 277. The Jews have no thought for the observance of the feast when attacking and overcoming the Roman governor Cestius (B, II, 517).

Jews would rather die than violate the sabbath, "for it is for us a norm to rest on that day"[319]. Finally, he offers another formulation of this principle: the Romans are shooting their catapults against the temple, "and if it were not amongst us a national custom to rest on the sabbath, the earthworks would not have been finished, for the Jews would have stopped them; for the Law allows us to defend ourselves against those who wage war and attack us, but allows not defence against enemies who do other things"[320]. The Romans are acquainted with the custom, and so did not attack, but devoted their efforts to mounting their war machines so as to use them the day after[321].

The military techniques of the Romans also have their place. For instance, the Romans' techniques of assault using machines are dealt with at length and in detail[322]. But the thing which for Flavius Josephus is especially deserving of attention is the marching order which the Roman army observes when on the move. So extensive and detailed is the first text, that it constitutes a historiographic ecphrasis all on its own[323]. Here I shall make comment on a shorter one.

Titus advances through Samaria as far as Gophna, a city about twenty miles distant to the north of Jerusalem: "While Titus advances towards the enemy's territory, his vanguard were the royal contingents and the whole of the allied army, after which came the road-builders and the camp-measurers. Then, the baggage-carriers of the officers and, after the escort of soldiers of the latter, the commander-in-chief with the lancers and other picked men and, after him, the cavalry of the legion. The latter marched in front of the machines, and after came the tribunes and prefects of cohort with picked men, and, after these, the standards around the eagle[324], and, in front, the trumpets and, after them, the main body of the phalanx six lines abreast. The servants of each legion came after, and, before them, the beasts of burden, and, bringing up the rear, the mercenaries and the commander of the rearguard who protected their rear. Marching the army in this order as is the custom amongst the Romans..."[325]. The description is a fine one and a complete one, and is at the same time illuminating for the readers, above all non-Roman ones. I believe that Flavius Josephus, by means of the introduction of institutions such as this, pursues a didactic end, and, more specifically in the

---

[319] A, XII, 274.
[320] A, XIV, 63.
[321] A, XIV, 64-68. Cf. its parallel in B, I, 146-148.
[322] B, IV, 19 ff.
[323] B, III, 115-126.
[324] The same may be seen in B, III, 123, regarding the order of the standards.
[325] B, V, 47-50.

case we are dealing with, undertakes the task of advertising the phenomenon of Rome.

The observations of Flavius Josephus on divorce too are enlightening, at least it provides evidence on the Jewish practice in his time: "For, amongst us, the man is allowed to do so, but a divorced woman is not allowed to re-marry on her own initiative unless the husband consents to it"[326]. On the state of marriage too he affirms that "it is an ancestral custom of ours to have various wives at the same time"[327].

A useful contribution is that of the description of the baths of hot water which Herod took at Callirrhoe, especially with regard to the reference to the use of warm oil to revitalize the weakened body of the king. He writes: "There the doctors decided to heat his whole body, enfeebled as it was, with warm oil by placing him in a bath full of it, he fainted and rolled his eyes as if dead. There were great cries from those who were treating him, and he regained his senses..."[328].

Finally, I shall quote those paragraphs which, from an institutional point of view, contribute to the enrichment of the entire historiographic corpus of Flavius Josephus. Thus we may include the election by lots of the high priest, a system which was first introduced by the Zealots (B, IV, 153); the Jews show great respect for the deceased, so that even those wrongdoers who die on the cross receive burial before the setting of the sun (B, IV, 317); the custom of heralding the sabbath with clarion calls (B, IV, 582); the triumphant entry of Titus into Rome (B, VII, 119-162); the body preserved in honey (A, XIV, 124); the respect for the temple which Herod demanded of his foreign troops (A, XIV, 482); seven days of mourning (A, XVII, 200); the Jewish law prohibiting images and the representations of animals (A, XVIII, 55; Vit, 65); the customs of the Parthians of carrying with them the images of their gods wherever they went (A, XVIII, 344) and the division of Judaea into five parts by Gabinius, which meant an aristocratic organisation of the Jewish people (A, I, 169-170).

6. *Archaeology*

In this section, I shall investigate the manner in which Flavius Josephus fixes his attention on the description of archaeological anti-quities, and also how he inserts them into the historiographical thread

---

[326] A, XV, 259. There are diverse formulations concerning the question of divorce in the Jewish world in sources contemporary with Flavius Josephus, such as the Gospels, in which the character of adultery is insisted on (*Marc.* X, 12; *Matth.* V, 32; *Luc.* XVI, 18) if they re-marry, but it is permissible for the wife also to reject (*Marc.*) the husband.

[327] A, XVII, 14.

[328] B, I, 657-658.

and what finality is eventually accorded them. The expression *ar-chaeological antiquity* is of course used from present day historical perspec-tive, not the perspective of the author, since obviously it did not hold the same meaning for him as it does for us.

Basically, there are two systems to be found here of references to ob-jects which are classifiable for us within the archaeological world: a sim-ple mention, with a certain amount of explanation, but nevertheless very brief, and the lengthy and detailed description of those sites which affect the historical action.

The two systems are to be found already in the first book of the *Bellum Judaicum*. Descriptions of cities and buildings are scant in Flavius Josephus. For instance: "having advanced as far as Samaria, where the city of Sebaste now stands, founded by king Herod..."[329]; "having heard that Aristobulus had fled to Alexandreion, one of the fastnesses prepared with greatest interest, situated high up in the mountains"[330]. As regards the other use, the temple of Jerusalem is more deserving of the historian's attention: "He (Pompey) observed the unassailable solidity of the walls and the terrible ravine before them, and the temple behind the ravine walled in such a formidable way that it were, once the city were taken, a second refuge for the enemy"[331].

In this description, attention should be drawn to the insistence on the difficulty presented by the walls together with the strategic importance of the temple, protected by nature (the precipice) and also by man.

The remaining references are much simpler, and are useful only in-sofar as they serve to indicate the existence of cities and their names or any changes in the same[332].

On the other hand, within the long description of the life of king Herod, Flavius Josephus devotes a part to the description of the building carried out on the king's orders. It is a section which refers to a king who is the builder and restorer of cities, palaces, fastnesses, temples and har-bours.

As regards the temple of Jerusalem, after indicating that he doubled its extension at enormous cost, he adds: "Evidence (of it) were the great col-umns around the temple and the fortress which, on the northern side, overlooked it, since he rebuilt them from the very foundations, and he restored the fastness with great quantities of money, so it was the palace's inferior in no way, and he named it Antonia in honour of Antonius. His

[329] B, I, 64.
[330] B, I, 134.
[331] B, I, 141.
[332] B, I, 61, 75, 77, 80, 156, 265; B, II, 168; B, III, 290.

own palace, raised in the high part of the city, comprised two buildings, the greatest and the most beautiful, with which not even the temple could compete, and he named them with the names of his friends: one, Caesareum, and the other Agrippeum"[333].

Herod founded new cities and rebuilt others. Thus "in the district of Samaria, he built a walled city with magnificent walls, some twenty stadia long, and took there six hundred colonisers, and shared out amongst them very fertile land, and in the centre of the foundation he raised a great temple, and around it he consecrated land to Caesar of a stadium and a half, and he named the city Sebaste. He conferred on its inhabitants a privileged constitution"[334].

He rebuilt the city of Anthedon, destroyed by war, and named it Agrippium, and on the door of the temple he had the name of his friend Agrippa engraved[335].

Out of filial love, he founded a city which he named Antipatris, in honour of his father "on the loveliest plain in the whole of his kingdom[336], rich in rivers and in trees"[337], and "in Jericho he founded a fortress, notable for its solidity and beauty, which he dedicated to his mother, Cypros by name"[338].

In honour of his brother Phasael, he raised a tower of the same name in the city of Jerusalem, and built the city of Phasaelis, in a valley, to the north of Jericho[339].

In addition, he was generous towards numerous cities outside his own realm. The text is detailed: "He built gymnasia at Tripolis, Damascus and Ptolemais, a wall for Byblus, halls, porticoes, temples and squares for Berytus and Tyre, theatres for Sidon and Damascus, an aqueduct for maritime Laodicea, baths, sumptuous fountains and colonnades marvellous for their architecture and proportions for Ascalon; others have sacred woods, and he made meadows there. Many cities, as associates to his realm, also received lands from him. He showered attentions on others by establishing incomes for the annual and continuous office of gymnasiarch, as at Cos, so that this honour should never disappear..., and he provided Rhodes with economic means for the building of the fleet, in many places and very often, and rebuilt in a better fashion the Pythian temple, when it burned down, with his own money... And

---

[333] B, I, 401-402.
[334] B, I, 403.
[335] B, I, 416.
[336] Ras el ʿAin, to the north-west of Joppa, on the way from Jerusalem to Caesarea.
[337] B, I, 417.
[338] B, I, 417.
[339] B, I, 418. The tower is explained in detail in B, V, 166-168.

did he not pave the main street of Antioch in Syria, which had to be
avoided because of the mud, twenty stadia long, with polished marble,
and embellished it with a colonnade of equal length as a protection
against the rains?''[340].

In honour of Augustus he raised numerous buildings, dedicated
magnificent places and consecrated temples the length and breadth of his
realm[341].

Especially deserving of the attention of the historian are the works of
refurbishing and the new buildings raised by king Herod in the city of
Caesarea[342]. He built there a magnificent harbour, "larger than that of
Piraeus"[343], successfully overcoming the difficulties presented by the
nature of that part of the coast, and surrounded it with towers[344]. He
singles out the places for the ships to dock, places for the passengers, the
northery orientation of the harbour, since the wind is much more
favourable there, the statues on columns, at the entrance, the houses and
streets of the city converging on the harbour, and the temple of the
Caesar, where a statue of the emperor stood, "in no way inferior to that
of Olympian Zeus"[345]. And he concludes: "The remainder of the works,
the amphitheatre, the theatre and public squares, were constructed in a
style worthy of its name"[346].

Finally, Herod built two fortresses which bore his name. Flavius
Josephus dwells especially on the architectural description of the second
one, situated on an artificial breast-shaped hillock, and on the out-
buildings with which he provided it[347].

The descriptions of the billeting of troops in the city of Jerusalem are a
fruitful source for the reconstruction of its archaeological layout. Thus
the three divisions were placed in three different camps, to the north of
the temple, to the south, at the side of the hippodrome, and to the east,
beside the palace[348]. The siting of troops outside an enclosed area is also a
good occasion for describing the principal cities and places of it[349].

Mentions of cities and buildings then are scattered throughout the
works of Flavius Josephus. One may therefore conclude that initially

---

[340] B, I, 422-425.
[341] B, I, 407.
[342] B, I, 408-414.
[343] B, I, 410.
[344] B, I, 411-412.
[345] B, I, 414.
[346] B, I, 415.
[347] B, I, 419-421.
[348] B, II, 44 and its parallel A, XVII, 255. Similarly B, V, 110, 134, 252-254, 259; B,
VI, 354-355.
[349] B, V, 468, 504-508.

Flavius Josephus is a valuable documentary source for gleaning knowledge of the archaeology of the ancient kingdom of Israel. Understandably so, it is the city of Jerusalem together with the temple that is the object of the most detailed description.

To bring this section to a close, therefore, I shall analyse a lengthy archaeological ecphrasis, the longest of all, which appears in book V of the *Bellum Judaicum*[350]. The special place which in his heart Flavius Josephus kept for his native city is brought to the fore when he says: "For the moment, what I have said of the city is sufficient, for I intend to publish again each thing in a more precise way"[351]. Doubtless Flavius Josephus is here referring to his work "On customs and causes", often mentioned but seemingly unfinished.

The description of Jerusalem comprises various parts: the description of the hills on which the city rested, that of the three walls, that of the towers, that of Herod's palace, that of the temple with its porticoes, courtyards, gates, façade, inner sanctuary, the *sancta sanctorum*, priests' chambers, the outer part, the altar and so on.

Contact is first made with the archaeology of Jerusalem through its topography. Modern archaeology too begins with a topographical study of the site. Flavius Josephus writes: "The city, fortified by three towers, is surrounded by unscaleable ravines, for it constituted a single enclosure. It has been raised on two hills, one in front of the other, separated by a dividing ravine, at which the houses of both the one and the other came to an end. One of the hills, the one which contains the upper citadel, is much higher, and its length was much straighter. On account of its strong position, it was therefore named by king David the Stronghold... The other, named Acra, supported the upper citadel, in a convex shape. Opposite there was a third hill, by nature lower than Acra, and cut firstly by another wide ravine. Later however, during the reign of the Hasmonaeans, they filled in the ravine intending thus to unite the city to the temple... The ravine known as that of the Cheesemakers... stretches as far as Siloam: thus we named it sweet abundant flowing fount. On the outside, the two hills of the city are surrounded by deep ravines, and it was completely inaccessible because of the steepness of both sides"[352].

As can be readily seen, this text is of inestimable value for an archaeologist. The text may serve as a very good guide to the geographical

---

[350] B, V, 136-247.
[351] B, V, 247.
[352] B, V, 136-141.

substratum of the ancient city. The description therefore brings together all the ingredients of a modern-day archaeological description. Perhaps the only thing which need be added is information of the orientation with regard to the cardinal points for the description to be complete.

The second point is given over to the description of the walls. The three walls were not all built during the same period, and the latter two correspond to successive extensions to the city following the downward slope of the land. The descriptions provide the names of the kings who built them, where they began and where they ended, their direction, the places where they neared each other, the districts of the city which they enclosed, the material used in building them and their measurements[353].

The third point goes into a study of the tower. Data are abundant: the situation, measurement, materials, rooms, the number of towers and their situation with regard to the walls. The octagonal Psephinus tower was a watch-tower whence the Antonia and the limits of Hebrew territory as far as the sea could be spied out[354].

Herod raised three towers, and named them after a friend, Hippicus, a brother, Phasael, and a wife, Mariamme.

The tower bearing Hippicus' name was square and impressive in size[355], with a cistern under cover to collect rain-water. The roof was multi-coloured and was crowned with towers and battlements; everything is provided with detailed measurements.

The second tower, named after Phasael, is also described with its measurements, its shape, with the portico which a great tower had, with sumptuous palace-like chambers. This second tower is similar to that of Pharos, but greater in diameter[356].

The third tower, Mariamme's, still unidentified by archaeology, was square according to the measurements given by Flavius Josephus, and, if the upper buildings are included, measured fifty cubits. It stood out from the rest because of its decoration and sumptuosity, as befitting a building dedicated to a lady, but not because of its solidness[357].

Flavius Josephus rounds off his description with a general view of the towers, which seem to be even more massive than they really are due to their having been built on a hill. They were constructed in white marble, so well polished and fitted together that they gave the impression of being made of a single block[358].

---

[353] B, V, 142-155.
[354] B, V, 156-160.
[355] B, V, 163.
[356] B, V, 166-169.
[357] B, V, 170-171.
[358] B, V, 172-174.

Finally, before going on to the lengthy description of the temple of Jerusalem, Flavius Josephus casts his eye over the palace of Herod. Situated within the space marked out by the towers, towards the north, this palace "is beyond all description"[359] and far higher than all other buildings. Encircled by an extremely high towered wall, it had numerous rooms and chambers for guests. The interior, built in rare stone and a wide variety of design, filled with objects of gold and silver, defies description... All around there were intercommunicating circular porticoes with different columns, pergolas, canals, all decorated with bronze statues, with many dovecotes. Unfortunately, Flavius Josephus says he cannot forget the conflagration of the malefactors, the rebels who set fire to the Antonia tower, besieged the Romans in Herod's palace, and the fire destroyed it[360].

For Flavius Josephus, the description of the temple[361] of Jerusalem is of great importance. As a priest, he was well acquainted with it. Flavius Josephus, together with the *Middoth*, the treatise of the second century A.D., is the most complete archaeological source. However, archaeologists and humanists find themselves with a series of discrepancies between Flavius Josephus, the Middoth and archaeology, which lead to the supposition of an idealised description of the temple of Jerusalem[362]. This is a problem which has no place here however, and therefore will not be touched on.

The description given by Flavius Josephus is generally accepted as the most likely one. My appreciation of this description of the temple of Jerusalem will therefore be limited, from an archaeological point of view to a general overview, without going into detail.

The descriptive sections of the temple of Jerusalem which are of value to archaeology are the following:

– the temple was added to gradually, from the time of its founder Solomon right up to the time of the historian (B, V, 184-188);

– the foundations are massive rocks; a task which seemed interminable was carried through because of the enthusiasm of the people (*id.*, 189);

– the porticoes had a special charm, due to their width and span, and above all to the columns on which they rested; they formed the first courtyard (*id.*, 190-193);

---

[359] B, V, 176.
[360] B, V, 176-183.
[361] B, V, 184-247. Cf. too A, XV, 391-425.
[362] As to this question, cf. O. Holtzmann, *Middot*, Giessen, 1913, VI, and 15-44.

– then came the second courtyard, barred to outsiders, surrounded by steps which led on to a quadrangle, and all leading up to a higher level (*id.*, 194-198);

– finally, the women's courtyard; after explaining to what extent women were allowed to participate, he adds that the west wing of the building had no gate, that the porticoes which were between the two gates were supported by marvellous columns, they were simpler but by no means inferior to those of the lower courtyard (B, V, 199-200), except for their measurements;

– the gates are described separately (B, V, 201-206). They are new gates, embossed in gold and silver, as are their uprights and lintels. Especially valuable was the Corinthian gate, in bronze, the greatest of all. The dimensions of the gates are given, with the special feature that the gate which gave access from the women's courtyard, to the east, was both larger and more richly decorated. More details of archaeological value: "Fifteen steps rose to the greatest door from the wall of the women; they were lower then the five steps of the other gates"[363].

Once at the temple, there are:

– twelve steps,

– a description and the measurements of the façade,

– gates,

– inner chambers,

– the holy veil of the temple, with decoration and symbology,

– the interior of the temple, with its measurements and objects; the *sancta sanctorum*[364].

In the lowest part of the sanctuary, there were numerous rooms on three levels, with the necessary entrances and communications. Flavius Josephus emphasises the height of the building at its highest point, and says that, although it is narrower, it reaches a hundred cubits[365].

The outer part of the temple was covered in plaques of gold, and from afar it seemed to be a snow-covered mountain. The roof was scattered with plates of gold, so that the birds should not alight on it. Some of the stones were of enormous dimensions, and the altar was huge. The sanctuary and the altar were encircled by a stone parapet which separated the people from the priests[366].

Finally, he mentions the tower and the castle which are named Antonia[367]. The historian describes it for us with all kinds of details:

---

[363] B, V, 206.
[364] B, V, 207-219.
[365] B, V, 220-221.
[366] B, V, 222-226.
[367] B, V, 238-246.

- it is situated at the angle formed by the west and north porticoes of the first courtyard;
    - built with great stones, it is enclosed by scarps and a wall;
    - it is a work of the genius of Herod;
    - the interior befits a palace;
    - the tower was furnished with four smaller towers, situated on each of the four sides; the north one was the tallest and overlooked the whole area of the temple;
    - it had communicating stairways on the side giving on to the porticoes.

With this review of the archaeology of Jerusalem, Flavius Josephus becomes the richest source of archaeological interest in the whole of antiquity.

The description of Masada, the last stronghold of Jewish resistance, at the time of being besieged by the Roman general Silva, is a geographical and archaeological ecphrasis of inestimable value[368]. I shall here analyse no more than the latter aspect.

The historical and archaeological elements which are provided by this description to the general narrative, together with the harrowing situation of the moment, can be specified in the following points:
    - historical contributions: the high priest Jonathan built the fortress and named it Masada. Later on king Herod finished it (No. 285);
    - archaeological contributions: especially as regards the works carried out by Herod. He thus walls in the summit in white stone, crowned by thirty-seven towers (No. 287), with space sufficient to stock provisions; he also builds a palace there (No. 289) to the west, north-facing with four towers, one at each corner. The interior was sumptuous; the columns of a single block (No. 290); the water supply was especially worthy of attention: numerous cisterns, both within the palace and without; an underground passage led from the palace to the top of the hill (No. 291); a great tower was placed on the part open to the west, less than a thousand cubits distant from the summit (No. 293). The stores had supplies sufficient to resist for many years (No. 296); arms there were too for ten thousand men (No. 299).

7. Wars

Among the many elements with which the historian has to contend with there is the war element. Wars, as an activity which is inherent to

---

[368] B, VII, 280-303. Cf. geographical and geological questions in Chap. II, A, 4. Herod built this unrivalled fortress out of fear of the Jews and of the intentions of queen Cleopatra (Nos. 300-303).

man, are absent from no history whether ancient or modern. It becomes
a natural situation in the development of peoples and minority communities. It is in this spirit that Flavius Josephus deals with wars and the
elements of which they are composed. Nonetheless, this still has to be
demonstrated.

Before going on to the main points, I should like to point out that
Flavius Josephus devotes the entirety of one of his books to an analysis of
the war of Jerusalem, the *Bellum Judaicum.* It is a large-scale war, full of
innumerable battles. Since the theme of this war has already been dealt
with *in extenso* from an aetiological viewpoint[369], and so to avoid repetition
of facts already mentioned, here I shall not analyse it from the angle of
component elements. Therefore, let a mention of the component items
suffice, in note 369. Nonetheless, an analysis will be made of the remaining war material which is to be found, though having very inferior
historiographic qualities when compared with those which appear in the
war of Jerusalem, in the extensive work of Flavius Josephus, following a
chronological order.

The whole of the *Bellum Judaicum* is interwoven with violent actions:
the rhythm of violence in it appears to quicken in *crescendo*, and it reaches
its climax with the description of the fall of Jerusalem. An atmosphere of
tension permeates the work, and drama is to be found on every page. The
historian goes to great lengths to confer on his work the purifying traits of
drama. In the same war spirit, the *Antiquitates Judaicae* exude a different
atmosphere, since there is no attempt in them to describe a great conflagration around which the whole work revolves, but rather the life and
evolution of the Jewish people. Wars and all war material are therefore
political events which are included within the lives of rulers and of
peoples.

The deeds of Alexander Jannaeus are set out in a very schematic way,
and at times the historian simply records the names of cities captured (B,
I, 86-87). During the twenty-seven years of his reign, Alexander had to
put down the uprisings of the Jews against him, had to fight against Antiochus XII Dionysus (86-85 B.C.) and Aretas, king of the Nabataean
Arabs, and conquered several cities of Gaulanitis (B, I, 104-105).

The uprisings of the Jews find a propitious moment in the occasion of
the religious feasts, "for it is above all in their festivals that sedition takes
place"[370]. After killing six thousand of their number, he directed his ef-

---

[369] Chap. I, B, 1 (downfall of Jerusalem) and Chap. I, B, 2 (concerning the wars of the
Jewish people). As for the war of Jerusalem, see B, IV, 193-584, 658-663; B, V, 1-135,
248-572; B, VI, 1-408.

[370] B, I, 88.

forts towards the Arab countries where he subdued some peoples and imposed tributes on them (B, I, 89). Vanquished later on by Obedas, king
of Arabia, his subjects rebelled. In six years he killed fifty thousand
Jews, but even thus the Jews did not bow to him and requested aid from
Demetrius III, king of Syria[371]. The Jews go out to meet the army of
Demetrius, their ally, near Sichem. All told, the army was made up of
three thousand horsemen and fourteen thousand foot soldiers as against
the one thousand horsemen and eight thousand mercenary infantry of
Alexander. The war follows a ritual. Firstly both enemies carry on a
"cold" battle: by means of heralds, they join battle in the form of propaganda designed to win over deserters from both camps. However,
the Jews neither let themselves be taken in, nor do the Greek mercenaries renege on their fidelity. Thus, "they determined to force an
outcome by hurling themselves into the fray with their arms"[372].
Demetrius is the victor. Even so, the historian attempts to disconcert,
and adds that the outcome of the battle was quite different, "because
they did not remain with Demetrius, though he was the victor, those who
had acclaimed him, and, through compassion because of the change, six
thousand Jews passed over to the side of Alexander, who had fled to the
hills"[373].

Antiochus XII Dionysus, brother of Demetrius, undertook a campaign
against the Arabs, and Alexander, in alarm, placed obstacles in his path
through his territory. Even so, Antiochus overcomes the obstacles and
goes on to the encounter with the Arabs. A description which is rich in
detail is not to be found here either: the Arabs retreat to more favourable
ground, launch a surprise attack on the army of Antiochus, "and it
became a violent battle"[374]. Antiochus falls, and the whole army is
dismembered, and the majority dead on the battlefield; others, during
the flight, take refuge in Cana, but almost all of them starve to death[375].

Alexander cannot as yet rest from the wars, because Aretas, when succeeding Antiochus II of Syria, begins a campaign against Judaea[376],
defeats Alexander, and strikes a treaty. Then, and for three years, Alexander turned to the conquest of many other cities, and, covetous of the
treasures of Theodorus, blockades Gerasa "with a triple line of walls,

---

[371] B, I, 92-95.
[372] B, I, 94.
[373] B, I, 95.
[374] B, I, 101.
[375] B, I, 99-102.
[376] B, I, 103.

and takes the place without a battle''[377]; there too the historian lists a number of other conquests in Transjordan[378].

The narrative development of these battles is simple but complete. In the first, it is well established that Demetrius undertakes the campaign against Alexander at the invitation of the Jews themselves, who have their reasons: the criminal treatment which Alexander exercises over his subjects. So much for the introduction. Straightway comes the body of the battle, made up by varied elements. Finally, the conclusion: the Jews who have rebelled return to the obedience of their king.

The historian gives no clue as to the causes of the battle between Antiochus and the Arabs. There is therefore no preliminary part. We are given no more than the central body of the narrative and the conclusion, with a profusion of detail.

With regard to the other conquests and when the historian makes no mention of causes, then one must inevitably think that military exploits are a result of the expansionist imperatives of peoples. In the parallel passages in the *Antiquitates Judaicae*[379] which correspond to the war exploits of Alexander, the historian dwells only on those which refer to the conquests of cities, which are quoted very briefly in the *Bellum Judaicum*. The remaining campaigns are dealt with in a very similar manner and with no variants.

With reference to the attacks on the cities of the coast of Syria, Flavius Josephus says that Ptolemais, Gaza, Strato's Tower[380] and Dora were the only cities which did not come under the sway of Alexander. At the same time however, Antiochus VIII Philometor and Antiochus IX Cyzicenus were fighting, and for that reason could offer no help to Ptolemais, which was then being besieged by Alexander. Then however Zoilus, the ruler of Dora, appears on the scene, whose ambition it was to become absolute ruler by taking advantage of the war between the two Syrian kings, and offers token aid to the people of Ptolemais. The people of Ptolemais appeal to Ptolemy Lathyrus, ruler of Cyprus. In spite of his being informed of the change of heart of the people of Ptolemais, Ptolemy shows up with his army. Zoilus denounces the attacks of Alexander to him, and Alexander, through fear, raises the siege and returns home. Alexander tries to pact with Ptolemy, but through betrayal, which is the cause of the invasion of Judaea by Ptolemy. It is at this moment when Flavius Josephus is more explicit in his manner of describing battles.

---

[377] B, I, 104.
[378] B, I, 105.
[379] A, XIII, 324-364.
[380] The future Caesarea.

So far everything has been by way of introduction, with a concatenation of causes which lead to a great battle. Alexander goes out to meet with his enemy near the Jordan, at Asophon. First element: the geography. He led eight thousand front-line soldiers, bearing long bronze-clad shields. Ptolemy too had soldiers of this type, but was less cautious at times of danger[381]. The second element: military strength. Philostephanus the tactician had not quite managed to rally the soldiers before ordering them to cross the river which separated the two armies; Alexander did not order the crossing, preferring to await the enemy, who would then be obstructed by the river if it came to a retreat. The third element: tactical traits.

Battle is joined: "At the beginning, therefore, there were similar deeds of courage and daring on the part of both armies, and there was a great slaughter done by both armies, but since those of Alexander were superior in number, Philostephanus divided his force and skilfully aided those who were giving ground. Since no-one came to the aid of the Jews who were gradually being worn down, it so passed that they were forced to flee, and neither did they receive any aid from those on their side, but rather the latter joined them in flight, but the men of Ptolemy did quite the opposite, for they pursued the Jews and killed them, and, at the end, they pursued all those who had taken flight and killed them, until their swords became weakened with so many deaths and their hands could no more"[382]. The fourth element: dramatic description.

The conclusion to the scene comprises a reference to the number of soldiers who have fallen, to the number of prisoners taken, and to the number of fugitives.

The military scenes throughout the first and second books of the *Bellum Judaicum* fall within the class of austere descriptions which may be seen in the majority of biblical war scenes. Even so, the wars of Herod against the Arabs deserve analysis[383]. In this case, I shall proceed by making a comparison of both treatments, as presented by the historian. I shall give a summary of the description and translate the most significant points:

Bellum Judaicum	*Antiquitates Judaicae*
	Malcus, the Nabataean Arab king, tries to avoid paying the tribute of two hundred talents to Cleopatra, and Herod was in charge of exacting it.

---

[381] A, XIII, 339.
[382] A, XIII, 341-343.
[383] B, I, 364-385 is parallel to A, XV, 108-160.

At the beginning of the battle of Actium, Herod prepared an army for Antonius, now that Judaea was enjoying peace.

Cleopatra, whose intention it was to hold sway over Herod, persuades Antonius to charge Herod with the war against the Arabs, in the hope of becoming lady of Arabia and of Judaea.

"At the beginning, he retaliated against the enemy, and, since he had enlisted a great number of cavalry, he sent them against the enemy in the outskirts of Diospolis, and was victorious, in spite of the strong resistance"[385].

Herod prepares to attack, a second time, the Arabs gathered at Canatha, preparing the operation with great care and fortifying the camp. His orders, however, were not heeded, and the soldiers, confident because of their last victory, hurled themselves against the Arabs (No. 367).

At the outset the Arabs fled, but when they saw Herod attacked by the natives of Canatha who were instigated by Athenion, Cleopatra's general and an enemy of Herod, they returned and, after regrouping in a rocky place, attacked the Jews, and did great killing amongst them. The fugitive Jews took refuge in Ormiza, but the Arabs besieged them and annihilated them (No. 368). Shortly afterwards arrived Herod with help, but it was already too late.

Herod, therefore, prepares to attack him, but the battle of Actium delays him (Nos. 108-109). The battle of Actium took place in the 187th Olympiad, between Caesar and Antonius[384].

Herod prepares an army for Antonius (No. 109), who refuses it, and orders him to launch an attack on the disloyal Arab king (No. 110). Cleopatra asked for this, since she believed that in this way both Herod and Malcus would weaken each other.

Herod gathered together his army, provided it with cavalry and infantry, and headed for Diospolis.

"The Jews were victorious, after a violent battle"[386].

The Arabs met at Canatha. Herod decided to set up camp in a favourable place and raise a stockade. While he was giving orders for this to be done, the victors of the first battle, believing their organisation to be already a good one, asked him to lead them with no delay against the Arabs. In view of their shouts and their daring, the king thought to derive benefit therefrom, and armed himself and led them (Nos. 112-114).

The Arabs fled in consternation, although they had offered resistance. All would have died if Athenion, Cleopatra's general, in command of the troops there and an enemy of Herod, had not attacked the king. Althenion had intended to attack Herod were the Arabs to lose. Athenion fell suddenly on the Jews, and inflicted many losses. Meanwhile, the Arabs recovered and also caused a great many deaths. A few Jews escaped back to their camp. Herod tried to send them aid, but arrived too late: and the Jewish camp was taken.

---

[384] All the details appear in Flavius Josephus.
[385] B, I, 366.
[386] A, XV, 111.

"The reason for this calamity which befell him was the disobedience of the officers, for, if the rash attack had not taken place, then Athenion would not have had occasion for his plan"[387].

"Herod took his revenge straight away on the Arabs by constantly plundering their country, so as to remind them many times of their only victory"[388].

"Henceforth, Herod devoted himself to plundering, and, by dint of many sackings, devastated the territory of the Arabs with his raids, camping in the mountains, and always avoiding combat in the open, and, although he did not emerge unscathed because of the frequency of the incursions and his activity, he nevertheless took care of his men, making good all hurts by any means"[389].

While Herod was occupied in these affairs, and during the battle of Actium, there was an earthquake in Judaea which sowed panic amongst the population. The army was not affected since it lived in the open air. Then the Arabs recovered, and, thinking to take over a resistance-less Judaea, killed the Jewish emissaries and brought invasion closer. So demoralised were the Jewish people in the face of their immediate plight and the Arab attack, that Herod had to gather them together and talk to them. Flavius Josephus propounds the objectives of the speech in a different way according to the version:

"Herod strove to stimulate them to defence, by saying"[390].

"The king tried to convince the commanders with his words and to raise their fallen spirits. Having stirred and encouraged some of the best men, he now adventured to address himself to the majority, at first hesitatingly, for fear of causing harshness on account of the setbacks"[391].

The contents of the speeches, which are analysed elsewhere[392], obtained results which the historian does not allow to go by without a mention. Thus Flavius Josephus notes that:

---

[387] B, I, 369.
[388] B, I, 369.
[389] A, XV, 120.
[390] B, I, 372.
[391] A, XV, 126.
[392] Chap. II, A, 2a (pp. 102-103 and 107-108).

Herod, with his words, revived the flagging spirit of his army, saw its fervour, offered a sacrifice to God and, crossing the Jordan, camped at Philadelphia, near the enemy.

He began an attack on a fort which was between the two forces. The Arabs took themselves there, and Herod defeated them and took the hill.

Herod daily provoked the Arabs to attack. On receiving no response, since they had fallen victims to great consternation, Herod destroyed their stockades.

The enemy were forced into attacking, but they did so in a very inefficient manner. They offered only token resistance and, in their flight, many of them died at the hands of the Jews or were trampled underfoot by their own kind, five thousand in number.

Others took refuge in the camp, and Herod besieged them, but they, for lack of water, surrendered to him. The king showed contempt for the emissaries, in spite of the offer of five hundred talents.

With the speech[393], the Jews revived. Herod made the customary sacrifices and, quickly, marched against the Arabs, crossed the Jordan and camped near the enemy.

Herod intended to storm the fort which was between them, for it would be useful to him in the case of joining battle, and, if a retreat were necessary, it would serve him as a fortified camp. At the beginning he simply provoked them, until the Arabs attacked, but then fled in defeat. This contributed to the raising of the hopes of the Jews, and Herod, "considering that their forces would prefer anything to joining battle[394], began the more boldly the destruction of their stockade and to approach the camp so as to attack it".

Forced into it, the Arabs attacked in disarray and with little spirit for victory. They fought hand-to-hand, because they were many and necessity made them be daring. There was a hard battle, and many died on both sides. Finally, the Arabs fled, many of them dying along the way at the hands of the Jews and were trampled underfoot by the fleeing multitude, five thousand in number.

The remainder managed to reach their camp, without the Jews being able to enter therein with them. The latter laid siege, so as to impede any entry into or exit from the camp. The Arabs sent an ambassador with the intention of parleying so as to achieve a temporary reprieve, for the lack of water was pressing hard on them. Herod refused the envoys and the ransom for the prisoners, "for he intended to have his revenge on them for the crimes they had committed against them"[395]. Hard-pressed by difficulties, especially thirst, the Arabs surrendered.

---

[393] The narrativa of the *Antiquitates Judaicae* is a very faithful reproduction of that of the *Bellum Judaicum*, with improvements and enlargements. I shall mention both the most outstanding points and the differences: B, I, 380-385 = A, XV, 147-160.

[394] A, XV, 150.

[395] A, XV, 156.

In five days, four thousand Arabs surrendered to the Jews. The seven thousand who still resisted were killed by Herod.

In five days, four thousand surrendered, of the besieged, when, on the sixth day, the Arabs determined to attack rather than die without glory. They could not resist the force of the war, ''considering it a victory to die and a disgrace to live, and, in the terrible battle that followed, some seven thousand fell''[396].

He punished Arabia, and broke the spirit of its inhabitants, and so he won himself great renown, so that Herod was chosen protector of the Arab nation[397].

This defeat did away with all the confidence which the Arabs had had at the beginning. Then the Arabs, admiring the military qualities shown by Herod in the midst of his own reverses, submitted to him and proclaimed him protector of their nation[398].

This comparative analysis of the two narratives with regard to the war facet in the life of king Herod presents, along general lines, a tendency towards austerity in detail and a will to create a solid structure based on:
   – chronological references,
   – geographical data, corroborated by modern archaeology,
   – definite historical figures (Cleopatra),
   – historiographic causes,
   – intellectual reflexions of the actors in history when in the face of difficulties, and
   – its dramatic character, with the use of speeches and emphasis at given moments.

Without any doubt, the treatment given in the *Antiquitates Judaicae* is more extensive and richer in details, the aetiology provides a basis for the various situations, and the personalities and groups in history operate with reasonings which are previous to any action. Even so, there is one point which appears in the *Bellum Judaicum* (but not in the *Antiquitates Judaicae*) which should be appraised: it is that which refers to the defeat of Herod which is brought about by the disobedience of his officers, by launching an attack which had not been properly prepared (B, I, 369).

Book III of the *Bellum Judaicum* is dominated by the war around the city of Jotapata[399]. This event has no parallel in the *Antiquitates Judaicae*. In general terms, the following structure can be given: Jotapata, a town in

---

[396] A, XV, 158.
[397] B, I, 380-385.
[398] A, XV, 147-160.
[399] B, III, 110-114, 141-288, 316-339.

Galilee, is attacked by Placidus, the Roman tribune (B, III, 111-114),
and is destroyed by Vespasian (*id.*, 141-288, 316-339).

As to the first point, the historian notes that Placidus, after causing
many deaths in Galilee, "observed that the army against which he was
fighting always took refuge in the cities fortified by Josephus, and
marched against the most formidable of them all, Jotapata"[400]. Here
then we have an immediate cause for the beginnings of hostilities.
Placidus, what is more, carries out his reasonings—οἰόμενος—, with the
aim of capturing Jotapata by a surprise attack, something which would
bring him great renown and a considerable advantage for the future campaign, since, with the fall of the strongest city, the others would be forced
to submit. However the people of Jotapata had been forewarned, and,
encouraged by the defence of their homeland, of their wives and children,
they put the Romans to flight, wounding a great number, but causing
only seven deaths, because the Romans retreated in good order and were
well protected. Those within Jotapata, therefore, were careful to maintain their distance and to avoid hand-to-hand fighting on account of the
weakness of their equipment; they suffered three dead and a few wounded. Placidus withdraws[401].

In this first point, Flavius Josephus does not go into the details of the
struggle, but what he does do is to specify the cause which pushed
Placidus to hostilities; he gives detailed insight into his aspirations and into the consequences of the taking of the city in the immediate future; he
then goes into the field of the practice of war, and also gives detailed insight into the spirits of the defenders of the city: πρὸς μάχην ἕτοιμοι and
πρόθυμοι. Finally, the aftermath of battle: number of casualties on both
sides, with the respective causes.

Then Flavius Josephus goes into a detailed description of Roman
military discipline on the battle field[402]. Vespasian calls his forces to a
halt in front of the enemy, so as to intimidate them and make them
desert. At the same time he makes preparations for siege. Expectations
are fulfilled: many begin to regret the uprising, all are filled with
alarm[403]. Then the troops of Flavius Josephus desert him; he finds
himself with very depleted numbers, sees low morale in his men, most of
whom want to capitulate. Flavius Josephus seeks refuge in Tiberias.
Straightway, Vespasian takes Gabara and destroys it. Flavius Josephus
asks Jerusalem for instructions.

---

[400] B, III, 111.
[401] B, III, 111-114.
[402] B, III, 115-126. It is an institutional ecphrasis.
[403] B, III, 127.

The campaign against Jotapata begins[404]. Vespasian is impatient to destroy Jotapata. Motives: it is a refuge for enemies, it is a strong base, and its fall may mean the capture of the whole of Judaea. Vespasian orders some soldiers to prepare a road for the passage of the army, a task which is carried out in four days. Date: 8th June, in the year 67 A.D. Flavius Josephus reaches Jotapata, and his presence raises the spirits of the Jews. Intervening of the transcendent world in the human plane: a Jewish deserter informs of the arrival of Flavius Josephus at Jotapata and advises Vespasian to attack the city without delay, since the capture of it may mean the capture of the whole of Judaea; all this is received as message of good fortune, as if a divine order had shown that that very man who was considered to be the shrewdest of enemies had walked into a prison. Response: Vespasian sends a thousand cavalry to surround the city and to warn Flavius Josephus of the futility of secret flight.

On the following day (B, III, 145), Vespasian arrives at Jotapata, makes camp on a hill so as to be seen by the enemy and to intimidate them. Flavius Josephus himself remarks that "so great was the immediate terror which took hold of the Jews, that not one of them dared to show himself in front of the wall"[405]. Vespasian, seeing that he cannot attack that same day, encircles the city with a double rank of infantry and with a third rank of cavalry. He thus cuts off all the avenues of escape, but at the same time this was a stimulus to the Jews, "for nothing is there in war which fights better than necessity"[406].

On the following day comes the first attack. The paragraphs[407] which Flavius Josephus uses to describe the first hostile encounter form a perfect architectural backdrop. Let us see:

A. The beginning:

– the Romans come up against the Jews who are encamped outside the walls;

– Vespasian sends in his archers, slingers and all his marksmen;

– Vespasian together with his cavalry places himself opposite a weak point in the wall.

B. Reaction from the Jews is not long in coming:

– Flavius Josephus, in fright, comes out with the whole multitude of the Jews;

– the Jews force the Romans back from the walls and demonstrate their daring.

---

[404] B, III, 141-339.
[405] B, III, 147.
[406] B, III, 149.
[407] B, III, 150-154.

C. Flavius Josephus makes an evaluation of both factions by means of comparison:

– the Jews suffered greater casualties than they inflicted,

– ''for as much as despair of all salvation struck them, no less so shame the Romans, and experience with force armed the ones, whereas confidence the others, who fought with courage''[408].

D. Flavius Josephus brings the episode to a close with two points, a chronological one and a list of casualties:

– the battle lasted the whole day long, and only night separated the combatants;

– thirteen Roman dead and many wounded / seventeen Jewish dead and six hundred wounded.

The six days which followed carried on in the same pattern as the first day. Flavius Josephus brings the narrative to a close again with a comparison: ''Neither did the Jews have the strength of their enemy, nor did the Romans lose heart when confronted with the difficulty of taking the city''[409].

Then comes a descriptive ecphrasis of the impregnability of the city of Jotapata, so as to lend support to the idea of the difficulty of taking it— δυσάλωτον—which has just been expressed. Therefore the ecphrasis has a very real historiographic reason[410], since the strategic difficulties are in direct relation to the natural defences provided by its geographical position, and military tactics have to be planned out according to its dictates. The movements which Vespasian ordered his army to carry out were therefore conditioned by the privileged position of the city:

''Vespasian, fighting against the nature of the site and the daring of the Jews, decided to carry on the siege with greater vigour, and summoned his officers so as to deliberate on the attack''[411]. He orders earthworks to be raised against that part of the wall which was accessible and all the necessary material to be deployed. The mountains were plundered and enormous quantities of stones were piled up. Work distribution: some soldiers stood guard over those working in the temple, others brought the earth. While work was going on, the Jews throw all manner of objects against the Romans. This event has a certain dramatic touch in the eyes of the historian: ''Though they did not touch them, they made a great and terrifying noise which brought difficulties to those who were working''[412].

---

[408] B, III, 153.
[409] B, III, 155-157.
[410] B, III, 158-160. Cf. Chap. II, B, 3 (p. 170).
[411] B, III, 161.
[412] B, III, 165.

Vespasian then orders his artillery into action (160 war machines). A detailed dramatic description: lance-throwing catapults, stones the weight of a talent and fire, Arab archers and slingers support the attack. A response is not long in coming from the Jewish side: sorties in the form of raiding-parties destroy the defences set up to protect the workers on the embankment and all the works already carried out. Vespasian realised that it was necessary to bring his troops nearer so as to protect the earth-work workers.

But the first great Jewish offensive comes as a result of the personal ingenuity of Flavius Josephus, and was not due to any war machines, since they had none. Since the embankment which the Romans were raising had already reached the height of the wall, Flavius Josephus ordered the walls to be raised and various towers and parapets to be built, together with ingenious means of defence against the Roman bombardment. The Romans lost heart "when confronted with the inventiveness of Flavius Josephus and with the perseverence of the citizens"[413]. The Jewish attacks in the form of raiding parties redoubled, and caused great damage to the Romans. Then Vespasian determines to blockade the city and to starve it into submission[414].

The city was well-provisioned with everything except salt, and water was what it was most lacking in. The Romans were not ignorant of the situation of the Jews as regarded this lack of water. Then Flavius Josephus orders clothes soaked in water to be hung out over the wall, so that the Romans, on seeing that extraordinary squandering of water, should think that the Jews had a plentiful supply of it. The strategem worked: the Romans went back to armed attack, which is what the Jews wanted, since they preferred death in battle to death by hunger or thirst. In these circumstances Flavius Josephus manages to send messengers out of the city, by means of a ravine unknown to the Romans, covered with pelts so that, by night, they should be mistaken for dogs[415].

In this point, the narration relates the events in the Jewish camp. Flavius Josephus considers that if he were to leave the city, then the Romans would relent in their attacks and he would be able to gather together reinforcements in Galilee. The people of Jotapata are reluctant to let him go and beg him to stay. The whole scene is structured on the basis of a dialogue or speech, in which both sides express their reasons: they so that he should stay, and he so as to leave. The despair of the citizens, the intense dialogue and the negative vision which Flavius

---

[413] B, III, 175.
[414] B, III, 176.
[415] B, III, 190-192.

Josephus has of the future of the city all achieve the creation of an atmosphere of dramatic density, which gives rise to resolutions which are both heroic and tragic, expressed in the concluding words, in direct speech, whereas the entirety of the long previous part has been transcribed in indirect speech: "Now is the time to join battle, when there is no hope of salvation; it is a magnificent gesture to lay down one's life in exchange for glory, and that one should fall in the wake of a noble act which may be remembered in posterity"[416]. And, for various days and various nights the Jews carried on with their sorties as far as the Roman camp.

Yet again does the historian find himself in the obligation of recurring to comparison of the two sides, so as to lend support to the successful final attacks of the Jews. On the one hand, a comparison of tactics: the Romans are not swift in attack since their capacity of reaction is conditioned by the heavy arms they use; the Jews, in contrast, effect short sorties and return to the city. On the other hand, a moral comparison: Vespasian prohibits any major engagement with the enemy, who is now looking death in the face, since there is nothing more invincible than desperation; the Romans, in contrast, wage war not out of necessity but to increase their empire.

The siege and the Jewish lightning sorties constitute a situation which was untenable for Vespasian, since the effect was of he himself being besieged[417]. Then Vespasian orders the battering ram to be used on the wall. Flavius Josephus takes advantage of this occasion to describe this Roman military machine, greatly prized by them[418]. What is more, the Romans bring up their entire artillery and personnel, and the ram begins its work. A dramatic trait: "At the first blow the wall shook, and there arose a great wailing from those who were within, as if they had already been made prisoners"[419]. Jewish reaction: Flavius Josephus orders sacks of straw to be lowered to the place where the ram is battering. This is a serious setback for the Romans, who then work out a system for cutting the ropes from which the sacks hung. When the ram began its work again, the Jews resorted to a new weapon: fire. Dry wood, soaked in tar and pitch, had set fire in one hour to all the work which had cost the Romans so much effort.

Flavius Josephus also directs his attention to the heroic deeds of those on his side. Thus a Jewish hero, Eleazar son of Sameas, a native of Saba of Galilee, manages to break the head of the ram by hurling a heavy rock

[416] B, III, 204.
[417] B, III, 213: personal opinion of the historian.
[418] B, III, 214-218.
[419] B, III, 221.

at it. In the midst of the Roman enemy, he picks up the iron head, scales the wall, and displays it to all as a sign of his courage. Straightway he falls with the ram as a result of his injuries. The brothers Netiras and Philip, also Galileans from Ruma, both excelled in heroic deeds. Penetrating into the tenth legion, they sowed confusion[420].

Flavius Josephus then begins another offensive. The machines, shields and embankments of the fifth and tenth legions are burned. The Romans repair the ram and take up the battering once more. Just then Vespasian receives a chest wound, something which creates a certain amount of consternation in the Roman ranks. Dramatic traits: "Confronted with blood, those who were near were dismayed, and the news spread quickly throughout the army, and the majority of the soldiers, giving up the siege, ran towards their general in consternation and fear. The first of all was Titus, fearful for his father, so that the multitude was agitated by the affection they had for their guide and by the anguish of the son. With ease did the father calm the fear-filled son and the tumult of the army"[421]. Vespasian overcame his pain, showed himself to the army, who then went back into the fray with redoubled enthusiasm.

The beginnings of the weakening of the Jewish forces. From paragraph 240 onwards, the Jewish army begins to show signs of tiredness as well as many casualties. Physical and moral strength are debilitated. The fatal effects of the Roman machines are irreversible. Here too drama has its place: "The ones with the others, bodies thudded when falling at the wall, and, within, a terrible wailing of women arose, and the groans of those who were dying without resounded. All along the front-line perimeter of the battle there was a river of blood, and the wall became scaleable due to the mound of fallen bodies. The surrounding mountains made the wailing all the more terrible, and, that night, nothing was left that did not shock the ear or eye"[422]. However, in the long run, the wall gives way to the blows of the ram, and the besieged defend the breach with weapons and their own bodies.

Early in the morning, the wall was to be scaled and the city entered. This delicate moment is presented by the historian in two comparative sections. Firstly he presents the deployment of troops as ordered by Vespasian, and then the positions of the troops of Flavius Josephus. Then the terror of the women and children at the sight of the Roman troops (B, III, 253-263).

---

[420] B, III, 229-233.
[421] B, III, 237.
[422] B, III, 248.

Vespasian redistributes his forces:

– aim: to force the defenders back from the breach made by them in the wall;

– means: he deploys the élite of his cavalry in three divisions in front of the ruins of the wall in full armour, so as to be the first to enter the city, when the ladders are in place; then, the infantry; the remainder of the cavalry, in the mountains, so as to catch any escapees; in the rearguard and in a semicircle, the archers, slingers and the artillery. Then he ordered the ladders to be placed against that part of the wall which was still intact.

Flavius Josephus, seeing his intentions, reacts in the following manner:

a. he entrusts the defence of the intact section of the wall to the tired and the aged (No. 258);

b. in the breach he places the most vigorous men, at the head of whom he collocates groups of six men, chosen by lot, and among whom he himself is numbered (No. 258);

c. he advises his men not to heed the war cries which the Roman legions were wont to give (No. 259);

d. he advises them to avoid volleys by covering their bodies, ducking, giving a little ground until the archers should empty their quivers (No. 259);

e. when the Romans have placed their ladders, they must hurl themselves against the enemy with all the means they have at their disposal (No. 260).

But there is a third element which has its role in all city warfare: the non-combatants (i.e. the women and children). For the historian, the time has come to give a dramatic touch to his narrative. The commotion and fright of the multitude is expressed in a very specific way: when they saw the triple cordon of Romans around the city, the enemy with sword in hand, the mountain-tops glittering with weapons, the Arab archers aiming at the city, "they released a wailing, the final one, of capture, as if the catastrophe were not still imminent, but already a reality"[423]. Flavius Josephus had to order them back to their homes, for fear of disheartening the combatants. He took his place, paid no attention to those who were putting the ladders in place, and waited for the whistle of the arrows.

The detailed description of these three historiographic actors and the great thoroughness of the preparations on both sides give the impression that this is going to be the final, decisive encounter.

---

[423] B, III, 262.

The trumpets of all the legions blare, a blood-curdling cry goes up, and missiles fill the air and cut off the light. The comrades of Flavius Josephus, impassive, will attack only when the ramps have been placed in position; there is hand-to-hand fighting. Comparisons: the Jews demonstrate their courage, no less than the Romans, who also fight bravely, but for very different interests from their own; the Jews receive neither reinforcements nor replacements, and therefore are exhausted; the Romans, when tiring, in contrast, are replaced by fresh troops and reinforcements. But the *testudo* formation of the Romans overcomes the resistance of the Jews, and the ascent up the ramps begins[424].

In this critical situation, ἐν ταῖς ἀμηχανίαις (B, III, 271), Flavius Josephus orders boiling oil to be poured on top of the advancing *testudo* formation. Results: the Roman formation is broken, and the soldiers fall down the ramps head-over-heels. Here Flavius Josephus makes an effort to bring out the dramatic qualities of the situation, by explaining all the details which may have any bearing on it: the characteristics of the oil; the oil seeps in through the armour, burning flesh from head to toe; the victims, with shields and armour, cannot escape from the effects of the boiling oil and leap off the ramps; those who are burned and try to retreat find their way blocked by the compact formation of their comrades.

Another comparison has its place at this moment: the Romans are not abandoned by fortitude, but neither are the Jews lacking in ingenuity; the former, even though they see their comrades burned, carry on with their advance; the latter invent yet another strategy: they threw boiled fenugreek over the ramps, so that no one could stand upright due to its slipperiness.

Chronological data: towards evening, the Romans withdraw. This battle took place on the twentieth day of the month of Daesius[425].

Final appraisal: the Romans suffered many dead and even more wounded, the defenders of Jotapata lost and recovered only three hundred wounded.

The paragraphs from 283 to 288 constitute a summary of events on the days immediately following. It is not clear how many days the reconstruction of the whole Roman military apparatus lasted. What does seem to be certain is that Jotapata fell on the 20th July. Therefore, the last attack took place during these twelve days of difference and with it an end to the hostilities.

Vespasian, therefore, on seeing the readiness of his soldiers to go into action, orders embankments to be thrown up and fortified, and three

---

[424] B, III, 270.
[425] B, III, 280 and 282: the date falls on the 8th July, in the year 67 A.D.

towers to be built, fifty feet high and completely iron-clad, and has them placed on the embankments, supplying them with light artillery, archers and slingers. In the face of this irresistible onslaught, unassailable by the Jews, the latter abandon the wall and devote themselves to making sorties to attack those who are attempting to scale the wall.

Thus it was that Jotapata, day after day, gradually lost its defenders until none were left. At this moment, the description of the military events at Jotapata are interrupted by the introduction of another description about the taking of Japha by Trajan and Titus[426], but which I shall not analyse.

By the forty-seventh day of the siege, the Roman embankments were higher than the walls. On the same day, a Jewish deserter informed Vespasian of the small number of defenders and the state of the defences, and that, in view of the exhaustion of their strength, they would be hard put to resist a coordinated attack. Thus, he advises the attack to be made at the last watch, when the sentries give themselves over to rest.

Vespasian, distrusting the deserter, since he himself was well acquainted with the loyalty of the Jews to each other, as well as their indifference towards punishment, ordered him to be placed in custody, and made ready to storm the city[427].

The final attack. At the appointed time, they advance in silence towards the walls. The first to climb was Titus, together with Sabinus, followed by a few men of the fifteenth legion. They killed the sentries and entered the city. Sextus and Placidus also entered with their troops. The city was taken by the first light of day, without the inhabitants realising it. The historian is given over to a dramatic vision of the reality: "The majority of them were lost in weariness or sleep, and a thick mist covered the eyes of those who were awakening, by chance when it encircled the city, until the entire army had spread out, they arose to see only their misfortune and they believed that they had seen their downfall come"[428]. The Romans, recalling their sufferings throughout the siege, carried out a general massacre. Others died in the ravines, others committed suicide rather than fall into the hands of the Romans to die.

Some of the Jews, though few, took refuge in one of the towers, to the north, but eventually surrendered when surrounded by the Romans. The Romans, in contrast, could have boasted of not having a single casualty at the moment of taking the city, had not the centurion Antonius, deceived by a Jewish prisoner, been killed by treachery.

---

[426] B, III, 289-315.
[427] B, III, 316-322.
[428] B, III, 327-328.

It is the end of the city. The historian cuts things very short:

 – on that day, the Romans exterminated all whom they found;

 – on succeeding days, the Romans searched the whole city, and spared no-one, except for women and children; the number of prisoners rose to 1,200;

 – the total number of dead during the final days of the siege was 40,000;

 – Vespasian ordered the city to be razed to the ground;

 – Jotapata was taken in the thirteenth year of the reign of Nero, in the month of Panemus[429].

The whole of Judaea was brought under the sway of Rome by force of arms, except for the fortress of Masada, the stronghold of the last of the Jewish rebels: the *Sicarii*, at the orders of Eleazar. The general layout is the following:

 A. the introduction of the actors in the history (B, VII, 252-253),

 B. causes (*id.*, 254-258),

 C. ecphrasis concerning the other Jewish rebel factions (*id.*, 259-274),

 D. preparations by the Roman governor Silva for the siege (*id.*, 275-279),

 E. geographical, geological and archaeological ecphrasis concerning Masada (*id.*, 280-303),

 F. the siege (*id.*, 304-319),

 G. long speech by Eleazar (*id.*, 320-388),

 H. how the collective suicide is carried out and who the survivors are (*id.*, 389-401), and

 I. the entry of the Romans into Masada (*id.*, 402-406).

 A. Flavius Silva replaces the deceased Bassus as ruler of Judaea. The whole of Judaea was under Roman rule except for the fortress of Masada. Silva gathers together all his forces and marches on Masada.

The fortress was occupied by the *Sicarii*, headed by Eleazar, a descendant of Judas, he who had incited the Jews, in the time of Quirinius (6-9 A.D.), to rebel against the power of Rome.

 B. During that time, the *Sicarii* attacked those Jews who accepted the power of the Romans, "but, in reality, that was an excuse which they forwarded, so as to conceal their cruelty and covetousness; by their deeds did they show their true colours"[430]. The Jews who joined them so as to fight against Rome had to suffer worse atrocities at their hands. Once

---

[429] B, III, 339. The date corresponds to the 20th July, in the year 67 A.D., according to Niese.

[430] B, VII, 256.

their falseness was discovered, they were to give even more palpable evidence of their vile ways.

C. Even so, the *Sicarii* were not alone in perpetrating base deeds, but found company in a whole series of criminals. Leaders too oppressed the masses, and the masses wanted to destroy power. The *Sicarii* were the first to show their cruelty against their fellow citizens, but John of Gischala was even worse. Simon ben Gioras was also responsible for a whole list of crimes. To these should be added the notorious behaviour of the Idumaeans and the Zealots. God, however, gave them their retribution.

This ecphrasis has its historiographic justification, for Flavius Josephus attempts, with a few strokes, to describe the internal situation of Judaea. Groups lacking in all scruple took advantage of the moral prostration of the Jewish people, after the long and terrible war waged against the Romans. There was therefore an impelling necessity to put them in their place. And Masada came to represent the most dangerous focal point for the development of the "pax Romana".

D. Flavius Silva suddenly becomes master of the whole territory and makes his preparations for the siege of Masada:

– guard posts at convenient points;

– he builds a wall around the fortress and places sentries at it;

– he makes camp in a place suitable to direct the siege operations, where the rocks of the fortress were very near to the adjacent mountain, though not so favourable for the provision of resources, especially supplies such as water, since there was no fount in the neigbourhood;

– having finished these preliminaries, Silva devotes himself to the siege, which he sees as being difficult in view of the solidness of the fortress.

All these points are noted by the historian as being preliminary to the description of the assault. One has the impression that the ground is being carefully and thoroughly prepared for the final battle. One may also observe a certain leaning towards theatricals, since there is no hurry on the part of the historian to get to the historical event which he has intended to record, and he dwells on the smallest detail. This slow-motion is shown by the two ecphrases which he introduces in the middle of his description, as well as the insertion of the long speech by Eleazar, which has already been commented on in Chap. II, A, 2a (pp. 97-98).

E. The ecphrasis draws attention to the geological morphology of the place where the fortress stands, to its two access points, to the east and west, and to the upper flat, where the fortress stands, begun by the priest Jonathan and finished by Herod, and to its buildings.

The reason why this ecphrasis is placed here is quite clear: we are to witness the final war action for which Masada will provide the scene, and it represents the last expression of its grandeur. The description of the difficulties it provides, difficulties which are natural as well as man-made, is the most suitable one to all the preparations, military and strategic, which the Roman general has worked out.

F. The siege is laid. Only one place is suitable for an embankment: a rock, very broad, three hundred cubits under the height of Masada, named Leuce. Working intensely, they manage to throw up earthworks to a height of two hundred cubits. Since this is still not high enough, Silva has a platform built, fifty cubits wide by as many cubits high. The machines used were in general of the same kind as those built by Vespasian and Titus for their sieges. In addition, a tower sixty cubits high was built, clad in iron, from which the Romans could shoot their missiles and prevent the defenders from toppling it over. At the same time, Silva ordered a battering ram to be used continuously against the wall, which managed to open a breach in it. Very quickly the *Sicarii* built another wall on the inside which was capable of resisting the force of the blows, in the following manner: a double wall of wooden beams with a filling of earth; and, so as to prevent the earth from spilling out, other beams were placed transversally to the original ones. Thus the ram struck against shock-absorbing material and became ineffective. Silva considered that the best way to destroy this wall would be to set fire to it. And so it was, but the wind blew against the Romans, and there was a danger that the Roman machines would suffer the same fate. However, as if by divine providence, the wind changed direction and destroyed completely the wall of wood built by the Jews.

Then the Romans, blessing God, returned happily to camp, with the intention of attacking the enemy on the following day: "And during the night the watches were much more vigilant, so that none should escape secretly"[431].

G. Eleazar, on seeing the wall consumed by the flames, on seeing that they had no further defence to fall back on, and on seeing what the Romans would do to them, their women and children, determined on mass suicide. With this idea in mind, and so as to give it a justificatory support, the historian constructs a long speech, which gives a dramatic dimension to the historiographic scene. The structure of the speech has been expounded already in Chap. II, A, 2a; here I shall mention no more than its place within the narrative thread. It is, therefore, a fully dramatic

---

[431] B, VII, 319.

speech, which captures in itself all those elements of atmosphere and mood of the people to whom it is directed.

But the first part of the speech has no effect at all. And Flavius Josephus notes the indecision of the listeners, specifying in a very plastic way, with an attempt to infuse the drama with some life, with an attempt to copy reality with a linguistic structure, to imitate the variety of moods: some are in favour of it, others, weaker, feel compassion towards the women and their families as well as for themselves, and their tears indicate that the heart is unwilling. Eleazar is afraid that the crying of some will shake the resolution of the others, and with more passion in his words, launches into an elevated speech on the immortality of the soul.

Here then we have an extensive speech which apparently changes objective, but which continues to pursue it by means of other contents. Flavius Josephus shows his capacity for reflexion and dialectic, and manages to construct a speech which is well adapted to the dramatically historical moment.

H. After the second part of the speech, the listeners hasten to carry out the act of suicide[432]. The nervous movements of the personalities are revealed by means of a rich psychological and mystical vocabulary: possessed (δαιμονῶντες), courage (ἀνδρεία), wise decision (εὐβουλία), affection (φιλοστόργος), passion (ἔρως), emotion (πάθος), reason (λογισμός), reflexive resolve (ἀτενῆ τὴν γνώμην), they caressed (ἠσπάζοντο), they embraced (περιπτυσσόμενοι), they took their children into their arms (τέκνα προσηγκαλίζοντο), kisses (φιλήματα), crying (δακρύοντες), proposition (βούλευμα), intention (ἐπίνοια), daring (τόλμημα), unfortunate victims of necessity (ἄθλιοι τῆς ἀνάγκης), sorrow (ὀδύνη), miserable station (τὴν δύστηνον ὑπουργίαν), with firmness (ἀτρέπτως), they trusted (ἐθάρρουν), sagacity and wisdom (φρόνησις καὶ παιδεία). Here should be included too the number of times that mention is made of death, of throwing oneself on one's sword and so on.

As can be seen, many of these words come under the heading of descriptive words, so that here the historian replaces what in the theatre would be action with words. This text reveals a great effort at imitating reality in action. So here we are dealing with a narrative which has many points of contact with drama.

Finally, as is usually the case in Flavius Josephus, a toll is given of the victims; in this case they all belong to one of the sides: 960, with women and children. Only two women, one aged and the other a relative of Eleazar's, remained alive. The episode is brought to a close with the date: 2nd May in the year 73 A.D.[433].

---

[432] B, VII, 389-401.
[433] According to Schürer, or the year 72 A.D. according to Niese.

I. Then the Romans, at day-break, advance to the attack. The deathly silence makes the Romans guess at what has happened. Their shouts are answered only by the two women who survive, and who tell all that has come to pass. But they can hardly believe what they hear. They extinguish the fire and enter the palace of Herod. There they see the reality of the tragedy with their own eyes, and the historian uses the moment to convert it into a tragic scene indeed: "They admired the nobleness of their resolve and the unshaken contempt for death in so many to carry it out"[434].

B. HISTORICAL NARRATIVE

In this section I intend to make an analysis of the four most important points which make up the mainstay of a historical oeuvre as regards its structural aspects. In these points are postulated the principles of continuity and narrative richness and techniques.

1. *The narrative thread*

The oeuvre of any writer is stamped with his own recurring peculiarities. There are authors who are easy to read, and there are others who require more time. This fact is a result of diverse elements: narrative cadences, comparisons, specialised sections, the intention of avoiding certain dispensible elements, the wilful determination of the writer himself to leave no point unlinked and so on and so forth. In a certain sense, the stylistic rhythm reveals the narrative quality and the quality of the organisation of material in a writer.

This theory, for theory it is, may be more readily seen in specific literary phenomena in the work of Flavius Josephus. Thus there are specialised sections, markers of the beginning and ending of certain narratives, comparisons and other traits which I shall now go on to study.

In the first place, there may be observed in Flavius Josephus some chapters which have great narrative unity within themselves. For instance, chapter IV[435] of the first book of the *Bellum Judaicum* contains events which mark an historical unit: the reign of Alexander Jannaeus (104-78 B.C.). The chapter begins with his ascent to the throne, after the death of Aristobulus, and ends with his death. In practice the activity of Alexander is polarised between wars, so that even in the theme there is a single narrative line. Chapters VI and VII[436] of the *Bellum Judaicum* also

---

[434] B, VII, 406.
[435] B, I, 85-106.
[436] B, I, 120-158.

form a narrative unit, with its beginning, its intervening exposition, and its ending.

There are doubtless moments of specialisation, that is, when Flavius Josephus goes into long drawn-out expositions and dwells on a subject, leaving the narrative mainstream to one side. In fact, those who were charged with organising the work of Flavius Josephus into chapters and paragraphs brought together into chapters certain narrative units which properly speaking make up narrative digressions. To take an example, from a thematic point of view, that chapter which deals with relating the building carried out by king Herod is a specialised chapter[437], as is the one devoted to the description of his domestic tragedies[438]. The chapter given over to the description of the three Jewish sects[439] is a thematic insert, as is the chapter relating the adverse situation of the Jews at the Diaspora[440], and the three final chapters[441] which deal with the Jewish uprising throughout the whole of Palestine.

One aspect which characterises the narrative thread of Flavius Josephus is the alternating of news. It would seem that there are intervening pieces of news which provide the whole with a good dose of agility. Thus we may see that in book IV of the *Bellum Judaicum* the writer is concentrating on the domination over the various points and cities of Palestine by the Romans, but from time to time intercalates the state of political affairs in Rome. I have chosen this book in particular since it gives wider treatment to the progress of Roman domination over the Jews. Thus the historian, throughout the book, heralds the arrival of news from Occident: the news of the revolt of the Gauls (67-68 A.D.) reaches Vespasian just when he has completed the domination of Peraea and is making ready to go to Judaea[442]; the death of Nero[443] poses serious problems for Vespasian, who is encamped at Jericho, and makes him put off his march on Jerusalem[444]; the civil war in Italy, the death of Galba (15th January, 69 A.D.) and of Otho (17th April, 69 A.D.) and the advance of Vitellius on Rome[445] are all placed before the invasion of Judaea by Vespasian (*circa* 23rd June, 68 A.D.) which was prior to them from the point of view of chronology; news concerning the disaster at Rome brought about by Vitellius, the reaction of Vespasian and of his soldiers,

---

[437] B, I, 401-430.
[438] B, I, 431-444.
[439] B, I, 119-166.
[440] B, II, 457-512.
[441] B, II, 556-654.
[442] B, IV, 440 ff.
[443] B, IV, 490 ff.
[444] B, IV, 497 ff.
[445] B, IV, 545-549.

and their proclamation of Vespasian as emperor constitute another moment of respite within the tense atmosphere created by the whole process
of the occupation of Jerusalem[446]; finally, the outcome of political tension
in Italy[447] and, more specifically, of the struggle for power with the end of
Vitellius bring this book to a close with a great narrative unity, in spite of
such diverse historical leaps.

Another element which marks the cadence of internal rhythm is that
provided by narrative pause. Flavius Josephus is very reiterative in
bringing attention to this, indeed so much so that it is a constant in his
work to finish off a particular history with a specific phrase. Thus the
history of the death of Phasael is brought to a close with a few simple
words: "Thus, therefore, he died"[448]. The statistical table gives a large
group of items which bring the narrative to a close in such a simple
way[449]. Other concluding formulae are more explicit and extensive. In
this line there are formulae of the following type: "this is what there was
to say about the Jewish philosophical schools"[450]; "that place, therefore,
has this nature"[451]; "a catastrophe of a similar category was that which
occurred at Alexandria"[452].

So as to avoid overloading this section with phrases and expressions
which do no more than demonstrate what I have been saying up to this
point, I shall simply give a list of the main items which include these formulae: B, I, 510, 646, 673; B, II, 647 and 654; B, III, 58, 160, 218, 246,
262, 315, 428, 442, 461, 521, 531; B, IV, 49, 120, 224, 270, 325, 587,
601; B, V, 105, 439, 520; B, VI, 192, 266, 442; B, VII, 95, 218, 294,
303, 419, 432; A, I, 66, 103, 139, 147, 178, 179, 206, 212; A, II, 179,
181; A, III, 95, 114, 133, 150, 177, 178, 187, 227; A, IV, 52, 76, 94, 159,
302, 331; A, V, 32, 174, 253; A, VI, 294, 342, 378; A, VII, 36, 45, 257,
375, 394; A, VIII, 1, 26, 85, 129, 149, 155, 159, 190, 204, 212, 253, 265,
282, 287, 289, 298, 324, 354, 388, 392; A, IX, 6, 17, 183, 204, 214; A,
X, 23, 98, 130, 148, 228; A, XI, 18, 113, 119; A, XII, 7, 137, 145; A,
XIII, 21, 212, 267, 283, 432; A, XIV, 119, 139, 228, 293, 491; A, XV,
10, 38, 289, 425; A, XVI, 100; A, XVII, 130, 135, 199, 316, 338; A,
XVIII, 25, 62, 80, 84, 179, 223, 288, 305, 309, 379; A, XIX, 114, 126,
137, 185, 201, 263, 272, 286, 354; A, XX, 68, 99, 112, 127; Vit, 43, 138,
148, 154, 177, 367, 428, 430; Ap, I, 115, 142, 293; Ap, II, 28, 78, 144.

---

[446] B, IV, 585-604.
[447] B, IV, 630 ff.
[448] B, I, 273.
[449] B, I, 551; B, II, 92; A, II, 209; A, XII, 40; A, XIII, 129. This list is completed in
the following paragraph.
[450] B, II, 166.
[451] B, II, 191.
[452] B, II, 499. Similarly A, II, 171, 269; A, XIX, 312.

This stylistic recourse brings to mind, in a certain sense, the Homeric *ringkomposition*, that is, when the narrative thread is interrupted by an *excursus*, this *excursus* is rounded off with typical phrases, as we have already seen, or with conclusions which refer back to the subject announced at the beginning. The digression forms therefore a self-contained whole.

Other conclusions are more extensive, and they therefore at the same time constitute a summary and a closure of the whole of the preceding narrative. Thus Herod annihilated the Arabs at Philadelphia, and in view of his spectacular victory Flavius Josephus closes the story by saying: "Having punished Arabia by such a great blow and having pacified the mood of the people, such was the renown he won, that he was even chosen to be the protector of the nation (of the Arabs) by them"[453]. At the death of Pheroras (5 B.C.), and after the solemn funeral in his honour, by order of Herod, the historian, before embarking on the following narrative, concludes: "An end such as this befell one of the assassins of Alexander and Aristobulus"[454].

As can be seen from these two examples, the conclusion does not confine itself, as we have seen in previous paragraphs, to rounding off a narrative, but rather, in addition to closing it, makes a summary of it or else suggests a whole episode which has been narrated previously, as is the case with the second example.

A final example of what I have just mentioned is that which refers to the heroic death of Simon the Jewish rebel. After having killed each and every one of the members of his family he takes his own life. The scene is extremely dramatic and poignant. It is then that the historian concludes by saying: (So perished) "the young man who, deserving of commiseration for the strength of his body and the firmness of his will, suffered his fate as a consequence of the faith he placed in some foreigners"[455]. A conclusion remarkable in content is that which refers to the downfall of his native city. When the Romans have razed the city to the ground, Flavius Josephus concludes that: "Such, therefore, was the end of Jerusalem due to the madness of the revolutionaries, a city splendid and renowned throughout the whole world"[456]. Finally, the conclusion which seals the whole of the exposition concerning the tabernacle and the laws of the Jews given by Moses in an extensive code[457] refers to their divine provenance, an idea which has been oft-repeated throughout the work: "Moses learned this code of laws, whilst he had established the army at

---

[453] B, I, 385.
[454] B, I, 581.
[455] B, II, 476. The same scene is dealt with on page 240.
[456] B, VII, 4.
[457] A, III, 102-286.

the foot of Sinai, from God, and he wrote it down for the Jews and handed it to them''[458].

Another trait which maintains the continuity of the narrative thread is
provided by a certain manner of referring to already narrated events,
which serves simply to establish a point of thematic continuity. At times,
these references centre the image of a personality: "Alexander, son of
Aristobulus, who had escaped from Pompey..."[459]. In this example, the
idea of escape links up what he is going to say and what he has already
said concerning the personality (No. 158). At other times, an event,
which has been cut short by the introduction of another, is continued
later on with a few words of reference, so that in this manner the original
history is maintained in its expositive thread: "Moses no longer ascended
Sinai, but, having entered into the tabernacle, sought..."[460].

These references can be justified to a great extent if they are conceived
as repetitions brought about by later interpolations, or by changes in the
work projects which Flavius Josephus had. In fact, when Flavius
Josephus, throughout his works, promises to bring out new works dealing
with those subjects which cannot be dealt with at that time, he could not
foresee whether he would realise them or no. In reality, these works were
never published, and thus there was the obligation to insert, in later revi-
sions, certain material which he had originally intended for these
works[461].

Comparisons too contribute to the creation of a narrative rhythm.
Thus the comparisons between people (B, I, 532-533), between nations
(B, I, 358 ff.), literary comparisons (B, II, 396, 556; B, III, 385; B, V, 4,
85, 525; B, VI, 196; A, X, 279; Ap, I, 28), between military forces (B,
III, 15), between peoples (B, III, 153, 195, 276) and between political
systems (Ap, II, 164 ff.) are some of the stylistic recourses which create
an atmosphere of variety and lend coherent rhythm to the whole work.

One may also observe another tendency in Flavius Josephus, which is
shown on not a few occasions. It is a manner of introduction to the narrative on which he is about to embark. Nevertheless, the term *introduction*
here does not have the scope or the content of what is normally
understood by this word, but is rather a simple introductory phrase to
what is going to be described or else referring to what has immediately
preceded or what has been related some time before, a device which en-

---

[458] A, III, 286.
[459] B, I, 160. Similarly, the introduction on Roman general Ventidius (B, I, 288) and
the reference to Hyrcanus (B, I, 433).
[460] A, III, 222.
[461] In this same sense, R. Laqueur, *Der jüdische Historiker Flavius Josephus. Ein
biographischer Versuch auf neuer quellenkritischer Grundlage*, Giessen, 1920.

sures that an event is linked up by literary recourses and that the narrative thread, which may possible have been interrupted, is understood.

Within the first tendency, we find that Flavius Josephus devotes some thought to the hostile attitude taken by the sons of Mariamme at their mother's death on the orders of Herod, the outcome of which he will describe just then. Thus he says: "The sons inherited the wrath and the hatred of their mother, and in their thoughts had contempt for their father as if he were their enemy, and at the beginning when they were brought up in Rome, and more when they returned to Judaea"[462].

When Archelaus succeeds Herod, he finds himself obliged to go to Rome to confirm himself in his post[463]. This poses new problems for the Jews. These ideas form a preparation for the introduction of a speech by Archelaus to the people, and represent a literary linkup with the circumstances which surrounded the death and burial narrated in the preceding book.

The following words represent a very distant linking: "When the ethnarchy of Archelaus was converted into a province, the others, Philip and Herod named Antipas, were ruling their tetrarchies"[464]. These words act as a bridge as it were to link up with paragraph 117, where the event of the reduction of the territory of Archelaus to a province is dealt with.

To abbreviate, I shall gather together in a single group those referential introductions, apart from the two already mentioned, which are found at the beginning of various books and which serve to construct this bridge of relationships with past events or to tauten the narrative thread which then follows, so that the reader does not lose the continuity of the narrative: B, III, 1 (links up with B, II, 555); A, III, 1; A, V, 1; A, VI, 1 (with A, V, 356); A, VII, 1 (with A, VI, 368 ff.); A, IX, 1 (with A, VIII, 400); A, XII, 1 (with A, XI, 346); A, XIII, 1; A, XV, 1; A, XIX, 1.

Within the books themselves are to be found brief introductions to particular subjects. I believe that all of them form a group which is very similar to the following type: "The Jews, after the defeat of Cestius[465], exalted by their unexpected successes, were unable to control their impulses, and, carried along on the tide of fortune, they took the war further"[466]. This brief introduction, apart from acting as a reminder of an event which had happened some time before, sets the scene for what he is going on to say. The items are the following: B, III, 59 (No. 34), 127, 316

---

[462] B, I, 445.
[463] B, II, 1.
[464] B, II, 167.
[465] Links in with B, II, 540 ff.
[466] B, III, 9.

(No. 288), 432 (No. 408), 616 (No. 607), 440; B, VII, 304 (No. 275 ff.); A, II, 60; A, IV, 11-13; A, V, 175, 198; A, IX, 74; A, XII, 228; A, XIII, 171; A, XVI, 271; A, XIX, 338 (No. 335).

It should also be added that the dramatic descriptions, the ecphrases and the narrative anticipations together make a powerful contribution to the creation of this historiographical thread which in the present case is the hallmark of Flavius Josephus. Also, with regard to those coincident chronological periods in the *Bellum Judaicum* and the *Antiquitates Judaicae*, it should be said that they have their discrepancies and narrative variations, something which provides us with a richly varied writer who knows how to expand or contract his narrative at the approriate time. I shall quote here, to illustrate this point, only the different narratives concerning the Jewish sects[467], and concerning the fatal end of Mariamme, Herod's wife[468], as well as the donation of Antonius to Cleopatra of some parts of Syria[469].

Finally, the echo of classical Greek authors in the oeuvre of Flavius Josephus contributes too to infusing an elevated tone into this narrative thread which I have attempted to follow in his oeuvre[470]. When Flavius Josephus makes a personal address to Justus[471] or to the inhabitants of Tiberias[472] or else makes a rhapsody of official texts[473], we find ourselves again with elements which are most suitable for the creation of a whole art of historiography. A change in the order of sources so as to conserve the chronological order of events[474] is yet another element to be taken into account when it comes to appraising the historiographic narrative thread of Flavius Josephus.

2. *Dinosis*

There are moments when the historian gives especial attention to certain events which make the situation impinge in the mind of the reader in a surprising manner. At times it is a feeling of terror, of surprise or of puzzlement. It is no doubt a resort which is used by Flavius Josephus to gradually outline one of the objectives at which he is aiming and most im-

---

[467] B, II, 119-166 = A, XIII, 171-173 = A, XVIII, 11-25.
[468] B, I, 438 ff. = A, XV, 185-231.
[469] B, I, 359-363 = A, XV, 88-107.
[470] B, I, 371, 530; B, II, 187, 416; B, III, 237, 433; IV, 255, 618; B, V, 551; A, V, 227; A, VI, 272; VIII, 182; A, X, 163; A, XIII, 193; A, XV, 71, 74; A, XX, 145; Vit, 132, 182, 379, 380.
[471] Vit, 340.
[472] Vit, 353-354.
[473] Ap, I, 74 ff.
[474] A, XI, 88.

portant to him: his pedagogical line, that is, to make history, with all its complexity, a vehicle for the diffusion of his pedagogical ideas. At times, nevertheless, exaggeration is not entirely fruitful, and he simply falls into hyperbole. With regard to this, we are faced with a historian who is full of the desire to stamp his own personal idea for posterity.

Not all the episodes are treated with the same degree of exaggeration. Some subjects are more deserving of the attention of Flavius Josephus, and therefore it would seem that the historian goes much deeper into them. The subject which is most used by Flavius Josephus is that of human misfortune, such as calamities of peoples, personal wretchedness, and the destruction of cities. It is the tragic element which therefore receives the most extensive treatment in the oeuvre of Flavius Josephus.

It is not surprising therefore that the calamities suffered by the Jewish people should have exercised a strong attraction on Flavius Josephus. Thus in the introduction to the *Bellum Judaicum* he does not omit mentioning that the misfortunes of all nations are not comparable to those which the Jewish people have suffered[475], so that a critic of his oeuvre, if he feels no compassion for the great many disasters which are to be found in it, "should adjudicate the facts to history, and the laments to the historian"[476]. Flavius Josephus therefore recognises that when confronted with the sufferings of his people, greater than any suffering of other peoples, he cannot react in an objective, distant manner.

In a certain sense Flavius Josephus is confessing that he is exaggerating some basically tragic events, since he provides no point of comparison, and therefore he becomes lost, and is aware that his statement is false. He therefore has to say that the historian is the only person responsible for the degree to which all these painful situations suffered by the Jewish people are described, fully aware that his laments are not historiographical material.

The investigator will never be able to find a just interpretation for the *dinosis* which Flavius Josephus gives to certain situations, so that any analysis will be no more than an attempt at appraising them under specific subjects.

Jewish emissaries enumerate before Augustus the excesses of Herod, with the intention of preventing Archelaus, the son of such a tyrant, from succeeding his father. The entire speech, in indirect speech, is full of exaggerations. One may readily conclude that here the exaggerated style becomes a descriptive method: things make a greater impact on the audience and the readers if they are presented in the superlative. They say:

---

[475] Thucydides (in I, 1) expresses a similar opinion regarding intra-Greek wars.
[476] B, I, 12.

"Herod reduced the nation to poverty and to the lowest degree of iniquity... the misfortunes inflicted by Herod, in a few years, on the Jewish
people far surpassed all those suffered by their ancestors since the exit
from Babylon"[477]. Here, therefore, we have rhetorical *dinosis*.

In the naval battle carried on by the Romans against the Jews on the
Lake of Gennesaret, the description of the Jewish defeat becomes a carnage which reaches such extremes that Flavius Josephus, at a loss as to
which expressive means to resort to, by the use of a simple phrase paints
an over-stated picture: "The whole lake was to be seen mixed with blood
and full of bodies: for no-one was saved"[478].

A similar picture can be found in the destruction of Gamala by the armies of Titus: "In all the places, there was the immense groaning of
those who were dying, and the blood, flowing down the slope, flooded the
whole city"[479].

When Simon finds out that his wife has fallen into the hands of the
Zealots, he advances on Jerusalem "like a wounded beast, since he did
not capture his tormentors, and visited his fury on those whom he found.
All those who had ventured out beyond the gates to gather herbs and
wood, finding unarmed people and elderly people, he tormented them
and killed them, carried along by the excess of his rage, almost devouring
even the dead bodies"[480].

The behaviour of the Jews within the besieged city of Jerusalem offers
an indescribable picture. The Jews work against each other, bringing
about degradation of the Jewish race: "It is impossible to describe their
licentiousness, but to say it briefly, no other city has offered such
miseries, nor has there existed any generation, since the world began,
which has been more prolific in evil"[481].

Syrian and Arab soldiers of the Roman army, in the space of a single
night, killed some two thousand Jews who had taken refuge in their
camp, on discovering that one of them picked gold coins from his own excrement. Flavius Josephus adds: "In my opinion, no other calamity
greater than this ever befell the Jews"[482].

In the hecatomb of Jerusalem, the author is at a loss for words to
describe the most terrible scenes imaginable. The description is tragic indeed: "One could well believe that the hill of the temple boiled
everywhere, from the very foot, covered in fire, and that the blood was

---

[477] B, II, 86.
[478] B, III, 529.
[479] B, IV, 72.
[480] B, IV, 540. Similar hyperbole in B, VI, 373.
[481] B, V, 442.
[482] B, V, 552.

more abundant than the fire, and that the dead far outnumbered the
killers: for nowhere was the earth to be seen, so many were the dead, and
the soldiers, trampling underfoot the piles of bodies, chased after those
who took to flight''[483].

And the end of Jerusalem is closed with very fatalistic words indeed,
which indicated that the end was irreversible: ''Neither its ancientness,
nor its great wealth, nor its people flung all over the earth, nor the great
glory of its cult were enough to prevent its downfall''[484].

Naturally, exaggerations fall within the field of the irrational, giving
play to those intellectual powers of man which do not lend themselves to
being regularised or organised or systemised. They are the expression of
the irrational impulse of the mind. Thus it is comprehensible that exaggerations should double and redouble concerning a specific subject and
should reach a state of incredibility for the reader. As regards the present
subject, we find that the Jewish people has suffered on various occasions
the experience of tragedy far above any other experience which they have
undergone. At the death of Moses, the Hebrews did fall into the deepest
sadness, ''a sadness which was incomparable in depth to any other which
had taken hold of the Hebrews''[485].

Another carnage is echoed in an exaggerated phrase of Flavius
Josephus, when Abias undoes the army of Jeroboam: ''Most certainly
never has such a great killing been recorded in a war, be it of Greeks, or
of barbarians...''[486].

The reference to Greeks and barbarians is considered to cover the
whole of the then known world. Regarding this, it is repeated at the moment when John kills his brother Jesus whilst carrying out his duties as
priest at the temple[487]. It is, therefore, an action which had never come to
pass either amongst the Greeks or amongst the barbarians.

The second section of this chapter is given over to those *dinoses* which
Flavius Josephus constructs before certain physical, artistic or moral
qualities of people, objects, peoples and so on.

Thus the temple of Caesar at Caesarea contained a colossal statue of
the emperor, ''in no wise inferior to that of Zeus at Olympia, to which it
is similar, and another at Rome, the same as that of Hera of Argos''[488].

---

[483] B, VI, 275-276.
[484] B, VI, 442.
[485] A, IV, 330.
[486] A, VIII, 284.
[487] A, XI, 299.
[488] B, I, 414.

The physical strength of Herod is evidently over-stated[489], as is the universality of the Jewish race[490], the extraordinarily marvellous temple of Jerusalem[491], the altar of the same temple, revered by Greeks and barbarians[492], the temple of Peace which was raised by Vespasian, "greater than all human prevision"[493].

Referring to the patriarch Jacob, Flavius Josephus asserts that "he reached a degree of prosperity not easily accessible to another"[494]. In wealth he surpassed all his fellow-citizens, and the qualities of his sons won him the envy and admiration of all, "for they were lacking in absolutely nothing"[495].

The people of Israel, on their journey through the desert, also realised portentous works: "They vanquished those who attacked them, and terrified the neighbouring nations, and, by their efforts, acquired great and magnificent wealth, when capturing the camp of the enemy, and obtained great wealth for both public and private use, those who at first had no sufficient food"[496].

The Jewish people would still give examples of their ungovernable character by provoking sedition against themselves and their leader: "An uprising therefore which, according to our knowledge, has not happened neither amongst the Greeks nor amongst the barbarians..."[497].

Of all the disputes which the sons of Israel occasion throughout their journey in the desert, there is one which, in the hands of Flavius Josephus, takes on very relevant literary characteristics, and at the same time, from a historiographic viewpoint, gives the event a very particular character, and makes the episode highly attractive. When the question of the choosing of priests is raised, Moses proposes that the people should make their choice and that then a sacrifice should be made to God for him to confirm those who are chosen in their posts. Two hundred and fifty men were chosen, those of greatest category. Suddenly, whilst the incense was being offered, a flame sent by God consumed the two hundred and fifty chosen, together with Korah, leaving only Aaron alive. In this manner God instituted priesthood amongst his people. However, as

---

[489] B, I, 429.
[490] B, II, 398.
[491] B, VI, 267.
[492] B, V, 17.
[493] B, VII, 158.
[494] A, II, 7.
[495] A, II, 7.
[496] A, III, 55.
[497] A, IV, 12.

regards this description, the biblical text is far from the text of Flavius Josephus. A comparison:

Biblical text, LXX	Flavius Josephus
"Hardly had Moses spoken when the ground beneath them split; the earth opened its mouth and swallowed them and their homes—all the followers of Korah and all their property. ...Meanwhile fire had come out from the LORD and burnt up the two hundred and fifty men who were presenting the incense"[498].	"There leapt forth a fire so great, that the like of it had never been related by any one as being the handiwork of man, neither coming up from the bowels of the earth by an underground current of heat, nor spontaneously being produced by the friction of the trees of the woods caused by the violence of the storms, but thus, by the order of God, it blazed brilliant and resplendent. All, the two hundred and fifty together with Korah, were consumed by it when it engulfed them, and even their very bodies vanished"[499].

In the view of the commentators there is a lack of coherence in the text of Flavius Josephus, with regard to the preceding text; there is also a clear discrepancy between the biblical text and that of Flavius Josephus, since in the first text Korah dies before, together with Datham and Abiram (*Num.* XVI, 27, and especially XXVI, 10); there is also a clear imitation of Thucydides (II, 77) in the description of Flavius Josephus of the all-consuming fire.

Without doubt Flavius Josephus, in spite of what I have said in the preceding paragraph, makes a rediscovery of the subject *fire*, and creates about it a scene which is of value in itself. The narrative is cut short, and the historian plunges into a literary αὔξησις which makes him lose the order in his scale of historiographical values. Eventually, one asks oneself what is more important, the choosing of Aaron by God to be high-priest or the scene where the fire is the only protagonist.

Finally mention should be made here of the other exaggerated traits included in my statistical table: A, V, 125; A, VII, 44; 97; A, X, 72; A, XII, 119.

---

[498] *Num.* XVI, 31-35.
[499] A, IV, 55-56.

3. *Ecphrasis*

At times historical narrative calls for a narrative pause in the chain of events. The concept of history in the ancient writers rests essentially on one fact: that the works will be read both in public and in private, and the capacity of the reader has a certain limit which cannot be exceeded, otherwise the reading itself would easily produce psychological fatigue. For this anthropological-type reason, and for many other reasons of the demands of historiography, the historian finds himself compelled to give explanations, to give clarifications with regard to events, personalities, places, time, monuments and so on, so that the entire strictly historiographic corpus of data should gain in stature as a document, and so that the history should gradually acquire those elements which satisfy its pedagogical mission in any field. It should not be forgotten that the historical event is presented always wrapped up in its predicaments, and these are the means by which the reader will understand the history, otherwise it is reduced simply to a systematic collection of events.

It is under these premisses that the historical method of Flavius Josephus should be understood. Whenever necessary, Flavius Josephus digresses from the central subject, so as to enlarge on a detail of it, or simply to add a brief explanation to a term, a name, a city and so on. Therefore ecphrasis has the mission of educating, of enriching with knowledge the historical subject and of setting a rhythm in the historiographic process.

Therefore throughout the oeuvre of Flavius Josephus there are constants, subjects which are deserving of the attention of the historian. Geographical, archaeological, institutional, historical, family, religious and philological subjects are all targets for the erudition of Flavius Josephus[500]. Let us see.

Geographical data often occupy the attention of the historian Flavius Josephus, and are given divers treatment. This diversity refers to the material extension of the ecphrasis. There are simple enlargements on the geography of a city, a mountain or the fauna. I shall analyse the most important points.

Of Jericho he writes that "here there is the most fertile soil in Judaea, and it produces an abundance of palm-trees and balsam-trees. They cut the trunks with sharpened stones and collect the balsam which oozes from the cuts"[501]. The implication of this geographical explanation resides in

---

[500] In the same sense, cf. Lucian, *De hist. conscr.* 57, and G. Avenarius, *op. cit.*, 142-149.

[501] B, I, 138. Similar historiographical importance is found in the description of the Galilean city of Sepphoris (B, III, 34) and of maritime Caesarea (B, III, 409).

the fact that Pompey camped near Jericho on his march towards Jerusalem.

Flavius Josephus is more extensive in the ecphrasis on Ptolemais[502], on the occasion of the arrival of Petronius there, on his way to Judaea. This cut in the narrative thread comes at a time of great tension, when the Jews believe and do not believe in the imminence of war, and "fear quickly spread everywhere"[503]. He places Ptolemais within the four cardinal points, always with reference to other geographical points, and is more voluminous as regards the phenomenon of glass sand and its conversion into vitreous material. From a historiographical point of view, these four paragraphs constitute a respite from the presence of the Roman troops and the resulting tension.

On the occasion of the arrival of Vespasian at Ptolemais, and after having listened to the words of the inhabitants of the Galilean city of Sepphoris regarding their being at Rome's disposal, and before embarking on the description of the descruction of Galilee by the Romans stationed at Sepphoris, Flavius Josephus goes into a detailed description of the geography of Galilee, Peraea, Samaria and Judaea[504]. The description comprises the cities, the mountains, the plains, the district bounds, the inhabitants, the soil and the agriculture, hydrographic resources, Jerusalem the capital, the toparchies and so on.

This ecphrasis, an extensive one, sets the scene for the destruction which the Romans wreaked amongst the Jews. All this wealth will be no more! I believe that this is the historiographical value of the ecphrasis, that is, it places before the eyes of the reader a display of splendour which will be irretrievably lost.

In the battle of Jotapata, the Roman commander Vespasian[505] is obliged to lay siege to the city, since it has an unassailable position, surrounded as it is by protecting nature. It is at this moment that Flavius Josephus introduces a description of the natural and artificial defences of the city which will make the Roman occupation of it difficult. The ecphrasis is a very brief one, and does not interrupt the narrative flow in the slightest. This means that the introduction of it fits in extremely well with the whole, and does not clash in the slightest with the spirit which pervades the description.

Joppa is another city which is utterly destroyed by the Romans. Its geography is so simple that it does not have a natural harbour[506]. This

---

[502] B, II, 188-191.
[503] B, II, 187.
[504] B, III, 35-58.
[505] B, III, 158-160. Cf. pages 143-153.
[506] B, III, 419-422.

notwithstanding, Joppa was one of the most important ports of that zone of the Mediterranean. The historian, therefore, when the Roman troops appear so as to put an end to the piratery which the inhabitants of Joppa carried on against the vessels which made the trade run from Syria and Phoenicia as far as Egypt, he finds himself obliged to give a description of the shape and constitution of its beach and the winds which sweep it. When all the pirates have taken to their boats and sailed away so as to avoid falling into the hands of the Romans, "there falls, at dawn, a violent wind on those who had sailed far out from Joppa, called by those who sailed in those waters the Black from the North..."[507].

This brief ecphrasis is very discrete, and the narrative thread does not lose its continuity for a moment.

Once Tarichaeae, a city situated at the foot of the Lake of Gennesaret, is taken, there are still some factions left who flee, one of whom takes to the lake looking for a means to escape. It is Vespasian who gives the pertinent instructions for the construction of troop-carrying rafts so as to go in pursuit of the fugitives[508].

It seems, at least from the psychological point of view of the reader, that while the craft are being built, Flavius Josephus uses the waiting time to go into an extensive description of the Lake of Gennesaret, the River Jordan, and the extremely fertile region which the lake touches. The description lasts as long as the time for the construction of the boats. Once they are finished, then the narrative thread continues without interruption in continuity.

Here then is the geographical ecphrasis: "The Lake of Gennesaret takes its name from the adjacent region... (*he gives the measurements of its length*)..., the water is fresh and very potable..., it is clean and is surrounded by a beach and sand..., on extracting water, it is of an agreeable temperature, warmer than that of a river or a fountain..., it contains various species of fishes..., it is cut in the middle by the Jordan..., it seems that the source of the Jordan is the Paneion, and it runs underground to it, without being seen from the one called Phiale; the latter is one hundred and twenty stadia distant from Caesarea (of Philip).... In fact it is called Phiale due to its circular shape, since it is a round lakelet, and the water always comes up to its rim, without dropping and without overflowing..., later (the Jordan), having travelled through an extensive desert, flows into Lake Asphaltitis"[509].

---

[507] B, III, 422.

[508] B, III, 492-505.

[509] B, III, 506-515. Only those sentences providing geographical information have been translated. The text is enriched further by historical data and a wealth of expressions of praise.

And he adds: "At the side of the Lake of Gennesaret there stretches out a region of the same name, wonderful for its nature and beauty, for it refuses no plant on account of its fertility..., and the temperature of the air harmonizes too with the diverse species; walnut-trees..., palm-trees..., fig-trees and olive-trees..., to which a milder atmosphere is beneficial... Apart from the goodness of the airs, (the region) is also watered by a very fertilising source of water, called by the inhabitants Capharnaum; some believe it to be a branch of the Nile, because it produces a fish similar to the *coracin* of the Lake of Alexandria. The extension of the region... is of some thirty stadia, by twenty wide"[510].

Book IV of the *Bellum Judaicum* provides five digressions of a geographical nature: 2-10, concerning the city of Gamala; 54-55, concerning Mount Tabor; 105, concerning the city of Cydasa; 451-485, regarding the region of Jericho, the valley of the Jordan, the fount of the prophet Elijah, the produce of the region, Lake Asphaltitis and the region of Sodom; 607-615, concerning Egypt in general, with the port of Alexandria and Pharos.

The historiographic incidence of these ecphrases is very natural, and all of them are postulated by the historical event which takes place in each one of the places described. All of them provide significant geographical data for the historical or war event which happens in the respective places. The ecphrasis 451-485, concerning Jericho and outlying districts, does not imply any dislocation of the narrative thread, in spite of its length, and serves to mark the end of an historical narrative, so as to be able to embark on the final great high point of the war: Jerusalem. Finally, the importance of the final ecphrasis, 607-615, is remarked on by Flavius Josephus himself. Indeed, Egypt represented the corner-stone of the economic fan of Rome, and when Vespasian is proclaimed emperor by his own troops, it is understandable that he should wish to assure this part, since "he was aware that Egypt was the most important part of the empire on account of the supply of wheat it provided; once Egypt had been conquered, he hoped, if the war became protracted, to also defeat Vitellius by force of arms, for the population of Rome would not endure hunger"[511]. At this moment, Flavius Josephus introduces the description of Egypt, and in which he comes to the following conclusion: "With reason, therefore, did Vespasian aspire to the control of the affairs of Egypt, with a view to stabilising the whole empire"[512].

The fortress of Machaerus, to the east of the Dead Sea, near its northern tip, brought together geographical and archaeological conditions

---

[510] B, III, 516-521.
[511] B, IV, 605-606.
[512] B, IV, 616.

which were such that they might "incite many to uprising because of its firmness"[513]. Therefore, Lucilius Bassus, legate to Judaea, had to take himself there so as to destroy it. And here begins the ecphrasis concerning Machaerus, so as to inform and show the readers that the decision of the legate is founded on real dangers. This ecphrasis comprises a description of the geographical elements which offer great difficulties to the conquerors as regards approach (Nos. 164-170), the history of its buildings, from the time of king Alexander Jannaeus, who reigned from 104 to 78 B.C., to those built by king Herod (Nos. 171-177). Finally, a lengthy description of the curative properties (Nos. 178-185) and a reference to the fountains of hot and cold water and to the mines (Nos. 186-189).

When faced with the difficulties described in the ecphrasis, Flavius Josephus has Lucilius Bassus act in consequence: "Bassus, having reconnoitred the place, determined to make an approach by embanking the oriental ravine..."[514].

The final, extraordinarily-dimensioned, geographical ecphrasis found in the *Bellum Judaicum* is that concerning Masada, the fortress rebuilt by Herod[515]. Jerusalem has already been destroyed, and only Masada remains, in the hands of Eleazar and his *Sicarii*. Silva, the Roman general, sets up camp in front of it[516]. And Flavius Josephus says: "Having, therefore, made these previsions, Silva gave his attention to the siege, something which demanded great inventiveness and effort, on account of the fortification of the fortress, the nature of which was thus"[517].

The ecphrasis which follows is made up of various subjects, that is, after a section devoted to the constitution of the rock together with its geographical and geological characteristics, it goes on to a description of the building carried out from the times of the high priest Jonathan right up to those of king Herod. This second part, therefore, is an archaeological ecphrasis[518], which provides abundant archaeological material for knowledge of the architecture and the site. Thus Flavius Josephus can sum up with the following words: "In such wise, therefore, the fortress was protected against the attacks of enemies, as much by nature as by the hand of man"[519].

But what about the inside of the fortress? Flavius mentions immense stores, hewn out of the rock, stocked with victuals, some of which had

---

[513] B, VII, 164.
[514] B, VII, 190.
[515] B, VII, 280-303.
[516] B, VII, 277.
[517] B, VII, 279.
[518] Studied in Chap. II, A, 6 (p. 135).
[519] B, VII, 294.

been conserved for many years in good condition, due to the climate of those altitudes.

Finally, the narrative digression touches on some historical points, which are a response to the motive which led Herod to build a fortress of such size. The answer is an historical one. Herod had always feared the ambitions of Cleopatra and her designs on Judaea. In spite of this, and in spite of the amorous passion which Antonius felt towards Cleopatra, he never ceded to the whim of the annexation of Judaea which had been expounded by the Egyptian queen. And Flavius Josephus adds: "On account of these fears did Herod fortify Masada, and left to the Romans their last task in their war against the Jews"[520].

Indeed, the rock was impregnable, and this fact necessitated an historiographic pause so as to show it.

The geographical ecphrases to be found in the *Antiquitates Judaicae* are very brief, and are interesting in so far as they are provided by Flavius Josephus himself, *addenda* as it were to the biblical text which he paraphrases. Thus there is the description of the difficulties of travelling through Mesopotamia in winter as well as in summer (A, I, 244), the manner of overcoming the dangers of serpents by Moses, in his journey through the desert (A, II, 244-247), the strategic difficulties presented by the city of Saba (A, II, 249-250) by reason of its geography, the geographic danger of the Sinai (A, II, 264-265), and the very brief mention of the fertility of the soil of Jericho (A, IV, 100).

Another block of numerous ecphrases provides us with the archaeological aspects. Archaeology has already been given extensive treatment in Chap. II, A, 6, with the intention of demonstrating the contributions made by the historian in this field. In this present section, I shall make a study of the historiographical repercussions of this contribution.

The idea concerning the tower of Antonia is enlarged on as regards its being a fortress (B, I, 118), when queen Alexandra (78-69 B.C.) has the wife and the sons of Aristobulus shut up there; Jerusalem is admired for its fortifications, when Pompey besieges it (B, I, 141). An extremely long ecphrasis (B, I, 401-430) gathers together the building carried out by king Herod, at a moment when Flavius Josephus presents the king as being at the especially splendid apogee of his life[521]. The ecphrasis serves as a stepping stone between the splendour and his domestic tragedies (B, I, 431...) which Herod is burdened with. It should be added, however, that this ecphrasis takes up all of chapter XXI of the original distribution of the work of Flavius Josephus, something which indicates that the ancient

---

[520] B, VII, 303.
[521] Cf. its parallel in A, XV, 136-159.

distributor had already intuitively taken it as a unified block which was then fitted into an exclusive chapter.

There are also very short ecphrases which serve to bring out the importance of buildings (B, I, 81, 344), a fortress (A, XII, 230-233), a funeral monument (A, XIII, 211-212), a city (A, XVIII, 249) and the courtyard of the temple (Ap, II, 103-109). However with all these ecphrases, there is not the slightest break in the narrative thread; rather, they simply contribute erudition and complement the imagined picture which the reader has to conjure up in each historical episode.

The longest archaeological ecphrases are the following: on the city of Jerusalem (B, V, 136-247), Masada (B, VII, 280-303), and the temple built by king Herod (A, XV, 391-425), which have already been analysed with regard to their archaeological value, in Chap. II, A, 6.

I also consider ecphrases those descriptions of an historical, institutional, philological, literary, religious, family, and psychological type which, to a certain extent, briefly interrupt the narrative rhythm and contribute a wealth of documentary evidence from an historiographical point of view.

Those ecphrases with an historical subject usually introduce that history which bears little relation to the historical moment which is being related. The history of the false Alexander[522] is presented after the sharing out of the kingdom of Herod amongst his three sons. The false Alexander, physically very closely resembling the real Alexander the grandson of Herod, put to death on the orders of his own grandfather (B, I, 551), passes himself off as the prince and is a pretender to the inheritance which is due to him as a member of the royal family. To this effect he deceives various Jewish colonies and reaches Rome with similar pretentions. There he is unmasked by the emperor himself and condemned to death.

There then follows the intervention of one of the inheritors, Archelaus the ethnarch.

This historical fact, then, contributes a very particular event which could well be omitted without unduly detracting from the general history from the point of view of documentation.

The most considerable historical ecphrasis is made up of a numerous collection of small historical events, relating solely to the internal situation of the Jews[523]. It therefore comes to represent a long break in the historical thread, after the victory of the Jews over the Romans, who were

---

[522] B, II, 101-110. Cf. too its parallel in A, XVII, 324-338.
[523] B, II, 556-III, 1-8.

led by Cestius[524]. So much so that the historian, from a stylistic view-point, finds it necessary to use a linking phrase so as to take up again the history which he had left some time before: "The Jews, after the defeat of Cestius, carried along by their unexpected victories..."[525].

The ecphrasis comprises data relating to the situation of the Jews in Jerusalem and Damascus, to the attitude of the Jews with regard to the preparations for war, to the activity of Flavius Josephus and of John of Gischala in the face of events, to the rebellion of Tiberias, and finally to the appointment of Vespasian as general of the Roman forces in Syria.

It is true enough that this collection provides information which is useful for an understanding of the general movement of the history which is being described, but it also provides the reader with essential background information of the preceding history of the Jews, which is necessary for the understanding of later events. It is, therefore, a highly complementary ecphrasis.

Historical ecphrases which receive a preferably complementary treat-ment to the general history appear in the following books: B, IV, 530-533; B, VI, 288-315; B, VI, 435-442; B, VII, 259-274; A, IX, 208-214; A, X, 110-118, 151-153; A, XVIII, 310-379; A, XX, 224-251; Vit, 336-367. Historical ecphrases which synchronise historical events with those of the general narrative appear in the following books: B, III, 289-315; B, IV, 14-16, 545-555, 585-655; B, VII, 21-22, 75-95; A, XIII, 365-376; A, XVIII, 39-52.

As regards ecphrases concerning institutions, it should be mentioned that there are two principal subjects which are broached: those of Roman military matters and of Jewish institutional matters. The military subject is specified in the form of the Roman army, and constitutes one of the most original contributions on that army of the first century. The Jewish institutions touch on one of the pillars of the Jewish world. Let us see.

The Roman army, therefore, has an internal organisation, and its training is maintained in times of peace[526]; it organises its camps accord-ing to tested ideas on defence; marching order is strictly laid down, and arms and equipment derive from definite specialities and necessities; finally, in battle, nothing is done which has not been calculated and worked out beforehand, and discipline fuses the spirit of the soldiers together.

This ecphrasis supposes a definite historiographical interruption, brought about by the survey of the strength of the armies of Titus and

---

[524] B, II, 551-555.
[525] B, III, 9.
[526] B, III, 70-109.

Vespasian. It is long and contributes a good deal of information concerning the Roman army, but, far from making us lose the continuity of the narrative, it provides it with a projection along the line of concept which Flavius Josephus has of history, that of instructing. It is, therefore, an eminently documented and informative ecphrasis.

In this same line should be placed those digressions which deal with the order of march of the Roman army[527] and with the use of the battering ram[528] and the artillery in battle[529].

The shortest of the institutional ecphrases refers to the two stones, Urim and Thummim. which the high-priest carried on his shoulders, on which the names of the tribes of Israel were engraved, six on each one[530]. The reason for this ecphrasis is given by Flavius Josephus himself, when he says: "I want to recount what I forgot (to mention) concerning the vestments of the high-priest"[531]. And he brings the ecphrasis to a close by saying: "Concerning this, we shall speak at a suitable moment; and now I shall go back into the description"[532].

The ecphrasis which is really remarkable in length is the one dealing with the three branches of Jewish philosophy. The subject is to be found in three different places[533]. The first, and longest, is motivated by the occasion of the uprising of Judas the Galilean, after the death of Archelaus and Judaea's becoming a Roman province, under the administration of Coponius. Regarding Judas, he says: "He was a sophist, founder of his own sect, resembling the others in nothing"[534]. This notwithstanding, the sect of Judas is described, and even so only briefly, in A, XVIII, 23-25, and constituted the fourth sect or life-option of Jewish religious thought.

On putting an end to the description of the Jewish sects, Flavius Josephus finds it necessary to pick up his historical thread once more with an appropriate phrase, and says: "After the ethnarchy of Archelaus had been converted into a province..."[535]. And thus he links it up with the final idea immediately preceding the ecphrasis.

The ecphrasis in book XIII of the *Antiquitates Judaicae* is very short (Nos. 172-173), and to my mind is placed there without being overly

---

[527] B, III, 116-126 and B, V, 47-51.
[528] B, III, 214-217.
[529] B, V, 269-270.
[530] A, III, 214-218.
[531] A, III, 214.
[532] A, III, 218.
[533] B, II, 120-166; A, XIII, 172-173 and A, XVIII, 11-25 (there is here another branche).
[534] B, II, 118.
[535] B, II, 167.

justified from an historiographic point of view. Of course it supposes no impediment to the continuity of the descriptive flow. Even so, I believe that the ecphrasis may have been motivated by the fact that Jonathan appears in the previous act as the factotum of Jewish politics: he renews the treaty with Rome and establishes links with "all the kings of Asia and of Europe and all the magistrates of the cities"[536]. If this interpretation is admissible, then the ecphrasis would also suppose the existence, in the times of Jonathan, of organised groups amongst the Jews who had advisory capacity, as Flavius Josephus points out: "In those times, there were three options amongst the Jews, which held different opinions on human affairs"[537].

The remaining ecphrases will be briefly outlined. Some historiographical notes[538] to justify the subjects to be dealt with are drawn out until they become an ecphrasis proper. In the redaction the death of Nero is twice denounced, once before and again after the ecphrasis, in an attempt to pick up the narrative thread.

Before beginning the paraphrase in the *Antiquitates Judaicae*, Flavius Josephus devotes nine paragraphs to contrasting the person and the work of Moses with other legislators[539]. More probably here we have a set of praises and preferences which in fact cut short the introduction, as is recognised by Flavius Josephus himself when he says: "I shall now go back to the narration of events..."[540].

Flavius Josephus makes a digression concerning the absurdity of the legends on the leprosy of Moses and his followers[541] which, in fact, cuts the biblical paraphrase on purity short. It is doubtless an apologetic ecphrasis.

A literary ecphrasis would be provided by the introduction of the relating of the birth of the prophet Samuel in the middle of the history concerning the high-priest Eli and his sons. Flavius is well aware of it[542]: "But I should first of all narrate the history of the prophet, and thus later speak of the history of the sons of Eli..."[543].

The eulogy of the sorceress of Endor and reflexions on the heroism of king Saul make for a substantial interruption[544] of the narrative thread.

---

[536] A, III, 165.
[537] A, XIII, 171.
[538] B, IV, 492-496.
[539] A, I, 14-26.
[540] A, I, 26.
[541] A, III, 265-268.
[542] A, V, 341-351.
[543] A, V, 341.
[544] A, VI, 340-350.

Flavius Josephus recognises this fact: "I shall return anew to where I began the digression"[545].

The philological ecphrasis concerning the word *pharaoh*[546] is most curious. Here Flavius Josephus is seeking to instruct his readers, "so as to do away with their ignorance and clarify the reason for the name"[547], and he later on concludes, "so as to make clear that both our books and the books of the Egyptians agree on many things"[548].

The entire history of the biblical Book of Esther is introduced as if it were an ecphrasis[549], so that the historian is aware of the necessity of picking up the historical movement again with the mention of an event which had been already dealt with some time before, "with the death of the high-priest Eliasib..."[550].

The maintaining of the privileges of the Jews by Vespasian and Titus is introduced a long time before these two personalities appear on the scene[551].

On the occasion of the capture of Jerusalem by Pompey, in the year 63 B.C., the question of the Jewish sabbath and its observance is brought up[552]. It is a question of whether the Jews are allowed to defend themselves on the sabbath in the case of attack. In fact, in this case, the Romans do not attack and spend their time in the preparation of the war-machines (No. 64). It is at this time that Flavius Josephus goes into a lengthy description of the piety with which the Jews observe rest on the sabbath, as is also noted by Strabo, Nicolas and Titus Livius (No. 68). It is, therefore, a religious ecphrasis.

An extremely long literal transcription of the texts of Roman decrees, in which friendship with the Jewish people is made manifest, cuts the historical thread[553]. In fact, in the old division of the work, these texts were grouped together in a single chapter, the Xth. The reason for demonstrating that these decrees are based on friendship with Rome is a constant concern of the historian, since he mentions it in the first and last paragraphs.

Finally I should like to mention the principal ecphrases which remain, without any kind of comment, since this historiographical technique of

---

[545] A, VI, 350.
[546] A, VIII, 155-159.
[547] A, VIII, 155.
[548] A, VIII, 159.
[549] A, XI, 184-296.
[550] A, XI, 297 (Eliasib has been cited in No. 158).
[551] A, XII, 121-124.
[552] A, XIV, 64-67.
[553] A, XIV, 185-267.

Flavius Josephus has been sufficiently demonstrated in previous commentaries:

- ecphrases which develop a subject related to family life: A, XVI, 66-86; 188-228; 300-334 and 395-404 (concerning the family troubles of king Herod); A, XVII, 1-22 (concerning the intrigues of Antipater and the nine wives of king Herod); A, XVIII, 127-142 (digression concerning the descendants of Herod),

- literal quoting of the Roman decrees in favour of the Jews of the Diaspora, and their motive: A, XVI, 160-178,

- religious ecphrasis: A, XVIII, 116-119 (the defeat of Herod by Aretas is attributed to divine vengeance, for having had John the Baptist put to death),

- psychological ecphrasis: A, XVIII, 170-178 (concerning the character of Tiberius) and 328-334 (comparison between Agrippa and Herod)[554].

4. *Historical anticipation*

Historical anticipation is a recourse, the object of which is to anticipate certain events which, following the rigour of chronology, should be narrated at a later stage. I believe Giet's[555] observations to be of importance concerning this question, when making a wider application of the biblical commentary of Father Vaccari on a New Testament parable[556].

The aim of this recourse is clearly explained by Vaccari himself: "L'évangéliste n'a fait que suivre un procédé stylistique assez fréquent chez les écrivains bibliques qui consiste à *anticiper* au cours d'un même récit une partie des événements, pour quelque raison de convenance, surtout pour ne pas revenir sur un sujet qui disparait de la scène"[557].

Giet complements these ideas in the following way: "L'histoire progresse ainsi par une série de bonds suivis chacun d'un léger recul (on serait tenté de dire qu'elle fait trois pas en avant et deux en arrière). Or, dans les derniers exemples donnés, aucune transition n'éclaire ces différentes démarches: elles n'apparaissent qu'à la lumière de renseignements étrangers au texte". He later on concludes: "Le procédé d'*anticipation chronologique* se ramène à un exposé par notices qui se recouvrent partiellement les unes les autres..., un peu comme les ardoises d'un toit. C'est un

---

[554] There are books which are richer than others in ecphrases: B, II, seven ecphrases; B, III, ten ecphrases; B, IV, ten ecphrases; A, XVIII, seven ecphrases.

[555] S. Giet, "Un procédé littéraire d'exposition: l'anticipation chronologique", *REAug* 2 (1956), 243-249.

[556] Father Vaccari, in *Mélange Lebreton*, Paris, 1952, 138-145 (cited by Giet).

[557] Cited by S. Giet, *op. cit.*, 243-244.

procédé simpliste qui ne permet de reconnaître ni un gran écrivain ni un historien capable de dominer parfaitement son sujet. D'auteurs modernes, on dirait qu'ils se contentent de classer de fiches, et de les recopier sans se préoccuper de fondre l'ensemble de leurs informations. À défaut de fichier, les anciens usaient des emprunts qu'ils faisaient à leurs devanciers, ou de leurs informations personnelles, à peu près de la même manière''[558].

In this article Giet applies the theory of anticipation to book XVIII of the *Antiquitates Judaicae*, and shows conclusively, by means of a thorough analysis, that chronological anticipation is something quite natural in Flavius Josephus. He comes to this conclusion above all when he sees that the historian realises, at times, that the narrative thread has been somewhat multilated, a situation which has to be put to rights by the insertion of explicit phrases which point to the transition of events, whereas other sources, the majority, receive no attention.

In the present investigation too I have come across these narrative or chronological dislocations, and I have applied Giet's method to the *Bellum Judaicum*.

In addition to this technique, I have also picked out another type of anticipation, but strictly narrative, thematic or of historiographic style, by means of which the author provides the reader with the background of what he will presently narrate[559].

In the first book of the *Bellum Judaicum*, I have come across a point which is very similar to the one commented on by Vaccari concerning the parable of the king who was making the preparations for his son's wedding, and the guests who did not attend[560]. King Herod, during his flight towards Arabia[561], comes up against various groups of Jews who attack him in an even more harrowing manner than had the Parthians. Sixty stadia from the city of Jerusalem a military action takes place, which is long: ''Here Herod overcame them and slew many of them, and here, to commemorate the victory, he founded a city, and decorated it with the most costly palaces, and there raised up the most well-fortified citadel, and named it Herodion, after his own name''[562]. And Herod continues with his flight towards Idumaea.

---

[558] S. Giet, *op. cit.*, 247.

[559] Though the subject should be gone into in greater depth, I would venture that this second technique is another element which shows the degree of influence of rhetoric on historiography.

[560] *Matth.* XXII, 2-9.

[561] B, I, 263 ff.

[562] B, I, 265. A description with details in B, I, 419-421.

It is clear that Herod did not stop to do all that the historian says he did at that time. That came rather later. Flavius Josephus simply anticipates a very definite event, and not for reasons of space, since he later on devotes a description to him, but rather, to my mind, so as to integrate in a whole later events which are intimately related with those he has just described, and which are the causes of those later events. It is a centripetal narrative, so as to prevent dispersal.

Straight away Herod leaves his family at Masada (No. 267) and makes for Arabia; in the meantime, the Parthians give themselves over to the sacking of Jerusalem and place Antigonus on the throne (Nos. 268-270); Phasael dies (No. 271), and the Parthians return to Parthia taking Hyrcanus prisoner (No. 273). Herod is not received by the Arab king Malchus (No. 274), and via Egypt and Rhodes reaches Rome, where Antonius appoints him king of the Jews (No. 285). The whole of this history took place during the year 40 B.C.

Then Flavius Josephus makes use of a παρὰ δὲ τὸν χρόνον τοῦτον (No. 286) which goes back to some preceding events: "During this time, Antigonus was besieging the occupants of Masada, who were supplied with all that was necessary, but lacking in water"[563]. How far does this *during this time* stretch? Indubitably to the time when Herod leaves his family in the fortress, or shortly afterwards, as is said in No. 267. It is a question of no more than months, during which Flavius Josephus has opted for giving narrative preference to the journey of Herod to Rome, being the more immediate subject, so as not to delay the news of his appointment as king.

On the other hand, the paragraphs comprised between Nos. 387-430 form a global whole which is chronologically continuous. Then there is the opening of a long section dealing with the domestic tragedies of Herod (Nos. 431-537) which must be placed between the news of the block which immediately precedes. Both blocks comprise a period which goes from the year 30 B.C. up to 9 B.C. and various events which are narrated in the second block belong to the first block. The following schematic figure is the result:

No. 387: Friendship of Herod with Octavian (30 B.C.).
    Return of Herod from the campaign in Egypt in favour of Octavian (30 B.C.).

No. 431: Herod's domestic tragedies: execution of Hyrcanus (30 B.C.).

No. 444: Execution of Mariamme (29 B.C.).

---

[563] B, I, 286.

No. 398: Additions of Trachonitis to
Herod (24-23 B.C.).
No. 399: Caesar returns to Palestine
(20 B.C.).
No. 401: Building by Herod (20-19
B.C.).

No. 445: Hostile attitude of the sons of
Mariamme (18 B.C.).
No. 448: Herod summons Antipater
(14 B.C.), and names him his heir (13
B.C.).
No. 452: Alexander accused before
Caesar (12 B.C.).

No. 415: Quinquennial Games (10-9
B.C.).
....
No. 538: Herod summons the tribunal
at Berytus (7-6 B.C.).

If one takes a look at the numerical order of this layout, it will be seen
that the block formed from number 431 to number 452 contains historical
data which synchronise with the events narrated in the preceding block
made up starting with number 387 and ending with number 415. In this
case, none of the delayed news is introduced by a phrase which indicates
this chronological dislocation.

In book IV of the *Bellum Judaicum* there is an additional example of
chronological dislocation, more specifically in Chap. IX and the beginning of Chap. X (Nos. 486-584 and 585-629). The layout, in which the
numerical correlation is followed and where the paragraphs follow a
chronological order, is the following:

June 68: No. 491: death
of Nero (9th June).

July
......
January 69: Nos. 499-
502: death of Galba
(15th January).
February: Nos. 503-544:
new war in Jerusalem
led by Simon.

March: No. 545: death
of Galba (15th January)
April: No. 548: death

Nos. 550-555: ἐν δὲ τού-
τῳ, Vespasian invades
Judaea (23rd June).

Nos. 556-576: Simon at-
tacks Jerusalem again.

of Otho (17th April)

		Nos. 585-587: κατὰ δὲ τὸν αὐτὸν καιρόν, Vitellius takes Rome.
May:	Nos. 577-584: Simon, master of Jerusalem (April-May)	

The three columns serve to indicate the correlative numbering of the paragraphs, as well as showing plastically how the news overlaps.

Finally, throughout book VII of the *Bellum Judaicum* one may see the overlapping of historical news with chronological backward movements.

Thus the book opens with the razing to the ground of the city of Jerusalem (Nos. 1-19); Titus leaves for maritime Caesarea. Then comes a historical step back (Nos. 21-22), with a reiterative formula of temporal indication: "*When* Titus Caesar was laying siege assiduously to Jerusalem, *then* Vespasian embarked on a merchant ship, and from Alexandria crossed over to Rhodes"[564]. If on the 26th September in the year 70 A.D. Jerusalem was taken, then Vespasian's journey to Rome must be placed beforehand.

The narrative thread is taken up again with the news that Titus is going to Caesarea of Philip, where he stayed for a considerable length of time, and where he finds out that Simon has been captured[565]. The history of Simon is placed here, but taking it back chronologically to the time of the siege of Jerusalem[566]. Titus goes back to maritime Caesarea[567], celebrates his birthday there (October 70) and leaves for Berytus (November 70). The history of the Jews of Antioch is added here, who were in danger "at that time"[568], and which constitutes a long ecphrasis[569]. Finally, the history returns to Titus and to the reception of Vespasian in Rome as emperor[570].

A substantial step back comes then, with the introduction of the rebellion of the Germanics and the Gauls, during the years 69-71 A.D., by means of the formula πρὸ δὲ τούτων τῶν χρόνων[571]. Parallel to this narrative there is the introduction of the invasion of the Scythians by means of the following formula, "in those same days, together with the uprising of the Germanics mentioned beforehand"[572].

---

[564] B, VII, 21.
[565] B, VII, 23-25.
[566] B, VII, 26-35.
[567] B, VII, 37.
[568] B, VII, 41.
[569] B, VII, 41-62.
[570] B, VII, 63-74.
[571] B, VII, 75-88.
[572] B, VII, 89-95.

The narrative thread returns to Titus, in Berytus, and the historical chronology follows its rhythm[573], until it ends up with the dedication of the *Templum Pacis*, in the year 75 A.D.

So far there have been four historical waves which come and go bringing fresh news and carrying off as much. Then another step back as far as the total destruction of Jerusalem, and when Bassus is mentioned as taking over the legion which Titus has left there[574], that is, the historical narrative goes back to the year 70, so as to take the fortress of Machaerus. About the same time, περὶ δὲ τὸν αὐτὸν καιρόν[575], the Jewish territory is sold.

Chapter VII situates the historic rhythm in the year 72-73 A.D., when it mentions the disastrous situation surrounding the king of Comagene, Antiochus[576]. Round about those same days, κατὰ τούτους δὲ τοὺς χρόνους[577], the Alani invade Media.

The great feat which crowns the end of this book VII is the taking of the Jewish stronghold of Masada, the last fortress of resistance against the Romans. The Roman governor Flavius Silva takes it on the 2nd May in the year 72 or 73, according to the commentator[578].

The following scheme stems from an analysis of this book:

```
. . . .year 70 . . . . 71 . . . . 72 . . . . 73 . . . . 74 . . . . 75
             | Jerusalem
                Nos. 1-20
. . . . . . |  . . . . |  . . . . |  . . . . |  . . . . |  . . . . |
 | Vespasian
    Nos. 21-22
. . . . . . |  . . . . |  . . . . |  . . . . |  . . . . |  . . . . |
             | Titus
                Nos. 23-25
. . . . . . |  . . . . |  . . . . |  . . . . |  . . . . |  . . . . |
 | story of Simon
    Nos. 26-36
. . . . . . |  . . . . |  . . . . |  . . . . |  . . . . |  . . . . |
             | Titus
                Nos. 37-40
```

[573] B, VII, 96-162.
[574] B, VII, 163.
[575] B, VII, 216-218.
[576] B, VII, 219-243.
[577] B, VII, 244-251.
[578] B, VII, 252-406. For the chronology, cf. E. Schürer, *Geschichte des jüdischen Volkes im Zeitalter Jesu Christi*, I-III, Leipzig⁴, 1901-1909.

. . . . . . | . . . . | . . . | . . . | . . . | . . . | . . . . |
　　　　| Antioch
　　　　　Nos. 41-62

. . . . . | . . . . | . . . | . . . | . . . | . . . | . . . . |
　　| Titus; Vespasian
　　withdraws to Rome
　　Nos. 63-74

. . . . . . | . . . . | . . . | . . . | . . . | . . . | . . . . |
　　| rebellion of
　　Germanics and Gauls
　　Nos. 75-88

. . . . . . | . . . . | . . . | . . . | . . . | . . . | . . . . |
　　| invasion of Scythians
　　　Nos. 89-95

. . . . . . | . . . . | . . . | . . . | . . . | . . . | . . . . |
　　　　| Titus to Berytus　　　　　*Templum Pacis*
　　　　　Nos. 96-157　　　　　　　　Nos. 158-162

. . . . . | . . . | . . . . | . . . | . . . | . . . | . . . . |
　　　　| Bassus to Judaea
　　　　and to Machaerus
　　　　Nos. 163-215

. . . . . . | . . . | . . . | . . . | . . . | . . . | . . . . |
　　　　| Judaea is conquered
　　　　　Nos. 216-218

. . . . . . | . . . | . . . | . . . | . . . | . . . | . . . . |
　　　　| events abroad
　　　　　Nos. 219-243

. . . . . | . . . | . . . | . . . | . . . | . . . | . . . . |
　　　　| events abroad
　　　　　Nos. 244-251

. . . . . | . . . | . . . | . . . | . . . | . . . | . . . . |
　　　　| Judaea
　　　　　Nos. 252 ff.

This scheme serves as a guide when it comes to pinpointing the chronological jumps of book VII of the *Bellum Judaicum*, but from it we may deduce that this chronological system of presenting events is fairly widespread in the other books[579]. I do not mean to imply that this is a quality, but rather the contrary: negative points because of the distortion which they cause in the events narrated.

---

[579] Though incomplete, I shall mention the following places: B, III, 9, 432.

With regard to the biblical texts which are paraphrased in the *Antiquitates Judaicae*, the phenomenon of chronological anticipation may consist in either historical anticipation or postponement, even to the extent of going against the biblical order. Such is the case of the fate of the prophet Michaias[580] at the hands of king Achab, of the mention of the attack of Sennacherib against the Arabs, which came to pass later[581], the proposal of his general Rapsakes to the Jews[582] which was made previously in the Bible, the letter of Cyrus to the satraps of Syria[583], mentioned later on by the biblical writer, the death of the high-priest Alcimus, placed in the Book of the Maccabees after the death of Judas[584].

Anticipation is also to be found in those books which are not paraphrases of the Bible. For instance: "Then did Archelaus[585] and Nero Caesar[586] expel Artaxias and did place on the throne his youngest brother Tigranes. But this came to pass later"[587]. Flavius Josephus himself recognises his haste. He also anticipates the story which refers to the visit of Octavian to Egypt, narrated a short time afterwards[588].

Finally I have gathered together a whole host of data which should not be simply cast aside. I do not think that they come to constitute anticipation such as that which I have been describing up to now, but rather anticipation which moves in the literary field. It is thematic anticipation, which paves the way for the exposition which follows it, or will be developed in the course of the history of some personality or event. Thus when Herod investigates into the plot which Antipater has been weaving against him, a woman witness, before giving testimony, throws herself headlong, but does not die[589]. And Flavius adds: "But due to divine providence, so it would seem, which was after Antipater, (the woman) fell not head first, but on another side, and was thus saved"[590]. The whole of Antipater's future is prematurely sketched with this short sentence: his death, shortly before that of Herod, will be inevitable.

The fate of Alexander, who was denounced by the enemies of Herod, will also be anticipated: "The tempest of his house passed on Alexander, and the whole of it came down upon his head"[591]. Indeed, in the follow-

---

[580] A, VIII, 392 = 1*Reg.* XXII, 26.
[581] A, X, 4 = 2*Reg.* XIX, 8.
[582] A, X, 5-10 = 2*Reg.* XVIII, 17-37.
[583] A, XI, 12-18 = 1*Esdr.* VI, 1-18.
[584] A, XII, 413 = 1*Mach.* IX, 54.
[585] King of Cappadocia.
[586] The future emperor Tiberius Claudius Nero.
[587] A, XV, 105.
[588] A, XV, 196 = 199.
[589] B, I, 592-598.
[590] B, I, 593. Cf. the parallel in A, XVII, 61-77.
[591] B, I, 488.

ing paragraphs, Alexander is imprisoned, and, after recounting at length the vicissitudes of his life, he is executed[592].

So as to avoid being repetitive, I shall briefly mention here those aspects which appear on numerous occasions in the work of Flavius Josephus: B, I, 513; B, II, 494; B, IV, 60, 137, 158 ff., 399, 658; B, VII, 219; A, I, 223; A, II, 40, 238, 257; A, III, 208; A, IV, 101; A, V, 179, 306; A, VII, 46, 162; A, VIII, 265, 299; A, XII, 119; A, XIII, 300, 303, 321, 351; A, XIV, 9, 25, 175; A, XV, 105, 196, 252, 261, 319, 380; A, XVI, 72-73, 229, 271, 300, 313, 335; A, XVII, 7, 69; A, XIX, 366; A, XX, 105, 113, 118, 141, 160, 163, 252; Vit, 14, 125, 145, 381.

C. THE PERSONAL ELEMENTS IN FLAVIUS JOSEPHUS

Under this heading, I shall group together and analyse the personal contributions of Flavius Josephus. Here I shall go into the most personal aspects of the historical work, with the intention of discovering how much of Flavius Josephus himself is in his history.

1. Paradox and reason

Historians of the Greek and Roman worlds did not always have a method of selection which was objective and analytical. They introduced into their works narratives which were fantastic in character, extremely difficult to prove in reality. All of them use them to varying degrees and some of them are not averse to passing critical and rational judgement on the event in question.

Flavius Josephus introduces few narratives of this type into his work, in comparison with the sheer volume of it. Of course I am not referring to the prodigious events which Flavius Josephus copies from the Holy Scriptures, which in his eyes are reliably related. This notwithstanding, his rationalism gives rise to situations where the unreal aspects of certain biblical events are slightly modified and left open to a free interpretation[593]. By this, Flavius Josephus appears to allow the irrational into the life of man, and thus reveals himself in his work.

This tendency not to allow in marvellous events in an easy manner became a golden rule for historians. It is well demonstrated in the instance of Lucian of Samosata, who advises the historian to maintain a measure of self-control when dealing with that in which he really believes[594].

---

[592] B, I, 550-551. Parallel in A, XVI, 229-270, 300-334, 356-394.
[593] Cf. S. Rappaport, *Agada und Exegese bei Flavius Josephus*, Wien, 1930, and G. Tachauer, *Das Verhältnis von Flavius Josephus zur Bibel und Tradition*, Erlangen, 1871, 18 ff.
[594] *De hist. conscr.* 60.

Flavius Josephus recognises, and says so explicitly, that there are things in life which are beyond what one may reasonably expect or believe[595], but that nevertheless the reader will find nothing that is illogical and nothing that is discordant in what he relates in connection with divine majesty, since he affirms nothing that does not observe the laws of nature[596], at the same time endeavouring to avoid that mythology which is characteristic of other authors[597], ordering events according to a reason[598].

This notwithstanding, paradox in the work of Flavius Josephus is inevitable. The historian affirms that the descendants of Seth erected two pillars, one of bricks and the other of stone, as landmarks in the case of a second flood. And he says: "(The pillar of stone) has remained standing to this very day in the land of Seiris"[599]. Similar statements are to be found which refer to the remains of the ark of Noah[600]. As to the pillar of salt into which Lot's wife was turned, he has this to say: "I have seen it, for it remains still"[601]. Regarding the disaster of Sodom, he says that it may still be seen, and that the credibility of its legends springs from visual proof[602].

On the other hand, Flavius Josephus confesses that he is weak in the arguing of certain information. Thus he justifies the longevity of the patriarchs from the standpoint of divine will and the diet which they observed. Even so, he invokes the testimony of other historians, starting with Manetho, so as to assure the reader of the veracity of the information he is presenting him with. But he ends up with a sentence, half liberal and half sceptical, which is marked by a strong dose of agnosticism: "Concerning this, however, let each look at it as he deems fit"[603]. A similar formula is repeated time and again throughout the work of Flavius Josephus, above all when something of a miraculous or supernatural nature[604] is brought into question, or else when a dilemma is presented[605].

---

[595] περὶ πίστεως (A, I, 14). On these aspects studied in the present chapter, cf. G. Delling, "Josephus und das Wunderbare", *NT* 2 (1958), 291-309; O. Betz, "Das Problem des Wunders bei Flavius Josephus im Vergleich zum Wunderproblem bei den Rabbinen und im Johannesevangelium", *Festschr. O. Michel* (1974), 23-44.

[596] A, I, 24 and A, V, 280.

[597] A, I, 15.

[598] The true date of the deluge is that which was propounded by Moses (A, I, 80-82).

[599] A, I, 71.

[600] A, I, 92 and A, XX, 25.

[601] A, I, 203.

[602] B, IV, 484-485.

[603] A, I, 108.

[604] A, II, 348; A, III, 81; A, X, 281.

[605] B, V, 257; A, I, 108; A, III, 322; A, IV, 158; A, XII, 359. A similar formula is used by Dionysius of Halicarnassus in his *Antiquitates Romanae* (I, 48, 1) and became an historiographic rule when dealing with marvellous events (Luc., *De hist. conscr.* 60).

Both the paradoxical and the rational aspects should be broached in some depth. King Herod, on two occasions, miraculously avoids death. The text says: "There (in Jericho) did something providential also happen to him, by which motive he gained a reputation of being a man especially loved by God, since he was saved against all hope"[606]. And the house where he had supped with the magistrates came crashing down hardly had the guests left it. The salvation of Herod from this disaster was a sign of the future dangers awaiting him and of his salvation in the future.

Thus, though Flavius Josephus tries to rationalise many of the events given in the Holy Scriptures as miracles, as we shall later see, elsewhere he shows himself to be ingenuously credulous.

After recounting the crossing of the Red Sea by the Israelites, which occurred in a miraculous manner, according to the Scriptures, Flavius Josephus is not at all at ease. He affirms that he has done no more than to transmit what he has found in the Holy Books, and closes the narrative with the *de rigeur* agnostic phrase. He says: "Let no-one be surprised at the paradox of the narrative, if the road to salvation was found for the ancients and innocent of crime too across the sea, whether by the will of God or by chance, when to the men of Alexander king of Macedon, men who have lived quite recently, the Pamphylian Sea ceded at their passage and offered another path, to those who had none, through it, when God wished to bring about the destruction of the Persian empire, and all who narrate the events of Alexander are in agreement on this. Be that as it may, on this matter, let each accept it as he deems fit"[607].

After Hyrcanus had brought about the complete destruction of Samaria[608], and on the occasion of his offering incense in the temple as high-priest, he heard a voice which said to him "that his sons had defeated, at that moment, Antiochus"[609]. Flavius Josephus himself recognises that the event is unthinkable: "It is somewhat paradoxical that which is said of the high-priest Hyrcanus, of the manner in which the Deity communicated with him"[610].

Dreams too are gathered together by Flavius Josephus, he who was familiar with this medium of communication between the deity and men. The system is somewhat mysterious. Flavius Josephus allows dreams and visions as events which are computable from the historical viewpoint[611].

---

[606] B, I, 331. He also had a fantastic escape from death at the hands of his enemies (B, I, 340-341).

[607] A, II, 347-348.

[608] A, XIII, 281.

[609] A, XIII, 282.

[610] A, XIII, 282.

[611] A, XIII, 322.

He has no qualms in describing clearly that, in a marvellous dream, he heard a voice which urged him to set aside his sadness and gave him its message: "Remember that it behoves you too to fight against the Romans"[612].

Flavius Josephus calmly allows the inclusion of rain "sent by God during the night"[613] to bring about a change in the plans of Joseph the brother of Herod. Joseph, besieged by Antigonus at Masada, determines to flee to the territory of the Arabs, since the water supply is already insufficient. The sudden rain, however, in a country where rainfall is very light, is included by Flavius Josephus without the slightest sign of surprise.

Whether from Nicolas of Damascus or from another source, the news of the profanation of the tombs of king David and king Solomon by Herod is included by Flavius Josephus in the following terms: "Two of his guards, according to what is related, were struck down by a flash of flame when they entered"[614]. This event brought in its wake unfortunate consequences in the political management of the king, according to Flavius Josephus, a statement which indicates that the historian reaffirms his belief in extraordinary phenomena[615].

No doubt all that I am analysing here is complemented by the religious beliefs of Flavius Josephus, an historian with a great traditional training, influenced by the ideological currents of the Hellenistic Era, at a moment of crisis of traditional values, especially religious ones. Therefore, if he allows that the transcendent world intervene, a world which for him has a rich variety of nuances, in historical affairs, then it is logical that he should allow other small details of an extraordinary or marvellous character, as can be seen in these examples.

Another instance when this mixture can be seen, no doubt brought about by a series of fluctuations in the mind of Flavius Josephus, is on the occasion of the transferring of the Olympian Zeus to Rome on the orders of Gaius. The emperor would not see his orders complied with lest the statue suffer damage. However, Flavius Josephus adds: "It is said that Memmius postponed the transfer for that reason and also because there came to pass signs which were more extraordinary than could be allowed as being worthy of credit"[616]. Here, to a certain extent, Flavius Josephus does not accept the episode, but does not easily refute it.

---

[612] Vit, 209.
[613] A, XIV, 390-391.
[614] A, XVI, 182.
[615] A, XVI, 188.
[616] A, XIX, 9.

In book VI, 288-315 of the *Bellum Judaicum*, there is a whole stock of portentous narratives. They come one after another, clearly intended to be grouped together as those signs which foreshadowed the fall of Jerusalem.

Soldiers have already overrun the entire city, and the temple is a pall of smoke, full of bodies and rubble. The end has come. Flavius Josephus then makes a series of educational reflexions, since to his mind history is the teacher of life, and straight away he notes a stock of ominous premonitions concerning the catastrophe.

Firstly, charlatans and liars led the people astray, but the people did not respond to the warnings sent to them by God[617]. Therefore, a sword-shaped star, a long-lasting comet over the city, and a splendorous light around the altar and the sanctuary are all misinterpreted by those who witness them. Ordinary people believe them to be good omens; the scribes, on the contrary, interpret them as a portent of disaster[618]. All this happened on dates which are specified by the historian.

Again, a cow offered in sacrifice gives birth in the middle of the temple, and the enormous east gate, which can hardly be moved an inch by twenty men, opens by itself at a specific time of night. Here too the omens seem to be good ones for the non-initiates, but the experts interpret them as being the opposite[619].

In the month of Artemision, there were seen, before the setting of the sun, armed armies flying through the air[620]. At Pentecost the priests heard a voice which said to them: "We are departing hence"[621]. But what is even more important is the personal oral warning of Jesus son of Ananias, a man of the country who, four years before the war, walked about in Jerusalem warning of the imminent danger and repeating "Alas, o Jerusalem!"[622].

Finally there is the description of two oracles. The first[623] of them represents an admission of the downfall of the city, and the second is a

---

[617] B, VI, 288. The testimony of Tacitus (*Hist.* V, 13) coincides with that of Flavius Josephus: "Euenerant prodigia, quae neque hostiis neque uotis piare fas habet gens superstitioni obnoxia, religionibus aduersa".

[618] B, VI, 289-291.

[619] B, VI, 292-296.

[620] B, VI, 297-299. Tacitus (*Hist.* V, 13), basing himself partly on Virgil (*Aen.* VIII, 528 ff.), says: "Visae per caelum concurrere acies, rutilantia arma et subito nubium igne conlucere templum".

[621] B, VI, 300: μεταβαίνομεν ἐντεῦθεν. Tacitus (*ibidem*) writes: "Apertae repente delubri fores et audita maior humana uox excedere deos; simul ingens motus excedentium". Alternative reading: "Let us depart this place" (μεταβαίνωμεν, Hegesippus, V, 44, p. 364; Zonaras, VI, 24-II, 69 Dindorf; Eus., *Dem. Eu.* VIII, 2, 112).

[622] B, VI, 300-309.

[623] B, VI, 311.

sort of ambiguous prophecy, found in the Bible, and according to which "at that time, one from their country would rule over the world"[624]. But the most interesting thing from the point of view of this investigation is the interpretation which Flavius Josephus gives the second oracle. Whereas for some the reference is to a personality of their race, and the sages are at a loss, Flavius Josephus does not hesitate for a second, and applies the ambiguous oracle—χρησμὸς ἀμφίβολος—to the person of Vespasian, "who was proclaimed emperor over Judaea"[625].

He brings this long paradoxical ecphrasis to a close by repeating the widely-differing opinions which were legion amongst the Jewish people in the face of these happenings: "Some interpreted them to their satisfaction, others showed disdain for them, until such times as the destruction of the city and their own perdition showed their folly"[626]. Flavius Josephus therefore makes an appraisal of them, gives them real content, and situates them in a very well-integrated manner within the plan of his work.

Now the other side of the matter should be broached. There is certain information which Flavius Josephus shows himself to be very demanding with, and he lessens the force of all that which may conceal things of a mysterious nature. This tendency is especially observable in biblical stories, in spite of his concern to reproduce them faithfully. In the *Bellum Judaicum* too are to be found some stories which are treated in this same manner.

When king Herod has to address his troops, who are demoralised by the intimidation caused by the earthquake, Flavius places in his words a complete analysis of events. These phenomena, he says, should not cause any demoralisation or affliction; "for these accidents of the elements are physical, and visit on men no more than their own consequences. Of a plague, famine, or of underground disturbances there may be a preceding, very small, omen, but these catastrophes carry within themselves the limitations of their magnitude"[627]. Here we have an excellent instance of the rationalistic virtue of Flavius Josephus. He shows himself to be a man of analysis in the words of Herod, who reduces all supernatural overtones to ordinary events.

Going on now to deal with the scenes of a miraculous and extraordinary character in the *Antiquitates Judaicae*, one observes a two-fold attitude on the part of Flavius Josephus: on the one hand, he transcribes

---

[624] B, VI, 312.

[625] B, VI, 313. Similarly in Tacitus, *Hist.* V, 13, and in Suetonius, *Vesp.* 4. For the relations between Flavius Josephus and Tacitus, cf. E. Norden, *op. cit.*, and P. Corssen, *op. cit.*

[626] B, VI, 315.

[627] B, I, 377.

the fantastic episodes of the Bible uncritically; on the other hand, from time to time, his critical sense, the awareness that his readers will find things difficult to believe, gets the upper hand. So Flavius Josephus attempts to reconcile this fact by changing certain expressions or pointing out to the reader an interpretation which is more in keeping with a rationalistic attitude.

The problem of the bitter water at Marah is described at length by Flavius Josephus and very concisely by the Bible. Flavius Josephus states that not even the beasts of burden could drink that water[628], whereas the Bible does not paint such a bleak picture, and the water is converted into good water by the direct intervening of God. A comparison of the two versions:

Flavius Josephus	*Biblical text, LXX*
"He, therefore, began to pray to God for him to change the water from its present state of badness so that it should become drinkable. And, God having granted him his favour, Moses picked up a rod which was lying at his feet, he split it in half along its length, afterwards he placed it in the well and tried to persuade the Hebrews that God had heeded their prayers and had promised to give them the water as was their desire, if they fulfilled his commandments without delay and with enthusiasm. On asking him what they might do to make the water fit to drink, he ordered the young men to place themselves around and to extract the water, saying that the remaining water would be drinkable, once most of it had been emptied by them. And they did so, and the water, stirred and purified by continuous blows, then became fit to drink"[631].	"Moses cried to the Lord, and the Lord showed him a log, which he threw into the water ...."[629]. "He said,[630]: 'If only you will obey the Lord your God, if you will do what is right in his eyes, if you will listen to his commands and keep all his statutes, then I will never bring upon you any of the sufferings which I brought on the Egyptians; for I the Lord am your healer'". "... and then the water became sweet"[632].

---

[628] A, III, 4.

[629] *Ex.* XV, 25.

[630] *Ex.* XV, 26. This verse contains the idea used by Flavius Josephus. For that reason I have placed it in the middle of the previous verse, since the historian used the idea of the obedience of the people of Israel as an express commitment, and Marah, *the bitter*, remained as testimony of it.

[631] A, III, 6-8.

[632] The end of the text, *Ex.* XV, 25.

The abundant number of expressions which Flavius Josephus uses to surround the simple Biblical text can be appreciated here. Secondly it should be mentioned that Flavius Josephus lays down a condition for the water to be made drinkable: the acceptance of divine will. And finally the miraculous biblical event is distorted and taken out of context so as to be given a different, empirical explanation: good water already existed at the bottom, and there was only the need to remove the dirty, bitter water on top to get at it.

The same can be said of the natural explication for the hunting of the quail, in which Flavius Josephus attributes their appearance to the fact of their being tired, given that the crossing of the Red Sea was excessive for that kind of bird[633]. The miracle is therefore explained by natural causes.

The crossing of the Jordan in times of Joshua also loses its miraculous side. The waters were not divided when the ark passed over, but they simply dropped, and the current became transitable[634].

He also tries to give a reasonable explanation to the fact that Jonathan and his shield-bearer sowed panic amongst the army of the Philistines[635]. But even more rationalised and reduced to its minimum is the divine appearance to the prophet Elijah[636]. The biblical description is very rich in spectacular details; Flavius Josephus' description simply mentions an earth tremor and a huge shining brightness as the material signs of the presence of God.

As regards the miraculous ascension of Elijah and his consequent disappearance from the sight of men, Flavius Josephus says no more than this: ''In those times, Elijah disappeared from among men, and, to this very day, no-one has knowledge of his end... In fact, of Elijah and Enoch, who lived before the flood, in the Holy Books it is written that they became invisible, and no-one has knowledge of their deaths''[637]. Flavius Josephus therefore takes away all the transcendent force from the biblical story. What is more, he reluctantly relies on the biblical sources and their authority, since, although they give no definite news on the death of these people, they at least insist on their disappearance by divine intervention.

Finally it can be seen how often Flavius Josephus relapses into his tactic of rationalisation A, IX, 37 (= 2*Reg.* III, 17-20), A, IX, 289 (= 2*Reg.* XVII, 25), A, X, 21 (= 2 *Reg.* XIX, 35) and in A, X, 259 (= *Dan.* VI, 17 ff.).

---

[633] A, III, 25 = *Ex.* XVI, 13.
[634] A, V, 17 = *Jos.* III, 13 and 16.
[635] A, VI, 114 = 1*Sam.* XIV, 12-13.
[636] A, VIII, 351 = 1*Reg.* XIX, 11-12.
[637] A, IX, 28 (= 2*Reg.* II, 1; *Gen.* V, 24 = A, I, 79).

2. *Ethical and philosophical reflexions*

Historical events are not self-contained units. A complete historian makes an appraisal of the origins, developments, and outcomes of various actions together with pedagogical consequences for the future. A specific fact of a specific personality, of a specific city, of a specific social group may have a paradigmatic content for future generations. It is with this in mind that Flavius Josephus, throughout his works, adds personal reflexions, of an ethical and philosophical kind, which enrich his historical task. Some seventy quotes are sufficient to present a Flavius Josephus as an historian full of content, with a sense of transcendent and pedagogic projection onto history.

What lesson can an historian draw from a catastrophe? In the presence of the valiant and generous death of Eleazar, Flavius Josephus ends up by saying that "he did no more than to aspire to great things, placing his life after glory"[638]. Again, at the treacherous death of Antigonus at the hands of his brother Aristobulus, he says: "Calumny severs all links of affection and of nature, and none of our good feelings is so strong as to be able to oppose envy for ever"[639].

In the speech of Herod to his disheartened troops, Flavius Josephus puts into the words of the king reasonings of great calibre, and, at the same time, easily understood by the troops.

Thus, hope that is founded on the misfortunes of others rather than on one's own strength is misplaced hope. And luck and misfortune are not permanent in man. At the same time, overconfidence leads to unreadiness, whereas fear teaches caution[640].

The king himself is aware that the counsellors of his sons have to be good men, and states that the rivalries between rulers come from the evil influence of their partners, whereas good companions promote affection[641].

The theme of ever-changing fortune in human affairs is a constant preoccupation in the mind of Flavius Josephus. Thus, when Flavius Josephus himself falls into the hands of the Romans, it is natural that the historian should make certain reflexions concerning the power of chance, the vicissitudes of war and the instability of human affairs[642].

The drama suffered by the Jewish people causes a host of refugees amongst the Roman armies. But an extremely unpleasant incident, bas-

---

[638] B, I, 43.
[639] B, I, 77. The same theme appears in B, I, 208.
[640] B, I, 373-374.
[641] B, I, 460.
[642] B, III, 396.

ed on the search for gold coins in the excrement of the Jewish refugees, induced the Arab and Syrian soldiers in the Roman army to kill some two thousand of them, so as to thoroughly examine their intestines and pile up the coveted gold. Titus rebuked his troops harshly and threatened the perpetrators of these acts with death. It is this atmosphere which Flavius Josephus uses so as to make his reader reflect, so as to make his history more of a teacher of life: "But avarice, so it would seem, disdains all chastisement, and a terrible passion for gain is natural in men, and no other passion like covetousness is comparable to it"[643].

Within the atmosphere of war, the horrors caused by hunger are also worthy of reflexion: "Hunger certainly surpasses all the emotions, but does not destroy as much as shame: for what at other times is worthy of modesty, is now disdained"[644].

On personal happiness Antiochus IV "also demonstrated that, when old, no one may call himself happy before death"[645].

In the face of the chaos which the Jews suffered during the destruction of Jerusalem, there is nothing to be done except to reflect and rectify positions. That which, in prosperity, holds man steadfast, "in adversity is rapidly persuaded; but when the deceiver actually comes to picture release from prevailing horrors, then he who suffers wholly abandons himself to expectation"[646].

But adversity is inevitable, "for it is not possible for men to avoid fate, even though they foresee it"[647], to the extent that "all manner of death seems to be preferable to suffering from hunger"[648].

Personal behaviour and faithfulness to friends is an object of reflexion when it falls into self-centredness, "for evil cannot avoid the wrath of God, nor is justice weak, but as time goes on it takes its revenge on those who have infringed it and inflicts harsher punishment on the wrongdoers, when they imagine that they have escaped from it by not having been immediately chastised"[649].

In the *Antiquitates Judaicae*, Flavius Josephus also presents a series of reflexions which reveal a revisionist sense of the biblical data. On the occasion of the destruction of the tower of Babel, Nimrod is persuading the people on the thesis of "the fear of God can be put away from men only if they live dependent on their own power"[650].

---

[643] B, V, 558.
[644] B, V, 429.
[645] B, V, 461.
[646] B, VI, 287.
[647] B, VI, 314.
[648] B, VI, 368.
[649] B, VII, 34.
[650] A, I, 114.

Abraham defeats the Damascenes, he who had only a small group of men, because victory "does not depend on number or the quantity of hands, but rather the fire and resoluteness of the combatants surpasses all number..."[651].

It is not possible to escape one's own conscience, and even less so when one does wrong, as in the case of the brothers of Joseph[652]. Joseph, on the other hand, knew how to keep himself in virtue and demonstrated the greatness of his spirit, in spite of all the changes in chance which overtook him[653].

The power of God cannot be diverted from its objective, as the Egyptians tried to do in the case of the birth of Moses: "No man can dominate the will of God, even though he may use unlimited means"[654]. In the journey of the infant Moses in the basket along the Nile, under the loving vigilance of his sister Mariam, Flavius Josephus also finds a motive for reflexion in the sense that all that God wants reaches its perfect end, in spite of difficulties[655].

Human behaviour in everyday affairs is often the target for reflexions. Thus the life of king Saul is full of moralising thoughts[656]. At the end of his life, Flavius Josephus writes a long ecphrasis so as to evaluate the contradiction-filled life which the king had to lead[657]. A comment on this latter point:

Flavius Josephus says in very clear terms that he has found material in the life of king Saul which would be of use to states, peoples, nations and good people (A, VI, 343). Virtue, aspiration to glory, zeal for good and noble acts, confrontation with danger and death and disdain of terror are all found exemplified in the life of Saul (*id.*, 343-345). "To my mind", he says, "only a man such as this is just, valiant and intelligent, and, if anyone has been or will be such as this, he deserves to achieve the praise of all for his virtue. For those men who have gone off to war with great expectations, intending to conquer and return safe and sound, who have already realised brilliant exploits, it seems not to me that they do well those historians who treat such people by calling them valorous. It is just, however, that they should be well esteemed, but only those can be

---

[651] A, I, 178.

[652] A, II, 25.

[653] A, II, 40 and 42.

[654] A, II, 209.

[655] A, II, 222.

[656] A, V, 253, 317, 359; A, VI, 59, 116, 262, 286. The jealous behaviour of Korah is also the object of reflexion (A, IV, 17). Joab hides his betrayal by being friendly to Abenar, because often wrong-doers play the role of good men (A, VII, 34) to ward off suspicion.

[657] A, VI, 343-350.

named, in all justice, valorous, daring and disdainful of dangers, who have all imitated Saul''[658]. And then comes the personal reflexion of Flavius Josephus: Saul went off to war aware of what was going to happen to him, with full knowledge of what would befall him, death, and, in spite of all, he goes out to meet it, fully aware, since he knew that any man who aspired to fame after death had to do some extraordinary deed in his lifetime[659].

As a reflexion on the murder of Abenar by the ambitious Joab, Flavius Josephus says: ''From these events, one may understand how many and what deeds men will dare to do out of ambition and power and so as not to leave it to another; for in their desire to obtain it, they do so by means of thousands of misdeeds, and, fearful of losing it, they ensure possession by means of deeds which are far worse...''[660].

The paraphrase of the remaining biblical books gather even more reflexions of an ethical and philosophical nature which spring from the behaviour of some personality. The moral behaviour of Roboamus, instigated by a change in character, as is usually the case among men who wield power, occupies the plane of moralising thoughts[661]. The same thing may be observed in the life of king Ozias[662].

Outside now the biblical paraphrase, there is no lack of *sententiae*. The inhabitants of Gaza send ambassadors to Jonathan to propose an alliance, ''because men, before experiencing misfortunes, know not what is good for them, but when they find themselves caught in some misfortune, then, after fighting against that which they might have done when totally ill-treated, they finally choose to do that, once they have suffered the punishment''[663].

At the death of Antigonus, through calumnies and the envy of his brother Aristobulus, Flavius Josephus makes the following reflexion: ''His death demonstrated that nothing is there which is stronger than envy and calumnies, and that nothing is there which so breaks friendship and natural intimacy as these influences''[664].

The conduct of social groups and peoples in the face of adversity also deserves reflexion on the part of Flavius Josephus, since he believes it to be sufficiently instructive for posterity[665].

---

[658] A, VI, 346.

[659] A, VI, 348-349.

[660] A, VII, 37.

[661] A, VIII, 251-252. More examples: A, VI, 341; A, VIII, 300 ff., 418 ff.; A, X, 277 ff.; A, XI, 268.

[662] A, IX, 222 and 226.

[663] A, XIII, 152.

[664] A, XIII, 310. In this same vein, Flavius Josephus reflects on the domestic misfortunes of king Herod (A, XVI, 395 and 403).

[665] A, XV, 17, 304, 313 and 353; A, XVIII, 156.

The intervention of God is wont to be manipulated by those rulers who are lacking in virtue, when they are surprised in an illegal act or are in danger of being punished, as is the case of Antipater[666].

Also the good or bad administration of a post is related to its duration, if one keeps in mind a natural law according to which rulers inevitably fall into covetousness[667]. And again: "The virtue of moderation is a very difficult one for those who are in a position to move with facility without having to answer to anyone"[668].

Flavius Josephus states that it is a condition of fear in man that it should not allow him to reflect at the most difficult times of his life[669].

Confronted with the re-emergence of Agrippa and with the recovery of his honours, Flavius Josephus writes: "Because of that it may be thought that it is characteristic of human nature that greatness should be humbled for all and that fallen powers once again should be raised up"[670].

The powerful will not suffer being reminded of their failures, and do not allow their subjects to glory in the successes of their services[671].

Finally, I should mention three reflexions of Flavius Josephus which derive from human experience: change in fortune is common to all men[672], wrong-doers do away with those who censure them[673], and a high post is always a target of calumnies because of envy[674].

3. *Eulogy and censure*

One of the contributions which is most particular to Flavius Josephus is his treatment of personalities. A personality understood as the agent of history may be the object of praise or rebuke. It is with this in mind that I shall develop the present section, and I shall limit myself to those contributions which are Flavius Josephus' own, disregarding those which come from the Bible.

There are key-moments when Flavius Josephus eulogises or censures when dealing with a given personality. There are two of these moments: introduction or appearance of the personality and the death of the same[675].

---

[666] A, XVII, 129.
[667] A, XVIII, 172.
[668] A, XIX, 210.
[669] A, XIX, 107.
[670] A, XIX, 296.
[671] A, XIX, 319.
[672] A, XX, 61.
[673] A, XX, 162.
[674] Vit, 80.
[675] Concerning moderation in eulogy and censure, cf. Luc., *De hist. conscr.* 59. Cf. too G. Avenarius, *op. cit.*, 157-163.

The words of introduction serve to centre the person, and, to a certain extent, the whole of later activity depends on them. They constitute the summary of the image which will endure up until death. Thus Abraham "was a man intelligent in all things, and persuasive with those who would listen to him, and did not stray in his conjectures; for that he began to make higher reflexions on virtue than others and on the opinion that was held of God..."[676].

Evidently, the person of Moses is deserving of the most eloquent eulogies. Moses is the best of Hebrews, "and all agree that, according to the prediction of God, Moses is the most noble of the Hebrews for the greatness of his intellect and his contempt for fatigues"[677].

Judes, of the tribe of Benjamin, is introduced by means of his physical qualities: "The most valiant in deeds of daring and the most capable of using his body for action, having greater dexterity in his left hand and deriving all his strength from it"[678].

The case of Gedeon is set out in similar terms: "He was a moderate man and a paragon of virtue"[679]. These words do not have a corresponding biblical parallel[680].

The sons of Eli are presented in terms of censure: "They, insolent to men and impious towards the deity, did not abstain from any act of iniquity"[681]. Even so, these words take their inspiration from the paraphrased biblical text[682].

The introduction is sometimes quite simple: "Abenar, a man of action and of good character"[683]. No biblical parallel[684].

As can be seen, praise and censure in the introduction of a personality hinge on two aspects: physical qualities and moral and intellectual qualities. I shall group together the principal items of praise and censure under these two headings:

– physical qualities: Asaelos, A, VII, 14 (enlarging on the biblical text in 2*Sam.* II, 18); Absalom, A, VII, 189 (enlarging on the biblical text in 2*Sam.* XIV, 25-26); Aristobulus and Mariamme, A, XV, 23;

– moral and intellectual qualities: Solomon, A, VII, 42-44 (paraphrasing the biblical text of 1*Reg.* V, 9-14); Azaelos, A, IX, 93;

---

[676] A, I, 154-155. Similar ideas are to be found in A, I, 167. The sons of Abraham too are deserving of eulogy in A, I, 238.

[677] A, II, 229. Ideas complementaries with those of A, I, 18; A, III, 74, 212, 317, 322; A, IV, 25.

[678] A, V, 188. Without biblical parallel, *Jud.* III, 15 (Hebr. Ehud: LXX 'Αώδ).

[679] A, V, 230.

[680] *Jd.* VIII, 1.

[681] A, V, 339.

[682] 1*Sam.* II, 12.

[683] A, VII, 9. His image is completed in A, VII, 22.

[684] 2*Sam.* II, 8.

Jodas, A, IX, 166; Joazos, A, IX, 177; Manaemos (censure), A, IX, 232; Josias, A, X, 49-52 (based on biblical texts in 2*Reg.* XXII, 1-2: 2*Chron.* XXXIV, 1-2); Hyrcanus, A, XII, 190-193; Eleazar, A, XIV, 107; Herod, A, XIV, 159; Germanicus, A, XVIII, 207-209.

At the death of a personality, Flavius Josephus makes a summary of the main qualities which have prevailed throughout his life. John Hyrcanus was "verily blessed and did not suffer fortune to mock him. Indeed he was the only one to have three great privileges: the government of the nation, high priesthood, and that of prophecy..."[685].

The qualities of Abraham at his death are summed up in very few words: "A man excellent in all virtue and worthily honoured by God for his zeal shown in His service"[686].

At the death of Isaac, there also appears a very condensed summary of his virtues: "Isaac was a man loved by God and was deserving of His great providence after his father Abraham, but exceeding him in length of years, for, having lived one hundred and eighty-five years in virtue, he died thus"[687].

The deaths of Jacob and Joseph are separated only by a few paragraphs of narrative. Of Jacob he says that "he was in no wise inferior to any of his ancestors in his piety towards God, receiving the reward which was justly befitting those who had been so full of virtue"[688]. Of Joseph he mentions his moral qualities and his qualities as a statesman: "Admirable for his virtue, he administered all under the guidance of reason, and made moderate use of his authority"[689].

Moses is accorded extensive eulogies in comparison with the eulogy he is given in the Bible[690]. Of him he says: "He surpassed in intelligence the men of his time and used reflexions in the best possible way, he was graced, moreover, with the gift of words and of addressing the multitudes, and had control over his passions... and was a general as there have been few, and as a prophet there has been no other like him..."[691].

Moses' successor, Joshua, receives a homage from the historian at the end of his days, as a summary of his qualities and deeds. He says of Joshua: "He was a man not lacking in intelligence nor unskilled when expounding his ideas to the multitude with lucidity, but sublime in two aspects, in action and in dangers he was brave and daring, and in times

---

[685] B, I, 68. Cf. the parallel in A, XIII, 299-300.
[686] A, I, 256.
[687] A, I, 346.
[688] A, I, 196.
[689] A, II, 198.
[690] *Deut.* XXXIV, 10-12.
[691] A, IV, 328-331.

of peace he was the most skilled in government, and adapted his virtue to each occasion''[692].

I shall now give the main items of eulogy and censure at the death of the most outstanding personalities: A, V, 197, Judas; A, V, 317, Samson; A, VI, 292, the prophet Samuel; A, VII, 390, David; A, VIII, 286, Abira; A, VIII, 313, Amarinos; A, IX, 121, Ochozias; A, IX, 172, Joas; A, IX, 182, the prophet Elijah; A, X, 73, Josias; A, XII, 224, Joseph, father of Hyrcanus; A, XII, 385, Menelaus; A, XII, 430 and 433, Judas Maccabaeus; A, XIII, 430, queen Alexandra; A, XIV, 283, Antipater; A, XV, 236-237, Mariamme; A, XIX, 201 and 207, Gaius; Ap, II, 144, Apion.

There are also extensive eulogies dedicated to architectural works (B, II, 49; B, III, 29) so as to bring out their beauty and usefulness, to institutions (A, XIV, 490) and to the Jewish laws (Ap, II, 291).

Finally I should like to point out that a study of the praises and censures offers extremely valuable material as regards knowledge of the command which the writer had over psychology in history. Without any doubt, this vocabulary is extremely revealing to us as regards this line, as I have shown in Chap. II, A, 1, when dealing with historical personalities. For this reason, I shall give a list here of the maximum possible number of items which contain eulogies or censures: B, II, 26, Antipater; B, IV, 316-325, Ananus and Jesus; A, I, 8, Epaphroditus; A, II, 7, Jacob; A, II, 9, Joseph; A, III, 192, Aaron; A, VII, 43, 130, David; A, X, 83, Joachim; A, X, 186, to some young men; A, X, 251, Daniel; A, XI, 295, Mordecai; A, XII, 128, Vespasian and Titus; A, XII, 352, Judas Maccabaeus; A, XIV, 97, Aristobulus; A, XVIII, 256-257, Gaius; A, XIX, 328-330, comparison between Agrippa and Herod; A, XX, 252, Cleopatra wife of Florus; Vit, 191, Simon; Vit, 427, to the wife of Flavius Josephus; Ap, II, 73, to the Romans.

4. *Proems and epilogues*

In this chapter there will be an analysis made of the use of proems, epilogues and personal annotations which appear in the four works of Flavius Josephus. A preliminary review of writers before Flavius Josephus, poets as well as prose-writers, will help to situate his tendencies with regard to these aspects[693].

---

[692] A, V, 118.
[693] G. Engel, *De antiquorum epicorum, didacticorum, historicorum prooemiis*, (Diss.), Marburg, 1910. Cf. G. Avenarius, *op. cit.*, 113-118.

Engel[694] distinguishes between two classes of proem: those which introduce an entire, unabridged work, and those which are destined to particular books. Each of them may be composed of different types, nine in all, according to the subjects and aspects dealt with.

The two types of proems are very different from each other. Those proems which introduce an entire work contain those explanations which are necessary for the clarification of the intention of the author and to illuminate the use of the work. The proems to particular books usually serve to guide the reader from one book to another.

According to Engel, the proems may be classified as follows:

I,   they indicate the matter which they are going to deal with;
II,   they present the layout of the matter which will be dealt with;
III, they recall what has been said in previous books or works;
IV,   they expound the causes which have motivated the work;
V,   they dedicate the work;
VI,   they recommend the subject they are about to deal with;
VII, the writer speaks of himself;
VIII, an invocation to the gods, characteristic of poets, and
IX,   history and its usefulness is praised, characteristic of historians.

Precedents

In epic poetry, the invocation of the Muses[695] at the beginning of a work is traditional, although it does not always appear in all poems. The *Iliad* and the *Odyssey*, in addition to the invocation, both indicate the subject which will be developed. Hesiod invokes the Muses in *Erga* and in *Theogonia*.

It cannot be established whether the *Hecale* of Callimachus began with a proem. In contrast, there is no doubt that the first books of the *Aetia* had one[696]. Apollonius of Rhodes began books I, III and IV with peculiar *exordia*.

Thus, in book I he invokes Apollo (verses 1-4) and relates the causes which gave rise to the undertaking of the Argonauts (verses 5-17), which places it as numbers I and VII according to the classification of Engel. The same can be said of the proems to books III and IV.

---

[694] Engel mentions studies which have preceded his own, and special mention should be made of H. Lieberich, *Studien zu den Proömien in der griech. u. byzant. Geschichtsschreibung.* Teil I: Die griech. Geschichtsschreibung, München, 1899.

[695] Quint. IV, 4: "Nemo miretur poetas maximos saepe fecisse, ut non solum initiis operum suorum musas inuocarent, sed prouecti quoque longius, cum ad aliquem grauiorem uenissent locum, repeterent uota et uelut noua predicatione uterentur".

[696] *Anth. Pal.* VII, 42.

The *Idylls* of Theocritus have no proems, but some of them do have a sort of introduction, so as to focus the attention of the reader (VI, XI, XVI, XVII, XVIII, XXII, XXIX).

The use of proems is a constant in Latin poetry. Livius Andronicus and Gnaeus Naevius use types I and VIII; Ennius uses various types: 1st, VI, I, VIII; 6th, VI; 8th, VII; 10th, I, VIII; 16th, IV. Virgil follows Homer, i.e. he uses proems of type I and VIII. Ovid uses a great variety[697].

The authors of didactic works wrote richer proems than those of poetic works[698]. There are, therefore, proems to a whole work and proems to particular volumes, better written and very varied.

There is an abundance of prologues or introductions and epilogues in the historical work of Herodotus, and in them the author gathers together ethnological, geographical and marvellous aspects[699]. Thucydides introduces his work with a prologue belonging to type I, in which he provides a pre-history of Hellas and analyses its ethnography and geography[700]. The second book is also introduced by a type I prologue, in which he mentions where the war begins and what order it will follow.

Xenophon writes a single proem to the whole of the *Cyropaedia*, which is an amalgam of types VI (1-5), I (6) and VII. Critical study is hesitant and in disagreement as to whether the *Hellenica* have a proem or not. The lack of a traditional proem may be observed in his *Anabasis*, in spite of the beginning of the first book being clearer than a prologue could be. Throughout the rest of the work are to be found records of previously narrated events (books II, III, IV, VII), a sort of type III proem, based on formulae; the rhythm of the narrative is broken[701].

Rhetoric had a great influence here. Thus a substantial number of historians stated their concept of historiography around the doctrine of Isocrates, showing a greater interest in the manner of dealing with things than in the things themselves.

According to the testimony of Polybius[702], Ephorus prefaced the whole of his history with a proem of type IX. Diodorus says: καὶ βίβλους γέγραφε τριάκοντα, προοίμιον ἑκάστῃ προσθείς[703], but nothing can be said of its

---

[697] G. Engel, *op. cit.*, 11-14.

[698] G. Engel, *op. cit.*, 15-41.

[699] Cf. J. L. Myres, *Herodotus, father of History*, Oxford, 1953, and T. Sinko, "L'historiosophie dans le prologue et l'épilogue de l'oeuvre d'Hérodote d'Halicarnasse", *Eos* 50 (1959-60), 1, 3-20.

[700] I, 1-3.

[701] G. Engel, *op. cit.*, 43-45.

[702] IV, 20.

[703] XVI, 76.

nature. Schwartz[704] identifies the second fragment[705] as a proem of type VII for the entire work.

According to testimonies[706], Theopompus dealt with his own person and the opinions of others in a proem of type VII[707]. Polybius[708] attributes to him a proem of type IV.

From a fragment it is known that Duris expounded his personal ideas on the art of history-writing in a proem belonging to type VII[709].

Polybius[710] is the source for knowledge of the exordium to Timaeus in book VI, which may be classified as being between types IX and VII.

Polybius stands out as master of the art of proems[711]. He became the standard model for those historians who came after him by reason of the quality and quantity of his work. In the proem to the whole of his work alone, types IX, I, VI, II, IV and III are to be found. Proems of types I, II and III appear in all the exordia of books I-VI. The other proems are comprised in type VII according to which the writer expounds the difficulty of the material (book III), or passes judgement on the work of previous historians (book XXXIV) or defends the arrangement of his work (books IV, VI, XI, XIV) and the reasons for writing it (IX, XXXVI, XXXIX).

Very little is known of the Roman historians, above all those of the first era, in view of the scarcity of fragments preserved; no more than a few testimonies offer certain information[712].

Julius Caesar does not use proems. A simple description of Gaul acts as the introduction to his *commentaries*. In book VIII there is a letter which doubles as a proem, and which belongs to types IV, I and VII.

Sallust uses a proem which is a compound of types VII, I, IV and VI in *De coniuratione Catilinae*, and of types VII, I and VI in the *Bellum Jugurthinum*.

Titus Livius is a rich source of introductory expositions. Types I, IV, VII, VI, and VIII appear in the general proem. He writes a proem of types III, VII and I in book VI; in book XXI, types I and VI appear. All these proems, save isolated cases, are placed at the most important junctures of his works[713].

---

[704] *RE*, *s.u.* "Ephorus".

[705] *FHG* I, 234.

[706] Pol. IV, 20; Diod., *Bibl.* XVI, 76.

[707] Dion. Hal., *Ant. Rom.*, at the beginning; cf. too *FHG* I, 283.

[708] VIII, 11, 1.

[709] *FHG* II, 469.

[710] XII, 28, 8.

[711] G. Engel, *op. cit.*, 50-59.

[712] G. Engel, *op. cit.*, 59-62.

[713] Cf. P. G. Walsh, *Livy, his historical aims and method*, Cambridge University Press, 1963; G. Wille, *Der Aufbau des livianischen Geschichtswerks*, Amsterdam, 1973, 71.

Tacitus provides prefaces to his *Historiae* and *Annales*, but not for individual books. The organisation of the first proem can be broken down into the following types: I, IV, VII and VI. The second proem comprises types IV and I[714].

Diodorus and Dionysius should be singled out for mention from amongst the later Greek writers. Diodorus, by way of general introduction to the forty books of his *Bibliotheca*, devotes the first five chapters of the first book to the exposition of the importance and usefulness of universal history, which places them among those proems of types IX, I, IV, VII, II and VI. When a comparison is made with the general proem of Polybius, it will be seen that they are the same proem but in a different order. The prologues to individual books abound, and in them types I and III appear[715].

Dionysius of Halicarnassus follows a similar path. In his preface to the Περὶ Ῥωμαϊκῆς ἀρχαιολογίας, there are two distinct parts, comprising the following types: part 1, types VII, VI, I, IV and VI; part 2, types II and VI. There are also proems to individual books[716]. He places his name at the end of the preface, after the fashion of Hecataeus, Herodotus and Thucydides.

Of biblical literature, the Books of the Maccabees deserve an analysis. In the first book, the reader finds himself mediis in rebus from the very beginning. There is, of course, no prologue. In contrast, the second book offers a proem after the fashion of the Greek historians, and is made up of types I, IV, VI and VII[717].

One may observe that, in Christian literature contemporary with Flavius Josephus, the *Evangelia* have no constant. Only the Gospel of Luke[718] is introduced by a prologue. The author, in very correct style, mentions the motive and argument of his work, and states that he seeks truth. The proem corresponds to types IV, I, VI and V, practically the same as those of Xenophon's *Hippica*. The Πράξεις τῶν ἁγίων ἀποστόλων begin with a proem which comprises types III, I and V.

Flavius Josephus is very much aware of this historiographic technique. His works are introduced by the exposition of his ideas and criticisms, and are brought to a close too with suitable epilogues. The longest proems are those to be found in his two great works, the *Bellum Judaicum* and the *Antiquitates Judaicae*.

---

[714] Cf. I. Lana, *Le Historiae di Tacito*, Torino, 1967, 164 ff.
[715] G. Engel, *op. cit.*, 67-76.
[716] G. Engel, *op. cit.*, 76-79.
[717] *2Mach.* II, 19-32.
[718] *Luc.* I, 1-4.

a) *The proems*

The proem to the *Bellum Judaicum* begins with a justification of the work. There is a critique of the histories already existing on the subject based on four points which are grouped together under two aspects: those historians who have based themselves on oral sources—ἀκοή—have written histories εἰχαῖα καὶ ἀσύμφωνα, in a strongly rhetorical style—σοφιστικῶς—, whereas those who had first-hand knowledge of the events have allowed themselves to be carried away by their desire for adulation —κολακεία—of the Romans and hatred—μίσει—of the Jews. In the second aspect he criticises partiality in the historians. Even so, even Flavius Josephus himself will not be able to avoid it completely[719].

Flavius Josephus gives voice to a commonplace when he says that "the war under way is the greatest, not only of those which have come to pass among us, but also almost of those of which we have heard told"[720].

The concept—again a commonplace—expressed by τὸ ἀκριβές[721] indicates an event narrated in all its exactitude, incompatible with histories which are "casual and contradictory, edited in rhetorical style"[722].

Flavius Josephus then (I, 3) speaks of himself, of the first writing of the history in his native language—τῇ πατρίῳ—, and his own two-fold condition as an enemy of the Romans, at first, and as a survivor by necessity—ἐξ ἀνάγκης—of the war, with which he refutes the κολακεία and the ἀκοή of his historian predecessors, to become an eye-witness of the events he is about to record[723].

So far, then, Flavius Josephus indicates the reason for his undertaking and the subject of the same (I, 1-3). Dionysius follows the same path in his proem (13-19) for the expounding of causes. This first part of the proem in the *Bellum Judaicum* includes types I, IV, and VII of Engel's classification.

There follow two paragraphs (Nos. 4-5) which sum up the turbulent circumstances of the Roman empire of those days, which gave rise to various rebellions throughout its territory. There is a clear attempt to justify the uprising in Palestine on account of the internal instability of Rome.

The insult to the truth of historical events on the part of some historians is qualified as ἄτοπον, and, by going deeper into the idea, it can be seen how Flavius Josephus opposes the πλαζομένην ... τὴν ἀλήθειαν with

---

[719] B, I, 12.

[720] B, I, 1. Cf. B, VI, 199 (2*Reg.* VI, 28 ff; *Deut.* XXVIII, 57 and *Baruch*, II, 2 ff.), Thuc. I, 1.

[721] B, I, 1.

[722] B, I, 1: εἰχαῖα καὶ ἀσύμφωνα διηγήματα σοφιστικῶς ἀναγράφουσιν.

[723] Polybius lays greater store by visual testimony than by aural.

his own historiographic attitude, διὰ τῆς ἐμῆς ἐπιμελείας ἀκριβῶς, laying
down three basic principles which he wishes to follow, i.e. ''the origins of
the war, the different phases it has gone through, and how it has concluded''[724]. This point is closed with a dedication of the work to the Greeks
and the Romans who did not take part in the struggle, bringing them out
of the ignorance in which they might have remained by reading histories
full of adulation and artifice.

Then (Nos. 7-8) he insists on his criticism against the historians for
their partiality when dealing with an appraisal of the true conqueror.
This notwithstanding, Flavius Josephus also denounces his own partiality, aware of his human condition, by stating that the events which he narrates are historical, whereas the laments for his homeland are something
personal of his (Nos. 9-12), ''outside the law of history''[725]. He also advances the basic cause of the disaster: ''internal uprising ... the Jewish
tyrants''[726], and testimony of all this in Titus himself.

There then follows a long defence (Nos. 13-16) of the history which
narrates events which are contemporary with the historian[727], criticising
those who simply rehash the works of other writers. The historian must
narrate new things and has to forge his own structure: ''The ingenious
writer is not he who reworks the scheme and arrangement of another's
work, but he who uses new material and creates his own corpus for his
history''[728].

So far then we have type VII, to which should be added other aspects
which have not been mentioned by Engel, such as the narrating of circumstantial events (Nos. 4-5), the justification of his work and the critique made of other historians, and the defence of autopsy as the most
basic of sources for the historian.

The second part of the proem goes into the presentation of a detailed
scheme of the work, distributed in seven books (Nos. 17-29), which
brings to mind Engel's type II. He confirms its truthfulness (Nos. 26-30)
even before people who were also witnesses to the events, something
which corresponds to certain aspects which are characteristic of type VI.

By way of conclusion, the dominating idea throughout the proem can
be specified in two aspects: that of controversy and that of self-defence.

Controversy on account of the severe criticism of historians who have
dealt with the same subject inadequately, on account of the criticism of
other historians, especially Greek, who narrate events of which they have

---

[724] B, I, 6.
[725] B, I, 11.
[726] B, I, 10.
[727] On the autopsy, cf. Chap. III, *Precedents*.
[728] B, I, 15. The same idea in Luc., *De hist. conscr.* 48.

no first-hand knowledge. Self-defence, because he will make an adequate and objective narrative, since he was an eye-witness to the events.

Finally it should be mentioned that this type of proem falls within the type elaborated by Greek writers.

The prologue to the *Antiquitates Judaicae* is also extensive (I, 1-26). It begins with the exposition of the reasons which have led historians to undertake their work: some for their own literary glory (λόγων δεινότητα) and for fame (θηρευόμενοι δόξαν); others in acknowledgement of the people who participate in the narrative (χάριν ἐκείνοις φέροντες); others since they had taken part in historical events, and yet others to make known historical events of universal usefulness (εἰς κοινὴν ὠφέλειαν).

These last two reasons have been behind Flavius Josephus' writing of the *Bellum Judaicum, Prooem.* He now embarks on a more ambitious work: the narrating of the ancient history and the political constitution of the people of Israel, according to the biblical writings. He justifies the content of the *Antiquitates Judaicae* in which he will explain ''the origin of the Jews and the fortune which they have suffered''[729], and confesses his doubt and concern (No. 7) in the face of the magnitude of the work which he is about to commence. Thanks, however, to certain people who have encouraged him, above all Epaphroditus, he has rallied courage sufficient to carry out the task (No. 8).

This tone of humility which Flavius Josephus adopts when mentioning his sponsor is curious, since it is fabricated and not at all sincere, as can be seen from the many passages in his works where the high opinion he held of himself is evident.

He alludes to his initial lack of desire to work and desire to make any effort (No. 9), perhaps indicating moral and physical fatigue in his privileged position in Rome. But Flavius Josephus still has two objections to make, which may simply be a literary recourse: whether his predecessors would have communicated information on the people of Israel which he proposes to give in Greek, and whether any Greek has ever been curious enough to want to have knowledge of the history of the Jews. The fact that king Ptolemy II should have been able to translate the Bible into Greek, with the permission of the Jewish priest Eleazar, is sufficient justification for his undertaking (Nos. 10-13).

A point which Flavius Josephus dwells on at some length is that of the historical lesson which the people of Israel suppose for the reader: acting in accordance or in defiance of the will of God brings in its wake either beneficial or disastrous consequences. Moreover, Flavius Josephus recommends his readers to place their thoughts on God and to ponder

---

[729] A, I, 6.

whether Moses presents a God who is far removed from traditional mythological aspects (No. 14-16). By this means, Flavius Josephus imposes on his non-Jewish reader a rationalist and critical attitude rather than a merely receptive one. He is either fully convinced of its theological truthfulness or he is awaiting some kind of censure which he has not been able to formulate so far[730].

He then declares that the plan he intends to follow will be that of paraphrasing the biblical narrative without either additions or omissions (No. 17): a promise which he keeps in neither of the two aspects. Even so, one should understand this statement in the sense that he will omit nothing of importance, that he will add nothing that does not fall within the biblical coordinates[731].

Finally he goes into an extensive exposition (Nos. 18-24) of the profound character of the work written by the great law-giver Moses, who is by no means comparable with other law-givers of fables. He promises a third book on "*Customs and Origins*"[732], of a more philosophical bent (No. 25).

Taking the classification of Engel which is given at the beginning, this prologue, very rich in data, includes the following forms, given in order of appearance: IV, I, III, V, VII, VI, IX and II.

A brief introduction to book XIV of the *Antiquitates Judaicae* serves to a certain extent to interrupt the over-long flow of the preceding narrative, with a slight indication of what is to follow[733]. In it Flavius Josephus touches on methodological ideas, no doubt inherited. He calls for beauty in exposition (No. 2) which is born of the choice of words and their harmony, so that the readers receive the information with pleasure and satisfaction (No. 3). The other aspect refers to the substance: historians have to exercise rigour—ἀκρίβεια—in their recording of history, and must love nothing more than truth itself[734].

Following Engel's scheme, here we have a proem of types VII, I and III.

The introduction to book XV is very short, by means of a reference to the subject dealt with in the preceding book. Book XV will deal with

---

[730] On his rationalism, cf. Chap. II, C, 1.

[731] On the use of this formula, cf. W. C. van Unnik, "De la règle μήτε προσθεῖναι μήτε ἀφελεῖν dans l'histoire du canon", *VChr* III (1949), 1-36; — *Flavius Josephus als historischer Schriftsteller*, Heidelberg, 1978, 26-40.

[732] A, IV, 198.

[733] The Codex Parisinus (P), of the eleventh century, adds at the end of book XIII: ἔρχομαι δὲ λέξων τὰ τοῖς υἱέσιν αὐτῆς συμβεβηκότα Ἀριστοβούλῳ καὶ Ὑρκανῷ μετὰ τὴν ἐκείνης τελευτὴν ἐν τῇ μετὰ ταύτην μου βίβλῳ. An epilogue-cum-proem perhaps? In point of fact, the idea is taken up again at the beginning of the following book.

[734] Similar observations concerning the duty of the historian are to be found in B, I, 16 and in A, I, 4.

following events[735]. It cannot really be considered a full proem, but
rather some simple sentences of transition, after interrupting the narrative with some personal reflections on the beginning of the reign of
Herod.

The introduction to the *Vita* is a long one (1-12) and in it Flavius
Josephus summarises the most outstanding aspects of his childhood,
boyhood, and youth. Neither does he leave unmentioned the sources on
which he bases the origins of his family (No. 6), and begins the work with
his first visit to Rome, on an official mission, at the age of twenty-six.
This therefore corresponds to Engel's type VII.

The proem to the first book of *Contra Apionem* is the most extensive of all
(1-59). It is made up of five parts: a justification and general plan of the
work (Nos. 15-16), a critique of the Greek historians, of their discrepancies and of their preference for writing literature rather than searching
out the truth (Nos. 6-27), the ontological value of the biblical sources
(Nos. 28-43), an apology of his *Bellum Judaicum* (Nos. 44-56), and the
points which he will be dealing with in his present book (Nos. 57-59).

The work is addressed to Epaphroditus (No. 1), and is the response to
a need which the historian has to counter the calumnies (No. 2) which
certain individuals have proffered concerning the *Antiquitates Judaicae*. He
will base his refutations on those historians of greatest reputation (No. 4)
and will confound the false writers (No. 4). His immediate plan is to
review the historians who have not neglected Jewish history.

The first thing to be borne in mind is the recentness of the Greek
writers (Nos. 6-14), so that it is an absurdity to consider them as the sole
possessors of the knowledge of ancient history (No. 15); he again sees
many points of discrepancy amongst the Greek historians on the same
points (Nos. 16-18), due to the negligence of the Greeks in keeping accounts of public events (Nos. 19-22) and to their interest in showing off
their skills rather than searching for the truth (Nos. 23-27).

In contrast the Jewish people, like the Egyptians, the Babylonians, the
Chaldaeans and Phoenicians, have taken care to conserve their most ancient records (Nos. 28-29), to choose people to devote themselves to
divine service (Nos. 30-36), in ancient times as well as at the present moment. For that reason, the twenty-two books of the Holy Scripture are
not at ideological loggerheads (Nos. 37-39). He goes into an exposition of
the years which the biblical books occupy (Nos. 40-41), and emphasises
the veneration which the Jews had for them (Nos. 42-43).

He recalls the defects of the Greek historians, but adds another two
reasons why they should be considered unreliable: not having visited the

---

[735] A, XV, 1.

places nor having witnessed the events which they describe (Nos. 44-46). In contrast, Flavius Josephus has been witness to all that he recounts in his *Bellum Judaicum*, and has the testimony of other prestigious witnesses to the events, as well as having at his disposal the written record of the historical precedents, i.e., the Holy Scriptures, in which the Jews profess their deepest confidence (Nos. 47-52). His *Bellum Judaicum* is therefore no mere literary exercise (No. 53), but is based on the autopsy of events and even on the *commentarii* of the imperial generals (Nos. 53-56).

Finally, the points to be dealt with: an explication for the silence of the Greek historians concerning the Jews, quotes from the testimonies to his integrity, and, to end up, the destruction of the calumnies of the detractors of the Jewish race (Nos. 57-59).

According to Engel's classification, and respecting their order of appearance, the following types are to be found here: V, IV, I, II. The apologetic aspect which moves the whole of this proem is not mentioned in the classification of Engel.

The brief introduction to the second book of *Contra Apionem* begins with a mention of the name of Epaphroditus and with a reference to the subject dealt with in his first book (No. 1). He then goes on to devote his efforts to refuting the accusations which have been levelled against the Jewish people, above all by Apion (Nos. 2-7), which will continue up to No. 144, and by other detractors. He considers it difficult to sum up the accusations of Apion, but that they may be grouped under three headings: concerning the leaving of Egypt by his ancestors, concerning the Jewish residents in Alexandria, concerning the accusations against Jewish liturgy and legislation (Nos. 6-7).

Therefore, according to Engel's classification, types V, III, I, II and VI are to be found here.

In numbers 145-150, after the death of Apion, Flavius Josephus reassesses the work, pointing out that he has set himself the creation of a means of rebutting the detractors of the Jewish people. Flavius Josephus determines to write a summary of the Jewish constitution, so as to dismantle the unfavourable arguments of Molon, Lysimachus and others, who do no more than proffer calumnies against Moses (No. 145). The excellence of the Jewish code only serves to bring about good relations with the whole of mankind (No. 146). Flavius Josephus begs that he be read without envy (No. 147). He will make no panegyric of his laws, but he does believe that a refutation must be made of the numerous accusations, a refutation which in its terms should fall within the Jewish code (Nos. 147-148). He will use solely the comparative method as regards other legislations, when it comes to the need to demonstrate that the Jewish laws are in no wise inferior (No. 150).

These points should all indubitably be taken as a sort of introduction to the second part of the book, which comes to constitute a sort of treatise-appendix to the whole apology. This appendix will therefore comprise a vision of the person and the work of Moses, the Jewish concept of God, the temple and the divine cult, marriage, education, funeral ceremonies, punishments together with a critical comparison with other legislations concerning these same points.

This introduction to a part of the work should be considered as falling under types I, IV and VI as proposed by Engel.

b) *The epilogues*

The epilogue to the *Bellum Judaicum* is short. However, throughout the work there may be observed certain expressions which serve to bring to a close either a narration or a book. Thus, the lengthy history of king Herod (B, I, 204-673) is brought to a close by means of a simple, stereotyped phrase: "...and that was the end of Herod"[736], which is parallel to the phrase which ends book II: "...and thus were the affairs in Idumaea"[737].

In addition to the brief conclusion to the entire work, there is a previous one, after the fall of Jerusalem (B, VI, 435-442). The event is deserving of it. The historian goes through a list of the times when Jerusalem had previously been captured, five in all (Nos. 435-439), and with the present defeat it was the second time that it had been sacked. He recalls the founding of the city by the "king of justice", Melchisedek[738], priest and king. There follow chronological particulars on the city, from the reign of king David and from its foundation up to its destruction at the hands of Titus (Nos. 440-441). And he concludes with an impressive listing of the titles of glory of the city (ἡ ἀρχαιότης, ὁ πλοῦτος ὁ βαθύς, τὸ διαπεφοιτηκὸς ἔθνος, ἡ μεγάλη δόξα τῆς θρησκείας), which availed it nought against the fury of the Roman armies (No. 442).

The final epilogue (B, VII, 454-455) is a mention of the two concepts which had already been pointed out in the proem to the whole work: he has written his history in all exactitude (μετὰ πάσης ἀκριβείας) for those who wish to know the exact manner in which the war developed, and has no hesitation in saying that the truth (περὶ τῆς ἀληθείας) has been the only objective he has pursued, and he even allows, as proof of his faithfulness

---

[736] B, I, 673.

[737] In the long run, these phrases become an extremely useful recourse for the changing of subject. Elsewhere: A, XIII, 432; A, XIV, 491; A, XX, 251. Regarding this, see the study concerning these narrative endings, similar to the *Ringkomposition*, which was made in Chap. II, B, 1.

[738] Mistaken philological interpretation.

to those premisses which he laid down in the prologue, that the reader makes his own interpretation as he may.

Book VI of the *Antiquitates Judaicae* is brought to a close (No. 378) with a short summary concerning the reign of king Saul. Saul has died lamentably and according to the predictions made by Samuel, because he has disobeyed God, because he destroyed Abimelech, the high-priest, and his family, and the priestly family of Nob, according to rabbinical tradition.

A chronological relationship with the life of the prophet Samuel interrupts this book. Saul, therefore, reigned for sixteen years during the lifetime of Samuel, and for twenty-five years after the death of the prophet.

These details are, no doubt, Flavius Josephus' own, and reveal his meticulousness as a historian, and a great pedagogical sense as a writer who knows how to draw the attention of the reader throughout the reading of his work, taking pains to remind him of dates and facilitating the effort needed to make relationships and comparisons.

The first part of this number 378 is moralising in intention. Jewish religious sense can be seen here in its two-fold manifestation: in the sphere of the acceptance of divine will and in the sphere of human behaviour. Here then we have a moment used by Flavius Josephus to present, once more, historical pedagogy.

On the occasion of the death of king Achab[739], come about in spite of all the attempts to thwart fate, the latter is irremediably fulfilled. In the first place, in view of the fulfilling of the prophecies concerning the royal death, Flavius Josephus says that it is necessary to recognise and honour God everywhere, and that counsels given simply to please should not be placed before the truth, and it is through prophecies that God warns us of that which we must avoid.

Yet again Flavius Josephus praises religion and obedience of God as a path of personal behaviour, and the historical event of the death of Achab is to be the occasion which teaches us to behave with wisdom and with submission to divine will.

For Flavius Josephus, there is yet another lesson to be learned from the king's end. Fate is ineluctable, even though it may be foreseen. And he concludes: ''It is evident that the capacity for reasoning of Achab was deceived by fate, so that he should not heed those who foretold his defeat, and, in contrast, that he should die for having obeyed those who had made him prophecies to please him''[740].

---

[739] A, VIII, 418-420.
[740] A, VIII, 420.

In short, there is a manifest tendency in Flavius Josephus to make use of certain impressive events, especially when transcendent power appears on the scene, so as to convert an historical event into a religious, moral and civic lesson.

The extensive *Antiquitates Judaicae* is brought to a close with a solemn epilogue. In the first number, 259, after pointing out that the work ends at a point where the narrative of the *Bellum Judaicum* takes over, he specifies the chronological scope of the same: "Here end my *Antiquities*, after which I shall begin to write on the war. This book contains the transmission from the creation of man up to the twelfth year of the reign of Nero, of the happenings which have come to pass concerning us, the Jews, in Egypt, Syria and Palestine"[741]. In short, the sufferings of the Jews all over the ancient world up to the times of the Romans. He does not let his μετ' ἀκριβείας (XX, 260) go by without another mention. In short again, he has conserved the record of the succession of high-priests, spanning two thousand years, as well as that of kings, judges, as is to be found in the Holy Scriptures (XX, 261), because he had promised thus at the beginning (A, I, 5 ff.). He devotes from number 262 to number 266 to talking about himself, regarding his intellectual standing, his knowledge of Greek, his capacity for interpreting the Holy Scriptures, and promises that he will write his autobiography, which will comprise a new overview of the war and of events up to his own times, and likewise he will publish four books on theology and Jewish laws (XX, 267-268).

It is, therefore, more an epilogue of self-defence and promises. The first part (XX, 259-261) recalls the index of a book.

The end of the *Vita* comprises words addressed to Epaphroditus, to whom the *Antiquitates Judaicae* and the *Vita* are dedicated. The *Vita* should be, at least in its final edition, a sort of appendix to the *Antiquitates Judaicae*[742]. It repeats the idea of leaving judgement on his life to the will of each[743].

The first book of *Contra Apionem* has a merely formal conclusion. The book has become over-long, and a second book must be started to contain the material which remains[744].

The second book of *Contra Apionem* contains an epilogue which is fairly extensive, which can be divided into three: a recapitulation (II, 287-290), a eulogy to Jewish laws (II, 291-295) and the dedication of both books to Epaphroditus (II, 296).

---

[741] A, XX, 259.
[742] Cf. A, XX, 266.
[743] Cf. similar ideas in B, VII, 430.
[744] Ap, I, 320.

The recapitulation comprises a reference to the *Antiquitates Judaicae*, where he has described Jewish laws, but his intention in the study under way has been to prove that those writers who have attacked the Jews have gone against truth itself. He has demonstrated the ancientness of the Jewish people, substantiating it by means of numerous quotes from other authors. He lays emphasis on the outstanding qualities of Moses and of the Jewish people.

The second part is given over to eulogising the essence of the Jewish laws: they move to piety, to the sharing out of goods, they encourage men, thanks to which the Jews have introduced marvellous ideas into the world. The author proclaims his faith in a providential God. May all the detractors of the Jewish people fall into confusion!

5. *Historiographic pointers*

Throughout all of his works, Flavius Josephus takes great care to indicate the manner in which he will carry out his *opus*, how he intends to distribute the material, at what moment he will deal with a given subject, and so on, by means of phrases which are stereotyped to a greater or lesser degree. All these indicators make for a whole which presents a well-established organisation of material, and at the same time provide the reader with a well-marked path through the work.

From an intrinsic point of view, this manner of history-writing manifests no more than the desire of leaving a well-made work, in which seriousness and historical rigour—so often expounded by Flavius Josephus—should appear with structural cohesion, as well as showing constant concern for conciseness, together with abundant information, and concern for the orientation of the reader as regards the work.

In this section, then, I shall analyse the data, bearing in mind their subject-matter and intentionality.

In the first place it is necessary to set up two main groups of references or historiographic pointers: those pointers to historical information *which has already been treated in previous paragraphs or books*, and events which refer to subjects which *will be broached later on or complemented further along*.

The first aspect is very rich both in the quantity and quality of the items. On the one hand, expressions of the type ὡς ἔφαμεν and similar abound[745], as do others, with slight differences, of the type ἀνωτέρω,

---

[745] B, I, 344, 365, 411; B, II, 114; B, V, 1, 246, 251, 550; B, VI, 114, 117, 375; A, I, 344; A, III, 62, 147, 171, 188, 201, 209, 215, 248, 288, 295; A, IV, 159, 311; A, V, 89, 122, 155, 215, 343; A, VII, 243, 334, 364; A, VIII, 130, 246, 309; A, IX, 1, 29, 112, 117, 280; A, X, 18, 81, 148, 230; A, XI, 341; A, XII, 387; A, XIII, 62, 80, 112, 285, 288, 320, 372; A, XIV, 5; A, XV, 13, 182, 240, 254; A, XVI, 73, 206, 227; A, XVII, 32; A, XVIII, 29, 129, 134, 138; A, XIX, 123, 212, 297, 298; A, XX, 9, 71, 101, 102, 110, 117, 199, 227; Vit, 10, 28, 122, 216, 272.

πρότερον, μικρὸν ἔμπροσθεν, πρὸ τούτων, πρότερον ἐν ἄλλοις … δεδηλώκαμεν, δεδήλωται, προειρήκαμεν …[746] and others with specifications of the work or the book in which the subject has already been dealt with, with phrases of the type ὥς μοι καὶ πρότερον λέλεκται τὸν Ἰουδαϊκὸν ἀναγράφοντι πόλεμον[747], ὡς ἐν τῇ πρὸ ταύτης βίβλῳ δεδηλώκαμεν[748]. So far, the author always refers to an event which is to be found in the same book or in the same work. On the other hand too, the *Antiquitates Judaicae* and the *Vita* both contain references to the *Bellum Judaicum*[749], and *Contra Apionem* has a reference to the *Antiquitates Judaicae*[750].

Finally, some of the items do not have their correspondence, that is, it is not true that Flavius Josephus has already related elsewhere what he is narrating at the present moment. The fact cannot be put down solely to carelessness on the part of the writer, but may well correspond to a phrase extracted from the source which he uses. Some commentators get round the problem by saying that he is referring to the work of another historian and not to his own. Thus, phrases such as ''such as has already been shown elsewhere''[751] may have been taken from the literary source or else may refer to another author[752].

The second aspect of this classification covers those references to subjects which Flavius Josephus will deal with at a later stage. A distinction should be made between later references in general, and later places, but more suitable for dealing with the subject. Thus, this range of nuances should be located between phrases such as ἐν τοῖς ἑξῆς δηλώσομεν, περὶ οὗ δηλώσομεν ὕστερον, αὖθις μετ' οὐ πολὺ δηλώσομεν and other similar ones[753]. The most suitable place is expounded in phrases such as κατὰ χώραν δηλώσομεν, κατὰ καιρὸν οἰκεῖον, περὶ ὧν ἐροῦμεν εὐκαιρότερον and other similar ones[754]. Finally, neither does Flavius Josephus keep his promise here, and some of the items do not have their later correspondence[755].

---

[746] B, VI, 400; B, VII, 244, 253; A, I, 135; A, II, 198; A, VI, 1, 105; A, VII, 330; A, VIII, 325.

[747] A, I, 203.

[748] A, IV, 74; A, VIII, 1; A, XIII, 1, 72; A, XIV, 1; A, XV, 1 (variant); A, XX, 1.

[749] A, XX, 239, 248; Vit, 61, 413.

[750] Ap, I, 127.

[751] A, XII, 390.

[752] A, XII, 244; A, XIII, 36, 61, 108, 119, 186, 253, 271, 347, 371. For all these aspects, cf. H. Drüner, *op. cit.*, 82-94, and J. von Destinon, *Die Quellen des Flavius Josephus in der Jüd. Arch. Buch XII-XVII = Jüd. Krieg Buch I*, Kiel, 1882, 19-29.

[753] B, I, 406, 418; B, II, 651; B, V, 20; A, I, 137, 142, 175, 195; A, III, 74, 218; A, V, 31; A, VI, 322; A, VII, 344; A, VIII, 211; A, IX, 266, 291; A, X, 30, 35, 107; A, XII, 388; A, XIII, 11, 296; A, XIV, 78; A, XV, 371; A, XVI, 404; A, XVII, 28, 60; A, XVIII, 373; A, XX, 48, 53, 96; Vit, 83; Ap, I, 92.

[754] B, I, 33, 182; B, II, 557; B, V, 237, 445; A, III, 94, 218; A, VII, 103, 105, 244; A, X, 80; A, XII, 237; A, XIII, 275; A, XIV, 388.

[755] A, VII, 89; A, XIX, 366; A, XX, 144, 147.

Apart from these numerous items which lend themselves so well to grouping, there is still a host of references which correspond to very specific places and times. I refer to phrases which are intended to clarify a specific point or smooth over some small methodological difficulty. Here then are the main instances of these items: so as to justify an ecphrasis (B, III, 109; B, VII, 274; A, VI, 350), to say that a subject has been dealt with sufficiently (B, III, 475; B, V, 247; A, II, 257; A, III, 187, 257; A, VII, 306, 394; A, VIII, 245; A, IX, 242; A, XI, 206; A, XII, 153; A, XIII, 73), to invoke brevity in the exposition (B, V, 442; Ap, I, 251), to limit the subject of the *Bellum Judaicum* (B, I, 17-18), to limit the subject of the *Antiquitates Judaicae* (A, I, 7), to promise another work (B, V, 237, 247; A, I, 25, 29, 160, 192, 214; A, III, 94, 143, 205, 223, 230, 257, 259, 264; A, IV, 198, 302; A, XX, 267, 268), to return to the subject which he has left off previously (B, II, 251; A, I, 67; A, III, 218; A, VIII, 298, 393; A, IX, 276; A, XVIII, 80), to limit a subject (A, I, 68; A, VII, 307, 369; A, IX, 158), to indicate that he has already spoken of the subject in the *Bellum Judaicum* (A, XIII, 173, 298; A, XVIII, 11; A, XX, 258; Vit, 27, 412), to justify what he is narrating (A, II, 293; A, V, 337; A, VIII, 26, 56, 159, 178), to indicate that he will speak of the subject later on (A, I, 133; A, II, 200; A, III, 213; A, VII, 69; A, XI, 185; A, XII, 137; Vit, 390; Ap, II, 145), to indicate the subject he will deal with straight away (A, I, 148; A, II, 8; A, III, 173, 175, 214, 225; A, IV, 13, 68, 196; A, VIII, 265; A, XII, 42, 60, 245; A, XVIII, 127, 129, 142, 310; A, XIX, 15; Ap, I, 153).

6. *Novelistic elements*

In broad outline, the Hellenistic Era may be said to have been full of violent conflicts which brought about all manner of upheavals amongst peoples, and above all the inner vacuum of feeling themselves invaded by ideological currents which were totally bereft of any connotations with their own peculiarities as a people. But there was no lack of those who would make them feel their own profound ideals, thus preventing their nationalist feelings from being completely extinguished.

On a popular level, this gave rise to the creation of a national history mixed with all sorts of legends and myths. This popular literature therefore constituted the nourishment which sustained their strength in the face of foreign domination. These legendary histories revived the ancient epic concept of the hero, around whom the episodes which take place are very similar from nation to nation.

On a more cultured literary level, something similar came to pass. During the reign of the Seleucids, Berosus wrote Βαβυλωνιακά, in which he praises the politics of the day. Manetho, in his work Αἰγυπτιακά, exalts the politics of the Ptolemies[756]. And, in the Jewish world, Flavius Josephus dedicates his work, the *Bellum Judaicum*, to the praise of Rome and the Flavii[757].

Thus, thanks to Plutarch[758], the names of some of the heroes appearing in various works in novel form in ancient times are known: Semiramis in Assyria, Sesostris in Egypt, Manes in Phrygia, Cyrus in Persia, Alexander in Macedonia[759]. The fact that there is no mention made of the Jewish national hero, Moses, may be due to the reserve of the Jewish world with a view to the non-Jewish world. It should also be pointed out that Jewish literature produced no nationalist work during the period of the Persians, and, in contrast, due to the socio-political changes brought about by the conquest of Alexander, it was capable of producing works of an uncompromising nationalist spirit, such as the books of Daniel, Judith and Maccabees.

Indubitably all this literature—possibly very abundant—must have influenced historians, not so much because of the specific contribution of data and events as because of the way in which personalities and historical passages are presented. In a certain sense, this literature contributes methodological elements to historical science, so making the historian pay closer attention to circumstantial elements and making him give greater appreciation to concomitant events: all this would lead to the creation of a history based on personalities.

Within, then, the history-novel, and above all in view of the true novels created in the Hellenistic Era, it seems that there are two predominant elements in them: the hero, who is the nucleus of the narrative, on whom the remaining elements converge, and those subjects or scenes of erotic interest, where the struggle between virtue and vice may appear.

Fictional writing in the Semitic world in the Hellenistic Era is gathered together in the *Testaments of the Twelve Patriarchs*[760].

Flavius Josephus is not immune to these literary attractions, and from his standpoint as an intellectual tries to recreate histories which, although both Jewish sources proper and the influences of Greek literature are

---

[756] Cf. *RE*, *s.uu.* "Berossos" and "Manethon".

[757] Flavius Josephus suffers from the Hellenistic influence in the treatment of certain episodes. On this point, cf. H. Sprödowsky, *Die Hellenisierung der Geschichte von Joseph in Ägypten bei Flavius Josephus*, Berlin, 1937.

[758] *De Is. et Osir.*, 24, 360 B.

[759] Cf. M. Braun, *History and Romance in Graeco-oriental Literature*, Oxford, 1938 (*Griechischer Roman und hellenistische Geschichtsschreibung*, Frankfurt a. M., 1934). For the Greek literature, cf. W. Aly, *Sage und Novelle bei Herodot und seinen Zeitgenossen*, Göttingen, 1969.

[760] Cf. M. Braun, *op. cit.*, 44-48.

borne in mind, become rhetorical novels, far removed from legend and the popular novel. Therefore Flavius Josephus does not continue the artistic Haggadah tradition of the Jewish narrators, but rather its antithesis, and does no more than borrow basic material from them. Flavius Josephus rewrites the same themes with the psychology of the Greek novelists, infusing biblical and Haggadah narratives with a Hellenistic spirit rather than a Jewish one[761].

All these aspects are scattered throughout the work of Flavius Josephus, which imposes limitations on this investigation to the extent of dealing with only the most representative episodes. Reference is made therefore to the following personalites: Joseph and the wife of Potiphar, Moses and Tharbis, the episode of Balaam and the Moabites, Antonius and Cleopatra, Herod, Titus.

The story of Joseph and its erotic implications, briefly reported in the Bible (*Gen.* XXXIX, 7-20), is given much fuller treatment in Jewish literature of the Hellenistic Era. I am referring to the *Testament of Joseph*, included in the *Testaments of the Twelve Patriarchs*[762].

The points of doctrine into which Braun breaks down the *Testament of Joseph* show a cleary dogmatic aim, an aspect which is deliberately pursued by the Hellenistic Jewish writers. The points are the following: (I) promises from the adulteress, so as to weaken Joseph's will, and threats so as to intimidate him; (II) the woman insists; (III) she herself praises Joseph in the presence of her husband, and later, when they are alone, tempts him; (IV) when failing to achieve her goal, the Egyptian woman presents herself to Joseph with the excuse of asking for instruction on the word of God; (V) the woman says that she intends to poison her husband and will make Joseph her spouse, if he acceeds to her sexual desires; (VI) the woman sends Joseph a meal in which a love-potion has been put; (VII) the woman apparently falls ill and announces her suicide to Joseph; (VIII) the woman once again tempts Joseph by displaying her body to him. Chapter IX deals with the story of Joseph in prison. Braun concludes that the Genesis story has all the characteristics of a novel, though with simple and archaic traits.

On the other hand, in the biblical narrative the following aspects stand out: the event is begun by the words (A): "Now Joseph was handsome

---

[761] For the treatment of some biblical personalities in Flavius Josephus, cf. L. H. Feldman, "*Hellenizations in Josephus' Portrayal of Man's Decline*", *Religions in Antiquity* (Essays in Memory of E. R. Goodenough), Leiden, 1968, 336-353. — "Hellenization in Josephus' Version of Esther", *TAPhA* 101 (1970), 143-170.

[762] M. Braun, *op. cit.*, 44 ff. I shall make a short summary of the study of this author; I shall, however, concentrate on the treatment which Flavius Josephus gives to the story of Joseph.

and good-looking''[763]. Shortly after Joseph had risen to power (B), ''his master's wife took notice of him''[764]. Straightway the proposition (C): ''Come and lie with me''[765]. Joseph refuses (D)[766], and adds that he has been entrusted with everything (E), ''except you, because you are his wife''[767]. From the moral standpoint, the woman's proposal is unacceptable to Joseph (F): ''How can I do anything so wicked, and sin against God?''[768]. The woman insists day after day, but he (G) ''refused to lie with her and be in her company''[769]. Another day, when there was no-one in the house, and Joseph was quite alone, the woman (H) ''caught him by his cloak, saying 'Come and lie with me' ''[770]. This time temptation is thwarted by Joseph's exit from the house. His cloak, however, remained in the hands of the woman, so as to provide proof in her later calumny before her husband. Then the woman called to the men of the household[771], and said to them: (I) ''Look at this! My husband has brought in a Hebrew to make mockery of us. He came in here to lie with me, but I gave a loud scream''[772]; and she shows them Joseph's cloak as proof of her words. When the husband arrived, she showed him the cloak and told him what had happened (J). And Joseph was imprisoned.

Flavius Josephus' Joseph is handsome and skilled in management (a)[773], and because of these things the wife of Potiphar falls in love for him. She believes that Joseph will consider it good fortune that the wife of his master should declare her passion to him (b). Joseph, however, believes that to succumb would be to betray his master (c), and advises her to control her passion, telling her that she should not cherish the hope of carrying her desire to fulfilment, because, when there is no hope, passion is extinguished (d)[774], and that he will abide by his decision. Joseph will go even further: even though a slave should do nothing which is against the will of his mistress, opposing her in the execution of orders of

---

[763] LXX, *Gen.* XXXIX, 6-18.

[764] LXX, *Gen.* XXXIX, 6.

[765] *Id.*, 7.

[766] *Ibid.*: κοιμήθητι μετ' ἐμοῦ.

[767] *Id.*, 8.

[768] *Id.*, 9.

[769] *Ibid.*: καὶ πῶς ποιήσω τὸ ῥῆμα τὸ πονηρὸν τοῦτο καὶ ἁμαρτήσομαι ἐναντίον τοῦ θεοῦ;

[770] *Id.*, 10.

[771] *Id.*, 12.

[772] In verse 11 (LXX and Hebrew), it has been said that there was no-one at home. Here, in contrast, two verses later, there is a contradiction, καὶ ἐκάλεσε τοὺς ὄντας ἐν τῇ οἰκίᾳ (LXX, ''she called out to the men of the household''). A curious contradiction, no doubt intentional, with the aim of providing drama, in which the impression sought after is held above logic. These traits indubitably have great novelistic force.

[773] In Flavius Josephus, the story is notably more extensive (A, II, 39-59) and is richer in details.

[774] A, II, 43.

this type will have a great many excuses (e). But the unexpected opposition of Joseph inflames the woman's passion even more, and, "terribly besieged by wrong"[775], tries a second temptation (f).

On the occasion of a public feast, which women were allowed to attend[776], she pretends illness, so as to be able to solicit Joseph in solitude (g). The idea of a house empty of people is simplified by the term "solitude" (μόνωσις, 45) (h). This time the proposition is made with "words smoother than the first ones" (i)[777]. The woman tries to persuade him: she is mistress and her passion is great, he should not have refused her first proposition; but Joseph is still in time to make good his lack of consideration (j). As proof of her love, she had feigned illness and had preferred to be with him than in the public feast (k). Then comes a mixture of promises and threats: if Joseph "requites her love"[778], he will enjoy immediate benefits and ever greater ones later on (l); but if he refuses, she will have her revenge on him and will hate him, and she will become his chief accuser in the presence of her husband, who will be more likely to accept her word against his (m). Joseph refuses by all sorts of reasonings, and insists principally on the spiritual benefits which chastity will bring him and tells her that she will be obeyed with more authority over him, her servant (n). The woman, however, becomes exasperated and tries to force him: Joseph flees in haste, leaving his cloak in the hands of the woman (o), which will later serve as evidence in the presence of her husband. The lament of the woman, in the midst of tears, is pure rhetorical artifice in reported speech (p). Pentephres believes his wife and imprisons Joseph (q)[779].

If these three texts are considered globally, certain similarities and dissimilarities may be observed. The biblical text is very short, and is therefore lacking in details and nuances. The remaining two texts are splendid as regards the treatment of the psychological world of the two main characters. Both the reasons of the woman and the refusals of Joseph are enriched with the whole range of human responses, and the scene takes on a realistic and human quality, so that the reader feels in close contact with the event.

---

[775] A, II, 44.

[776] This feast is abiblical, and belongs to the rabbinical explanations, so as to be able to justify the phrase "when none of the men of the household was there indoors" (LXX: καὶ οὐθεὶς ἦν τῶν ἐν τῇ οἰκίᾳ ἔσω).

[777] A, II, 45.

[778] A, II, 48.

[779] The punishment certainly does not fit the crime, another detail which increases the amount of novelistic traits in this episode.

The similarities in the three versions are the following[780]: Joseph is handsome (A-a); enamouring of the woman (B-b); proposition of adultery (I-C-b); the woman insists in her objective with various temptations (II-III-IV-VIII-G-H-f-g-i-j); proof of her love towards him is her feigned illness (VII-g-k); threats in view of Joseph's refusals (I-m); promises of the woman (V-l); resistence of Joseph (*passim* D-F-G-H-c-d-e-n-o); logical reasonings of Joseph so as to justify his refusal to commit adultery (E-F-c-d-e-n); the house is empty (H-h); violence on the part of the woman in her last attempt (H-o); accusation by the woman in public against Joseph (I-J-p); imprisonment of Joseph (all three sources).

The dissimilarities are as follows: praise of Joseph by the woman in the presence of her husband (III); the would-be adulteress asks Joseph for religious instruction so as to proposition him (IV); the woman will poison her husband to marry Joseph (V); a meal with a love-potion included (VI); the woman announces her suicide (VII); temptation accompanied by nudity (VIII); the story occurred shortly after Joseph rose to power (B); fornication is a sin against God (F); the woman considers her proposal an honour for Joseph (b); the woman's desire is not requited (d); Joseph justifies his non-compliance with the proposal of his mistress (e); the refusal of Joseph inflames the woman's passion even more (f); a public feast which women were allowed to attend (g); chastity brings benefits (n).

Taking into account solely the biblical text and Flavius Josephus, it must be concluded that the LXX very schematically give the basic points of the episode, which are very suitable for literary enlargement. One may note that Flavius Josephus extends the narrative to the detriment of the moral content which the biblical text contains: Flavius Josephus does not mention the idea of sinning against God, but goes into extensive consideration concerning chastity, remorse, and faithfulness to the husband.

The introduction of the feast into the text of Flavius Josephus answers the desire of the writer to give a certain logic to the fact of the house being empty. This, however, raises an unanswerable question: how is it that Joseph was not present at the public feast, in view of his being an authority amongst those people?

Doubtless the *Testament of Joseph* has many particular points which are not echoed in Flavius Josephus, something which leads us to the belief that Flavius Josephus had no knowledge of this source. On the other hand, even the points in which both sources agree suggest that they used the same sources separately.

---

[780] The order of numbers and letters follows that of the order I have used previously when setting out the three narratives.

Finally, the punishment does not fit the crime. A case such as this is punishable by death. The biblical writer did not bear this in mind when he introduced this literary genre—the novel—before describing the great ennoblement of Joseph by express divine will. The writer resorted to the most commonplace subject—sexual sin—, but did not take into account the terrible end which was awaiting anyone guilty of such an act.

The simple punishment of imprisonment kept the transgressor alive. It may well be that this biblical novella occupies the place of the real reason behind Joseph's imprisonment, although this is not strictly necessary. We cannot demand historical rigour of a history of the patriarchs of Israel, of a popular history nor of a religious history because, in this second part of Genesis, the only intention is that of showing basic truths: the origins and the migration of the ancestors of Israel, their geographical and ethnic relationships, and their moral and religious behaviour[781].

In the life of Moses there is to be found a legend which gathers all the basic elements of any novelistic writing. This narrative is indubitably an invention of the Jewish colony in Alexandria, possibly brought about by the allusion to the marriage of Moses to the Cushite woman in *Num.* XII, 1[782]. The division into short chapters of the *Antiquitates Judaicae* already includes this episode (A, II, 238-253 = X, 1-2) in one of them only.

Moses is presented there as the author of the salvation of the Hebrews and of the humiliation of the Egyptians (A, II, 238). Egyptian territory is invaded by the Ethiopians (*id.*, 239-240). The Egyptians, after consulting their oracles, receive the order from God to ask for help from the Jews in the person of the *Hebrew*, i.e. Moses (*id.*, 241-242). Moses accepts the leadership of the hostilities, and Flavius Josephus places in him all the hopes of all the Hebrews of ridding themselves of the yoke of the Egyptians if they had him as general. So a first intensified element: Moses as the leader of the people of Israel to salvation (*id.*, 243). A second point touches on the intellectual qualities of the leader: "Then he (Moses) gave an admirable instance of his wisdom"[783]. By his stratagem, Moses unexpectedly defeats the Ethiopians (*id.*, 248), and reaches the gates of the capital, Saba, which is very well-protected (*id.*, 249-250). We are therefore presented with a victorious Moses, who has to take the decisive step towards his own consecration as soldier and leader. Moses, before

---

[781] *La Sainte Bible*, École Biblique de Jérusalem, Paris, 1956, 5-6. Cf. too *La Sainte Bible Polyglotte*, ed. F. Vigouroux, Paris, vol. I, vol. I, 1900, 205, note 7.
[782] H. St. J. Thackeray, *Josephus*, The Loeb Classical Library, vol. IV, London-Cambridge / Massachusetts, 1967 (4th ed.), 269, note b.
[783] A, II, 244.

Saba, could not bear[784] the idea of his army having nothing to do, since the Ethiopians would not engage in battle in the open. At this moment the second part of the episode begins: the erotic-amorous side. Here then is the text[785]:

"Tharbis was the daughter of the king of Ethiopia. She, on seeing that Moses, near her walls, was in command of the army and fought with bravery, full of admiration for the cleverness of his manoeuvres, and understanding that he was for the Egyptians, who had desisted in their attempts to gain their freedom, the cause of their success, and for the Ethiopians, who boasted of their actions against them, being reduced to the last straits, fell into a deep love for him and, under the power of passion, sent him her most faithful servants so as to propose marriage to him. He accepted her proposal on the condition that she should surrender the city, and he swore firm oaths to marry in truth here, and that he, lord of the city, would not violate the pacts; whereupon action outstripped parley. And Moses, after punishing the Ethiopians, gave thanks to God, held the marriage and led the Egyptians to their land."

One can see here various decisive elements so as to incite the daughter of the king to take her decisions: a. Moses was a brave general and warrior[786]; b. his strategic intelligence is admired[787]; c. Moses is the answer (αἴτιον) to the situation, both for the Egyptians and the Ethiopians[788]; d. Tharbis falls madly in love[789]; e. an illogical action: the sending of the messengers with the immediate proposal of marriage, explained by the domination of her amorous passion which enslaves her[790]; f. the rapid acceptance of Moses and the surrender of the city sound unreal, and cannot be historical[791].

With a little bit of insistence on these points, it can be seen that the episode has a "happy ending" with an erotic air. The characteristic words appear together with the presentation of female sentimental weakness in the presence of a hero with strong streaks of masculinity. One may also ask after the reasons why the woman was so suddenly overcome by love. But in fact the historian has already pointed them out after his fashion: because of his manner of fighting (μαχόμενον γενναίως ἀποσκοποῦσα), because of the cleverness of his actions (τῆς ἐπινοίας τῶν

---

[784] A, II, 251.

[785] A, II, 252-253.

[786] A, II, 252.

[787] Ibid.: τῆς ἐπινοίας τῶν ἐγχειρήσεων θαυμάζουσα.

[788] Ibid.: καὶ τοῖς τε Αἰγυπτίοις αἴτιον ... καὶ τοῖς Αἰθίοψιν.

[789] Ibid.: εἰς ἔρωτα δεινὸν ὤλισθεν αὐτοῦ.

[790] Ibid.: πέμπει πρὸς αὐτὸν τῶν οἰκετῶν τοὺς πιστοτάτους διαλεγομένη περὶ γάμου.

[791] A, II, 253.

ἐγχειρήσεων θαυμάζουσα) and because she could see that Moses would be the bringer of victory to the Egyptians and of defeat to the Ethiopians[792].

In conclusion, the episode represents an incomparable literary piece. The contribution of the literary source and the part added by Flavius Josephus cannot be specified. This notwithstanding, a tone can be seen here which is similar to that of other passages where the novelistic element is a personal contribution of Flavius Josephus. I should like to mention two things with regard to this: the treatment of Moses is conceived according to the spiritual and human prestige which he receives from the author throughout the work, and, on the other hand, the image of the woman answers to a cliché of Flavius Josephus which is repeated at moments which have strong erotic and novelistic overtones.

Another episode which is given extensive novelistic treatment by Flavius Josephus is the whole affair of the prophet Balaam with the Moabite king Balak[793]. A simple comparison of the length of the episode in the biblical text with that of Flavius Josephus is revealing: *Num.* XXV, 1-15 = *Antiquitates Judaicae*, IV, 101-158.

Here I shall analyse fundamentally the central point of the question, i.e. from paragraph 126 to paragraph 140, which come to represent a paraphrased enlargement on the first two verses of the Book of *Numbers*. I shall end this study with an analysis of the fragment comprising paragraphs 141-155. The first biblical verse says thus: "When the Israelites were in Shittim, the people began to have intercourse with the Moabite women"[794]. Corresponding to this bare piece of information, we have paragraphs 126-138 in the *Antiquitates Judaicae*. The second verse says: "...who invited them (i.e. the Israelites) to the sacrifices offered to their gods"[795]. To this verse correspond paragraphs 139-140 in the work of Flavius Josephus.

The content of the first part is fairly clear, though not entirely so. The Israelites began to have *sexual* intercourse with the Moabite women, to put it bluntly.

What literary means could Flavius Josephus have had to hand to develop a lengthy novelistic episode? In the Book of *Numbers*, XXXI, 16, there is an indication whereby Moses says that the women of Midian, following the counsel of Balaam, seduced the Israelites away from the cult of the LORD. This is the only indication to be found in the whole of

---

[792] A, II, 252. Cf. Braun, *op. cit.*, 97-102.
[793] A, IV, 101-158.
[794] *Num.* XXV, 1.
[795] *Num.* XXV, 2.

the Holy Scriptures, and later literature would take it on itself to fill in
this information gap. Thus the completed episode is found in Philo[796] and
in the Talmud, and there is belief in the possibility of a pre-Christian
Palestinian Haggadah, which is echoed in Judaeo-Hellenistic, rabbinical[797] and New Testament literature[798].

More specifically, rabbinical tradition presents the history of Balaam
with a great wealth of details, according to what I have been able to
derive from a study of Braun, already mentioned. The same author insists on the fact that the question of sex occupies a preeminent place in
Philo and in Flavius Josephus; for the former, above all, the moral
aspects of sex, a very attractive subject for a Hellenistic writer.

The first biblical verse presents the sexual question. Flavius Josephus
develops it as follows:

– Balak dismisses Balaam because the Israelites have not been
destroyed (No. 126);

– before passing the Euphrates, Balaam makes a long speech addressed to Balak and the Midianites, which has the following counsel as
its principal point: since it is impossible to do anything against Israel,
because the LORD is with them, attempt to gain a small victory by sending them your daughters, the prettiest and most capable of constraining
and conquering the will of those who might see them, so that when the
young men are carried away by their appetites, the girls should leave
them, and that when the youths beg them to stay, the girls should persuade them to renounce the laws of their fathers and to honour your gods,
before they gave in. And Flavius Josephus indicated what can cause
harm to Israel: ''For thus God will be kindled against them''[799], which is
tantamount to saying that the people of Israel will receive heavy punishment (Nos. 127-130);

– indeed, the young Midianite girls are successful, and their beaux
make all kinds of promises to them (Nos. 131-133);

– when the girls saw that the youths were slaves to their passions, they
then began to impose their conditions in a long speech: if you are so
vociferous in your love for us, think that you must adapt yourselves to
our way of life, since you are a people with very special customs, not
found in many peoples; one of the things which you must do is venerate
our gods, and that will be the best proof of your affection towards us, and
no man may reproach you that you venerate the gods of the place where

---

[796] *Vit. Moys.* I, 294; *De uirt.* 34.
[797] Cf. Braun, *op. cit.*, 102-104.
[798] *Apoc.* II, 14.
[799] A, IV, 130.

you live, above all when our gods are common to many peoples, whereas yours are yours alone (Nos. 134-138).

The first biblical verse is enlarged on up to this point. The second verse is amplified in the following way:

– the young men transgressed the laws of their fathers and accepted the plurality of gods (No. 139);

– the example spread throughout the whole of the Jewish army, with the danger of a complete collapse of the institutions of the people of Israel; even some of the most important men succumbed to the contagion (No. 140);

– from paragraph 141 through to number 155, Flavius Josephus describes the fate of Zambrias and of the Midianite Chosbia, together with the reaction of Phinees and other youths who were lovers of honour and heroism. This long fragment is the equivalent of only four biblical verses, and its characteristic note is the long speech given by Zambrias (Nos. 145-149).

One aspect which should be pointed out in the whole of this narrative is the abundance of speeches, which, naturally, have no corresponding speeches in the Bible. The entire narrative has a dramatic structure, in which the erotic elements serve as the cause of a whole series of consequences. Moses himself, in reported speech, declares that they have preferred voluptuousness (τὴν ἡδονὴν προτιμήσαντες τοῦ θεοῦ, No. 143) to God.

The speeches have the following structures:

– Balaam, direct (Nos. 126-130),

– the Midianites, direct (Nos. 134-136), reported (No. 136), direct (Nos. 137-138), reported (No. 138),

– Moses, reported (Nos. 142-144),

– Zambrias, direct (Nos. 145-149).

The narrative is brought to a close with another characteristic typical of the novel: the concept of heroism and of love of honour born in the light of the glorious deed of Phinees, who punished the transgressor of the law, Zambrias. The other youths, on seeing the deed, followed the example and purified the people of Israel[800].

All through his works, Flavius Josephus gives his attention to various anecdotes or historical events, and brings out in them traits which are characteristic of the novel or of novelistic currents of the age. I cannot here go into the question of the literary source or the contribution of the literary assistants, so as to elucidate the extent to which they must have insisted on the erotic or heroic aspects, characteristic of the novel.

---

[800] A, IV, 154-155.

According to Hadas, Hellenistic historiography developed the novel as an apologetic method, in which the historical elements are overshadowed by the erotic elements, so as to become propaganda instruments in the hands of minorities or unpopular cults[801]. Even though this theory is not fulfilled in all its points, in the case of Flavius Josephus, and, in broad outline, one may appreciate a tendentious feeling in the majority of the situations where the subject may benefit someone or even discredit them. Without any doubt, the three situations I have analysed above offer a great sense of apology of virtue, of the sense of redemption in Moses and of the intrinsic values of the people of Israel. In practice these three aims will be found whenever Flavius Josephus insists on the felicitous and glorious deeds of a Jewish personality.

In the *Bellum Judaicum*, Antonius and Cleopatra, Herod and Titus, amongst others are dealt with in the erotic and heroic characteristics of the novel.

With regard to the Antonius-Cleopatra tandem, Flavius Josephus picks up the tradition of the love affair between the two personalities with well-known expressions, which rather bring to mind novelistic situations. Cleopatra attempts to annex the territories of Syria and Judaea by dominating Antonius, who, "undone by love of Cleopatra, was slave to his passion"[802]. In the *Antiquitates Judaicae*, Flavius Josephus says that Cleopatra "had great influence (over him) because of his passion for her"[803]. And, after enumerating her excesses, he concludes, "nothing was sufficient for a woman extravagant and the slave of her passions, so that all things were deprived of that which she desired to satisfy her imagination"[804]. He also specifies the state of Antonius: "Antonius' dilemma... was that he was dominated by this woman, so that not only did he seem to obey her in all her wishes by her intimacy, but also by the influence of drugs"[805].

Here then we have a whole novel-like panorama based on a single element, eroticism, by means of which the queen seeks power over the world. On the other hand, the image of Antonius is highly caricaturised, and is based on the extreme exaggeration of his sentimental side.

So as to complete the character of queen Cleopatra, her relationship with Herod should also be examined. The text is very expressive: "She

---

[801] M. Hadas, *Three Greek Romances*, New York, 1953, 8, cited by Horst R. Moehring, *Novelistic Elements in the Writings of Flavius Josephus*, (Diss.), Chicago, 1957, 65-66; also B. Justus, "Zur Erzählkunst des Flavius Josephus", *Theokratia*, 2, (1973), 107-136.

[802] B, I, 359.

[803] A, XV, 88.

[804] A, XV, 91.

[805] A, XV, 93.

attempted to have sexual relations with the king, for, by nature, she delighted very openly in this manner of pleasures, and it may also be that she had a passion for him..., in short, she showed herself to be conquered by desire''[806]. The advice of the friends of Herod convinced him not to give in to this invitation.

Reference to the passion of Cleopatra seems to have a certain consistence, but the historical truth is presented in too fictional a way, and everything points to the reality having had a different slant[807].

Book V of the *Bellum Judaicum* is dominated by the figure of Titus, the son of Vespasian. His deeds are hero-like in their characteristics: he sets about reorganising the Roman army, bringing each legion up to full strength, reconnoitres the defence qualities of Jerusalem, and displays his war-power to the Jews so as to infuse them with fear[808].

However, during this reconnoitring, the situation goes against Titus, and a host of Jews attack him. While he is fighting off his enemies, Flavius Josephus brings out the following points:

a. the leader receives no wound, "because the situations of wars and the dangers of kings are in the care of God"[809],

b. with his sword he disperses the enemies who surround him and vanquishes many of them[810],

c. the Jews concentrate their attacks on him[811],

d. Titus returns happily to the Roman camp[812].

The onslaught begins, and a whole Roman legion would have found itself in grave peril,

e. had not Titus gone to their aid: he makes those Romans who are fleeing out of cowardice go back, he hurls himself against the Jews, killing and wounding and breaking the enemy ranks[813].

The Jewish attacks come thick and fast, and increase in cruelty, and the counsellors of Titus fear for his life and advise him to withdraw,

f. "lord who is of the war and of the world, let not one on whom all depends face such a dire situation"[814],

g. Titus pays no heed to the advice, attacks the enemy, and brings off a great victory[815],

---

[806] A, XV, 97.
[807] Cf. H. R. Moehring, *op. cit.*, 76.
[808] B, V, 39-46 and 52.
[809] B, V, 60.
[810] B, V, 62.
[811] B, V, 63.
[812] B, V, 65.
[813] B, V, 81-82.
[814] B, V, 88.
[815] B, V, 89-90.

h. the troops who had been fortifying their camp were petrified at the thought that Titus may have been killed, but on seeing him in the thick of the fight and the danger he was in, they went back in shame to the aid of their Caesar; the Jews had to withdraw[816].

In the presence of such a glorious deed, Flavius Josephus cannot help saying:

i. "Thus, if the truth has to be told without being added to out of flattery nor detracted from out of envy, the Caesar in person twice saved the entire legion from grave danger and gave them the security of returning to their camp"[817].

This information is sufficient to centre the person of Titus, to whom the historian gradually applies human qualities, but always very lofty ones, so that the reader comes away with the impression that the war is the hero, that is, Titus.

Now a commentary on these preceding points:

The fact of divine protection should be remarked on (a). This point alone is sufficient to indicate an exceptional person, that is, a hero. Together with this aspect, the historian has the whole future of the war hinge on Titus (f), and at the same time makes him the indisputable saviour of his army (e, i). Titus also appears as a military model for those faint-hearted soldiers (e, h), and is the perpetrator of the most successful military actions (b, c, d, g).

The life of Herod is given extensive treatment in both of the main works of Flavius Josephus, and moreover is full of novelistic traits, especially in the texts which refer to his relations with his wife Mariamme. His life was greatly echoed in dramatic literature and even in medieval liturgical drama[818].

Moehring makes a detailed study of those main passages of the life of Herod which are adorned with novelistic elements. Here I shall simply review them, so as to analyse other passages which have not yet come under study.

Thus Moehring studies the whole episode of the sending of the portraits of Mariamme and her brother to Antonius[819], and emphasises that both narratives are based on three things: the amorous passion of the king for his wife, his jealousy and his suspicion[820].

---

[816] B, V, 91-95.

[817] B, V, 97.

[818] For the bibliography on these aspects, see H. R. Moehring, *op. cit.*, 83.

[819] B, I, 438-440; A, XV, 23-38.

[820] H. R. Moehring, *op. cit.*, 84-92; the author also quotes the non-historical character of this matter.

The following study makes an analysis of the characteristics of the three death sentences dictated by Herod against Mariamme: B, I, 441-444; A, XV, 65-87; A, XV, 183-208[821]. Moehring draws attention to the novelistic traits and the historical basis. Confronted with the discrepancies of the texts, he propounds that Flavius Josephus arranged his material in accordance with the subject and not in accordance with the chronology.

Moehring's study also analyses other points of the work of Flavius Josephus, and comes to the conclusion that Flavius Josephus is the author of all the erotic aspects in his works, in spite of the literary sources and the "literary assistants" who polished them[822].

From the *Antiquitates Judaicae* I have taken various items which may be included under the heading which is being dealt with at present. A good many of them have their reference in the biblical text, which clearly shows up the variations introduced by Flavius Josephus into the subject.

The story of Jacob and Rachel is novelistic in tone, especially with regard to their first encounter[823]. Jacob reaches Haran, and near a well finds some shepherds who are waiting to water their flocks. They cannot begin until all the flocks are there. Jacob asks them whether they know his uncle Laban. They tell him that they do know him, for he is a man who cannot remain unknown, and that his daughter is grazing the flocks with them, and find it strange that she has not yet arrived.

The biblical text is not so explicit in these kinds of details. I should like to underline the final idea of Flavius Josephus' text: "They were surprised that she had not yet arrived"[824]. This phrase confers on the text an air of mystery which is not to be found in the biblical text. Jacob's spirits are therefore put on tenterhooks. The two texts, apart from slight variants which have no bearing on the subject, agree on the fact of watering the flocks. However, the following verses require a comparison:

Biblical text, LXX[825]	*Flavius Josephus*[826]
	"She, innocently pleased by the presence of Jacob, asked him who he was and whence he came to them and what business brought him hither,

---

[821] R. M. Moehring, *op. cit.*, 92-123.
[822] R. M. Moehring, *op. cit.*, 141-146.
[823] A, I, 285-292 = *Gen.* XXIX, 1-14.
[824] A, I, 286.
[825] The text of the LXX agrees with that of the Hebrew text: *Gen.* XXIX, 11-12.
[826] A, I, 287-292.

and told him that it was possible for them to offer him all that he was in need of. Jacob, conquered not by kinship nor by the affection derived from it, but out of love for the young girl, was struck by her great beauty as was possessed by very few other women then, and said...

"(Jacob) kissed Rachel, and was moved to tears. He told her that he was her father's kinsman and Rebecca's son; so she ran and told her father."

She... for the love which she had for her father began to shed tears, and embraced Jacob, and kissing him told him that he had brought with him the most desirable satisfaction and the greatest pleasure to her father and to all those of the house...".

Here I have translated no more than that part which enlarges on the verses of the Bible. The first difference is that of extension, and the second that of function: in Flavius Josephus it is Rachel who speaks, who weeps and embraces Jacob. There is yet a third difference: the biblical text has very few words, but, in contrast, the text of Flavius Josephus bases the whole scene on a dialogue, transmitted by the historian with a combination which is characteristic of it: reported speech (No. 287), direct speech (Nos. 288-290), reported speech (Nos. 291-292).

The novelistic aspects of this episode may be explicitly seen in the use of eroticism. Words such as ἔρωτι ἡττηθεὶς ἐκπέπληκτο, κάλλος, ὑπὸ εὐνοίας ἔνδακρυς περιβάλλει, κατασπασαμένη, ἡδονή constitute the coordinates which are characteristic of a novel or of a narrative with a novelistic slant. With regard to this same point, the aspects to be emphasised are the female attitude towards the man, the heightening of the amorous feelings of the girl as regards Jacob, whom she knows only by name (No. 291), and the appreciably physical satisfaction of the young girl, which is revealed through her acts, which take on an erotic air.

By way of conclusion to this analysis of novel-like historical situations, and to avoid being over-repetitious, I shall now give the bibliographical reference of other passages in which there appears a novel-like treatment of personalities and of situations, making it quite clear that eroticism and heroism are both inherent to the work of Flavius Josephus, deeply rooted in an intentionality of the author.

Therefore the story of Samson (A, V, 285-317) should be considered as falling under this heading, as should the relations between Solomon and the queen of Sheba (A, VIII, 165-175), the events which occurred in the court of Artaxerxes (A, XI, 184-296), the story of Joseph son of Tobias

(A, XII, 160-222), the whole affair of Paulina and Fulvia (A, XVIII, 66-84) studied by Moehring and Justus[827], and expressions of praise of heroism (A, IV, 154-155) and of the beauty of women (A, XV, 25 ff.; 50 ff.; A, XVIII, 341 ff.).

7. *History and drama*

This subject should be approached beginning with the view of Aristotle, when he makes a comparison between history and tragedy. The second person to raise the issue was Isocrates, thanks to whom historiography assumed many tragic traits. Polybius explicitly opposes himself to this, but is not wholly successful in maintaining himself completely unaffected by these influences.

Aristotle points out that imitation is essential to poetry[828] and that the poet imitates the acts of men[829] giving them a certain magnitude, so that by eliciting the pity and fear of the spectators, they produce a κάθαρσις of those emotions[830]. Aristotle adds that history describes the events that have happened, whereas poetry describes what might have happened. The work of Herodotus, for instance, would not be poetry even though it were to be written in verse. It should also be borne in mind that history deals with particular things, and that poetry with universals[831]. All this implies that history, just like treatises on medicine or physics, even if it were written in verse, is not poetry because it does not imitate acts[832] and does not bring about in people's minds either the pity or the fear that is to be found in tragic poetry[833]. What is more, fear and pity cause a greater impact if they are unexpected (παρὰ τὴν δόξαν), because they are then all the more admirable, θαυμαστόν[834]. Aristotle goes on to state that those situations which cause neither fear nor pity, but only sensationalism (τερατῶδες), cannot be included in tragedy[835]. Finally, tragedy expounds action which has a beginning, middle and end, whereas history is not necessarily thus[836].

---

[827] H. R. Moehring, *op. cit.*, 56-68; B. Justus, *op. cit.*, 112-122.

[828] *Poet.* 1, 1447a 17.

[829] *Poet.* 2, 1448a 1.

[830] *Poet.* 6, 1449b 27; 1450a 15 ff.

[831] *Poet.* 9, 3. 1451b, 5-7.

[832] *Poet.* 1, 1447b 16.

[833] History, since it has no beginning, no middle and no end, does not represent an action, but rather a period in which there are even non-related events (23, 1459a 21).

[834] *Poet.* 9, 1452a 4; cf. 24, 1460a 12. For θαυμαστόν and τέρας, see 14, 1453b 9.

[835] *Poet.* 14, 1453b 1.

[836] All these data have been borrowed from the studies of B. L. Ullman, "History and Tragedy", *TAPhA* 73 (1942), 25-53, and of F. W. Walbank, "History and Tragedy", *Historia* 9 (1960), 216-234.

So much for the theory, but practice is not always subject to this doctrine, since tragedy makes itself felt within history. Herodotus and Aeschylus dealt with the invasion of the Persians in the style which was befitting to each of them, i.e., according to the literary genre they worked in, but it can be seen that the historian, in his latter books, shows the influence of the tragedies of Phrynichus and Aeschylus[837]. It should also be remembered that *speeches*, so frequently found in the Greek and Roman historians, are the product of drama technique[838].

It seems to be evident that the introduction of rhetorical elements and poetical effects in historical prose is due to Isocrates. Technically, the speech announces the recourse to the admirable anecdotes (θαυμαστά) so as to heighten feelings and attract the attention of the listener[839]. The most ancient historians are a good example of the use of these extraordinary elements. Isocrates comes to represent the restorer of these aspects in history. Moreover, it is his disciples who made a decisive contribution to the creation of rhetorical history[840]. In short then, it should be said that tragic history is that which expounds sensationalist exaggerations (ὑπερβολὴ τερατείας), in a declamatory tone (ἐπιδεικτικαὶ συντάξεις), so as to make an impression on (ἔκπληξις) the greatest number of people[841].

Another theory brings new arguments to bear in favour of a peripatetic origin to "tragic history"[842]. Aristotle remarks that poetry is more philosophical and loftier than history, "for poetry speaks rather of that which is universal, whereas history of that which is particular"[843]. The question hinges on the value which is given to μᾶλλον. Von Fritz sees here the foundations on which the peripatetic theory concerning tragic history is built. If history is less philosophical than poetry it is because the latter deals with that which is universal. Therefore, to enhance history, it must be made more universal and more similar to poetry.

The theories propounded by investigators eventually hinge on two key-personalites, whom they consider as the "inventors" of tragic history. Callisthenes, nephew and disciple of Aristotle, was the first. In his history of Alexander, he uses extraordinary elements so as to arouse admiration

---

[837] J. B. Bury, *The Ancient Greek Historians*, New York, 1909, 33 and 68.

[838] Cf. J. B. Bury, *op. cit.*, 116; F. M. Cornford, *Thucydides Mythistoricus*, London, 1907, 137.

[839] *Rhet.*, 3, 14, 1415b 2.

[840] W. von Christ, *Geschichte der griechischen Literatur*, 1, München, 1920, 527.

[841] Pol., 16, 17, 9, 18, 3. Cf. Fritz Wehrli, "Die Geschichtsschreibung im Lichte der antiken Theorie", *Festgabe für E. Howald*, *Eumusia* 68 (1947), 54-71.

[842] Kurt von Fritz, "Die Bedeutung der Aristoteles für die Geschichtsschreibung", *Histoire et historiens dans l'antiquité* (Entretiens sur l'Antiquité classique 4), Vandœuvres-Genève, 1956, 85-145.

[843] *Poet.* 9, 3, 1451b 5-7.

and pity. Even so, it is thought that his points of view concerning tragic history have their origins in Isocrates[844].

The second "inventor" was Duris of Samos, a disciple of Theophrastus[845]. In a harsh piece of criticism directed against Ephorus and Theopompus, on account of the inferiority of their narrative to the events it contained, he says: "For they would have no hand in any imitation nor in the pleasure of the expression, but they concerned themselves only with the writing itself"[846]. Duris clearly thought that μίμησις was an integral part of the task of the historian. Von Fritz has connected μίμησις with τὰ καθ᾽ ὅλον in order to fill in the gap between Aristotle's distinction between poetry and history in terms of particular and universal, and the insistence of Duris concerning the need for μίμησις and ἡδονή in history.

What therefore should be understood by μίμησις? For Gomme, μίμησις means *representation*[847]. For von Fritz, complementing Gomme, tragic μίμησις which inspires fear and pity in the audience means the "concentrated representation" of that which in real life is less concentrated, and it is from this concentrated representation whence springs universality: "The universality of tragedy consists of the fact that it represents what stands as an extreme possibility behind every life and perhaps also in a less extreme form becomes reality in every life"[848]. If this is the case, Duris would ask that history presents the facts as they might have been (οἷα ἂν γένοιτο). In spite of that, if we bear in mind the subjects he describes—marvellous stories, travelogues, prodigious births, scandalous customs, love-intrigues and so on—we would have to conclude that Duris, when he uses the word μίμησις, had something simpler in mind: a vivid presentation of events.

Polybius is the greatest censor of tragic history, since he believes that the historian should neither arouse emotions nor transmit sensationalistic stories[849]. He criticises historians who present an unexpectedly triumphant Scipio (παραλόγως), treating him as a marvellous being (θαυμαστοτέρους)[850]. Similarly those writers who provide unexpected solutions to real historical problems are acting after the manner of the writers of tragedy and at bottom impose a *deus ex machina*[851] on the natural course of history. Those historians also come in for their share of criticism

---

[844] Cf. B. L. Ullman, *op. cit.*, 34-37. Cicero himself (*De orat.* 2, 58) described the history of Callisthenes as *rhetorico paene more*, like that of Ephorus and Theopompus.

[845] *Athen.* 8, 18, 377d; 4, 1, 128a.

[846] *FGH* 76 F 1 = Phot., *Bibl.* 176 p. 121a 41.

[847] A. W. Gomme, *The Greek attitude to poetry and history*, Berkeley, 1954, 53 ff.

[848] A. W. Gomme, *op. cit.*, 120.

[849] Pol. 1, 35, 1-7; 1, 87, 1; 2, 35, 8; 2, 56; 15, 34, 1-2.

[850] Pol. 10, 2, 5-6.

[851] Pol. 3, 48, 8 and 3, 58, 9.

who aggrandise small subjects (ὑπόθεσις) by means of tragic
(τραγῳδοῦντες) and sensational (τερατεία) elements, so as to arouse feelings of pity and cruelty[852]. Nor does he spare historians who are concerned about their style: they destroy reality[853]. This notwithstanding,
Polybius will commit that very same error he criticises when he describes
the history of Philip V of Macedon and the war of Numantia.

Now that the principal interpretative difficulties have been expounded
at this level, we have an adequate methodological perspective from which
to look at the information which the work of Flavius Josephus offers us.
Thus an investigation must be carried out to see to what extent Flavius
Josephus attempts to arouse narrative emotion, in any of its facets.

Flavius Josephus is sensitive to human suffering, and takes note of
crisis situations. So he records aspects of depression in moments of
violence, thus endowing it with a dramatic character. In this manner one
sees that violence done to someone's person is elaborated with particular
traits, and the historian duly records the reaction of the person affected
(B, I, 57-60).

Deaths are described in great detail, so that the entire scene takes on
an extraordinary hue. The death of Aristobulus is preceded by the
description of some kind of prophecy which contributes to the creation of
an atmosphere of mystery. The entire scene is related in reported speech,
which endows an everyday event with a histrionic character (B, I, 78-84).

Death too for a political ideal has its impact on people who only see it
from far-off, as is the case of king Herod when faced with the death which
a desperate father inflicts on his sons, on his wife and on himself for having refused to submit (B, I, 312-313).

Popular and multitudinous agitation also has its dramatic side in the
work of Flavius Josephus. The sieges seem to take on an air of being
stage-managed, with crowd scenes, always wishing for a solution of
divine or exceptional origin, and military strength, both of the revolutionaries and the attackers (B, I, 347 ff.; B, III, 247-252). All this is
heightened by the various attacks, with their successes and failures.

An extensive reference should be made here to the setting of the war of
Jerusalem. The material preparations for the siege, from the winter of
66-67, are plastically rich (B, II, 647-651). The description of the fervour
of the Jews and of their feverish activities throughout the country create a
tense situation, which is made even tenser by the frequent attacks by both
sides (B, III, 13-28).

---

[852] Pol. 7, 7, 1-2, 6; 7, 7, 6; 29, 12, 2.
[853] Pol. 16, 14, 1; 17, 9; 18, 2; 29, 12, 1-3.

Natural disasters also provide a motive for drama due to the situation of alarm which is produced in those who suffer them. In the case of an earthquake, and its aftermath, the troops of Herod are panic-stricken to such a point that it becomes necessary to bring in a speech of consolation (B, I, 369-379).

The personal situation of Herod, with his anxiety concerning his political security, helps towards the creation of dramatic atmosphere, so characteristic of these scenes (B, I, 386 ff.). The speeches give the finishing touch to the background of the historical event in question.

Indubitably the family tragedies of Herod make for a good dramatic plot, as I have said on previous occasions. The references to suspicions and denunciations (with or without Herod's pardon), executions and arrests, trials and sentences, enmities and tortures, reconciliations and conspiracies, mediations and denunciations, fear and repentance, the situation of parentless children, intrigues and exiles, poisoning attempts, disclosing of secrets, confessions and the forging of letters and giving of false news, speeches and their replies, sicknesses, popular uprisings, suicides and testaments together constitute the framework of a grand drama, which, as I have already said, takes up a great part of the work of Flavius Josephus (B, I, and A, XIV-XVII).

Reference should also be made here to the speeches, in order to indicate that all the situations which are based on them, together with the corresponding setting, attempt to approximate the reality which gave rise to them. It is in the speeches that the realisation of the μίμησις which I analysed at the beginning of this section is to be seen in all its plasticity. The historian imitates reality by alluding to the physical situation of the orator and his audience, to the exchange of speeches, to the reactions of the various interested parties, to the incidents during the session, to the motives which gave rise to the speech and to the conclusions which are finally reached. In fact, if there had been no will to imitate, then the situations based on speeches and dialogues could be summed up in very few words, which would reduce the phonetic expressions to their essential concepts. If we cannot speak of a conscious will to imitate, we may certainly conclude that the technique of reproducing such events is essentially mimetic, and that in the final analysis it is a technique which says more for man's expressive limitations than for his capacity. It is, therefore, a method more in keeping with the requirements of psychological needs than with an imperative of historical truth.

The emotional impact of the aftermath of war is incomparable. The atmosphere is the same atmosphere which pervades tragedies, and unwittingly creates in the reader the feeling of the emotion, the fear, the vexation, the weeping and the impotence which is to be found in real life (B,

II, 457-468, 494-498). In such situations, individual deeds take on the
virtues and the defects of the dramatic protagonist. So too, the spirit and
sensibility of the reader is moved in the same manner as those of the audience.

Simon is the protagonist of a brief tragedy which has war for a setting.
On finding himself undone, Simon makes a short speech, puts to death
his parents, his wife and his sons, and finally commits suicide over the
beloved bodies (B, II, 469-476).

Before this horrifying spectacle, the historian draws the lesson, which
is basically tragic κάθαρσις: ''(The death of) a young man worthy of commiseration for his strength of body and his resoluteness of mind, who suffered his alloted fate for having placed his trust in foreign people''[854]. The
conclusion is therefore moralising.

Flavius Josephus' personal situation during hostilities also goes
through dramatic moments. The animadversion of the Jews created a
chaotic situation around him, and put his life in danger, which makes one
think of a justification of his conduct and of a demonstration of in-
gratitude on the part of the people towards a man who has done a great
deal for the country (B, II, 590-613). In contrast, the multitudinous
demonstrations of acceptance of his condition as leader give rise to some
intensely dramatic scenes (B, III, 201-206).

When Flavius Josephus and his comrades find themselves in dire
straits, the historian opts for surrender to the Romans, but comes up
against the opposition of the others, who even go so far as to accuse him
of being a traitor. The scene is markedly dramatic, and develops in the
midst of a long speech (B, III, 350-391). All his comrades take each
other's lives, following the order established by drawing lots, and Flavius
Josephus is last in line. Flavius Josephus then surrenders to the Romans.

These moments are grave in the extreme, and according to the
historian's description, the reactions of the Roman soldiers were very
disparate on seeing the Jewish general their prisoner (B, III, 392-408).
This entire scene revolves around one word, μεταβολή (B, III, 394), in
its tragic sense, that is ''change of fortune'', since the situation of Flavius
Josephus is quite the opposite of what it had been up to then: from
general to prisoner. This aspect is a constant one in the setting of the
classical tragedies.

So as to abbreviate and avoid repetition, I shall give the principal items
of those moments which I believe have achieved a dramatic climax, as
evidence of the abundant material of this type in the work of Flavius
Josephus: B, III, 221; B, IV, 106 ff., 305-313, 556-565; B, V, 16-19,

---

[854] B, II, 476.

25-35, 291-295, 420-438, 512-518, 568-572; B, VII, 112-115, 320-406; A, III, 83-88, 315-326; A, VII, 324-328; A, IX, 209-210; A, XIII, 314-319; A, XIV, 429-430, 479-481; A, XVI, 87-129; A, XVII, 93-141; A, XIX, 343-351.

I should finally like to mention that book VI of the *Bellum Judaicum* is rich in dramatic situations. The book opens with a view of the suffering of Jerùsalem together with a description of the pitiful spectacle offered by the interior (Nos. 1-9), and of the state of mind of the armies (Nos. 19-53). The havoc created amongst the Jewish multitude by hunger (Nos. 193-219) is described in minute detail, together with a description of the attitude of Titus and the conduct of the Roman armies (Nos. 253-270). The massacre of the Jews follows, with the burning and sacking of Jerusalem (Nos. 271-285, 363-369), and the final conduct of the victorious army once inside the city itself (Nos. 403-408).

CHAPTER THREE

CONCLUSIONS: THE METHODOLOGY OF
FLAVIUS JOSEPHUS

This final chapter will be devoted to discussion of the conclusions reached after the previous analysis and will be summed up under three main headings.

First of all there is the question of the type of history which Flavius Josephus writes, or again the type of content which is made up by the historical material with which he has formed a unified corpus by means of a rich historiographic web, as we have already seen. Point A. will be devoted to this heading.

The second summary deals with the manner in which Flavius Josephus has constructed his work. Here I shall be touching on the use of the predicaments. Whereas in the previous paragraph there was a summing up of the substance of the work, here the form in which it is presented will be dealt with. Point B. will correspond to this subject.

The third heading will cover the various historical issues, the solutions to historical problems and to their demonstrative technique by means of the use of literary sources and various argumentations. Point C. will study this subject.

Point D. will look at one of the most important themes in Flavius Josephus, the sources he used, but solely from a formal standpoint. Finally, point E. will cover the historiographic attitude and impartiality of Flavius Josephus.

Precedents

Nonetheless, these aspects should be assessed from an historical perspective. And so the classical precedents will provide the light necessary for a full understanding of them. But first of all something should be said of the concept of history as it stood in antiquity.

The fundamental value of the word ἱστορία is that of *seeing*, so that it seems that history must be based, from the very beginning, on the testimony of a person who has been witness to the events[1], and then to

---

[1] E. Benvéniste, *Noms d'action et noms d'agents en indo-européen*, Paris, 1948, 29, 32, 33 and 51.

this testimony must be added any knowledge which has been obtained by means other than autopsy[2].

In the *Iliad*, the word ἵστωρ has the value of *witness*[3] and of *arbiter* or *judge*[4], or else that of *one who testifies*[5]. In the *Homeric Hymn* XXXII, 2, the Muses are named ἵστορες ᾠδῆς, i.e., *verseds or experts in song*. In Hesiod, it means a man *full of knowledge*[6].

Archaeology has shown that ancient Greek poetry contained a certain amount of historical elements, even though they were completely divorced from reality[7]. What is most important of all, however, is the continued search for relationships between the events and their causes. By this token, it is evident that Homer is the initiator of the historiographical method[8].

Periegetical and genealogical literature represents a second attempt to rationalise history. The geography and ethnology contained in these travels were the beginnings of the two incipient scientific disciplines, and the expositive form of those first notes was determined by the order of succession of the places which the curious traveller either visited or spied out from his vessel[9].

In his *Genealogies*, Hecataeus attempted to provide inherited myths with a realistic and historical basis, by using the chronological method of the succession of generations, each lasting for forty years. What is important here is not the result, but rather the effort, a clearly historiographical one, together with the critical method he employed, both basic elements in future historiographical theory.

It should also be said that Hecataeus was not the only forerunner of Herodotus[10], which implies a long period of formation of the historiographic method, without which the historiographic maturity of the work of Thucydides would not have been possible.

Whereas the work of Hecataeus is geography with historical *excursus*, that of Herodotus centred on history and conceded some *excursus* to

---

[2] B. Snell, *Die Ausdrücke für den Begriff des Wissens in der vorplatonischen Philosophie*, Berlin, 1924, 59.

[3] Ψ, 486. In Flavius Josephus, *accessory* (A, XVII, 78).

[4] Σ, 499.

[5] H, 499; K, 328.

[6] *Erga* 792. Too Bacchylides, VIII, 44; Sophocles, *El.* 850; φ, 26.

[7] W. Schadewaldt, "Die Anfänge der Geschichtsschreibung bei den Griechen", *Ant* 10 (1934), 144-153. The theory according to which ancient poetry was attributed to priestly authority (F. Creuzer, *Die historische Kunst der Griechen*, Leipzig, 1803, 3) has been discredited (N. Falk, *De historiae inter Graecos origine et natura*, Kiliae, 1809, 20-21).

[8] A. Lesky, *Storia della Letteratura Greca*, Milano, 1965, 245. On the historical values of ancient poetry, cf. the work of Falk already mentioned, 21-35.

[9] Hecat., *FGH* 127, on the Pelasgians.

[10] Dion. Hal., *De Thuc.* 5.

ethnographical and topographical aspects[11]. Thus, autopsy found its way into history through the periegetic tradition, at the same time as rationalism found its way there via Hecataeus.

In Herodotus, the word ἱστορίη is used again and again in the sense of *research, investigation* or *inquiry*[12]. Once only does it seem to be used in the narrative sense of the word[13]. The inheritor of a long logographical tradition, Herodotus provided autopsy with historiographical consecration, by making it the first postulate of historical method. The second point of his method was aural information, sought out from among existing testimonies. He makes the following, very clear, statement on the matter: ὦτα ἀπιστότερα ὀφθαλμῶν[14], and even made a distinction between information gathered visually and aurally[15].

G. Nenci[16] has summed up all these ideas thus: "Ma Erodoto distingue ulteriormente quel che si dice[17] da quel che si dice e gli pare vero[18] e ancora da ciò che si dice ed egli ha potuto controllare *de visu*[19]". Again a distinction is made between eye-witness reports and third-hand information[20]. This shows that Herodotus was well aware of the difficulty of a real historical method, and did not omit a declaration of the methodological principles which lead to truth: ὄψις ἐμὴ καὶ γνώμη καὶ ἱστορίη[21].

By way of conclusion, Herodotus is eager to make known his viewpoint concerning historical methodology. In contrast, Thucydides is extremely unforthcoming in this respect; excepting chapters 20, 21 and 29 of the first book, the places where he gives insights into his method are few and far between.

Thucydides did not use the word ἱστορίη, but σύγγραμμα and συγγραφεῖν[22]. It may be that the Ionic word repelled Thucydides. If we

---

[11] G. Nenci, "Il motivo de l'autopsia nella storiografia greca", *SCO* 3 (1953), 29; E. Schwartz, "Geschichtsschreibung und Geschichte bei den Hellenen", *Ant* 4 (1928), 14-30; W. Schadewaldt, *op. cit.*, 156-165.

[12] W. von Christ, *op. cit.*, 425 adn. 2. In Herodotus, see I, 24, 56, 61, 122; II, 18.

[13] Hrdt. VII, 96.

[14] Hrdt. I, 8.

[15] Hrdt. II, 29: αὐτόπτης, ἀκοῇ; II, 99: ὄψις, ἤκουον, ὄψιος; II, 19: ἐπυθόμην; II, 75: πυνθανόμενος; II, 118: εἰρομένου δέ μευ; II, 73: ἐμοὶ οὐ πιστὰ λέγοντες; II, 142: οἱ ἱερέες ἔλεγον; II, 147: προσέσται δέ τι αὐτοῖσι καὶ τῆς ἐμῆς ὄψιος; II, 156: εἶδον ... ἀκούων; see VI, 47 and VIII, 109.

[16] *Op. cit.*, 30-35.

[17] Hrdt. I, 5; IV, 195; V, 10. He believes that the historian is free to believe what he is told (II, 123; VII, 152a). Again: ἐγὼ δὲ ὀφείλω λέγειν τὰ λεγόμενα, πείθεσθαί γε μὲν οὐ παντάπασι ὀφείλω, x. μοι τ. τὸ ἔπος ἐχέτω ἐς πάντα λόγον (VII, 152).

[18] Hrdt. II, 15: ὡς αὐτοὶ λέγουσι Αἰγύπτιοι καὶ ἐμοὶ δοκέει. See too VI, 64.

[19] II, 102, or simply to control, II, 44.

[20] IV, 16 and II, 119.

[21] II, 99.

[22] Thuc. I, 1, 97; V, 41; VIII, 67. Cf. B. Snell, *op. cit.*, 65.

add to this the fact of his very different approach from that of Herodotus, in the sense that while Thucydides steeped himself in his near-contemporary history, Herodotus was an untiring traveller in quest of historical data, then we have the explanation of why this word from Ionia had so little success in Thucydides' work[23].

After, the semantic difference between ἱστοριογράφος and συγγραφεύς was defined. The first word refers above all to a writer of *past events*; the second word, to the historian of events *contemporary with him*, so that there is the possibility of checking by the historian himself[24]. This distinction probably came from grammarians of the first century A.D.[25].

Though his attitude was one of reliance on eye-witness sources, Thucydides does not completely abandon written accounts of events, and even submits to them[26].

There is still one aspect which is an integral part of his historiographic concept and method. Thucydides, in spite of the great value he placed on autopsy, also proposed that the intellectual personality of the historian be integrated into the historiographic method, without meaning to conceal the relative nature which may be deduced from it. No doubt the creation of his direct speeches were pointers in this direction, and he manifests openly that it was not his intention to faithfully reproduce words[27]. His relativism however, far from being a comfortable stance, is the product of the philosophical process of the Sophists, which had begun with Empedocles and Parmenides and had been carried on by the majority of the pre-Socratics, and which holds that reason was greater than the sensorial fact. Seeing and feeling therefore are subordinate to the personal νοῦς of the historian.

Therefore, in conclusion, Thucydides demands autopsy, rejects doubtful tradition and propounds the strength of one's νοῦς which brings to light the deep reasons of the history of an era, even though they have never been personally witnessed by the historian[28].

In Hippocratic treatises, the word ἱστορίη means *science*, a very logical meaning concerning writings which were entirely based on the compilation of tested data[29].

---

[23] F. Muller, ''De ''historiae'' vocabulo atque notione'', *Mnemosyne* 54 (1926), 243.

[24] Cf. K. Nickau, *Ammonii qui dicitur liber De adfinium uocabulorum differentia*, Lipsiae, 1966, *s. uu.*

[25] *RE*, *s.u.* ''Ammonius''.

[26] Thuc. I, 73.

[27] Thuc. I, 22, 1.

[28] Cf. the study on historical aetiology in Chap. I and Parmenides, B, 6, 6-7. The same idea is beautifully expressed in a verse by Epicharmus: νοῦς ὁρῇ καὶ νοῦς ἀκούει· τἄλλα κωφὰ καὶ τυφλά (B, 12).

[29] *V. Med.* XX, Littré I, 622.

Philosophical vocabulary was very reluctant to admit the word ἱστορίη. The number of times that it is used by philosophers is few, and when it is used, it continually bears the meaning of *science* and *knowledge*. Thus Heraclitus, according to the testimony of Clement of Alexandria[30], calls the εὖ μάλα πολλῶν ἵστορες philosophers[31], with the meaning of *knowing*.

Here the word μάθησις may come into the fray; it means to carry something to memory without going any deeper into its causes, i.e. *to learn*. The Pythagorean school accorded the words μάθησις and μαθήματα great dignity[32]. Finally, Heraclitus describes Pythagoras as a good investigator, when he says ἱστορίην ἤσκησεν[33]. Neither did Plato give ἱστορίη its later historiographic value, but rather the meaning of *knowledge* or *science*. He also gave it the value of *philosophy*[34].

At the same time, the tragic writers showed great indifference to the use of the word ἱστορίη. Examples are very scarce. Aeschylus gives it its original meaning of *to know, because it has been seen*[35]. Sophocles uses it with a similar meaning[36]. In Euripides, it has the meaning of *investigation*[37].

The participle εἰδότες in Attic oratory means the person who gives testimony as possessing a guarantee from the gods[38]. Demosthenes used the word ἱστορία with the meaning of *science* or *knowledge*[39].

Aristotle made great use of it. The word ἱστορία appeared in the titles of his works on biology[40], but it does not reflect the concept of history of events, even though it was translated into Latin as *Historia/animalium/*. The word ἱστορεῖν and the compound προιστορεῖν appear only in the apocryphal works[41].

Even so, a certain number of passages with the words ἱστορία and ἱστορικός offer what is almost the modern meaning of *history*[42]. In his *Poetica*, Aristotle defines the genre of history in opposition to poetry:

---

[30] *Strom.* V, 141.

[31] *Fr.* 35, Diels.

[32] B. Snell, *op. cit.*, 72 ff.

[33] *Fr.* 22 B 128, Diels.

[34] *Phaed.* 96a: τῆς σοφίας, ἣν δὴ καλοῦσι περὶ φύσεως ἱστορίαν. See in this same sense: *Phaedr.* 244c; *Cratyl.* 437b, 406b, 407c ἵστωρ; *Sophist.* 267e ἱστορικός.

[35] *Eum.* 455: 'Αργεῖός εἰμι, πατέρα δ' ἱστορεῖς καλῶς. Cf. *Ag.* 1090 and J. Brunel, *L'aspect verbal et l'emploi des préverbes en grec, spécialement en attique*, Paris, 1939, 39.

[36] *Oed. R.* 1484: ὃς ὑμῖν, ὦ τέκν', οὔθ' ὁρῶν οὔθ' ἱστορῶν πατὴρ ἐφάνθην, ἔνθεν αὐτὸς ἠρόθην. Cf. too *El.* 850.

[37] *Fr.* 910, Nauck: ὄλβιος ὅστις τῆς ἱστορίας / ἔσχε μάθησιν.

[38] Dem., 55, 9, 11 ff.; 35. Isocr., 17, 44; 19, 29, 34, 73, 99, 113, 118.

[39] XVIII, 144.

[40] P. Moraux, *Les listes anciennes des ouvrages d'Aristote*, Louvain, 1951.

[41] P. Louis, "Le mot ἱστορία chez Aristote", *RPh* 29 (1955), 39-44. Apocryphal works of Aristotle: *De mundo* 4, 396a 20 and 3, 393b 13; *De plant.* I, 3, 818b 28; *De hist. mir.* 37, 833a 12.

[42] *Rhet.* I, 4, 1359b 22, 1360a 24; III, 9, 1409a 28; *Probl.* XVIII, 917b 8.

history narrates past events; poetry, events which may come to pass; the latter is more philosophical and more universal, history, more particular; in history, a great diversity of actions have to be synchronised into a single space of time, whereas in tragedy and epic poetry no more than a single act should be presented at a time[43].

Other texts provide the meaning of *knowledge*[44] and of *research* or of *science*[45]. This notwithstanding, the words ἱστορία and ἐπιστήμη are not synonymous in Aristotle. The difference between them is based on the fact that ἐπιστήμη refers to universal things[46], and ἱστορία to particular things.

In conclusion, from the original etymological value of *witness* to the Aristotelian *science*, one sees that the word ἱστορία takes on the meaning of *knowledge* and of *investigation*, giving particular importance to the autopsy of events on the part of the writer; within the lapse of a century, the historian has managed to lay the foundations for his particular method.

To try and give a definition of *quid sit* history is no easy task. There is no widely shared opinion even within the camp of scientific historians. What some consider to be history is less considered so by others. And the whole of this shifting world is borne to nothing else but to the very nature of history. There is no doubt that it is here where the historian's role is essential, because history is not a "narrating of the human past"[47], nor is it "a literary work"[48], even though the historian adopts a form and develops a style. History is not writing, but rather "knowing the human past"[49]. It is in this sense, then, that the historian has in his mind a perfectly thought-out vision of human history, which he gradually shapes by means of a rigorous and systematic method. With history considered in this light, then that initial meaning of *research* is no more than a means, and not an end in itself.

Here a brief digression should be made concerning the ideas which classical writers had on kinds of history and on the elements which the historian had at his disposal when it came to writing his history.

---

[43] *Poet.* 9, 1451b 1-7; 23, 1459a 21-24.

[44] *De anima* 1, 402a 1 (εἴδησις = ἱστορία = γνῶσις); *H. an.* I, 6, 491a 12; *G. an.* III, 8, 757b 35 (ἱστορικῶς).

[45] *Anal. Pr.* 30, 46a 24; *De caelo* III, 1, 298b 2.

[46] *Met.* II, 6, 1003a 15; X, 1, 1059b 26; 2, 1060b 20; XII, 9, 1086b 9, 1086b 23; *De anima* II, 5, 417b 23.

[47] O. Philippe, *L'homme et l'histoire*, Actes du Congrès de Strasbourg, 1952, 36 (cited by H.-I. Marrou).

[48] R. Jolivet, *L'homme et l'histoire*, Actes du Congrès de Strasbourg, 1952, 11 (cited by H.-I. Marrou).

[49] H.-I. Marrou, *op. cit.*, 27-39. Cf. K. Löwith, *El sentido de la historia*, Madrid, 1973 (orig. ed. 1949).

In general terms then, the Greek historians showed a similar way of writing to that of the dramatists: letting persons and events speak for themselves. Like plastic artists, the historian imitates life[50], the πάθος of which he may use solely insofar as it does not take him away from the integrity of the truth[51].

The two kinds of history created in Greece, narrative history (Herodotus) and philosophical-scientific history (Thucydides), were not given as absolutes, and both tendencies are found mixed with each other. The difference between them stems rather from the basic attitude of the historian when faced with the events he is to narrate[52].

Even though Herodotus has many points in common with Hecataeus, his differences are more important. Herodotus expounds information which has been collected by himself, ἱστορίης ἀπόδειξις. From among his similarities to Hecataeus, special mention should be made of his extensive ethnological *logos*[53], independent creations belonging to the times when he was a traveller, according to Jacoby[54]. As regards differences, Herodotus is above all a writer of the "affairs of men", especially of "great and marvellous works", which he provides with a serious and profound foundation, that of *cause.*

Man, as the centre of his work, appears immersed in nature, hence the attention which Herodotus pays to geography and to geophysical realities[55].

Parallel to his capacity as narrator, there is his facility for novelistic creations, based on the destiny of man. He distinguished between those parts investigated by himself and information coming from written sources[56], keeping in mind that the first aspect included personal observation (ὄψις), his opinion (γνώμη) and his own investigation (ἱστορίη), and that he regarded the second point with some scepticism[57].

For all his critical sense, the work of Herodotus contains considerable quantities of myth[58], perhaps due to the fact that it was not his intention to aspire to absolute rationality.

---

[50] Luc., *De hist. conscr.* 51; Plut., 1, 1.

[51] Diod., *Bibl.* XX, 43.

[52] Cf. N. Falk, *op. cit.*, 44-50, and H. R. Immerwahr, *Form and Thought in Herodotus*, Cleveland, Ohio, 1966.

[53] K. Trüdinger, *Studien zur Geschichte der griech.-röm. Ethnographie*, Basel, 1918.

[54] F. Jacoby, *RE*, Suppl. 2, *s.u.* "Herodotos".

[55] II, 21; IV, 36. Cicero considered the *regionum descriptionem* as one of the characteristics of history (*De orat.* II, 15, 63).

[56] II, 99.

[57] VII, 152.

[58] III, 84; VI, 61; VII, 129. In this same sense, cf. R. Crahay, *La littérature oraculaire chez Hérodote*, Paris, 1956, and P. Frisch, *Die Träume bei Herodot*, Meisenheim am Glan, 1968.

On the other hand, Thucydides sees his work as falling into two parts: the description of events and the part made up by the totality of the speeches. He also recognised a third type of history, *mythical* history, which he could not allow, since his history was "composed as a possession for ever rather than a prize-performance for the moment"[59].

The first two parts are found also testimonied in Plato[60], Ephorus[61], Theopompus[62], Polybius[63], Dionysius[64], and Quintilian[65].

Polybius is the artificer of the classification of histories, and establishes three clearly differentiated groups. The first group comprises histories which are genealogical in character; the second those which narrate the foundings of cities and conquests; the third covers those which are entirely given over to the acts (πράξεις) of peoples, cities and rulers[66].

Polybius placed himself in the third category, that of the pragmatic genre[67]. Concerning the interpretation of his ὁ πραγματικὸς τρόπος, Pédech[68], after a lengthy exposition of opinions, concludes that Polybius is against the histories of foundings and genealogical histories, and that he indicates the study of public and political events, which constitute the material of historical narrative.

Diodorus divided history into ἀρχαιόταται πράξεις and into νεώτεραι πράξεις (IV, 1, 2, 4), adding that the criterion followed by Ephorus separated history into two stages, the dividing point being the arrival of the Heraclides, a thing which was to be identified with the era of Greek colonisation.

Dionysius of Halicarnassus distinguishes two parts, τὸ πραγματικὸν μέρος and τὸ λεκτικὸν μέρος, the first being understood as the historical content researched and the strict ordering of the same, and the second the style and form[69].

Asclepiades of Myrleia[70] proposes a real history, a false history and another quasi-real history. The real history speaks of the gods, heroes and famous men, deals with places and chronologies and narrates τὰς

---

[59] Thuc. I, 22, 4.
[60] *Tim.* 19c.
[61] Harpocr., *s.u.* "ἀρχαίως".
[62] Pol., XII, 27, 8.
[63] XIV, 1a, 3.
[64] *De Imit.* III, 3; 209, 20; *Ad Pomp.* 3, 20; *De Thuc.* 25; 364; 7, 55; 418, 13.
[65] X, 1, 101.
[66] IX, 1, 3 ff.
[67] I, 2, 8; 35, 9; III, 8; IX, 2, 4; XII, 25e, 1; 27a, 1; XXXVI, 17, 1; XXXIX, 1, 4.
[68] *Op. cit.*, 22-32.
[69] *De Thuc.* 1, 34; 9, 21; 21, 357, 19; *ibid.*, 358, 8; 381, 15; *Ad Pomp.* 3, 15, 6, 8-9; *De Imit.* I, 197, 2, B, III; *Comp. verb.* 1, 3.
[70] S. Emp., *Adu. Math.* I, 252-253; *Adu. Gramm.* 655, 25B.

πράξεις. The false history is that of myths and genealogies. The quasi-real history is that of comedy and mime[71].

Sextus Empiricus numbers four parts of history: τοπική, χρονική, περὶ τὰ πρόσωπα, περὶ τὰς πράξεις[72]. Eustathius too is of the same opinion: ἐκτοπικοῦ καὶ πραγματικοῦ καὶ χρονικοῦ καὶ γενεαλογικοῦ[73].

Hellenistic science too exercises a good influence in this matter by attributing to the word ἱστορία the possibility of describing places and countries, as well as the narration of events themselves. The description of places included θαύματα and παράδοξα as a means of making history more pleasant and elaborate[74]. This latter point was allowed by Thucydides, Polybius and Diodorus[75] only when it contributed to the clarification of the placing of historical causes. Cicero and Tacitus recognise in it the value of decorating the simple ἔκφρασις[76], and Lucian recommended sparing use of it[77].

Regarding the integrant elements of history, first of all should be mentioned the great influence which rhetoric exercised over historians from the fifth century onwards.

Rhetoric teaches the art of reasoning out an event until a definition of it is reached. Evidence should therefore be provided and causes looked into carefully so as to be able to establish the authenticity and significance of an event[78].

Rhetoric also demands an analysis of the conditions in which the event has taken place[79]. This will give rise to classifications of motives, of influences, of the forces of social pressure, whether circumstantial or simply environmental, which have a bearing on the event. Even so, Aristotle insists on the fact that the cause of the event should not be confused with one or other of its antecedents[80].

---

[71] Cicero classes the annals as *monumenta temporum, hominum, locorum gestarumque hominum* (*De orat.* II, 12, 63; II, 15, 63).

[72] *Adu. Math.* I, 257; *Adu. Gramm.* 657, 2B.

[73] *In Dionys. Perieg.* (*GGM*), II, 215, 14; 427a, 12. On this author, cf. P. Scheller, *op. cit.*, 19-21.

[74] Hrdt., I, 93; II, 35; IV, 82; Dion. Hal., *Ad Pomp.* 6, 4; Diod., *Bibl.* IV, 1, 5.

[75] Pol., V, 21, 3-9; cf. I, 41, 7; X, 9, 8; Diod., *Bibl.* XVIII, 5, 1.

[76] *De orat.* 20, 66; *Ann.* IV, 33.

[77] *De hist. conscr.* 57.

[78] Cic., *Inv.*, I, 28, 43; Quint. VII, 2, 3. For the development of rhetoric and its application to history, cf. B. P. Reardon, *Courants littéraires grecs des II⁄ᵉ et III⁄ᵉ siècles après J.-C.*, Paris, 1971, 64 ff.

[79] Isocr. II, 276.

[80] Arstt., *Rhet.* II, 24, 1401b, 29.

These contributions are clearly the result of an intellectual concept of history, and reveal the mental activity by means of which the historian will painstakingly qualify and assess the historical event[81].

It should not be forgotten that in fifth-century Greece there arose no clear distinction between the orator and the historian which might have lead to two distinct and separate professions. Corax, Tisias and Gorgias were founders of schools of history and oratory in Sicily. Isocrates himself practised both professions. Theopompus fused them both in himself. Ephorus, as a disciple of Isocrates, poured into his history all his stylistic beauty (panegyrics, battle descriptions, speeches and so on), revealing as great a capacity for rhetoric as his master. Hence the reason for the need to bring out the rhetorical and descriptive aspects when making an analysis of an historical work[82].

Thus, within the limits of history, the area of historical and epideictic influence comprises two fundamental moments in historiographic technique: formal descriptions (ecphrases) and speeches.

The ecphrasis refers to places, landscapes, special objects and so on, and may appear in the comparisons and in the encomiastic passages. Numerous speeches in praise of cities, countries and the like simply answer to the imperatives of the ecphrasis. Within the conditions imposed by the historiographic method, terminological clarity and vividness are both absolutely essential. There are numerous quotes concerning this matter.

By way of example, one may observe in the work of Herodotus, at times of description, an impressive variety, in spite of the manifest archaic nature which surrounds the whole of his work, and at times achieves particular intimacy[83].

Thucydides is not over-generous in descriptions, but the few that he does give are manifestly rich in detail[84].

A. Pragmatic history

Firstly the historical content should be investigated which is most predominant in Flavius Josephus and his work. This, however, is provided by the author himself when he offers a general table of contents in his

---

[81] Lucian is critical of the opinion which holds that the task of the historian is a simple one, and states that the historian has to make a strenuous mental effort, πολλῆς τῆς φροντίδος (De hist. conscr. 5).

[82] Indubitably rhetoric was one of the most influential successes achieved by the Sophists, in spite of the opposition of some profound thinkers.

[83] I, 24; IV, 71, 2; VI, 125; VII, 210-212, 223-225.

[84] I, 70; II, 47; VII, 43, 44.

principal works. With regard to this point an analysis should be made of the following fragments: B, I, 19-30; A, I, 5-9, 14-16; A, XX, 259-266.

In the *Bellum Judaicum*[85], Flavius Josephus specifies the subjects dealt with in each book:

I. comprises events from the times of Antiochus Epiphanes, when he assumes control of Jerusalem, to the Hasmonaeans, who brought Roman intervention onto the scene; it also includes the ousting of the Hasmonaeans from power by the action of the Idumaean Herod;

II. will narrate the rebellion of the Jewish people and the death of Herod, the beginnings of the war, under the rulership of Nero and the first military successes of the Jews in the first encounters in war;

III. will cover the fortification of Judaea on the part of the Jews; Nero places Vespasian in charge of the war; the invasion of the Romans, their military discipline; the sufferings of the prisoners, witnessed or suffered by Flavius Josephus himself;

IV. will deal with the misfortunes of the Jews, the death of Nero, the imperial dignity of Vespasian, the civil war amongst the Jews and the appearance of the tyrants who wanted power and the second invasion of Judaea by Titus;

V. the situation of Jerusalem, after the civil war, the effects of the different attacks of the Romans; the temple and some ritual aspects, the ill-treatment of the citizens by the tyrants, and the clemency of the Romans;

VI. the fortune of the Jewish deserters, the punishments of the prisoners, the burning of the temple of Jerusalem; the capture of the city and of the tyrants;

VII. the ending of the war by the Romans, the restoration of law and order by Titus, and his return to Italy and his official triumph.

In this table of contents can be seen nothing but verifiable events, military events, political events, social events, without giving place to fantastic or unverifiable events.

Flavius Josephus is not so explicit when it comes to the *Antiquitates Judaicae*. In general terms he says that this work "will comprise the whole of our ancient history and political constitution, translated from the Hebrew books"[86].

At the end of the *Antiquitates Judaicae*, Flavius Josephus once more recalls, in general terms, the contents of his work. After saying that this work ends where the *Bellum Judaicum* begins, he adds that "this work embraces the tradition, from the first creation of man to the twelfth year of

---

[85] B, I, 19-30. Cf. B. Niese, "Der jüdische Historiker Josephus", *HZ* 40 (1896), 193-237.

[86] A, I, 5. Too A, I, 26; A, II, 347; A, IV, 36; A, VIII, 159; A, X, 218; Ap, I, 54.

the reign of Nero, of the events which came to pass amongst us, the Jews, in Egypt, Syria and Palestine, and all that we have suffered at the hands of the Assyrians and Babylonians, and the ill-treatment that the Persians and the Macedonians have accorded us, and after them, the Romans''[87]. He then adds that he has kept the record of the line of succession of the high-priests for two thousand years, as well as that of judges and kings[88], as he had promised at the beginning of his history.

The second aspect is the aim which Flavius Josephus is pursuing in his works. In the preface to the *Bellum Judaicum*, he criticises harshly those historians who, without having taken any part in the war, have produced a rhetorical-type history, or if they have witnessed the war, then they have written history which is full of inventions and eulogies, a very far cry from historical rigour[89]. As a consequence, his work in history-writing is aimed at clarifying the truth of events, that is, has a classificatory and educational objective.

In the *Antiquitates Judaicae*, Flavius Josephus specifies the great lesson which he intends the reader to draw from his work: that he who obeys the will of God and does not transgress his laws will prosper in all. He adds that the words of Moses are perfectly adapted to the concept of divine nature, avoiding the mythology which is usually the case with other authors and the invention of fiction[90].

The objective behind *Contra Apionem* is also pedagogic, since Flavius Josephus wishes to make known the ancient history of the Jewish people, in spite of the malicious calumnies of certain writers[91], and intends to support his theories with the authority of the most important Greek writers[92].

In conclusion, therefore, one may find in the works of Flavius Josephus subjects which are basically political and social, and from his investigation has as his aim the clarification of events and pedagogic enlightenment of the history of the Jewish people.

On the other hand, Flavius Josephus endows his work with many names, something which is very suggestive when it comes to specifying the kind of history he is writing. Therefore the words πραγματεία, ἱστορία, συγγράφω and συγγραφεύς throw sufficient light, from a purely philological point of view, on the question to be able to elucidate the historical content of the works of Flavius Josephus.

---

[87] A, XX, 259-260.
[88] A, XX, 261.
[89] B, I, 1-2.
[90] A, I, 15-16.
[91] Ap, I, 1-2.
[92] Ap, I, 4. The *Vita* should be located within these coordinates, with a keen sense of self-defence.

The words συγγραφεῖν and συγγραφεύς have already been clarified previously in *Precedents*. Flavius Josephus maintains the use of συγγραφεῖν (B, VII, 448; A, I, 1, 6, 107; A, II, 348; A, X, 20, 93, 267, 277; A, XI, 208; A, XII, 5, 100; Vit, 338, 358, 365; Ap, I, 7, 18, 37, 40, 45, 183, 252), συγγραφεύς (B, I, 13, 18; A, XII, 38; A, XIII, 337; A, XIV, 3, 68, 111), συγγραφή (A, XIV, 265) and σύγγραμμα (Ap, I, 161) for contemporary events with the historian; sometimes the meaning they have is of a more general nature.

The word ἱστορία appears eighty times, not counting the corresponding verb[93]. Its meanings include those of *investigation* (B, IV, 477), *inspection* (B, III, 443), *narration*, *knowledge*, *historical events* and *historical work*. It therefore falls within the possibilities of the meanings discussed in *Precedents*.

The word πραγματεία is richer in semantic possibilities, although its specific meanings do not contribute a decisive content: *activity*, *effort*, *historical work*[94]. I believe, however, that this word should be understood in very close connection with the use made of the word πρᾶγμα throughout all his works. Apart from the generic meaning, πρᾶγμα means: *political circumstances*, *public affairs*, *government*, and *political power*[95]. In the classical writers and Polybius, the semantic trajectory of the word πραγματεία is the following: occupation, study, work and effort, manner of dealing with a subject, result of a study and historical work, particularly political, diplomatic or philosophical[96].

Thus we have a clear definition of the meaning of this word, according to which concrete values and the events in life would be included as opposed to theoretical and speculative knowledge.

For the Peripatetics, "pragmatic" was opposed to "logical" in the sense that a pragmatic discussion was founded on the nature of the things itself (πρᾶγμα), and logical discussion would start from the information of communal thought with a view to persuasion[97].

The expression πραγματικὴ ἱστορία is attributed to Polybius, with the meaning of instructive and pedagogic history, even though he himself is more concrete and less philosophical, understanding it in opposition to the mythological and genealogical histories, of colonisations and the founding of cities. Polybius' conception of history is that of a history

---

[93] Cf. *Concordance*, *s.u.*

[94] Cf. *Concordance*, *s.u.*

[95] Cf. *Concordance*, *s.u.*

[96] Plat., *Crat.* 408a; *Gorg.* 453a; *Rsp.* 500c; *Ant.*, 120, 14; Isocr., 11d, 83e; Arstt., *Pol.* 3, 1, 1; *Rhet.* 1, 15, 21; *Metaph.* 1, 6, 1; *Phys.* 2, 7, 3; Pol., 1, 1, 4; 1, 3, 1; Luc., *De hist. conscr.* 13.

[97] Simplicius, *Comm. de Phys.*, p. 22.1.29; 23.1.29; 26.1.11; 115.10 ed. Diels.

made up of events, and especially of political events. Thus history brings some benefit[98].

Now that the limits within which the word πραγματεία moves have been seen, an analysis should now be made of the essence of the events which are meant by it. In view of its connection with πρᾶγμα, under the broad heading of happenings, that is, a set of actions which constitute periods or historiographic corpuses, a qualification should be made of the type of happening to which it gives rise within the context in which it is found.

In the first place, the term πραγματεία[99], with its variants in meaning:

1. "and I have undertaken *this work* thinking that it will appear in the eyes of all Greeks worthy of attention"[100];

2. "I have narrated, therefore, these things, because I wish readers to know that I have said nothing but the truth, nor have I tried to avoid a critical investigation by intercalating the history with passages which seduce or lead to untruths and distraction, but indeed I deserve to be believed all along, and I crave no indulgence, if I have with impunity strayed from that which is proper to *historical narration*, and I do not expect to be received favourably, if I cannot make known truth with demonstrations and evident truths"[101];

3. "however, concerning these matters, I shall give a more exact demonstration in the second book of the *Bellum Judaicum*"[102].

4. "Joseph, while he was at the head of the administration of the affairs of the realm, and, for that very reason, often found himself with Mariamme to despatch *public affairs...*"[103];

5. "having reached this point in my narrative, I wish to address Justus, who has also written the *exposition* of these events..."[104];

6. "afterwards, during my rest at Rome, when I had all the *historical material* in order..."[105].

One may observe that there is an abundance of texts which confer on the term πραγματεία the value of historical work (Nos. 1, 2, 3, 5 and 6) or a similar value, but number 4 is highly significant because of its specific thematic value, and I shall relate to it all the parallel contents which may be inferred from the term πρᾶγμα, which is semantically involved with it in many cases.

---

[98] P. Pédech, *op. cit.*, 21-32.
[99] It is not used in the *Bellum Judaicum*.
[100] A, I, 5. Cf. too A, I, 17, 25; A, IV, 198; A, XII, 245; Ap, I, 54.
[101] A, VIII, 56.
[102] A, XIII, 173. Cf. too A, XIV, 218.
[103] A, XV, 68. Cf. too A, XVI, 45.
[104] Vit, 336. Cf. too Vit, 357.
[105] Ap, I, 50.

Depending on the context, therefore, the word πρᾶγμα[106] refers to the following concepts:

I. historical actions in general,

II. war actions and situations of misfortune,

III. fortune and destiny, and

IV. political events and affairs of government.

I. The historical actions refer to events, affairs of acts in any given situation, be they favourable or unfavourable, referring to interventions of God, to deeds and interests of some personality or of a people[107].

II. The numerous actions of war and their consequences are also included in the word πρᾶγμα. Therefore the tribulations of the victims, their misfortunes and the chaotic situation are realities which are fully assumed by this word which, from a generalising value, is confined to a concrete and restricted one[108].

III. The destiny and fortune of people is also included here, as well as their aspirations and their behaviour, be they individuals or a whole people[109].

IV. Finally, a great number of items refer to actions which are properly of a political or governmental character. It is on this point that I want to base my conclusion, according to which Flavius Josephus writes pragmatic history, in so far as he includes fundamentally, in his narrative, events which develop in the field of politics and are realised by men in power[110].

---

[106] I shall analyse a selection; I also include πρᾶξις and πεπραγμένα. Cf. too *Concordance, s. uu.*

[107] B, I, 3, 8, 19; B, V, 68, 445; A, I, 26; A, III, 5, 66, 95; A, IV, 10, 24, 36, 102, 142; A, V, 185, 197, 307, 319; A, VI, 131, 213, 265; A, VII, 90, 257; A, VIII, 4, 209; A, IX, 46 (πράξεις); A, X, 53, 222, 278; A, XIII, 22, 115; A, XIV, 2, 373; A, XV, 380 (πράξεις); A, XVI, 187 (πράξεις), 261; A, XVII, 273; A, XVIII, 154; A, XIX, 51; Vit, 63, 222, 412, 430 (πεπραγμένα); Ap, I, 6, 15, 183; Ap, II, 204 (πράξεις).

[108] B, I, 1, 2, 6, 9, 12, 13, 30; B, II, 113, 334; B, III, 138; A, IV, 96; A, V, 143, 338; A, VI, 100; A, VII, 132, 281; A, XI, 303; A, XII, 224, 267; A, XIII, 7, 84; A, XIV, 327; A, XV, 162; A, XVII, 2, 99, 206, 299; 325; A, XIX, 91; A, XX, 109; Vit, 36, 70, 87, 134, 192, 391.

[109] B, I, 23; A, V, 121, 322; A, VI, 329, A, VII, 44, 65; A, VIII, 9, 203, 205, 235; A, XII, 130, 402; A, XIII, 171, 431; A, XIV, 124; A, XV, 318; A, XVII, 272; A, XVIII, 269, 346; A, XIX, 246; Vit, 311 (πεπραγμένοις), 333 (πεπραγμένων); Ap, II, 281.

[110] B, I, 242, 561, 569, 665; B, II, 28, 61, 168, 233, 272-273, 481, 594; B, IV, 208, 230, 247, 278, 339, 492; A, IV, 165; A, V, 234; A, VI, 35, 81; A, VII, 28, 31, 96, 259, 389; A, VIII, 2, 21, 134, 221, 251, 263, 278 (πραττομένων); A, IX, 5-6, 216, 223; A, XI, 111, 217, 275; A, XII, 84, 285, 295, 379, 380, 386; A, XIII, 34, 36, 220, 261, 273, 300, 387, 407, 422, 429; A, XIV, 268, 273, 326; A, XV, 32, 42, 65, 68, 78, 92, 109, 165 (πολυπραγμονεῖν), 183, 184, 189, 191, 192, 218, 248, 264, 323; A, XVI, 1, 21, 22, 56, 115; A, XVII, 23, 32, 42, 221, 224; A, XVIII, 42, 43, 124, 215, 217, 222, 256, 338; A, XIX, 46, 161, 162, 196; A, XX, 1, 105, 160, 162, 261; Vit, 314; Ap, I, 186; Ap, II, 177.

B. HISTORIOGRAPHIC EXPLANATION

History as the personal work of the writer should reproduce the truth of history with accuracy and a wealth of information. History will therefore comprise a system of abstract relationships which the historian tries to detect or establish amongst the events chosen for narration. History which is therefore presented in its ''natural state'' as it were is not sufficient, since the intelligent mind demands a system of relationships amongst events. It is here that the analysis procedure which the historian has set himself comes into play, here the attitude of his mind as regards his documents is revealed. Here the philosophical character of history arises, thanks to which man may discover those particular moments in which his own history is to be found, the history of his historical times, whence it is going, and where, when and how it may finish.

Historians who preceded Polybius did not manage to intuit the elements of historical explanation, and their historiographical theory is limited to no more than emitting their opinion as regards the use of certain historiographic elements, the external aspect which the historical work must present, the layout and plan of the same: the sole thing which came in for their consideration were the rules of historical exposition, but not the exigencies of an understanding of the events, which came to constitute properly speaking the task of the intellectual.

Polybius sets out the demands of the work of the historian with great accuracy, when he specifies that the characters of the abstract relationships which the historian must discover amongst the events should be modal, temporal and causal: πῶς καὶ πότε διὰ τί[111]. Later on he will also mention the value, in historical description, of the conditions of the place, ποῦ, where events have happened[112].

Cicero speaks in much the same terms when he defined historical method[113] and when he gave advice to the lawyer and enumerated the parts of any act[114].

One may appreciate yet again the remarkable influence which rhetoric had on historiography and on research into its method and its means, much more so than pure philosophy. Philosophers themselves reflected on rhetoric.

To conclude it should be mentioned that research into the causes determines the conviction of the historian and of the reader, but causes do not

---

[111] Pol. III, 1-4. Cf. P. Pédech, *op. cit.*, 33 ff.
[112] Pol. III, 36, 1-38, 5.
[113] Cic. *De orat.* II, 15, 63.
[114] Cic., *Inv.* I, 26, 37-38. Cf. Quint. IV, 2, 2; V, 10, 94.

make known the means which the historian has used or his attitude in the face of the truth which he seeks to publish. The elements of historical explanation are, therefore, elements which are essential to history proper.

Flavius Josephus makes abundant use of the terms ἀκρίβεια, ἀκριβής and ἀκριβόω to point out that his historical opus is exact, correct, detailed, complete, real, faithful, scrupulous, meticulous, that it presents a real state of affairs, in short, that what he is saying is the truth[115].

On the other hand it is true enough that these words constituted a favourite term of all historians, a fact which makes for such an accumulation of historiographical tradition that they are frequently used with a purely literary value, or resulting from the modesty proper to the professional standing of the historian, who always wishes to offer his truth. This notwithstanding, historical accuracy demands a full explanation of events, both temporal, modal, causal, and local, exegetical, descriptive and critical.

Another aspect which affects the content of these words is the subjective force with which the author infuses them. When he offers accuracy in his work, the historian is simple proclaiming one of his basic principles, the history is the product of the historian, and that depending on the historian the same events may vary completely from the pen of another writer. The sincerity therefore with which these words are used must be judged from the perspective of each individual historian.

Historical explanation, in the case of Flavius Josephus, will also include a task of exegesis and philology, so that certain Jewish institutions and certain proper names, understood only by the Jews, should be made comprehensible too to foreign readers.

On the other hand, Flavius Josephus, who has personally taken part in the war, is able to offer the readers of Orient and Occident a careful narrative of events, from the moment they began, of the various phases they went through and their outcome[116]. Neither does Flavius Josephus forget that his own feelings may colour events, nor duly begs our pardon for them[117].

The work of Flavius Josephus becomes interesting from the moment when it is the fruit of his solid intellectual training. The more learned the historian, the more questions he may raise concerning historical events, and the entirety of his stock of learning gives birth to answers and ideological links in the most unexpected places. The erudition of rabbi

---

[115] Cf. *Concordance, s.uu.* To the mind of Flavius Josephus, the sole purpose of his history is the truth (cf. quote 235).

[116] B, I, 6; A, I, V, and see the value which he attributes to autopsy (cf. Chap. III, *Precedents* and E).

[117] B, I, 9-12.

Flavius Josephus throws light on the hidden obscurities of the Scriptures for his foreign readers, seeks out relationships and criticisms concerning those Greek writers who have given their attention to the Jewish people, and will give him breadth of vision so as to collocate the power of Rome in its place.

I shall here mention only the speeches, where the extent of Flavius Josephus' capacity of explanation may be appreciated.

Flavius Josephus goes on to say that he will observe the narrative order of the Holy Scriptures, leaving everything in its place, such as all kinds of social and war upheavals, heroic successes of generals and political changes[118], and the vision of a God completely free of the trammels of mythology, such as flowed from the stylus of Moses[119]. Finally, his attitude before the material offered by the Holy Scriptures will be one of respect, ''adding nothing and taking nothing away''[120]. In practice, nevertheless, he will add some legends, especially concerning Moses, borrowed from the Haggadah, Mishnah and Talmud, as well as omitting other small details[121].

Attention should be given now to the examination of each one of the characteristics of Flavius Josephus' historical explanation, minus the question of causes, which I have already dealt with at length in the whole of Chapter I.

Moreover, if we invoke the Aristotelian classification of the predicaments, we may clearly establish the degree of perfection which the author achieves. For Aristotle, nature is divided into ten predicaments: substance, quantity, quality, relation, time, space, place, habit, action and consequences[122]. If by substance we understand the content of an historical work, the remaining predicaments should be looked for in concrete situations.

Previous to going into this matter, it should not be forgotten that however complete historical explanation might be, it nevertheless has to follow certain criteria of selection, since not everything contributes to the clarification of an event, there being many things which simply encumber it. To the mind of Flavius Josephus, something which is common knowledge can be left out, thus avoiding interruption of the narrative

---

[118] A, I, 13.

[119] A, I, 15-16.

[120] A, I, 17: οὐδὲν προσθεὶς οὐδ' αὖ παραλιπών. On the same idea, see B, I, 26; A, IV, 196-197; A, X, 218; A, XII, 109; Ap, I, 42. Cf. W. Cornelis van Unnik, *Flavius Josephus als historischer Schriftsteller*, Heidelberg, 1978, 26-40, and *De la règle* Μήτε προσθεῖναι μήτε ἀφελεῖν ..., 1-36.

[121] In this sense, cf. Chap. III, D.

[122] *Cat.* 4, 1b 25; Luc., *De hist. conscr.* 47.

thread[123]. But here he is not uniform either, since elsewhere he does not practice what he preaches. Reason, in the present case, would mean a will to smooth over the memories of the scandalous life of Nero[124]. When he thinks fit, on the other hand, he cuts the narrative with long explanations. These digressions certainly interrupt the narrative, but contribute a great quantity of details and reveal the extensive knowledge of the author[125].

His words referring to the scope of historiographical explanation are suggestive in this respect: the reason behind his history is that men should know "whence the war came... through which circumstances it passes and how it ended"[126].

Dealing now specifically with the manner in which Flavius Josephus uses the predicaments, we may say that the use of clarifications in difficult questions and misunderstandings is frequent[127], when a personality or a group of people is to be described in few words[128], in questions relating to institutions[129], in explaining things in general[130], in details of place and manner of doing something[131], of number[132], to justify his way of history-writing[133], to explain in detail the workings of war artefacts[134], to refer to classical myths[135], in questions of etymology or the interpretation of certain words[136], the names as well as the personal details

---

[123] B, II, 251.

[124] The text A, XX, 154-157 may support this opinion. Moreover, the whole dark life of Nero brought to a close in a single point (A, XX, 153).

[125] Cf. Chap. II, B, 3.

[126] B, I, 6.

[127] B, I, 80, 581; A, III, 282; A, V, 11, 16, 18; A, VI, 195, 205, 337; A, XVII, 65, 106.

[128] B, I, 574; B, VI, 262; B, VII, 244; A, VI, 375; A, VII, 100, 216; A, XII, 204; A, XIII, 144; A, XIV, 107; A, XVIII, 32.

[129] B, II, 42, 313, 425; B, VI, 362; B, VII, 124; A, I, 33; A, II, 205, 311; A, IV, 29, 143, 144, 156, 162, 164-172, 195, 234, 239, 248, 252, 321; A, IV, 84; A, VII, 131, 171; A, VIII, 4, 100, 385; A, IX, 86, 224; A, XI, 107, 109, 148; A, XII, 412; A, XIV, 105-106; A, XV, 50, 314; A, XVII, 213, 254; A, XVIII, 344; A, XIX, 214; A, XX, 186, 198, 215; Vit, 65.

[130] B, II, 595; B, III, 262; B, V, 550; B, VI, 68, 131, 237, 293, 420 ss; B, VII, 148 ss., 306-307; A, III, 33; A, V, 343; A, XIX, 127.

[131] B, II, 619; B, IV, 84, 581-582; A, XV, 297; A, XVII, 198-199; Vit, 281.

[132] B, II, 635; B, III, 59, 166, 531, 540; B, IV, 80, 333, 435-436, 643; B, VI, 5, 358, 386, 420; B, VII, 38; A, II, 317, 324; A, VII, 196; A, IX, 220, 247; A, XII, 366; A, XIII, 333, 364; A, XIV, 72, 102; A, XVII, 270.

[133] B, III, 108-109; A, XI, 152.

[134] B, III, 167 ss., 213-221.

[135] B, III, 420.

[136] B, IV, 5, 11; B, V, 51, 299, 474; B, VI, 201; A, I, 34, 36, 38, 52, 174, 177, 180, 190, 204, 205, 212, 213, 258, 262, 284, 304, 324, 333, 334; A, II, 3, 91, 92, 228, 278, 313; A, III, 3, 32, 151, 152, 153, 163, 283; A, V, 34, 121, 200, 201, 285, 323, 336, 346, 360; A, VI, 22, 156, 320; A, VII, 67; A, VIII, 95, 142; A, IX, 19, 290; A, X, 243-244; A, XI, 173, 203, 286, 329; A, XIII, 370; A, XVIII, 47; Vit, 54; Ap, I, 167.

of people[137], the contents of a letter[138], literary comparisons[139], giving geographical details[140], attacks in war[141], to take up again the thread he has left off[142], in details concerning the Jewish Diaspora[143], in distances[144], so as to explain eponyms[145], so as to explain the properties of materials[146], in the descriptions of animals[147], and plants[148], in the description of an object[149], or a building[150], in describing illnesses[151] or ventriloquists[152], to give a detailed explanation of the functioning of musical instruments[153], to complete an action and its consequences[154], to specify chronology[155], to throw light on the power of the Jewish high-priests[156], in embellishing details[157], to specify genealogy[158], and social groups[159], to expound tragic situations[160] and pains[161], to specify an inheritance[162], to describe works of art[163], when making historical references[164], and finally

---

[137] B, IV, 145, 235; B, V, 474; A, II, 95, 210, 258, 264; A, VI, 107; A, VII, 10, 299; A, IX, 95, 142, 177; A, XII, 354; A, XIII, 62; A, XVI, 294; A, XIX, 100, 121, 137, 148, 163, 208; Vit, 204.
[138] B, IV, 228; A, XVI, 296.
[139] B, IV, 326, 397.
[140] B, IV, 413, 552, 554, 634; B, V, 55, 67, 107-108, 504-505; A, I, 160; A, II, 249, 305, 315; A, III, 9, 76; A, IV, 95, 161, 176, 325; A, V, 48; A, VI, 17, 374; A, VII, 71, 174, 283; A, VIII, 154, 312; A, IX, 7, 39, 206, 251, 279; A, X, 84, 269; A, XI, 340; A, XIII, 154, 188, 338; A, XIV, 18, 49, 57, 88, 91; A, XV, 112, 363; A, XVIII, 252; A, XX, 68, 118, 130; Vit, 16, 123, 188, 346; Ap, II, 25.
[141] B, IV, 429.
[142] B, IV, 556, 585.
[143] B, VII, 43-62.
[144] B, VII, 101; A, XII, 369; A, XV, 168; Vit, 157, 281, 349.
[145] A, I, 122-139, 221.
[146] A, II, 221.
[147] A, III, 25; A, XVIII, 195.
[148] A, III, 28, 173-178, 197; A, VIII, 176-177; A, XV, 96.
[149] A, III, 220.
[150] A, V, 314; A, X, 264; A, XV, 318, 324, 331; A, XVII, 257, 262; A, XIX, 88-90; A, XX, 110, 221.
[151] A, VI, 3.
[152] A, VI, 329-330.
[153] A, VII, 306.
[154] A, IX, 78, 103, 224; A, XIII, 302, 364; A, XVII, 183, 265; A, XIX, 335-337; Vit, 24, 40.
[155] A, XI, 1.
[156] A, XI, 111-112.
[157] A, XI, 235, 331; A, XIV, 107; A, XVII, 197.
[158] A, XI, 302.
[159] A, XV, 371; A, XVI, 277; A, XVIII, 22.
[160] A, XVI, 374.
[161] A, XVII, 169. Cf. M. Neuburger, *Die Medizin im Flavius Josephus*, Bad Reichenhall, 1919.
[162] A, XVII, 321.
[163] A, XIX, 8.
[164] A, XIX, 223.

in the use of specifications of the environment as an integral element in historical action[165].

Flavius Josephus also takes advantage of the names of important buildings so as to surround them with a brief explanation concerning their origins and functions, and to relate them to other similar places[166]; when mentioning a place, he includes the agricultural characteristics of the area[167], he goes into the details of the defensive aspects of a city[168], and makes lengthy descriptions when presenting constructions which have been carried out by Herod[169], mentions the climatological characteristics of a region[170], describes a river[171], furnishes a great many city names[172], is rich in the general descriptions of places where historical action takes place[173], mentions some ethnological aspects[174] and disagreeable subjects, such as suicides, both individual and collective, to the tune of twenty-three[175], and finally, pays a great deal of attention to the mention of the cardinal points, both with geographical and chronological value[176].

Finally, I should like to draw attention to three important aspects, on account of their implication in the historical event which is being narrated. In the first place, Flavius Josephus mixes up autobiographical elements in the narrative thread[177]. In the second place, the mention of political institutions as well as religious institutions is an integral part of the historical action[178]. In the third place, the use of the literary ''I'' of the author, in a great many places in his works, gives a personal and intimate character to his historiográphic style.

---

[165] B, I, 287, 330, 339, 370-371; B, III, 181, 312-313. 413; B, IV, 22, 43, 76, 90, 293, 299, 310; B, VI, 374; B, VII, 20, 164, 298, 317; A, I, 244; A, V, 16, 68, 71, 124, 205; A, VI, 14, 109, 135; A, VII, 186.

[166] B, I, 118.

[167] B, I, 138.

[168] B, I, 141, 147.

[169] B, I, 401-425.

[170] B, III, 181; B, IV, 451-485.

[171] B, VII, 96-99.

[172] B, I, 134; A, XVIII, 372.

[173] B, I, 145, 177-178.

[174] B, IV, 5; A, I, 244, 310; A, II, 257, 259, 263, 322; A, IX, 40; A, XVI, 277.

[175] Cf., in this sense, L. D. Hankoff, "The theme of suicide in the works of Flavius Josephus", *CM* 11 (1976), 15-24.

[176] Cf. *Concordance*, *s.uu.* ἑώθινος, ἕως and derived, ἀνατολή, μεσημβρινός, μεσημβρία, νότιος, νότος, δύσις; ἑσπέρα; προσάρκτιος, ἄρκτος, μελαμβόρειον, βορέας, βόρειος. Cf. B. Brüne, *op. cit.*, *Josephus, der Geschichtsschreiber...*, 37-39.

[177] The most notable places are the following: B, II, 568; B, III, 171, 406, 438; B, IV, 629; B, V, 332; B, VI, 81, 112; B, VII, 448.

[178] B, I, 60, 124, 146, 169-170, 184, 194, 229, 253, 270, 477; B, II, 10, 409, 456, 515; B, III, 270; B, IV, 99-100, 136, 205, 402, 499; B, V, 99; A, XIII, 12, 234, 235, 252, 257, 337, 372, 397; A, XIV, 25, 63, 475, 482-483; A, XV, 7, 281; A, XVII, 14, 200; A, XX, 106; Ap, 137.

C. Apodictic history

The intention to seek out the truth, to base events on reality and to construct an exposition which is rich in all manner of aspects and circumstances should not be enough for the historian. The argumentation of the facts which he puts forth, the demonstration that what he says is true is also an imperative with the historian. Here the question is raised of the use of the sources and the historian's intention in using them, aspects which will be dealt with later on when the use of sources is covered. Here it is rather a question of appraising the attitude according to which the historian presents historical events as problems to be solved.

Pédech in his already-mentioned work on Polybius[179], sums up the concept of apodictic history in the following terms: "L'ἀποδεικτικὴ διήγησις s'oppose donc à l'exposé qui consiste dans l'énoncé pur et simple des faits, l'affirmation non démontrée dans laquelle l'auteur n'apporte aucune preuve et n'emploie d'autre argument que sa propre autorité, sans se donner la peine de la justifier. Polybe réprouve cette méthode peu scientifique; elle ne lui paraît pas convenir à son temps de découvertes géographiques. Mais cette exigence va bien au-delà de la simple explication des causes et des effets; elle enveloppe tout l'appareil de preuves, arguments, témoignages, références, que l'historien et, en général, le savant présentent à l'appui de leurs affirmations; elle comprend aussi la réfutation des opinions contraires". Therefore, this manner of history-writing is in opposition to that of the laudatory genre, proper to rhetoric, and postulates the demonstration of historical truth by means of all manner of evidence. With historical perspective, Pédech also indicates that Herodotus had already organised, even though he did not use the term ἀπόδειξις in the sense of argumentation, demonstrative history thanks to his critical attitude. Naturally, the term and the concept were used and enriched by later authors, both historians and philosophers and orators.

Apart from the meaning of *exposition*, the term ἀπόδειξις[180] in Flavius Josephus also has the meaning of *argumentation*, *demonstration* and *evidence*. Flavius Josephus comes up against historical problems throughout his works, and undertakes the argumentation which is necessary to elucidate them. Thus, after expounding on the correspondence between Hiram king of Tyre and Solomon, he states that anyone wishing to check that what he is saying is true may consult the official archives, where the correspondence in question is kept. And he adds: "I have gone into these things in detail, because I want the reader to know that we have said nothing outside the bounds of truth, and that we have not tried to divert

---

[179] P. Pédech, *op. cit.*, 43-44.
[180] And ἀποδείχνυμι; cf. *Concordance, s.uu.*

the investigation by intercepting the narrative with seductive events which lead to deceit and distraction..., but rather we invite that we be not well accepted if we cannot establish the truth with solid demonstrations and evidence''[181]. It is therefore a personal formulation of his historical method: investigation (ἐξέτασις) and the providing of evidence.

The text which is expounded serves as the demonstration of the fact which is raised by Flavius Josephus earlier on[182]: Hiram, king of Tyre, is pleased that Solomon should have inherited the kingdom of his father David.

It is clear that Flavius Josephus holds the demonstrative power of documents, conserved in official places, in high esteem: ''By these documents, I shall also provide the proof of my affirmations''[183].

But the written document is not the only demonstrative document; equally demonstrative are all the logical and historical argumentations which prepare and develop the historical event. Thus, at the beginning of book II of the *Bellum Judaicum*, Flavius Josephus presents the succession of Archelaus to the throne as being full of popular disturbances. This is the historical problem of which the why and the how must be demonstrated. The historian, with regard to this, expounds the speech of Archelaus in the temple, the demands of the Jews, the rebellion of some of the Jews as a result of the crimes committed by Herod, the sending of people by Archelaus to cool tempers and their consequent ill-treatment by the rebels, the presence of multitudes on the occasion of the Passover, the presence of a cohort, which is destroyed by the mobs, and finally the military attack of the forces of Archelaus, which brings the death toll to three thousand and scatters the rest. All this material is forwarded by the historian so as to demonstrate that the disastrous beginnings of the reign of Archelaus with which the exposition began are demonstrable.

When Aristobulus associated his brother Antigonus to the throne[184], Flavius Josephus bases the whole of his exposition on an apparent brotherly affection on the part of Aristobulus, and raises the problem of the death of Antigonus on the orders of his brother, in spite of the love which he bore him. Flavius Josephus contributes all the details, emphasising the occasion (πρόφασις, No. 73) and the means (ἀφορμή, Nos. 75-76). The death of Antigonus comes to pass at the hands of the guard alerted by Aristobulus. And Flavius Josephus concludes: with that ''there is solid proof that calumny severs all links of benevolence and of nature, and that there is no feeling of ours which is so strong that it may

---

[181] A, VIII, 55-56.
[182] A, VIII, 50.
[183] A, XIV, 188. Cf. too A, XIV, 218; Ap, I, 155, 215.
[184] B, I, 70-80.

resist envy absolutely'' (No. 77). So it is demonstrated that wrong-doing springs from the inner evil of the executor.

The Holy Scriptures are also an object of argumentation on the part of Flavius Josephus. Thus, so as to give demonstrative support to the whole question relating to the universal flood, Flavius Josephus quotes the external testimony of Berosus, Hieronymus the Egyptian, Mnaseas, Nicolas of Damascus and many others[185].

Similarly, when dealing with the longevity of the patriarchs[186], Flavius Josephus uses three argumentations so as to elucidate the length of the lives of the patriarchs: firstly, because they were the chosen ones of God (theological argument) and because their diet was suitable to such duration (natural medicine argument); secondly, because their knowledge of astronomy and geometry would have been of no use, because they could not have predicted anything with any certainty had they not lived 600 years (intellectual argument); thirdly, other authors give the same testimony (argument based on written sources).

As regards the peopling of the earth, the biblical text says: ''and from them came the separate nations on earth after the flood''[187]. Flavius Josephus mentions that, because of the diversity of tongues, the descendants of Noah went off to found colonies around the world, urged on by God, and occupied the interiors and the coasts of the continents and islands. The original names given to the foundations are still conserved in many places, others have been modified to make them more intelligible, through the fault of the Greeks[188].

Having now finished with the biblical paraphrase, Flavius Josephus continues to base his narrative on quotations from written sources[189]. Argumentation is not missing wherever, since it is a constant characteristic in his methodology. Thus, when dealing with the matter of the Jewish emigrants to Seleucia, a city where they were ill-treated and murdered, Flavius Josephus previously argues the disastrous consequences[190]. The city was made up of Greeks and Syrians, the latter also

---

[185] A, I, 93-95. He similarly relies on sources to argue his statements: A, I, 118-119, 158-160, 240-241; A, II, 348; A, III, 38; A, VII, 101; A, VIII, 144, 147, 157, 253, 260-262; A, X, 18, 20, 34, 219, 227, 228; A, XII, 5, 38, 112-113, 127, 135, 137, 358; A, XIII, 249, 286, 344, 347. Cf. K. Albert, *Strabo als Quelle des Flavius Josephus*, Aschaffenburg, 1902.

[186] A, I, 104-108.

[187] *Gen.* X, 32.

[188] A, I, 120-121.

[189] A, XIV, 9, 35, 68, 104, 111, 114, 138, 265, 323; A, XV, 9, 174; A, XVI, 183.

[190] A, XVIII, 371-379.

enjoying the benefits of civil rights. Even so, the Greeks dominated the social situation, and that was the reason for their being cut off from the Syrian community. Then the Syrians felt impelled to establish ties of friendship with the Jewish community. The Greek reaction was not long in coming, and negotiations began with the Syrians, with the aim of severing the ties of friendship with the Jews. The Syrians gave way easily, and both groups offered as proof of their faithfulness to show enmity towards the Jews. The Jews were ill-treated and murdered, and were forced to flee to other, calmer, cities. In this way, Flavius Josephus bases the truth on the bad situation of the Jewish Diaspora.

From the philological standpoint, there are certain key-words thanks to which one may appreciate the continuous tendency in Flavius Josephus to the argumentation and consolidation of history. So as to avoid being over-repetitive on this matter, I shall simply mention items: πίστις, σημεῖον, τεκμήριον, μαρτύριον, δεῖγμα, δῆλον, εἰκότως, ὁμολογεῖσθαι, στοχάζεσθαι[191].

It should also be pointed out that the ecphrases may be a response to the need imposed by historiographic demonstration. I refer back to Chap. II, B, 3, in this regard.

Finally, it should be said that sometimes Flavius Josephus argues on unspecified literary sources, and leaves the bibliographical reference ambiguous with phrases of the kind ''we have received (from history)''[192], ''as some historians have said''[193], ''this is demonstrated elsewhere too''[194].

D. Use of sources

This section will take a look at the use of sources in the work of Flavius Josephus. However, it is not a question of studying the sources for their own sake, nor whence they come, but rather of the manner in which the historian makes use of them. Source-study already has a long and fecund bibliographical tradition[195]. This study should also make a special analysis of the first thirteen books of the *Antiquitates Judaicae*, since it is a paraphrase of a very specific source, the Bible. I shall therefore make a study of the use and non-use of the biblical text.

If one looks carefully at the narrative content of the *Bellum Judaicum*, one may find there certain personal attitudes of Flavius Josephus in the

---

[191] Cf. *Concordance*, *s.uu.*
[192] A, X, 183 and 248.
[193] A, XIII, 337.
[194] A, XIV, 98. Similarly, too, A, XIV, 119, 122, 270.
[195] Cf. H. Schreckenberg, *Bibliographie...*, *passim*, and T. W. Franxman, *Genesis and the ''Jewish Antiquities'' of Flavius Josephus*, Rome, 1979.

face of the material which the sources offer him. It is true that the author, throughout the work, omits mention of the sources which he uses, but we know from other writers that he uses the *memoirs* or *commentaries* of the Roman generals Vespasian and Titus[196], the vast work of Nicolas of Damascus, the abundant correspondence with his friend king Agrippa II[197], the testimony of deserters and his own knowledge as an eye-witness of a good many of the events which he narrates.

In spite of these premises and the fact that we do not have these sources, so as to make a comparison, there are clear indications of how Flavius Josephus organises the raw material so as to make up his own historiographic corpus, as he postulates[198]. For instance one may detect a series of points which are classifiable under the heading of historical errors, others which are interpretations, and others under the heading of the personal contribution of Flavius Josephus. The heading of historical errors may be attributed to Flavius Josephus, but always with certain reservations, and not forgetting that we are still in the area of hypotheses.

By grouping together the three headings I have mentioned, there are anachronisms relating to personalities who are placed outside their time[199], narrative differences and discrepancies with the information given in other books by the same author[200], alliances which are anticipated chronologically[201], the attribution of Jewish religious feelings to the Roman generals Vespasian and Titus[202], to the Roman multitudes[203], errors in the succession of kings[204], discrepancy with the source[205], errors in imperial details[206], exaggerations[207] and personal interpretations of Flavius Josephus' own[208].

---

[196] Vit, 342, 358; Ap, I, 56. On these questions, I have consulted H. St. J. Thackeray, *Josephus, the Man...*, 38-40. Cf. too H. Bardon, *La littérature latine inconnue II: L'époque impériale*, Paris, 1956, 209-210 and 271-272; H. Lindner, *op. cit.*, 16.

[197] Vit, 361-367.

[198] B, I, 15.

[199] B, I, 35, 62.

[200] B, I, 36 (A, XII, 270): officer unnamed in 1*Mach*. II, 25; B, I, 47 (A, XII, 422): disagrees with 1*Mach*. IX, 5; B, I, 62, (A, XIII, 250 ss); B, I, 351 (A, XIV, 487); B, I, 363, (A, XV, 104); B, I, 401 (A, XV, 380); B, I, 444 (A, XV, 240 ss.); B, II, 111 (A, XVII, 342; Vit, 5); B, II, 118 (A, XVIII, 23); B, III, 141 (Vit, 234); B, VII, 44 (Ap, II, 39); B, VII, 427 (B, I, 33; A, XII, 388; A, XIII, 63; A, XX, 236); B, II, 183 (A, XVIII, 252); B, II, 592-594 (Vit, 74-76); B, II, 612 (Vit, 147).

[201] B, I, 38.

[202] B, III, 444, 484, 495; B, VI, 215.

[203] B, VII, 73.

[204] B, I, 48.

[205] B, II, 86; A, XI, 120 (1*Esdr*. VIII, 1).

[206] B, III, 5.

[207] B, IV, 313 (B, IV, 206); B, VII, 88.

[208] B, I, 45, 81, 112, 148, 235, 282, 365, 408, 507, 599, 609, 610, 614; B, II, 38, 198, 282, 293, 296, 406, 531, 539, 545; B, III, 2, 6, 65, 111, 127, 136, 320, 504; B, IV, 318,

If we centre this analysis on the *Antiquitates Judaicae*, and more specifically on the manner of using the biblical text throughout the first thirteen books, we shall find there a long list of possibilities. One could even evaluate the extent to which Flavius Josephus acts in consequence with his declaration of faithfulness to his sources, when he says: ''This I have found written in the Holy Books''[209]. Throughout his works he will frequently invoke the authority of the biblical sources[210] and of other historical sources[211]. But nevertheless it is Flavius Josephus himself who divulges to us the method which he has followed in his paraphrasing of the text of the code of Moses, something which illuminates the whole of his method regarding the manner of using the biblical sources: ''We have added nothing which simply embellishes, and nothing which has not been handed down to us by Moses. The only innovation which we have contributed has been to put in order the several subjects, since his writings have been left in a haphazard manner, in the same way as he received each instruction from God''[212].

Here, without going into the question of why the historian acts in such a variegated manner, I shall first of all offer the following classification concerning the uses[213] of the biblical text:

– additions to the biblical text: A, I, 17, 50, 52, 54, 166-168, 176, 311, 319; A, II, 199; A, III, 26, 162, 193, 203; A, IV, 53, 78, 202, 252, 305; A, V, 11, 44, 64, 66, 117, 124, 240, 247, 248; A, VI, 48, 63, 79, 80, 97, 98, 116, 124, 204, 209, 215, 247, 268, 271, 278, 280, 293, 323, 327, 332, 340, 352; A, VII, 12, 27, 29, 30, 31, 34, 43, 54-55, 74, 77, 86, 87, 104, 106, 107, 130, 147, 154, 158, 166, 171, 191, 233, 235, 247, 298, 312, 319, 342, 352, 358, 371; A, VIII, 37, 95, 102, 105, 141, 187, 196, 218, 228, 235, 237, 241, 243, 288, 294, 302, 327, 340, 365, 368, 374, 395, 409; A, IX, 2, 6, 7, 30-31, 38, 41, 64, 72, 93, 94, 112-114, 132, 209, 218, 219, 249, 253, 264; A, X, 2, 24, 25, 29, 32, 37, 60, 98, 110, 116, 124, 128, 139, 145, 158, 194, 202, 208, 229, 230, 240, 247, 261, 272-274; A, XI, 3, 32, 80, 86, 87, 102, 104, 108, 133, 141, 149, 168, 173, 174, 189,

---

370, 602, 616, 626, 652; B, V, 3, 26, 28, 97, 118, 410-411, 442, 517, 519; B, VII, 4, 73, 421, 427.

[209] A, I, 26: ταῦτα δ' ἐν ταῖς ἱεραῖς βίβλοις εὗρον ἀναγεγραμμένα.

[210] A, I, 82; A, II, 347; A, III, 38, 81, 105; A, IV, 303; A, V, 61; A, VIII, 129; A, IX, 28, 46, 208, 214; A, X, 210, 218; A, XIII, 297; A, XX, 261. Cf. R. Plaut, *Flavius Josephus und die Bibel. Eine kritisch-exegetische Studie*, (Diss. Leipzig), Berlin, 1867; G. Tachauer, *op. cit.*, 18.

[211] A, IX, 283; A, XI, 99; Vit, 6. Cf. K. Patsch, ''Zu Nicolaus von Damascus'', *WS* 12 (1889), 231-239; P. Otto, *Quaestiones Strabonianae*, (Diss.), Leipzig, 1889, 225.

[212] A, IV, 196-197.

[213] Cf. J. D. Fréderic Burger, *Essai sur l'usage que l'historien Flave Josèphe a fait des livres canoniques de l'Ancien-Testament*, Strasbourg, 1836, 12-15.

200, 201, 203, 205, 214, 232, 247, 253, 257, 278, 280; A, XII, 91, 117, 168, 250, 251, 270, 309, 318, 319, 329, 339, 398, 411, 413, 419, 434; A, XIII, 21, 25, 88, 94, 129, 145-147, 152, 155-157, 169, 175, 180-181, 189, 197, 206, 208, 211;

– mixture of another source or of other biblical quotes: A, I, 41, 265; A, III, 294; A, IV, 49, 69, 74, 284; A, V, 66, 342; A, VI, 128, 161, 171, 227; A, VII, 389; A, IX, 102, 170, 257; A, X, 231; A, XI, 90, 204, 208, 221; A, XIII, 121;

– contribution and personal interpretation of Flavius Josephus: A, I, 54, 103, 128, 129, 168, 197, 198, 203, 215, 232, 253, 255, 261, 265, 317, 343; A, II, 3, 17, 99, 125, 189, 193, 194, 255, 275, 276, 342; A, III, 52, 55, 57, 90, 96, 137, 180, 187, 315; A, IV, 11, 36, 39, 82, 164, 205, 240, 245, 253, 259, 262, 301, 322, 588-589; A, V, 71, 209, 234, 253, 289, 303, 317, 337; A, VI, 58, 63, 236, 296, 326; A, VII, 5-6, 44, 46, 52, 67, 73-74, 147, 214, 234, 242; A, VIII, 155, 161, 166, 216, 225, 241, 290, 297, 327, 418; A, IX, 104, 238; A, X, 19, 27, 57, 76, 132, 142, 157, 186, 188, 210, 241, 262; A, XI, 96, 139, 142, 174, 185, 209, 237, 268; A, XII, 58, 253, 290, 312; A, XIII, 158, 288, 311, 314, 380;

– errors: A, I, 67, 113, 128, 165; A, II, 229, 255; A, III, 236, 247, 255, 282, 320-322; A, IV, 123, 303; A, V, 3-4, 17, 34, 115, 139, 150, 233, 319, 321, 323, 347; A, VI, 18, 56; A, VII, 36, 189, 393; A, VIII, 72; A, IX, 6, 17, 19, 213, 215, 234, 242, 271; A, X, 50, 67, 83, 116, 171, 211, 231; A, XI, 26, 137, 151, 198, 201, 246; A, XII, 25, 27, 33, 93, 196, 225, 234-235, 248, 393, 422; A, XIII, 14, 55, 138, 163, 212, 218;

– condensing of texts from the Scriptures: A, I, 91, 199, 257; A, III, 91; A, IV, 287; A, V, 349; A, VI, 84, 157; A, VII, 102, 142, 382; A, IX, 130, 155, 167 ff.; A, X, 215, 216; A, XI, 162, 172, 180; A, XII, 286, 317;

– enlarging: A, I, 122, 164, 192, 219, 223, 226, 255, 340; A, II, 34, 36, 39, 45, 63, 75, 212, 218, 232; A, III, 2, 32, 139, 154, 261, 276, 282, 288, 290; A, IV, 204, 208, 211, 214, 220, 226-227, 228, 246-249, 263, 271-274, 281, 282, 314; A, V, 36, 46, 65, 135, 149, 151, 197, 198, 199, 204, 207, 215, 216, 235, 271, 276, 283, 326, 332, 334-335, 354; A, VI, 2, 7, 17, 18, 27, 37, 57, 61, 108, 136, 140, 160, 180, 184, 185, 193, 202, 217, 230, 241, 272, 281, 286, 290, 296, 299, 317, 321, 355; A, VII, 49, 79, 81, 84, 97, 131, 135, 140, 145, 152, 159, 185, 192, 202, 213, 216, 220, 226, 234, 238, 252, 256, 259, 271, 295, 317, 323, 326, 353, 356, 373; A, VIII, 6, 8, 20, 41, 45, 63, 88, 106, 108, 112, 121, 202, 204, 206, 221, 252, 254, 256, 273, 278, 281, 300, 311, 339, 343, 356, 387, 405; A, IX, 74, 97, 125, 132, 136, 151, 160, 180, 192, 197, 200, 201, 212, 231, 254, 291; A, X, 61, 69, 102, 106, 122-123, 134, 137, 167, 190, 204, 251, 253, 254, 263; A, XI, 15, 83, 161, 171, 194, 196, 205, 210, 245, 254,

256; A, XII, 256, 277, 285, 292, 302, 309, 315, 327, 363, 371, 378, 387, 402, 404, 414, 421, 431; A, XIII, 6, 96, 130, 132, 143, 145-147, 148, 161-162, 163, 168, 169, 170, 178, 180-181, 187;

– narrative variants: A, I, 248-249, 293; A, III, 63, 208, 270; A, IV, 9, 54, 64, 307; A, V, 168, 182, 250, 334-335; A, VI, 58, 76, 77, 78, 82, 260, 284, 310; A, VII, 1, 56, 57, 59, 72, 73, 167, 191, 209, 241, 254, 294, 301, 307, 311, 320, 321, 335, 378; A, VIII, 15, 27, 31, 64, 117, 134, 191, 204, 230, 250, 266, 308, 331, 347, 381; A, IX, 20, 69, 90, 139, 143, 146, 152, 161, 171, 172, 175, 183, 193, 260; A, X, 46, 130, 157, 189, 207, 271; A, XI, 73, 190, 266, 284; A, XII, 366, 375;

– anachronisms: A, I, 73; A, II, 346; A, III, 157, 389; A, IV, 96, 218; A, V, 223; A, VI, 26, 40; A, VII, 220; A, VIII, 133; A, XI, 333;

– contradictions: A, II, 189; A, X, 120; A, XIII, 148, 217, 249;

– abiblical aspects: A, III, 115, 262, 297; A, IV, 71, 112, 142; A, V, 79, 288, 348, 360, 361; A, VI, 16, 111, 119, 122, 127, 133, 165, 166, 192, 232, 236, 238, 239, 258, 290, 301, 305, 306, 311, 315, 318, 320, 325, 357, 370; A, VII, 92, 131, 177, 179, 218, 225, 227, 235, 243, 257, 262, 291, 293, 300, 303, 378; A, VIII, 4, 14, 32, 40, 54, 65, 66, 74, 85, 89, 131, 133, 138, 177, 180, 214, 221, 226, 236, 238, 240, 242, 258, 282, 294, 303, 320, 321, 347, 354, 356, 358, 361, 363, 373, 378, 383, 386, 388, 392, 398, 402, 403, 408, 409, 415; A, IX, 9, 32, 34, 51, 58, 60, 61, 65, 80, 88, 93, 106, 127, 137, 151, 160, 162, 183, 192, 224, 256, 260, 266, 289; A, X, 5, 12, 17, 30-31, 53, 77, 99, 100, 111, 114, 154, 162, 164, 169, 199, 200, 233, 238; A, XI, 7, 13, 26, 30, 33, 56, 62, 68, 89, 121, 147, 158, 160, 163, 164, 165, 167, 176, 177, 181, 211, 223, 248, 249, 252, 265, 270; A, XIII, 101, 129, 133, 138, 150, 155-157, 166-167, 192[214];

– omissions: A, II, 293; A, III, 300; A, IV, 63, 161, 271-274; A, V, 20, 26, 44, 89, 146, 177, 214, 236, 254, 269, 295, 346; A, VI, 15, 135, 155, 193, 195, 196, 223, 240, 244, 301, 316, 324, 367; A, VII, 46, 58, 59, 79, 119, 191, 302; A, VIII, 12, 35, 66, 191, 216, 254, 267, 284, 290, 295, 297, 299, 304, 314, 318, 336, 349, 354, 356, 374, 386, 395, 396, 397, 404, 414; A, IX, 2, 8, 17, 26, 37, 87, 105, 109, 132, 138, 143, 146, 149, 155, 157, 174, 188, 211, 214, 217, 235, 250, 252, 259, 263, 267, 279; A, X, 21, 37, 65, 71, 86, 101, 114, 135, 170, 180, 202, 209, 213, 269; A, XI, 26, 61, 73, 79, 102, 127, 130, 136, 158, 162, 165, 187, 199, 215, 262, 272, 277, 279, 288; A, XII, 31, 40, 85, 100, 278, 299, 300, 318, 335-336, 353, 370, 371, 414, 416, 418, 420, 422; A, XIII, 16, 52, 183, 184, 227;

---

[214] On the use of the text of the Maccabees, cf. M. Nussbaum, *Observationes in Flavii Josephi Antiquitates Lib. XII, 3-XIII, 14*, (Diss. Göttingen), Warburg, 1875.

- mixture of sources: A, IV, 25;
- emphasis: A, IV, 207;
- amalgam of themes: A, IV, 278;
- invention: A, VI, 137; A, VII, 14, 127; A, VIII, 91, 197;
- harmonising of sources: A, V, 124; A, VII, 89; A, VIII, 76;
- change of order: A, V, 341; A, VI, 55; A, VIII, 130, 176, 225, 246, 285, 289; A, X, 268; A, XI, 88;
- use of the LXX text and Hebrew text: A, I, 27-36, 96, 120; A, II, 184; A, VI, 134, 186, 195, 245, 251, 274, 291, 310; A, VII, 48; A, VIII, 85, 203, 209, 259, 339, 351, 355, 360, 412; A, IX, 188;
- inversion of source: A, VI, 192;
- remoulding of the sources: A, II, 303, 307, 349; A, III, 150; A, IV, 53; A, VI, 371; A, VIII, 414; A, IX, 163, 165, 170; A, XI, 156, 261, 291; A, XII, 217, 282, 383; A, XIII, 58, 62, 214;
- biblical and non biblical literal quotes: A, I, 240; A, VII, 101; A, VIII, 144, 262, 324; A, IX, 239; A, XI, 3, 22, 99, 118, 123; A, XII, 36, 45, 51, 136, 138, 145, 147; A, XIV, 112, 138, 149, 190, 306; A, XVI, 162; A, XVII, 134, 137; A, XVIII, 304; A, XIX, 280, 286, 303[215] (even so, these literal quotes do not mean a literal transcription of the sources);
- simplification of the sources: A, IV, 253; A, V, 4; A, VI, 106; A, VII, 381; A, VIII, 342, 352; A, X, 5; A, XI, 75, 233;
- anticipation of the source: A, V, 135; A, VII, 153; A, XI, 12, 165, 184;
- discrepancies with the biblical text: A, II, 302, 304; A, V, 228; A, VI, 140; A, VIII, 62, 224; A, X, 146, 152, 249; A, XI, 37, 198; A, XIII, 226, 236, 254;
- postponement: A, VIII, 76, 403; A, IX, 263, 268; A, X, 9;
- filling in of events: A, I, 157, 192, 228, 271;
- correction of source-text: A, XI, 21, 69, 98, 106, 120;
- lack of concordance between the *Bellum Judaicum* and the *Antiquitates Judaicae*: A, VIII, 61, 62; A, XIII, 258, 266, 277, 318, 358, 372-373, 377, 379, 395, 407, 412-418, 418-421, 432[216].

The other books of the *Antiquitates Judaicae* present a different treatment of the sources. Even so, it is difficult to specify the use made of them, due to the impossibility of access to the sources. My objective will be centred on eliciting the main points:

---

[215] On the use and omissions of Aristeas' letter, cf. A. Pelletier, *Flavius Josèphe, adaptateur de la Lettre d'Aristée. Une réaction atticisante contre la Koinè*, Paris, 1962, 199-206.

[216] On the discrepancies between the two works, cf. P. Otto, *op. cit.*, 234. The paraphrasis of the *Bellum Judaicum* in the *Antiquitates Judaicae* has the same traits as the biblical paraphrasis (cf. Shave F. B. Cohen, *op. cit.*, 48-66).

– there is an abundance of discrepancies and variants in relation with the parallel text of the *Bellum Judaicum* (A, XIV, 7, 30, 55, 82, 140, 144, 163, 165, 167, 168, 170, 180, 278, 287, 346, 436, 449, 476; A, XV, 148, 198, 200, 246, 392; A, XVIII, 252), which implies a change of attitude and a self-criticism of the historian himself[217]; there are also some enlargements (A, XIV, 353, 422, 473);

– there appear some anachronisms: A, XIV, 145, 267;

– criticisms of various sources concerning the authenticity of the information they forward: A, XIV, 9; A, XVIII, 43, 46; A, XIX, 106, 111; A, XX, 154;

– the personal contributions of the historian and his own interpretations: A, XIV, 370, 374; A, XV, 65, 110, 116, 157, 298, 372, 380, 422; A, XVI, 76, 153; A, XVII, 180, 236, 277, 354; A, XVIII, 24, 29, 310, 377; A, XIX, 162; A, XX, 94, 153, 214, 226, 237, 260.

Finally, in the *Vita* and *Contra Apionem*[218], though cast in the same mould, one may observe the following points:

– literal quotes from the sources: Vit, 217, 226, 229, 235, 365-366; Ap, I, 75 ff., 93, 135, 146, 165, 169, 173, 177, 185, 187-189, 196, 197, 209, 237, 313; Ap, II, 10, 21, 33, 50;

– quotes from sources: Vit, 342, 358; Ap, I, 142-144;

– criticisms of the sources: Ap, I, 6, 68, 213, 219, 254, 267, 293, 300, 304, 312; Ap, II, 34, 79;

– personal contribution of the historian: Ap, I, 26, 28, 44, 49, 55;

– comparison of sources: Ap, I, 28, 44, 154, 293; Ap, II, 38 ff., 164, 237, 275.

E. HISTORIOGRAPHIC ATTITUDE AND IMPARTIALITY

After the analysis of the work of Flavius Josephus, his personal attitude as the one responsible for his legacy should be studied. Polybius has already reflected on this point, and in Ephorus praises three qualities: his diction, the organisation of the historical material and his perspicacity in the choosing of the material[219]. Language, method and skill are therefore the three basic virtues of an historian. These three qualities reappear later on, when speaking of his work as an historian[220]. Even so, these

---

[217] On the parallels between the two works, cf. R. Laqueur, *op. cit.*, 138-221; on the use of their mutual dependence, cf. H. Drüner, *op. cit.*, 51-56.

[218] On the contradictions between *Contra Apionem* and the *Antiquitates Judaicae*, cf. S. Belkin, "The Alexandrian Source for Contra Apionem II", *JQR* 27 (1936-1937), 1-32. On the discrepancies between the *Vita* and the *Bellum Judaicum*, cf. Shave F. B. Cohen, *op. cit.*, 3-33, and on their relationship, 67-83.

[219] Pol. XII, 28, 10.

[220] Pol. XXIX, 12, 10.

three ideas are not exclusive to historians, since Isocrates had already postulated them for the good orator[221] and Cicero would also echo them when speaking of Timaeus[222].

Critical investigation has therefore to be made in three directions, according to Polybius[223]: the heuristic direction, of the written sources (ὑπομνήματα), a personal vision (θέα) of the cities and places, and careful attention concerning political events (αἱ πράξεις αἱ πολιτικαί). Thus, Ctesias boasts of having used ταῖς βασιλικαῖς διφθέραις[224], and of having personally inspected matters and of having used very reliable authors[225]. Ephorus[226] and Theopompus[227] follow the same line, and Timaeus travelled around the countries of the Ligurians and the Celts in search of sources[228].

Finally, the moral and intellectual attitudes of the historian pervade historical work. Moderation (ἐπιείκεια) must be ever-present in the exposition of events, of causes and of the positive aspects of historical personalities and peoples[229]. Dionysius even advocated silence on the defects of one's homeland[230], but Polybius represented a firm attitude in the face of truth, even though it should be damaging for personal affection[231]. Moderation is also postulated for rhetoric[232].

By way of conclusion, I shall set out the ideas concerning these aspects which are contained in the only treatise preserved on the historiography of classical antiquity. It is attributed to Lucian of Samosata[233], and gives the following canon: skill (Nos. 4, 5, 32), diligence (No. 4), exactitude (No. 47), love of truth (No. 39), impartiality (Nos. 39, 41, 49), understanding of the material (No. 47), command of the narrative (No. 56), power of expression (Nos. 6, 9, 34, 44, 45, 49, 51, 59), sense of being useful (No. 9)[234], not over-valuing (Nos. 11, 12, 13, 19, 57), criteria to

---

[221] *Orat.* IV, 9 and, similarly, *Orat.* XIII, 16. In this same sense, cf. P. Scheller, *op. cit.*, 26-28.

[222] *De orat.* II, 14, 58.

[223] XII, 25e, 1 ff.; XX, 12, 8; XII, 28, 3 and 10.

[224] Diod., *Bibl.* II, 32, 4: "the royal parchments".

[225] Phot., *Bibl.* 36, 3B.

[226] Pol. XII, 27, 7.

[227] Pol. XII, 27, 8; Dion. Hal., *Ad Pomp.* 6, 2-3.

[228] Pol. XII, 28a, 3.

[229] Dion. Hal., *Ad Pomp.* 3, 15; 4, 2; *Arch.* I, 6, 5; *De Thuc.* 8.

[230] *Ad Pomp.* 3, 8.

[231] Pol. XXXVIII, 6, 1 ff; 3, 5; XVI, 14, 6; 17, 8; 18, 1.

[232] Arstt., *Rhet.* 1356a 6; Dion. Hal., *De Lys.* 24; 31, 11.

[233] *De hist. conscr.* Cf. too Dion. Hal., *De Thuc.* 8; Cic., *De leg.* I, 1, 5; Quint. X, 1, 31. Cicero (*De orat.* II, 15, 62 ff.), more concisely, had also laid down an historiographic canon, practically included in that of Lucian.

[234] Cf. J. de Romilly, "L'utilité de l'histoire selon Thucydide", *Histoire et historiens dans l'antiquité* (Entretiens sur l'Antiquité classique 4), Vandoeuvres-Genève, 1956, 41.

judge what is important and what is not good (Nos. 25, 27), incorruptibility and absence of fear (Nos. 37, 39, 41), perspicacity (No. 55), political shrewdness (No. 34) and to think that the work is for the future (Nos. 39, 61).

Fortunately, Flavius Josephus does not keep silent concerning his own historiographical attitude throughout his work, and gives sufficient material to be able to elaborate the fundamental traits of his attitude concerning historical material. The first point to be studied is that relating to his global concept of history, that is, his object. The second point should deal with the importance which he accords to the various sources he uses, and thirdly, the value he places on the formal aspect of his work. There is a final point which is basic in all historians, that of his impartiality.

I have already commented in various sections that Flavius Josephus went to great lengths so that his narrative should conform to the exigencies of historical truth. This is therefore his prime objective as historian[235]. Consequently one may deduce that here is an educational objective for his future readers, and he says as much explicitly at certain historical moments, moments which the historian uses to make some moral reflexion.

On the occasion of the dream dreamed by Glaphyra, the daughter of king Archelaus, Flavius Josephus finds it necessary to justify the inclusion of the event in the mainstream of the narrative. And he says: ''I do not consider these events alien to my history, because they refer to royalty, and, what is more, they provide an example of that which leads souls to immortality and providence with which God embraces human affairs; I thought it fitting to mention them. He who does not believe these things, being pleased in his own opinion, could not be any impediment to him who adds these things for the demonstration of virtue''[236].

It is true that Flavius Josephus refers to the fact of the credibility of dreams, that is, something which is not subject to objective rules, but he also uses the occasion to leave it well-established that all historical events, of whatever kind, contribute to knowledge of transcendency and good, and are therefore educational circumstances.

Elsewhere, and again to justify his historical task, he says: ''I shall narrate the whole of his story, so that it serves as an example to the whole of human kind, to live with virtue in all circumstances''[237].

---

[235] Truth is a worry for Flavius Josephus: B, I, 6, 16, 17, 30; B, VII, 455; A, I, 4; A, VIII, 56; A, XIV, 3, 68; XX, 157; Vit, 40, 336-337, 339, 361, 385; Ap, I, 3, 6, 24, 47, 52, 56, 154, 214, 217; Ap, II, 287, 296. Cf. G. Avenarius, *op. cit.*, 40-46; W. Speyer, *Die literarische Fälschung im Altertum*, München, 1971, 60-61 (''exordial Topik'').

[236] A, XVII, 354.

[237] A, XVII, 60.

The whole weight of ancestral structure cannot be lightly changed. If innovations are introduced, the downfall of the people will ensue. Therefore a suitable lesson must be learned so as to avoid it[238].

Flavius Josephus has a didactic reason, among others, for the narration of the death of Gaius: "I wish to describe with accuracy all that has been said about him, principally because it contains great evidence of the power of God, and comfort for those who find themselves in unfortunate moments, and a lesson in wisdom for those who believe that good fortune is everlasting..."[239].

Flavius Josephus also believes that a lesson can be learned from the occasion of the famous judgement of Solomon: "I have thought it necessary to expound the subject through which it came to pass that justice should be done, so that readers should have knowledge of the difficulty of the judgement and, when finding themselves in the midst of similar situations, they should strive, in emulation of the wisdom of the king, to be capable of easily demonstrating the things which they investigate"[240].

In the introduction to the *Antiquitates Judaicae*, Flavius Josephus devotes a great many paragraphs to the consideration of the need to make known the laws and the political constitution of the Jews; in other words, he expresses a desire to carry out, by means of his history, a task of diffusion of the historical and cultural world of the Jews. And he adds: "...but, in general, one may learn from this history... that those who follow the will of God and do not venture to transgress well-established laws prosper far beyond the bounds of belief, and happiness is accorded them on the part of God as reward"[241]. Naturally, those who transgress the laws come to a sorry end, and he adds: "I therefore exhort those who would read these books to fix their thoughts on God and examine whether our lawgiver conceived His nature rightly..."[242].

Flavius Josephus gives extraordinary value to one particular type of source: autopsy. Consequently, oral and written sources coming from testimonies coeval with the historical events are included. The other source which is considered perfect is that constituted by the biblical books. Finally, there are the written sources of diverse origins.

Given these possibilities, his works can be grouped under the following headings:

– those which depend above all on visual sources, that is on autopsy: the *Bellum Judaicum* and the *Vita*;

---

[238] A, XVIII, 9.
[239] A, XIX, 16.
[240] A, VIII, 26.
[241] A, I, 14. Similar ideas in A, I, 20.
[242] A, I, 15.

– those which owe a debt to the biblical sources: the *Antiquitates Judaicae*;

– those indebted to other sources: the *Antiquitates Judaicae* and *Contra Apionem*.

In *Contra Apionem*, Flavius Josephus makes an apology of his principal works, and leaving a precious testimony of his historiographic method[243]. As a contrast to the Greek historians, Flavius Josephus explains how he has written his works:

– he has written a complete and detailed work on the war, and has been present at events (τοῖς πράγμασιν αὐτὸς ἅπασι παρατυχών, No. 47);

– the *Bellum Judaicum* is the product of autopsy: "During this time, not one of the events escaped my knowledge. Indeed, I carefully noted down what I saw in the camp of the Romans and was the only person to receive the information which the deserters gave"[244];

– historical method demands exact and personal knowledge of events, whether one has been in contact with them or whether they have been learned from those who were witness to them. Flavius Josephus was true to his words in his two great works[245];

– of the *Antiquitates Judaicae* he says: "I have made a translation of the Holy Books, being as I am a priest by family line and participant in the philosophy contained in these books"[246]. Flavius Josephus therefore has the credentials for exact knowledge of the history of the people of Israel;

– of the *Bellum Judaicum* he says that "I have been the actor in many events, an eye-witness to the most part of them, and, in short, I have had knowledge of all that has been said or done"[247].

Another type of source is the literary one, and Flavius Josephus continuously appraises and indicates the use which should be made of it, as well as noting its finality.

Thus, when praising the task of the historian, Flavius Josephus says: "The industrious historian is not he who remodels the scheme and the arrangement of another work, but rather he who uses new materials and elaborated the corpus itself of his history"[248]. So Flavius Josephus identifies himself with the idea of history as a single corpus and a living corpus, according to the opinion of Dionysius of Halicarnassus[249].

---

[243] Ap, I, 47-56.
[244] Ap, I, 49. On the value of the autopsy, cf. B, I, 3, 14, 30; B, VI, 200.
[245] A, VIII, 46; Ap, I, 53-54.
[246] Ap, I, 54.
[247] Ap, I, 55.
[248] B, I, 15. On the σῶμα τῆς ἱστορίας... ἴδιον, cf. W. Weber, *op. cit.*, 58-59.
[249] Cf. Chap. II, *Precedents* (p. 65).

In book XIV of the *Antiquitates Judaicae*, Flavius Josephus provides a great number of Roman decrees, in which favours conferred on Jews everywhere figure. The important thing are the reasons given by Flavius Josephus as a justification for their inclusion in his history: "...so that other nations should know that the kings of Asia and of Europe have held us in benevolence and have loved our courage and our loyalty. Because many, because of their enmity towards us, do not believe the writings of the Persians and Macedonians concerning us, because these writings are not to be found anywhere nor in public places, but amongst us and amongst some other barbarian peoples, but against the decrees of the Romans nothing can possibly be said, for they are engraved in public places in the cities and even now are written on bronze tablets in the Capitolium..., of these too I provide proof"[250]. With these words Flavius Josephus shows that he accords great apodictic value to the sources which he uses. Further along[251], when transcribing two decrees of Marcus Antonius, he says: "We have also mentioned these documents in the suitable place, so that they be a testimony of what we say..."[252].

As regards the formal aspect of the historical opus, Flavius Josephus notes the most relevant traits, either directly or indirectly when criticising the works of another. In the introduction to the *Bellum Judaicum*, Flavius Josephus criticises those historians who have collected information from people who were not witness to the events and so "have written about them in a rhetorical style"[253], whereas others, "who have witnessed the events, distort them to praise the Romans or out of hatred for the Jews, and their writings contain invectives here, eulogies there..."[254]. He also emphasises that over-concern for stylistic aspects determines the choice of the subjects, so as to compete with rivals, so that mythological history is the result, yet others devote their efforts to the praise of cities and monarchs, avoiding any criticism of the events[255]. And he defines: "For proof of real history is whether all say and write the same thing concerning the same events"[256].

It is obvious that the objective which the historian pursues will determine the formal aspect of the work. If the historian places any other ob-

---

[250] A, XIV, 186-189. The reason for the discrepancies amongst the different Greek historians stems from the fact that the Greeks neglected to keep records of public events and paid more attention to style than to historical truth. On the Roman decrees, cf. L. Mendelssohn, *De senati consultis Romanorum ab Josepho Antiq. XIII, 9, 2; XIV, 10, 22 relatis commentatio*, Leipzig, 1874.

[251] A, XIV, 306-322.

[252] A, XIV, 323.

[253] B, I, 1.

[254] B, I, 2.

[255] Ap, I, 25.

[256] Ap, I, 26.

jective before historical truth, then his work will present a preponderance of stylistic traits, and consequently his objective will be more to please his reader than to transmit the truth.

As regards the question of style, I have already shown (Chap. II, A, 2), that Flavius Josephus is sparing in the use of speeches, as we have seen too that the descriptions of wars (Chap. II, A, 7) are very close to the subject, that the ecphrases (Chap. II, B, 3) answer the need for enlightenment, that the eulogies and censures (Chap. II, C, 3) do not go beyond the bounds of moderation and that the novelistic elements (Chap. II, C, 6) and the dramatic elements (Chap. II, C, 7) preserve sufficient historical elements so as not to become simple entertaining stories.

Nor can we forget the concern of Flavius Josephus for the literary correctness of the Greek language. This fact has given rise to a whole theory concerning his literary assistants, amply developed by Thackeray, to whom I refer in this regard[257]. As for his appreciation of the value of style, Flavius Josephus writes: ''For it is necessary that history and the record of events unknown to the majority should have, because of the ancientness of the events, beauty in exposition, that which arises from the choice of words and their arrangement, and other things which, in addition to these, provide the narrative with elegance..., so that the readers receive the knowledge with delight and pleasure...''[258].

Finally, impartiality in historical work should be commented on. I have already done so concerning paragraph B, I, 12[259], in which Flavius Josephus declares the impossibility of repressing his own personal feelings when dealing with certain events which affected him very acutely. It has also been said that the historian is the measure of history, and, moreover, it is he who qualifies the events he narrates. Consequently history is, in a sense, what the historian himself wants it to be.

Therefore Flavius Josephus cannot remain indifferent to this reality, and throughout his works certain moments and viewpoints may be perceived which answer more to the very personal vision of the historian. Here I shall simply give the items which, in my opinion, contain a statement of intent by the historian, according to their common traits:

– admiration for Rome and for her generals, and justification of their acts: B, I, 9-12, 135, 495-498; B, IV, 92, 320; B, V, 19, 257; B, VI, 284, 215-216, 313, 371; B, VII, 112-113; A, XIV, 72;

---

[257] H. St. J. Thackeray, *op. cit.*, *Josephus, the Man...*, 100; R. J. H. Shutt, *Studies in Josephus*, London, 1961, 79-109.

[258] A, XIV, 2-3.

[259] Cf. Chap. II, B, 2, and B, V, 20.

– self-justification and opinion concerning himself: B, III, 136-137, 175, 200-201, 205-206, 340, 351 ff., 387-391; A, XX, 260 ff.; Vit, 99, 339;

– anti-Samaritan attitude: B, III, 308; A, IX, 290 ff.; A, XI, 114, 341, 346;

– over-valuing of the Jewish world: B, II, 398; B, VI, 13, 241; A, VIII, 161; A, XII, 119 ff.; A, XIV, 110-111, 185-186; A, XVI, 158;

– anti-Herod attitude: A, XIV, 156, 382.

– anti-Hellenic attitude: A, I, 121; A, XVI, 174.

– God is on the side of the Romans: B, II, 390; B, III, 484; B, V, 19, 367, 412, 559; B, VI, 371, 411.

Finally, expressions of the kind οἴομαι and ὡς ἐμοὶ δοκεῖ should also be included, since they are indicative of an affective or intentional charge on the part of Flavius Josephus[260].

Certain exaggerated passages, which have been commented on in Chapter II, B, 2, may also be the bearers of points of view which are partial or else have little justification[261].

---

[260] Cf. *Concordance, s.uu.* οἴομαι and δοκέω.

[261] The works of Flavius Josephus indubitably have a marked apologetic bent, which is toned down by the author by means of insinuations, harmonisings, allegories and other literary means. On this point, cf. B. Heller, "Grundzüge der Aggada des Flavius Josephus", *MGWJ* 80 (1936), 237-246 and 363. Concerning his criticism of Justus of Tiberias, cf. A. Schalit, "Josephus und Justus", *Klio* 26 (Neue Folge VIII) (1933), 67-95. Cf. too H. Vincent, "Chronologie des oeuvres de Josèphe", *RBi* 8 (1911), 382-383. Concerning the degree of impartiality among the Latin historians, cf. R. Syme, *Tacito*, Brescia, 1967, 270, and, more particularly in the case of Sallust, R. Syme, *Sallust*, Berkeley, 1974², 43-59, 121-137, and also J. I. Ciruelo, *Salustio, política e historiografía*, Barcelona, 1973, 112 ("ethical imbalance").

BIBLIOGRAPHY

I. *Editions and Translations*

Hegesippus qui dicitur sive Egesippus de bello Judaico ope codicis Cassellani recognitus. Edidit Carolus Fridericus Weber. Opus morte Weberi interruptum absolvit Julius Caesar. Marburg, 1864.

Joannis Zonarae Epitome Historiarum. Edidit Ludovicus Dindorfius, 5 vol., Leipzig, 1868-1974.

Flavii Josephi Opera, ed. B. Niese, 7 vol., Berlin, 1887-1895.

Oeuvres complètes de Flavius Josèphe, ed. T. Reinach, 7 vol., Paris, 1900-1932.

Josephus, ed. H. St. J. Thackeray, R. Marcus, A. Wikgren, L. H. Feldman, 9 vol., The Loeb Classical Library, London-Cambridge/Massachusetts, 1926-1965.

Flavio Giuseppe, La Guerra Giudaica, ed. G. Ricciotti, 3 vol., Torino, 1963.

II. *Old and New Testament*

Sainte Bible Polyglotte, La, ed. F. Vigouroux, 8 vol., Paris, 1900-1909.

Bíblia, La, versió dels textos originals i comentari pels monjos de Montserrat, Montserrat, 1926 ff.

Sainte Bible, La, École Biblique de Jérusalem, Paris, 1956.

Novum Testamentum Graece, ed. E. Nestle, and Erwin Nestle and K. Aland, Stuttgart, 1960.

New English Bible with the Apocrypha, Oxford University Press, Cambridge University Press, 1970.

Septuaginta, ed. A. Rahlfs, 2 vol., Stuttgart, 1971 (9th. ed.).

III. *Works of Reference*

A Complete Concordance to Flavius Josephus, Suppl. I: Namenwörterbuch zu Flavius Josephus, A. Schalit, ed. K. H. Rengstorf, Leiden, 1968.

A Complete Concordance to Flavius Josephus, 4 vol., ed. K. H. Rengstorf, Leiden, 1973-1983.

Bardon, H., *La littérature latine inconnue II: l'époque impériale,* Paris, 1956.

Christ, W. von, *Geschichte der griechischen Literatur,* 2 vol., München, 1920-1924.

Croiset, M., *Histoire de la Littérature grecque,* Paris, 1947 (4th ed.).

Daremberg, M. M. Ch. et Edm. Saglio, *Dictionnaire des Antiquités Grecques et Romaines,* Paris, 1896

Diels, H. - W. Kranz, *Die Fragmente der Vorsokratiker,* 3 vol., Zürich/Berlin, 1960-1964.

Díez Macho, A., *Neophyti 1, Targum palestinense, ms. de la Biblioteca Vaticana,* vol 1, Génesis, Madrid-Barcelona, 1968.

Hatch, E. and H. A. Redpath, *A Concordance to the Septuagint,* Graz-Austria, 1954.

Jacoby, F., *Die Fragmente der Griechischen Historiker,* (*FGH*), Berlin-Leiden, 1923-1958.

Lesky, A., *Storia della Letteratura greca,* 3 vol., Milano, 1965.

Littré, É., *Oeuvres complètes d'Hippocrate,* 10 vol., Paris, 1839-1861.

Müller, C., *Fragmenta historicorum graecorum,* (*FHG*), Paris, 1874. — *Geographi graeci minores,* (*GGM*), 2 vol., Paris, 1882.

Nauck, A., *Tragicorum Graecorum Fragmenta,* Hildesheim, 1964.

Nickau, K., *Ammonii qui dicitur liber De adfinium uocabulorum differentia,* Lipsiae, 1966.

Paulys Realencyclopädie der classischen Altertumswissenschaft, (*RE*), ed. A. Pauly and G. Wissowa, Stuttgart, 1893 ff.

Suidae Lexicon, ed. A. Adler, 3 vol., Lipsiae, 1928-1933.

Usener, H. and L. Radermacher, *Dionysi Halicarnensis Opuscula Rhetorica,* Lipsiae, 1899-1929.

IV. Books and Articles

Alba, V., *La concepción historiográfica de Lucio Anneo Floro*, Madrid, 1953.

Albert, K., *Strabo als Quelle des Flavius Josephus*, Aschaffenburg, 1902.

Aly, W, *Sage und Novelle bei Herodot und seinen Zeitgenossen*, Göttingen, 1969.

Avenarius, G., *Lukians Schrift zur Geschichtsschreibung*, Meisenheim-Glan, 1956.

Balsdon, J. P. V. D., *The Emperor Gaius (Caligula)*, Univ. Pr., 1964 (1rst. ed. 1934).

Bardy, G., "Le souvenir de Josèphe chez les Pères", *RHE* 43 (1948), 179-191.

Bauernfeind, O. and O. Michel, "Die beiden Eleazarreden in Jos. bell. 7. 323-336; 7, 341-388", *ZNTW* 58 (1967), 267-272.

Belkin, S., "The Alexandrian Source for Contra Apionem II", *JQR* 27 (1936-1937), 1-32.

Benvéniste, E., *Noms d'action et noms d'agents en indo-européen*, Paris, 1948.

Betz, O. "Das Problem des Wunders bei Flavius Josephus im Vergleich zum Wunderproblem bei den Rabbinen und im Johannesevangelium", *Festschr. O. Michel*, Göttingen, (1974), 23-44.

Bischoff, H., *Der Warner bei Herodot*, Marburg, 1932.

Brady, Th. A., "The reception of the Egyptian cults by the Greeks (330-30 b. Ch.)", *The University of Missouri studies* 10 (1935).

Braun, M., *History and Romance in Graeco-oriental Literature*, Oxford, 1938. Original title: *Griechischer Roman und hellenistische Geschichtsschreibung*, Frankfurt a.M., 1934. — "The Prophet who became a historian", *The Listener* 56 (1956), 53-57.

Brüne, B., *Josephus der Geschichtsschreiber des heiligen Krieges und seine Vaterstadt Jerusalem*, Wiesbaden, 1912. — *Flavius Josephus und seine Schriften in ihrem Verhältnis zum Judentume, zur griechisch-römischen Welt und zum Christentume mit griechischer Wortkonkordanz zum Neuen Testamente und I. Clemensbriefe nebst Sach- und Namen-Verzeichnis*. Appendix: *Josephus der Geschichtsschreiber*, Gütersloh, 1913.

Brunel, J., *L'aspect verbal et l'emploi des préverbes en grec, spécialement en attique*, Paris, 1939.

Burger, J. D. Fréderic, *Essai sur l'usage que l'historien Flave Josèphe a fait des livres canoniques de l'Ancien-Testament*, (Thèse), Strasbourg, 1836.

Burgess, Th. Ch., "The Epideictic Element in History", *StudCPh* 3 (1902), 195-214.

Bury, J. B., *The Ancient Greek Historians*, New York, 1909.

Charles, R. H., *Eschatology*, New York, 1963 (2nd ed.).

Ciruelo, J. I., *Salustio, política e historiografía*, Barcelona, 1973.

Cohen, Shave F. B., *Josephus in Galilee and Rome. His vita and development as a historian*, Leiden, 1979.

Coleman-Norton, P. R., "St. Chrysostom's use of Josephus", *CPh* 26 (1931), 85-89.

Collomp. P., "La place de Josèphe dans la technique de l'historiographie hellénistique" (Publ. de la Fac. des Lettres de l'Université Strasbourg 106), *Mélanges 1945, III. Études historiques*, Paris (1947), 81-92.

Cornford, F. M., *Thucydides Mythistoricus*, London, 1907.

Corssen, P., "Die Zeugnisse des Tacitus und Pseudo-Josephus über Christus", *ZNTW* 15 (1914), 114-140.

Crahay, R., *La littérature oraculaire chez Hérodote*, Paris, 1956.

Creuzer, F., *Die historische Kunst der Griechen*, Leipzig, 1803.

Daube, D., *Typologie im Werk des Flavius Josephus*, Bayerische Akad. d. Wissenschaften, 6, München, 1977.

Delling, G., "Josephus und das Wunderbare", *NT* 2 (1958), 291-309.

Destinon, J. von, *Die Quellen des Flavius Josephus in der Jüd. Arch. Buch XII-XVII = Jüd. Krieg Buch I*, Kiel, 1882.

Drexler, H., "Untersuchungen zu Josephus und zur Geschichte des jüdischen Aufstandes 66-70", *Klio* 19 (1925), 277-312.

Drüner, H., *Untersuchungen über Josephus*, Marburg, 1896.

Duschak, M., *Mor Deror. Josephus Flavius und die Tradition*, Wien, 1864. — "Flavius Josephus. Seine Zeit und seine Bedeutung als Historiograph", *IMGIJ* 1 (1865), 53-59, 119-126, 300-306.

Edersheim, A., *s.v.* "Josephus", in *A Dictionary of Christian Biography*, III, ed. W. Smith and H. Wace, London, 1882, 441-460.

Engel, G., *De antiquorum epicorum, didacticorum, historicorum prooemiis*, (Diss.), Marburg, 1910.

Ernesti, J. Aug., *Observationes philologico-criticae in Aristophanis Nubes et Flavii Josephi Antiquitates Judaicae*, Leipzig, 1795.

Falk, N., *De historiae inter graecos origine et natura*, Kiliae, 1809.

Feldman, L. H., "Abraham the Greek philosopher in Josephus", *TAPhA* 99 (1968), 143-156. — "Hellenizations in Josephus' portrayal of Man's Decline", *Religions in Antiquity* (Essays in Memory of E. R. Goodenough), ed. J. Neusner, Leiden, 1968, 336-353. — "Hellenization in Josephus' version of Esther", *TAPhA* 101 (1970), 143-170.

Fischer, J. B., "The Term δεσπότης in Josephus", *JQR* 49 (1958/9), 132-138.

Franxman, T. W., *Genesis and the "Jewish Antiquities" of Flavius Josephus*, Rome, 1979.

Frisch, P., *Die Träume bei Herodot*, Meisenheim am Glan, 1968.

Fritz, K. von, "Die Bedeutung des Aristoteles für die Geschichtsschreibung", *Histoire et historiens dans l'antiquité* (Entretiens sur l'Antiquité classique 4), Vandoeuvres-Genève, 1956, 85-145. — *Aristotle's contribution to the practice and theory of historiography*, Berkeley, 1958.

Gabba, E., "L'impero romano nel discorso di Agrippa II (Joseph., B, II, 345-401)", *RSA* 6-7 (1976-1977), 189-194.

Giet, S., "Un procédé littéraire d'exposition: l'anticipation chronologique", *REAug* 2 (1956), 243-249.

Gomme, P., *The Greek attitude to poetry and history*, Berkeley, 1954.

Hadas, M., *Three Greek Romances*, New York, 1953.

Hankoff, L. D., "The theme of suicide in the works of Flavius Josephus", *CM* 11 (1976), 15-24.

Heller, B., "Grundzüge der Aggada des Flavius Josephus", *MGWJ* 80 (1936), 237-246, 363.

Hellmann, F., "Geschichte und Schicksal bei Herodot", in *Herodot. Eine Auswahl aus der neueren Forschung*, ed. W. Marg, München, 1965, 40-56.

Holtzmann, O., *Middot*, Giessen, 1913.

Holwerda, "Observationes criticae in Flavii Josephi Ant. librum XVIII", *Mnemosyne* 2 (1853), 111-141.

Huart, P., *Le vocabulaire de l'analyse psychologique dans l'oeuvre de Thucydide*, Paris, 1868.

Immerwahr, H. R., "Historical causation in Herodotus", *TAPhA* 87 (1956), 244-247. — *Form and Thought in Herodotus,* Cleveland, Ohio, 1966.

Jolivet, R., *L'homme et l'histoire*, Actes du Congrès de Strasbourg, 1952.

Justus, B., "Zur Erzählkunst des Flavius Josephus", *Theokratia* 2 (1973), 107-136.

Kirkwood, G. M., "Thucydides' words for cause", *AJPh* 73 (1952), 205-223.

Ladoucer, D. J., *Studies in the Language and Historiography of Flavius Josephus* (Diss. Providence, 1977), Ann Arbor, Michigan, 1979.

Lambert, A., *Die indirekte Rede als künstlerisches Stilmittel des Livius*, (Diss.), Zürich, 1946.

Lana, I., *Le Historiae di Tacito*, Torino, 1967.

Laqueur, R., *Der jüdische Historiker Flavius Josephus. Ein biographischer Versuch auf neuer quellenkritischer Grundlage*, Giessen, 1920.

Leuty, H., *An inquiry into the historical methods and contributions of Flavius Josephus*, (Thesis Calif. State Coll., at Fullerton), 1971 (Microfilm).

Lieberich, H., *Studien zu den Proömien in der griech. u. byzant. Geschichtsschreibung*. Teil I: Die griech. Geschichtsschreibung, München, 1899.

Lindner, H., *Die Geschichtsauffassung des Flavius Josephus im Bellum Judaicum*, AGJU 12, Leiden, 1972.

Louis, P., "Le mot ἱστορία chez Aristote", *RPh* 29 (1955), 39-44.

Löwith, K., *El sentido de la historia*, Madrid, 1973, (orig. ed. 1949).

Lucas, J., *Les obsessions de Tacite*, Leiden, 1974.

Marrou, H. I., *El conocimiento histórico*, Barcelona, 1968.

Mendelssohn, L., *De senati consultis Romanorum ab Josepho Antiq. XIII*, 9, 2: *XIV, 10, 22 relatis commentatio*, Leipzig, 1874.

Mess, A. v., "Die Anfänge der Biographie und der psychologischen Geschichtsschreibung in der griechischen Literatur", *RhM* 70 (1915), 337-367.

Meyer, E., *El historiador y la historia antigua*, Buenos Aires, 1955.

Moehring, H. R., *Novelistic Elements in the Writings of Flavius Josephus*, (Diss.), Chicago, 1957.

Moore, G. F., "Fate and Free Will in the Jewish Philosophies according to Josephus", *HThR* 22 (1929), 371-389.

Moraux, P., *Les listes anciennes des ouvrages d'Aristote*, Louvain, 1951.

Morel, W., "Eine Rede bei Josephus (Bell. Jud., VII, 341 sqq.)", *RhM* 75 (1926), 106-114.

Muller, F., "De "historiae" vocabulo atque notione", *Mnemosyne* 54 (1926), 234-257.

Myres, J. L., *Herodotus, father of History*, Oxford, 1953.

Naber, S. A., "Observationes criticae in Flavium Josephum", *Mnemosyne* 13 (1885), 263-284, 353-399.

Nadel, B., "Quid Flavius Josephus sermoni atque colori dicendi invectivarum Romanorum debuerit", *Eos* 56 (1966), 256-272.

Nenci, G., "Il motivo de l'autopsia nella storiografia greca", *SCO* 3 (1953), 14-46.

Nestle, W., *Griechische Religiosität von Alexander dem Großen bis Proklos*, Berlin, 1934.

Neuburger, M., *Die Medizin im Flavius Josephus*, Bad Reichenhall, 1919.

Niese, B., "Bemerkungen über die Urkunden bei Josephus Archaeol. B. XIII. XIV. XVI"., *Hermes* 11 (1876), 466-488. — "Zur Chronologie des Josephus", *Hermes* 28 (1893), 194-229. — "Der jüdische Historiker Josephus", *HZ* 40 (1896), 193-237.

Norden, E., "Josephus und Tacitus über Jesus Christus und eine messianische Prophetie", *NJ* 16 (1913), 637-666.

Nordh, A., "Virtus and Fortuna in Florus", *Eranos* 50 (1952), 111-128.

Nussbaum, M., *Observationes in Flavii Josephi Antiquitates Li. XII, 3-XIII, 14*, (Diss. Göttingen), Warburg, 1875.

Otto, O., *Quaestiones Strabonianae*, (Diss.), Leipzig, 1889.

Pallavicini, B., *Is liver continet: De Flenda cruce Baptistae... Quaedam ex Josepho de Jesu Christo*, Wien, 1511.

Patsch, K., "Zu Nicolaus von Damascus", *WS* 12 (1889), 231-239.

Paur, H., *Observationes et adnotationes ad Flavii Josephi elocutionem*, Nürnberg, 1892.

Pearson, L., "Prophasis and Aitia", *TAPhA* 83 (1952), 205-223.

Pédech, P., *La méthode historique de Polybe*, Paris, 1964.

Pelletier, A., *Flavius Josèphe, adaptateur de la Lettre d'Aristée. Une réaction atticisante contre la Koinè*, Paris, 1962.

Philippe, O., *L'homme et l'histoire*, Actes du Congrès de Strasbourg, 1952.

Plaut, R., *Flavius Josephus und die Bibel. Eine kritisch-exegetische Studie*, (Diss. Leipzig), Berlin, 1867.

Pohlenz, M., *Die Stoa*, II, Göttingen, 1955.

Posner, A., "Römische Persönlichkeiten in Josephus' bellum", *MGWJ* 80 (1936), 246-261.

Raab, C., *De Flavii Josephi elocutione quaestiones criticae et observationes grammaticae*, (Diss.), Erlangen, 1890.

Rappaport, S., *Agada und Exegese bei Flavius Josephus*, Wien, 1930.

Reardon, B. P., *Courants littéraires grecs des IIe et IIIe siècles après J.-C.*, Paris, 1971.

Richards, G. C., R. J. H. Shutt, "Critical notes on Josephus' Antiquities", *CQ* 31 (1937), 170-177.

Ripoll Perelló, E., *Sobre els orígens i significat de l'art paleolític*, Barcelona, 1981.

Romilly, J. de, *Thucydide et l'impérialisme athénien*, Paris, 1947. — "L'utilité de l'histoire selon Thucydide", *Histoire et historiens dans l'antiquité* (Entretiens sur l'Antiquité classique 4), Vandoeuvres-Genève, 1956, 41-81.

Rösiger, F., *Die Bedeutung der Tyche bei den späteren griechischen Historikern, besonders bei Demetrios von Phaleron*, Konstanz, 1880.

Runnalls, D. R., *Hebrew and Greek sources in the speeches of Josephus' War*, (Diss. Univ. of Toronto), 1971.

Russell, D. S., *The Method and Message of Jewish Apocalyptic*, London, 1964.

Schadewaldt, W., "Die Anfänge der Geschichtsschreibung bei den Griechen", *Ant* 10 (1934), 144-168.

Schalit, A., "Josephus und Justus", *Klio* 26 (Neue Folge, VIII), (1933), 67-95.

Scheffer, Th. von, *Hellenismus, Mysterien und Orakel*, Stuttgart, 1940.

Scheller, P., *De hellenistica historiae conscribendae arte*, Leipzig, 1911.

Schemann, F., *Die Quellen des Flavius Josephus in der jüdischen Archaeologie, Buch XVIII-XX = Polemos II, cap. VII-XIV, 3*, (Diss.), Hagen, 1887.

Schlatter, A., *Wie sprach Josephus von Gott?*, BzFchrTh 14, Heft 1, Gütersloh, 1910. — *Die Theologie des Judentums nach dem Bericht des Josefus*, BzFchrTh 2, Reihe Bd. 26, Gütersloh, 1932.

Schmidt, G., *De Flavii Josephi elocutione observationes criticae*. Pars prior. (Diss. Göttingen), Leipzig, 1893; completed in *JCPh*, Suppl. 19 (1894).

Schreckenberg, H., *Bibliographie zu Flavius Josephus*, ALGH 1, Leiden, 1968. — *Die Flavius-Josephus-Tradition in Antike und Mittelalter*, ALGH 5, Leiden, 1972. — *Bibliographie zu Flavius Josephus*, ALGH 14, Suppl. mit Gesamtregister, Leiden, 1979.

Schürer, E., *Geschichte des jüdischen Volkes im Zeitalter Jesu Christi*, I-III, Leipzig,[4] 1901-1909.

Schwartz, E., "Geschichtsschreibung und Gesch. bei den Hellenen", *Ant* 4 (1928), 14-30.

Shutt, R. J. H., *Studies in Josephus*, London, 1961.

Sinko, T., "L'historiosophie dans le prologue et l'épilogue de l'oeuvre d'Hérodote d'Halicarnasse", *Eos* 50, (1959-1960), 3-20.

Snell, B., *Die Ausdrücke für den Begriff des Wissens in der vorplatonischen Philosophie*, Berlin, 1924.

Soulis, E. M., *Xenophon and Thucydides*, Athens, 1972.

Speyer, W., *Die literarische Fälschung im Altertum*, München, 1971.

Spródowsky, H., *Die Hellenisierung der Geschichte von Joseph in Ägypten bei Flavius Josephus*, Berlin, 1937.

Stählin, G., "Das Schicksal im Neuen Testament und bei Josephus", *Festschr. O. Michel*, Göttingen, (1974), 319-343.

Stein, E., "De Flavii Josephi arte narrandi", *Eos* 33, (1930-1931), 641-650.

Stern, M., "Flavius Josephus' Method of Writing History" (in Hebrew), *IHS* (1962-1963), 22-28.

Syme, R., *Tacito*, Brescia, 1967. — *Sallust*, Berkeley, 1974[2].

Tachauer, G., *Das Verhältnis von Flavius Josephus zur Bibel und Tradition*, Erlangen, 1871.

Thackeray, H. St. J., s.u. "Josephus", in *A Dictionary of the Bible*, Extra Volume, ed. J. Hastings, Edinburgh, 1904. — *Josephus, the Man and the Historian*, New York, 1967.

Tränkle, H., *Livius and Polybius*, Basel-Stuttgart, 1977.

Trüdinger, K., *Studien zur Geschichte der griech.-röm. Ethnographie*, Basel, 1918.

Ullman, B. L., "History and Tragedy", *TAPhA* 73 (1942), 25-53.

Ullmann, R., *La technique des discours dans Sallust, Tite Live et Tacite*, Oslo, 1927.

Unnik, W. C. van, "De la règle Μήτε προσθεῖναι μήτε ἀφελεῖν dans l'histoire du canon", *VChr* 3 (1949), 1-36. — *Flavius Josephus als historischer Schriftsteller*, Heidelberg, 1978.

Veyne, P., *Comment on écrit l'histoire*, Paris, 1971.

Vidal-Naquet, P., *Du bon usage de la trahison*, in *La guerre des Juifs*, transl. by P. Savinel, Paris, 1977.

Viereck, P., *Sermo graecus quo senatus populusque Romanus magistratusque populi Romani usque ad Tiberii Caesaris aetatem in scriptis publicis usi sunt examinatur*, Göttingen, 1888.

Vincent, H., "Chronologie des oeuvres de Josèphe", *RBi* 8 (1911), 366-383.

Vossius, G. I., *Ars historica*, Lugduni Batavorum, 1623.

Wächter, L., "Die unterschiedliche Haltung der Pharisäer, Sadduzäer und Essener zur Heimarmene nach dem Bericht des Josephus", *ZRGG* 21 (1969), 97-114.

Walbank, F. W., "History and Tragedy", *Historia* 9 (1960), 216-234.

Walsh, P. G., *Livy, his historical aims and method*, Cambridge University Press, 1963.

Weber, W., *Josephus und Vespasian. Untersuchungen zu dem jüdischen Krieg des Flavius Josephus*, Stuttgart, 1921.

Wehrli, F. W., "Die Geschichtsschreibung im Lichte der antiken Theorie", *Festgabe für E. Howald, Eumusia* 68 (1947), 54-71.

Weidauer, K., *Thukydides und die hippokratischen Schriften*, Heidelberg, 1954.

Wille, G., *Der Aufbau des livianischen Geschichtswerks*, Amsterdam, 1973.

GENERAL INDEX

This *General Index* lists proper names, geographical names, basic concepts, titles of works and the most important events. The main Greek terms have been placed at the very end. Numbers refer to pages.

INDEX OF GREEK WORDS